SEX, POWER, CONFLICT

SEX, POWER, CONFLICT

Evolutionary and Feminist Perspectives

Edited by
DAVID M. BUSS
NEIL M. MALAMUTH

New York   Oxford
OXFORD UNIVERSITY PRESS
1996

Oxford University Press

Oxford   New York
Athens   Auckland   Bangkok   Bombay
Calcutta   Cape Town   Dar es Salaam   Delhi
Florence   Hong Kong   Istanbul   Karachi
Kuala Lumpur   Madras   Madrid   Melbourne
Mexico City   Nairobi   Paris   Singapore
Taipei   Tokyo   Toronto

and associated companies in
Berlin   Ibadan

Published by Oxford University Press, Inc.,
198 Madison Avenue, New York, New York 10016

Oxford is a registered trademark of Oxford University Press

Library of Congress Cataloging-in-Publication Data
Sex, power, conflict : evolutionary and feminist perspectives /
edited by David M. Buss, Neil M. Malamuth.
p.   cm.
Includes bibliographical references (p.   ) and index.
ISBN 0-19-509581-2; ISBN 0-19-510357-2 (pbk.)
1. Man-woman relationships.   2. Acquaintance rape.   3. Dating
violence.   4. Family violence.   5. Sexual harassment.   6. Sex
(Psychology)   7. Genetic psychology.   8. Feminist theory.   I. Buss,
David M.   II. Malamuth, Neil M.
HQ801.83.S49   1996
306.7—dc20   95-15685

2 4 6 8 9 7 5 3 1

Printed in the United States of America
on acid-free paper

Contents

SEX, POWER, CONFLICT

Introduction

At no other time in human history have issues of conflict between the sexes become so salient in social science and public discourse. Sexual harassment in the workplace, rape in the dating scene, and violence in the home dominate the headlines and galvanize discussions. The conflict seems to center on two key themes that are often intertwined: power and sex.

The prevalence and importance of these issues have not escaped the attention of scholars and researchers. Indeed, more research is being done on such topics as rape, sexual harassment, and violence among intimates than at any other time in the history of the social sciences.

It is apparent, however, that researchers approach these issues through different theoretical lenses. Two emergent perspectives on the "battles between the sexes" dominate recent discussion: feminism and evolutionary psychology. Despite the fact that these two perspectives grapple with many of the same issues (e.g., sexual harassment, marital conflict, and power imbalances), they have remained strangely isolated, failing to inform one another of the insights they might have to offer.

Part of the reason for this conceptual isolation is that evolutionary psychology and feminism operate on different planes. Evolutionary psychology is a *scientific discipline* and hence is primarily concerned with describing and explaining *what exists*. Feminism shares with evolutionary psychology a concern with describing and explaining what exists, but it also carries a social and political agenda. Hence, feminism is partly concerned with what *ought* to exist.

For these and other reasons, the two perspectives have remained more than merely isolated. Adherents of one sometimes display outright hostility to the other perspective in the belief that the two are inherently antithetical. Feminists, for example, sometimes view evolutionary perspectives as dangerous because they might be used to justify the status quo or further the oppression of women. Moreover, feminists sometimes worry that if certain human patterns are anchored in our evolved psychology, then they will be less amenable to change.

Evolutionary psychologists, in turn, worry that mingling a political agenda with the scientific enterprise sacrifices and distorts the objective search for the truth. Hence, evolutionary psychologists typically sharply distinguish between "what exists" and "what ought to exist." Conflating the two is deemed the *naturalistic fallacy*. Feminists sometimes respond that no science is value free, that the entire scientific enterprise is infused with unrecognized biases, and that to pretend otherwise is self-delusional. So, the two perspectives march along in their parallel paths, failing to intersect.

The goal of this book is to bring together in a single volume some of the key leaders from each of the perspectives. One of our goals is to open up the discourse about sex, power, and conflict, establishing lines of communication between feminist and evolutionary perspectives. If we achieve this goal, our volume will have succeeded in our eyes. Our second and somewhat more ambitious goal, though, stems from the view that genuine insights can be immediately gained by individuals with the flexibility to view sex, power, and conflict through *both* lenses. If even a small fraction of readers starts to do this, we will have succeeded in this second goal.

To accomplish the goals of this book, we brought together leading scientists who focus on sex, power, and conflict. The book is divided into three parts. The first includes contributions by leading evolutionary psychologists. Martin Daly and Margo Wilson explain how evolutionary psychology illuminates marital conflict by showing how the interests of the husband and wife depart from one another under certain conditions, such as in the case of stepchildren. Douglas Kenrick, Melanie Trost, and Virgil Sheets examine the evolutionary psychology of mate selection and argue that women are not merely passive pawns in a man's game of power and harassment. Michael Studd presents an insightful analysis of the evolutionary psychology of sexual harassment and shows that many of its features are explicable within an evolutionary framework. Nancy Thornhill concludes this part with an evolutionary analysis of sexual coercion and the psychological trauma experienced by rape victims. Taken together, the four contributions provide a powerful case that evolutionary psychology has much to offer in our attempts to understand the major forms of conflict between the sexes.

The second part is represented by a group of scientists explicitly guided by a feminist perspective. Janet Hyde, a leading scientist in the study of sex differences, summarizes the research on the domains in which sex differences do and do not exist. Interestingly, given the focus of this volume, sex differences seem strongest in the domains of sexuality and aggression. The next three chapters deal with the commingling of sex and aggression in the form of rape. Charlene Muehlenhard, Sharon Danoff-Burg, and Irene Powch offer an insightful analysis of the controversy about whether rape is sex or violence. Antonia Abbey, Lisa Ross, Donna McDuffie, and Pam McAuslan summarize a fascinating program of research on the role of alcohol in rape and how it can affect women's and men's perceptions and attributions of blame. Gerd Bohner and Norbert Schwarz analyze the psychological impact of the threat of rape on women who have not actually been raped. Although all authors in this section are self-described feminists, it is apparent from these chapters that feminism is not a monolithic entity, and that there is great diversity under the umbrella label *feminism*.

The final third of the book contains chapters by scientists who are explicitly wrestling with the cross-fertilization between evolutionary and feminist perspectives. Felicia Pratto provides an integrative theory of "social dominance" that is anchored simultaneously in the evolutionary theory of sexual selection and the feminist view of male dominance. Barbara Smuts, a self-described evolutionist and feminist, shows how an evolutionary consideration of our primate past can illuminate many aspects of men's aggression against women. Neil Malamuth integrates feminist and evolutionary perspectives in his "confluence model" of sexual aggression. Finally, David Buss concludes this part by revealing how aspects of feminism can be understood in the context of evolutionary psychology.

We do not claim that this volume offers a complete portrait of the complex commingling of sex, power, and conflict. Nor does it offer the final word on the potential (or lack of potential) for integrating evolutionary and feminist perspectives. What we hope we have done is to lay the groundwork for a deeper, more complex, more multifaceted understanding of the conflicts between men and women that touch the lives of everyone.

Ann Arbor, Michigan   D. M. B.
Ann Arbor, Michigan   N. M. M.
August 1995

I

Evolutionary Perspectives

1

Evolutionary Psychology and Marital Conflict: The Relevance of Stepchildren

MARTIN DALY AND MARGO WILSON

The specific focus of this chapter concerns one particular source of conflict between women and men in marital or marital-like relationships, namely the existence or presence of children from prior unions. In explaining our rationale for suggesting that such children might be expected to engender or exacerbate marital conflict, however, we have to synopsize theories of much broader applicability. Our argument is predicated on a more general account of the nature of the marital relationship from the perspective of evolutionary biology, which in turn is predicated on a still more general evolutionary understanding of the nature of sociality and of the male–female phenomenon. Thus, we start with these most basic issues and work toward the specific question of the possible relevance of stepchildren to marital disharmony.

NATURAL SELECTION AND ADAPTATION

To attain a deep understanding of the relationship between women and men, it seems to us essential that the issue be situated within larger biological issues, namely the comparative characterization of the human animal and the general significances of sex and sociality in the living world.

The unifying conceptual framework of the life sciences is the theory of *evolution by selection*. Human beings and other organisms are extremely complex systems, and it has long been evident that the complex adaptive organization of living creatures requires explanation. Pre-Darwinian thinkers (e.g., Paley, 1802) could see no alternative to the hypothesis that one or more creatures analogous to ourselves, but unimaginably more powerful, must have designed and created terrestrial life. Such "creationist" theories were obviously unsatisfactory since they begged the question of the sources of the alleged creators' complexity and thus solved nothing, and since they were devoid of testable implications that would enable one to choose among the numerous competing versions. But no one had a better solution until Charles Darwin and Alfred Russel Wallace (1858) announced their independent discovery of the natural process that generates complex adaptation automatically and without intentionality: Random variation is ceaselessly generated in populations of reproducing organisms and is then winnowed by nonrandom differential survival and reproduction, with the result that the more successful forms proliferate while their alternatives perish, and adaptive complexity is cumulative over generations. Darwin called this process, which has since been amply confirmed and elaborated in each of its essentials, *natural selection.*

It is crucial to note that Darwinian selection is not just a matter of differential survival, as might be inferred from its popular epitomization as "survival of the fittest." Over generations, it is successful attributes that "survive," not individuals, and this sort of long-term survival depends not merely on the longevity of those with a given attribute, but on the abundance of their progeny. Suppose, for example, that a new, combative mutant variety of male were to appear in a population of pacifists and that the new mutant variety were to fertilize more females than the pacifist variety, on average, despite tending to die younger. In such a case, the mutation would spread through the population over generations and male lifespan would decline. The point of this little thought experiment is not that aggressivity must supplant pacifism; on the contrary, we could just as easily have framed the hypothetical case in such a way that the pacifists won out, and indeed there are both combative and pacifist equilibria in natural animal populations. Rather, the general point is that adaptive attributes of living creatures have been "designed" by the Darwinian historical process to contribute to a single outcome: outreproducing other members of one's species (sometimes called *fitness*) in environments whose relevant aspects are not crucially different from those in which the history of selection has occurred.

Every living creature has been shaped by such a history of Darwinian selection and so has every complex functioning constituent part of every living creature. Thus, the "adaptationist" enterprise of elucidating the evolved functional designs of organisms and their constituent parts is the cornerstone of biological discovery and always was, even before Darwin's theory made it evident *why* this strategy of functional parsing of the organism works (Mayr, 1983). For a highly readable, book-length elaboration of modern adaptationism, see Dawkins (1986).

WOMEN AND MEN IN COMPARATIVE BIOLOGICAL PERSPECTIVE

Given this little introduction to evolution, consider the human animal in comparative perspective. People readily characterize their species as a relatively hairless primate, as unusually bipedal, complexly social, and so forth, characterizations that entail implicit or explicit comparison to other animal species, not necessarily limited to closely related ones. It is also popular to attempt to "define" our species by its apparent uniqueness: *Homo* the tool user, the toolmaker, the user of arbitrary referential signs, and so forth. These attributes have an unsettling history of losing their uniqueness as knowledge of other animals accumulates, but there is little doubt that the human animal is indeed exceptional in its language, complex culture, and other attributes. However, there is much more to the business of situating human beings in comparative perspective than cataloging our peculiarities.

The first thing to note about *Homo sapiens* as a species is that people reproduce sexually. This may seem trite, but not all creatures reproduce sexually, and the fact of sexual reproduction has some profound implications. Unlike ourselves, asexual organisms produce offspring that are genetically identical to the mother, with the result that whatever resource allocations or other states of affairs (e.g., habitats occupied, foods selected, social circumstances preferred, etc.) are optimal for maternal fitness will necessarily be optimal for offspring fitness, too, since the mother's and the offspring's fitnesses are isomorphic. In sexual reproducers, by contrast, the lack of genetic identity between parent and offspring makes "parent–offspring conflict" (Trivers, 1974) endemic: The resource allocations and other states of affairs that would maximize parental fitness are *not* identical to those that would maximize offspring fitness.

The consequence of this conflict in the natural selective structure of sexual reproduction is that parental and offspring attributes necessarily evolve not simply to complement each other, but also, to some degree, to counter each other. These considerations have innumerable consequences for maternal and infantile physiology and psychology, as illustrated by Haig's (1993) remarkable exposition of how "maternal–fetal conflict" plays itself out in the specific case of human beings.

Besides engendering parent–offspring conflict, sexual reproduction introduces an additional social relationship, namely that between mates. Because preferences have been shaped by selection to promote expected fitness and because the well-being, survival, and eventual reproduction of an offspring contribute to the fitness of both its parents, the resource allocations and other states of affairs that appeal to one parent are likely to have appeal for the other as well. In this sense, there is a fundamental commonality of purpose between mates, which is—like the commonality of purpose between parent and child or other genetic relatives—ultimately traceable to correlated fitnesses. However, the relationship between mates also entails endemic conflicts, which are again—as in the parent–offspring relationship—ultimately traceable to the genetic nonidentity of the participants. In particular, the fact that both parties accrue expected fitness from either's investments in the welfare of their joint offspring opens the door to the evolution of "parasitic" exploitation of one sex's reproductive efforts by the other sex and thus to escalated "evolutionary arms races" between the sexes. These conflicts apply to all sexual reproducers, from single-cell organisms to ourselves.

The second thing to note about *Homo sapiens* in comparative biological perspective is that people are *dioecious*: Individuals come in two varieties, female and male, and successful reproduction requires one of each. Not all sexually reproducing creatures are dioecious, and the considerations just discussed, including parasitic exploitation of a mate and evolutionary arms races, apply just as much to monomorphic hermaphrodites (e.g., Fischer, 1988) as they apply to bimorphic dioecious species such as people. The additional twist that dioecy adds is the evolution of two distinct morphs, with distinct attributes that are partly complementary and partly antagonistic.

In dioecious organisms, the female is, by definition, the sex that produces the larger gamete: Eggs are bigger than sperm. One consequence is that in cases in which internal fertilization (the union of parental gametes inside one parent's body) has evolved—as it has done many times independently—it almost invariably occurs within the female. This in turn sets the evolutionary stage for the sexually differentiated elaboration of additional modes of internal nurturance, such as mammalian pregnancy and lactation, with the female literally left holding the baby. This sexual differentiation of the evolved mechanisms of "parental investment" (Trivers, 1972) opens the door to the evolution of parasitic exploitation of the female's reproductive efforts by the male: Females commonly invest vastly more time and energy in the nurturance of each offspring than do males, who can disappear after conception and still gain the full fitness benefit of successfully raised young. Various sex differences in the psychophysiological paraphernalia that we call *sexuality* (e.g., Symons, 1979) follow logically from this asymmetry.

In other words, insofar as reproductive efforts can be partitioned into the pursuit of matings versus parental investment (Trivers, 1972; Low, 1978), males in taxa with internal fertilization generally specialize in the former and females in the latter. One significant implication is that the principal factor limiting male fitness is often the number of mating partners, whereas female fitness seldom profits analogously from increased numbers of mating partners and is instead generally limited by nutrient availability. Since the minimal time and energy cost of producing a viable offspring is much lower for a male than for a female, the ceiling on potential reproduction is higher. Hence, the variance in reproductive success is usually higher for males (*effective polygyny*; see Daly & Wilson, 1983, pp. 151–152) and the proportion who die childless is also higher, engendering more intense male–male competition and the selective favoring of more expensive, dangerous, and competitive tactics. That is why musculature and specialized weaponry for same-sex combat are so often sexually differentiated. Moreover, insofar as males are specialized morphologically and psychologically for violent competition with other males, and insofar as male fitness is largely determined by the frequency and exclusivity of mating access, it is hardly surprising that males also commonly apply their aptitude in violent conflict to the task of direct aggressive control of the females themselves. It is also noteworthy—and, without an evolutionary perspective, paradoxical—that greater size and aggressivity of males tend to be associated with greater vulnerability to extraspecific threats of starvation, disease, and even predation, as the demands of intrasexual competitive prowess compromise male design efficiency with respect to other aspects of the ecological niche of the species (e.g., Gaulin & Sailer, 1985).

This generic characterization must immediately be tempered, however, by the recognition of considerable cross-species diversity. The extent to which male mammals have higher fitness variance, grow larger, die younger, and otherwise differ from females varies greatly even among quite closely related species, and these various aspects of sexual differentiation are apparently strongly correlated with one another. Most notably, wherever pairs remain together and care for their young cooperatively—as foxes and various monkeys and beavers and a smattering of other mammals do—these sex differences are diminished or abolished. Such biparental care is atypical in mammals and other animals with internal fertilization, presumably at least partly because it is difficult for males in such cases to have reliable cues of paternity, with the result that fathers are vulnerable to *cuckoldry* (unwitting investment in young sired by rivals) and paternal investment is therefore *evolutionarily unstable*.

The third thing to note about *Homo sapiens* in comparative perspective then—and the first in which we differ from closely related species—is that people form mateships of some stability with biparental investment in young. Our nearest relatives, chimpanzees and gorillas, cleave much closer to the mammalian stereotype, with males very much larger than females and parental investment predominantly or solely maternal.

Admittedly, ours is hardly an exemplary monogamous species. The prevalence of adulterous fantasy and action demonstrates that marriage does not abolish interest in the opposite sex, and the same is implied by the ubiquity of countermeasures to adultery (e.g., Wilson & Daly, 1992a). Moreover, the ethnographic record reveals that men are ardent polygamists when the opportunity presents itself: In the majority of known human societies—including all those who subsist by foraging, as all people did until the relatively recent invention of agriculture—most marriages are (at least serially) monogamous, and yet some men of high status manage to have multiple wives simultaneously (Betzig, 1986). Nor does it seem quite correct to claim, as did Dorothy Parker, that woman's nature is monogamous even if man's is not (e.g., Baker & Bellis, 1989, 1994), although women are clearly less polygamously inclined than men (Daly & Wilson, 1983).

The human animal exhibits a number of sex differences that may be interpreted as evolutionary vestiges of a selective history as an effectively polygynous species—that is, as a species in which male fitness has generally been more variable than female fitness and hence intrasexual competition has generally been more intense among males than among females. These vestiges include sex differences in body size, in maturation schedules, in intrasexual combat, and in rates of senescence. In all of these, the sexes differ more in human beings than in monogamous mammals, but much less than in extremely polygynous mammals such as bison or various seals or our cousins the great apes. Likely implications are that the human species evolved as a slightly polygynous one, and, more specifically, that pair formation with biparental care is an ancient hominid adaptation but that competitively ascendant men continued to be polygamists. And that, of course, is also what is suggested by the ethnographic record of marriage practices.

MARITAL ALLIANCE IS A PANHUMAN INSTITUTION

In all societies, women and men enter into individualized marital alliances, which entail entitlements and obligations recognized and acknowledged by the marrying couple and by others.

A central component of marital alliance is that it bestows legitimate sexual access (often, but not always, exclusive). Not coincidentally, marriage is also the relationship within which reproduction is deemed legitimate, normal, or appropriate, and marriage entails the expectation that the couple's reciprocal obligations will extend far beyond conception. In other words, the relationship between marital partners develops, in the event of reproduction, into a relationship of biparental obligations. Moreover, marital alliance is the relationship that determines and/or legitimizes the cross-generational transfer of heritable material and social resources.

Many writers have maintained that because human marriage is an economic as well as a reproductive union—or even because it is primarily or fundamentally economic in its motivations—it is therefore unique and incommensurate with the merely reproductive partnerships of other animal species. Such claims are predicated on ignorance of the lives of nonhuman animals and on misunderstanding of the nature of the relationship between production and reproduction. All animals accumulate and allocate resources, hence engage in "economic" activities. These activities may often have priority over reproductive activities in the limited sense that sex and reproduction are matters to which animals turn their attention only when material concerns are adequately under control. But reproduction has priority over production in another sense: Economic activities and motives have come into existence and have been shaped over evolutionary time as means to reproductive ends.

In addition to the economics of individual life, sexual reproduction commonly entails complex accessory exchanges. A male hornbill forages and feeds his mate while she sits on their tree-hole nest incubating their eggs. A pair of beavers cooperatively maintains their dam and domicile throughout the winter. These unions, with their divisions of labor and exchanges of benefits, are neither more nor less economic than the relationship between human husbands and wives. In nonhuman animals, as in people, the mundane interactions of mated pairs seldom serve immediately reproductive purposes, and yet the union itself and the partners' reciprocities can only be understood as predicated on reproductive partnership. (What *is* exceptional about human marriage is the degree of involvement of parties other than the marriage partners themselves in these economic exchanges.)

The cross-culturally general features of marital alliance add up to a complex panhuman institution. To be sure, many additional details of marriage vary between times and places and even between segments of the population, including the specific obligations and entitlements of wives, husbands, and other interested parties; whether the start of a marriage is marked by a discrete ceremonial event; the number of simultaneous marital partners permitted to each sex; rules of marital eligibility; the legitimacy and prevalence of marital dissolution; and even whether marriage partners reside together. But acknowledgment of this diversity should not distract us from recognition of the core phenomenon. The enduring aspect of marriage and its attendant implication of biparental obligations contrast with the usual mammalian state of affairs. Admittedly, marriages fail, but, unlike most mammalian sexual alliances, they are nowhere entered into with the expectation or intent of dissolution when conception or some other reproductive landmark has been attained. Notwithstanding its variable aspects, then, marriage is everywhere intelligible as a socially recognized alliance between a woman and a man, instituted and acknowledged as a vehicle for producing and rearing children.

MARITAL CONFLICT

If marriage is fundamentally to be understood as a cooperative reproductive venture in which the joint offspring are equally the vehicles of both parties' fitness prospects, whence comes marital conflict? Insofar as marital harmony derives ultimately from correlated expected fitnesses, then marital disharmony may be expected to derive from phenomena that tend to counter that correlation. Unfortunately, the list of potential threats to correlated fitness, and hence to harmony between mates, is substantial.

One reason that reproductive partnership does not impart perfect commonality of interests is that personal reproduction is only one component of expected fitness (Hamilton, 1964). One's impacts on the reproduction of one's relatives affect fitness, too. Marriage partners have separate kindred, in whom they are likely to retain their benevolent interests, and each may then resent the other's continued "nepotistic" investment of time, attention, and material resources in collateral kin. This is the evolutionary theoretical gloss on a cross-culturally ubiquitous and widely recognized source of marital friction: in-laws.

Moreover, even if marriage partners eschew collateral nepotism, their reproductive alliance may be fragile. If both parties want out, conflict may be minimal, but the inclination to separate is probably more often asymmetrical. This can arise because the partners have — or perceive themselves to have — different "mate values" in the marriage market and hence unequal opportunities for striking a better deal (e.g., Buss & Schmitt, 1993). When the woman is the partner for whom separation is relatively tempting, the man may resort to violent coercion to deter and retain her (e.g., Wilson & Daly, 1993).

Regardless of whether either party is tempted to end the marriage, there may be conflict over the husband's inclination to be a polygamist, when feasible. More generally, even monogamously married men are often tempted to allocate resources to extramarital mating effort rather than to the wife and her children. This, of course, is one major source of wifely grievance about inequitable investment in the marriage and may again contribute to asymmetrical inclination to end the marriage.

More generally, power asymmetries and resultant dissatisfactions are important direct sources of conflict and important contributors to asymmetrical inclinations to separate, too. One partner, usually the wife, is apt to be tempted to terminate the marriage because unequal power within the relationship sustains an asymmetry of investment in the couple's joint venture that the less powerful partner finds unacceptable and irremediable. In a sense, this is the same issue as that of male parasitism of female parental investment discussed above; however, by invoking these specifically reproductive conflicts, we do not imply that the detailed substance of marital discord must reflect them directly. Rather, we are invoking reproductive partnership and conflicts as the natural selective underpinnings of the psychology of sexual partnership, but it is again necessary to note that although the couple's joint venture is functionally reproductive, its substance includes all the mundane business of subsistence. Wives' grievances about exploitative asymmetry in marriage (e.g., Friedan, 1963) clearly encompass more content domains than just inequities in the sharing of parental duties.

One way in which the functional centrality of reproduction in marital partnership is reflected is in the emotional force attached to sexual and reproductive betrayals. The most explosively dangerous source of marital conflict is apparently wifely infidelity (Daly & Wilson, 1988c; Wilson & Daly, 1992a). This has always been an especially potent threat to a husband's fitness insofar as it entails risk that he will make a prolonged investment in the upbringing of unrelated children ("cuckoldry"), and this threat is presumably of evolutionary relevance to the fact that the jealousy of men is more focused on the copulatory act than is that of women (Buss, Larsen, Westen, & Semmelroth, 1992; Daly, Wilson, & Weghorst, 1982; Teismann & Mosher, 1978).

And then, over and above the problems of in-laws, infidelity, inequitable power, and asymmetrical inclination to separate, there may be children of prior unions.

Stepchildren and Marital Conflict

We have been arguing that reproductive partners share a profound, beneficent interest in the welfare of their offspring. It follows that children of the present marriage are likely to be sources of spousal harmony rather than discord because they facilitate consensus on the crucial question of how the couple's resources should be allocated. Children from former mateships, on the other hand, are a potential source of conflict about resource allocation, especially, but not only, if they reside with the married couple.

These hypotheses are predicated on the assumption that parental psychologies can distinguish genetic children from stepchildren and tend to value the former more highly. It would be surprising to a Darwinian if this were not the case since parental investment is a potentially valuable resource and selection must favor those psyches that succeed in allocating it discriminately where it will enhance parental fitness. Cues that offspring are indeed one's own constitute just one of several classes of cues of expected fitness that are processed by complex, evolved psychological adaptations of *discriminative parental solicitude* in animals (Daly & Wilson 1988a, 1994, 1995).

In addition to its theoretical plausibility, the idea that stepchildren might face discrimination gibes with folk understandings of human affairs. "Cruel stepparents" are staple characters in folklore from every corner of the globe (Thompson, 1955), and the prefix "step-" evokes negative attributions in the contemporary Western world as well (e.g., Bryan, Coleman, Ganong, & Bryan, 1986; Fine, 1986). Remarkably, however, social scientists lacking a Darwinian perspective have never asked what, if any, basis in fact this negative "stereotype" of steprelationships might have.

Are parents more likely to neglect, assault, exploit, and otherwise mistreat their stepchildren than their genetic children? One might suppose that this rather obvious question would have received considerable attention during the explosion of child abuse research that followed Kempe, Silverman, Steele, Droegemuller, and Silver's (1962) agenda-setting proclamation of "the battered-child syndrome." But it did not. The first published study addressing it was our demonstration (Wilson, Daly, & Weghorst, 1980) that stepchildren constituted an enormously higher proportion of child abuse victims in the United States than their numbers in the population-at-large would warrant. Much subsequent research (e.g., Creighton, 1985; Daly & Wilson, 1985, 1988a, 1988b, 1988c, 1991; Ferri, 1984; Flinn, 1988; Gordon, 1989; Hill & Kaplan, 1988; Russell, 1984; Wilson & Daly, 1987) has confirmed and extended these results, demonstrating that excess risk to stepchildren is cross-nationally ubiquitous, is not an artifact of poverty or any other suggested correlate of steprelationship, and extends to a variety of mistreatments but is especially extreme in the most assaultive and dangerous ones.

Conflict in steprelationships is not confined to the violent extremes assayed by child abuse and homicide samples. There is a large amount of literature on American stepfamilies, mainly dealing with volunteer subjects with middle-class backgrounds and relatively minor problems, and this literature has a single focus: the conflicts and dissatisfactions of stepfamily life and how people cope with them (see, e.g., Giles-Sims & Crosbie-Burnett, 1989; Ihinger-Tallman, 1988; Pasley & Ihinger-Tallman, 1987; Wilson & Daly, 1987). Lest we paint too bleak a picture, it is important to stress that people do cope, for the most part reasonably well. Some stepparents, albeit a minority, even feel able to profess to "love" their wards (Duberman, 1975). But, although steprelationships are by no means inevitably hostile, the extensive literature is unanimous that they are, on average, more distant, more conflictual, and less satisfying than the corresponding genetic parent–child relationships.

What then of the effect of stepchildren on the relationship between marriage partners? Not surprisingly, the evidence is that their effect is negative.

Studies of divorce, for example, indicate that each child of the present union is associated with a decrease in the marital-duration-specific likelihood of divorce for first and subsequent marriages alike, at least for the first few children, whereas each child of former unions is associated with an increase in that same divorce risk (Becker, Landes, & Michael, 1977; White & Booth, 1985). The mere presence of children is not the problem then; their effect on marital instability depends on their origins.

More direct investigations of marital conflict tell a story that is consistent with the divorce data. Messinger (1976), for example, asked remarried Canadians who had children from previous marriages to rank the areas of overt conflict in each of their marriages. Children and money topped the list of arenas of conflict in the remarriages, yet they were scarcely mentioned when her respondents considered the conflicts in their failed first marriages. Moreover, it is clear from Messinger's report that the crux of these conflicts over children and over money were the same: The genetic mother wanted more of the stepfather's resources invested in her children than he was inclined to volunteer. For other studies leading to much the same conclusion, see Hobart (1991), White and Booth (1985), and Wilson and Daly (1987).

Stepchildren and Violence Against Wives

An obvious question in light of the above discussion is whether the existence of children sired by previous partners is a risk factor for violence against wives. Again, as with the question of risk to stepchildren themselves, this hypothesis seems never to have occurred to researchers lacking a Darwinian perspective. A review by Hotaling and Sugarman (1986), for example, listed 97 proposed "risk markers" for violence against wives, but parenthood of children was overlooked. Daly and Wilson (1988c) raised the issue and reviewed the fragmentary evidence from studies of spousal homicide, but no direct study appeared for another five years.

The homicide data are certainly suggestive. Lundsgaarde (1977), for example, examined the police files for a one-year sample of Houston homicides and wrote a monograph that includes capsule accounts of 33 conjugal cases. In 11 of these synopses, the brief narrative happened to indicate that there was a stepchild in the household (usually as a witness). One in three—a minimal estimate, since Lundsgaarde evinced no particular interest in the phenomenon and included these facts incidentally—is almost certainly a much higher proportion of stephouseholds than would be expected by chance, but no population-at-large comparison is available. Stepchildren pop up with a similarly uncanny frequency in other descriptive studies of spousal homicides, too (e.g., Chimbos, 1978; Polk, 1994), but the evidence has remained impressionistic.

Daly, Singh, and Wilson (1993) finally addressed this question directly in a study not of homicide victimization, but of Canadian women seeking shelter from assaultive husbands at a women's refuge over a period of one year. Out of 170 such women who reported having one or more children less than 18 years of age and a male partner coresiding at the time of the shelter admission,

48 (28%) had at least one child sired by a previous partner, almost four times the number that should have been expected by chance on the basis of a survey of the local population served by the refuge. The existence of one or more children of the present union, in addition to the stepchild(ren), reduced this overrepresentation only slightly, if at all (Figure 1.1).

Even the results in Figure 1.1 do not demonstrate conclusively that women who have children from previous unions are especially often assaulted, however. An alternative hypothesis is that the data reflect different thresholds for making use of shelter services. This alternative is plausible in view of the fact that the stepchildren themselves face a much higher risk of violence, as noted above, so that their mothers have special cause to fear for their safety. When mothers who sought refuge at the shelter in the Daly et al. (1993) study were asked whether the children, too, had been assaulted, those with children sired by previous partners were much more likely to reply in the affirmative (Figure 1.2).

It must not be forgotten that mistreatment encompasses more than violent assaults. Children are much more likely to be misused as sexual objects by stepfathers than by genetic fathers (Creighton, 1985; Daly & Wilson, 1985; Russell, 1984; Wilson, Daly, & Weghorst, 1981), and such sexual exploitation is a potent source of marital conflict. So although it may well be the case that women with children sired by previous partners are quicker than others

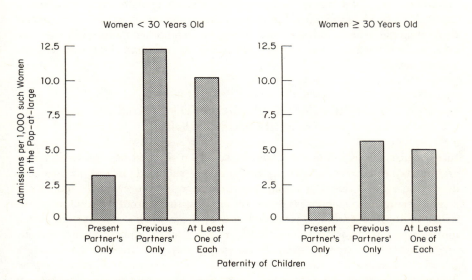

FIGURE 1.1.   The per annum rates at which three groups of Canadian women seeking refuge from assaultive partners entered a women's shelter (Daly, Singh, & Wilson, 1993). Only women coresiding with a male partner and one or more own children less than 18 years of age at the time of admission are represented here, and the three groups are distinguished on the basis of their children's paternity. Data for women below versus above the median age of the shelter clients are portrayed separately.

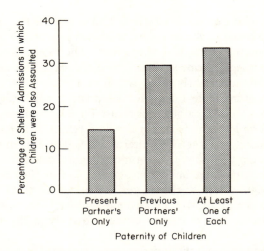

FIGURE 1.2.   The percentages of women seeking refuge from assaultive partners at a Canadian women's shelter who reported that their partners had assaulted the children, as well as themselves, in relation to the children's paternity. Data from Daly, Singh, & Wilson (1993).

to make use of shelter services, flight to the women's refuge can be seen as one of several tactics of maternal defense of the children against stepparental abuse (cf. Wilson & Daly, 1992b). Homicide case descriptions and other materials show that the genetic mother's inclination to defend her children in this and other ways is itself a source of overt marital conflict and an elicitor of violence against her.

IS THERE REALLY AN EVOLVED PSYCHOLOGY
OF STEPPARENTHOOD?

Just because the psyche has evolved by selection, it need not follow that our arguments are correct. Discriminative parental solicitude in response to cues of genetic versus steprelationship may or may not have evolved. People do, after all, enter into stepparental and other substitute parental roles, and, notwithstanding the problems reviewed above, these work out reasonably well more often than not. An evolutionist might suggest that, contrary to our arguments above, stepparenthood has simply not been the sort of recurring adaptive problem that would have inspired the evolution of psychological defenses against it. Nonnutritive saccharine, an evolutionarily unforeseen component of novel environments, activates our evolved system for the recognition of nutritive sugars. Might stepparenthood constitute a sort of "social saccharine," a novel social environment in which the evolved psychology of parenthood is activated maladaptively?

Such a hypothesis appears to gain plausibility when one turns to the social scientific literature on steprelationships. Cherlin (1978) proposed that stepparenthood is a novel role or status with ground rules yet to be established, and that difficulties attend steprelationships because of this "incomplete institutionalization" and attendant "role ambiguity." Many family sociologists have embraced and elaborated on this sort of interpretation, which is in effect a novel social environment argument, albeit a non-Darwinian one. Unfortunately, it is also a naive argument. Evolutionists, recognizing the different functions that different relationships serve for the individuals involved, have long been concerned to characterize the qualitatively distinct criteria defining an ideal mate (for example) versus an ideal daughter versus an ideal same-sex friend. However, mainstream social scientists have only recently recognized that different social relationships vary even quantitatively (e.g., in their degree of "intimacy"), and have yet to make the characterization of the essential distinguishing features of, say, peer versus mating versus filial versus sibling relationships and their respective psychologies a part of their analytic agenda. Thus, one implicit premise of Cherlin's "novel social role" argument is that social influences and expectations affect all roles and relationships in qualitatively similar ways. Reconciling this premise with elementary principles of social evolution would be difficult, if not impossible, but the social scientists who adhere to it have not yet perceived the problems facing their domain-general conception of sociality, let alone confronted them.

Of course, the fact that Cherlin's (1978) novel social role argument is uninformed by Darwinism does not mean that it must be wrong. Even on its own terms, however, this popular analysis is ahistorical, ethnocentric, and counterfactual. Steprelationships are not new. The mortality levels incurred by tribal hunter-gatherers guarantee that remarriage and stepparenthood have been common for as long as people have formed biparental, marital bonds; moreover, the ethnographies of recent and contemporary hunter-gatherers abound with anecdotal information on both the prevalence of steprelationships and their predictable conflicts (e.g., Hill & Kaplan, 1988). Nor is it correct to claim even that steprelationships are newly prevalent in "our society." Historical records indicate that stepparental relationships, consequent on both widowhood and divorce, have been numerous for centuries in the Western world (e.g., Dupâquier, Hélin, Laslett, Livi-Bacci, & Segner, 1981). Moreover, European historical archives show that having a stepparent was associated with mortality risk in fact and not just in fairy tale (Voland, 1988).

Attempts to account for stepfamily conflict in terms of the peculiarities of rapid social change in the contemporary West (or, more commonly, in terms of the peculiarities of the United States) are superfluous. All available evidence suggests that steprelationships are more conflictual than the corresponding genetic relationships in *all* societies, regardless of whether steprelationships are rare or common and regardless of their degree of institutionalization. The social saccharine hypothesis is without foundation.

But, if parasitism by stepchildren has been a chronic, significant threat to fitness, why doesn't human parental psychology reject them more consistently? Why, in other words, do people treat their stepchildren for the most part quite tolerantly and even make costly investments in their welfare? We suggest that the answer resides in the fact that a stepparent assumes pseudoparental obligations in the context of a complex array of costs and benefits, reciprocities and negotiations. If having dependent children of former unions decreases one's value on the marriage market (as it apparently does; see Wilson & Daly, 1987), then such children constitute a cost or deterrent to remarriage for the prospective stepparent. All parties are likely to recognize more or less explicitly that stepparental tolerance and investment constitute benefits bestowed on the genetic parent and the child, entitling the stepparent to a better bargain than the stepparent's mate value would otherwise warrant, whether in the form of a better quality of mate or of behavioral reciprocities. The genetic parent is likely to be grateful for stepparental investment, whereas comparable investment from a spouse who is the child's genetic parent would be considered only one's due. The interesting questions then are not why parental affection and action can ever be directed toward manifestly unrelated children, but whether the motives and emotions of stepparents vis-à-vis the children ordinarily (or indeed ever) become essentially like those of genetic parents and, if not, how they differ.

An obvious hypothesis from a Darwinian view of parental motives is that stepparental feelings will indeed differ from those of genetic parents, at least quantitatively and perhaps qualitatively, too. Indulgence toward stepchildren may be a good way to promote domestic solidarity and tranquility, but the circumstances must always have been rare in which a stepchild's welfare was as valuable to the adult's expected fitness as a genetic child's welfare would be. By this argument, one should not necessarily expect to see ubiquitous abuse of stepchildren, but one would not expect to see stepparents sacrificing as much for them as genetic parents either. So, is there in fact a large difference between genetic parents and stepparents in willingness to incur major costs (e.g., life-threatening risks) on the children's behalf? We expect that there is, but we know of no relevant research. There is, however, plenty of evidence that stepparents and stepchildren alike view their relationships as less loving and as a less dependable source of material and emotional support than genetic parent–offspring relationships (e.g., Duberman, 1975; Ferri, 1984; Flinn, 1988; Perkins & Kahan, 1979; Santrock & Sitterle, 1987).

WHY SHOULD SOCIAL SCIENTISTS LEARN TO THINK EVOLUTIONARILY?

One answer to this question is in the findings. Living with a stepparent has turned out to be the most powerful predictor of severe child abuse risk yet discovered, but two decades of intensive child abuse research conducted without the heuristic assistance of Darwinian insights never discovered it. Likewise, the intensive epidemiological search for risk markers for violence against wives overlooked the same factor until evolutionary thinking led us to look.

The human psyche—the species-characteristic bundle of mind/brain mechanisms that produces human behavior—has evolved by selection. That is not controversial. Whether thinking evolutionarily will prove to be useful for generating sound psychological hypotheses relevant to topics such as violence against wives is, however, a genuine issue; obviously, we think it already has been useful and will continue to be. But even if willing to grant that evolutionary sophistication is a valuable aid to psychological science, social scientists may question whether psychological reductionism is an appropriate approach to the questions that interest them. We would argue (with Tooby & Cosmides, 1992) that sociological, economic, and political hypotheses are necessarily built on implicit psychological hypotheses about how individual human actors perceive and are affected by social, economic, and political variables, and that social scientific theories can be better developed and tested if they make their implicit assumptions about psychology explicit.

An impediment to evolutionary sophistication within psychology itself has been a suspicion of purposive concepts that explain action in terms of its ends. Hard sciences have supposedly progressed by shedding this sort of "teleological" thinking and adhering to a mechanistic causality. From this perspective, Darwin's discovery of natural selection was an orthodox event in the advance of scientific understanding for it replaced a supernatural purposive creator with a blind mechanism. What many psychologists have yet to grasp, however, is that the mechanistic process of selection resolves psychology's perennial confusion about how to deal with the manifest fact that living things have complex "purpose" instantiated in their structures, thus rendering doctrinaire antagonism to purposive concepts obsolete (Daly & Wilson, 1995). Darwin's theory made seemingly teleological reasoning scientific by showing that the consequences of biological phenomena constitute an essential part of their explanation: what they achieve is in a specific, concrete sense why they exist. Why an organ or a process or a preference exists or takes the form it does is just as legitimate a scientific question as how it works, and answers of the form "in order to . . . " are legitimate scientific answers. Wings are meaningfully hypothesized to exist for flying, livers to exist for detoxification, a "sweet tooth" to exist for promoting the ingestion of nutritive sugars, male sexual jealousy to exist for paternity assurance, and so forth.

Unfortunately, psychologists and social scientists have not always understood this implication of Darwinism. A common confusion is to imagine that the purposive functionality of evolutionary biology is isomorphic with an account of goals and drives. In other words, evolutionists are misunderstood to claim that fitness itself is what people and other animals strive for. In actuality, fitness consequences are properly invoked not as direct objectives or motivators, but as explanations of why certain proximal objectives and motivators have evolved to play their particular roles in the causal control of behavior. Selection designs organisms to cope with particular adaptive problems that have been sufficiently persistent across generations, both in their essential forms and in their significance, to have favored particular solutions. These evolved solutions necessarily entail contingent responsiveness to environmental features that were statistical predictors of the average fitness consequences of alternative courses of action in the past. Adaptation is not prospective; adaptive performance in contemporary environments depends on the persistence of essential features of past environments.

Also impeding an infusion of evolutionary sophistication among social scientists is the false dichotomy of "social" versus "biological" explanations. Subscribers to this dichotomy equate biology with its mechanistic subdisciplines such as genetics and endocrinology and think of biological influences as intrinsic and irremediable, to be contrasted with extrinsic and remediable social influences. Moreover, since putative biological influences are invariant and constraining, those who propose their existence (the so-called nature crowd) are unmasked as pessimists and reactionaries, while the advocates of "alternative" social influences (the so-called nurture crowd) are optimists and progressives. This ideology, predicated on a profound incomprehension of evolutionary biology, pervades the social sciences, in which it is often accepted by nature advocates as thoroughly and thoughtlessly as by their nurture foes. A presumption of this prevalent worldview is that biology (falsely defined as the study of the invariant innate) is mute about aspects of sociality and behavior manifesting developmentally, experientially, and circumstantially contingent variations. The very demonstration of any such contingency is seen as an exercise in the alternative, antibiological mode of explanation. The irony is that developmentally, experientially, and circumstantially contingent variation is precisely what evolutionary biological theories of social phenomena are about.

The above misunderstandings are particularly prevalent and destructive with respect to sex and gender. Mistakenly imagining that evolutionary biology is somehow more deterministic than, say, sociology and is therefore somehow reactionary, countless writers have deplored the supposed sexism of sociobiology, without troubling to attain a first-undergraduate-course level of familiarity with the relevant theories and research. (Ironically, the field's fundamental theories about sex—see Charnov, 1982—cannot be made to lend even superficial support to the notion that one sex is superior to the other. They can much more readily be taken to imply the ineluctably equal value of females and males, although the value in question is arguably incommensurate with moral worth in any case.)

As for feminism, evolutionary biology is of direct relevance to its central conceptual and practical concerns (Gowaty, 1992). Feminism has confronted the fact that women and men are different. Thinking selectively can help us see how and why they differ. Feminism has confronted the fact that men are motivated to limit women's autonomy. Thinking selectively can help elucidate when and where this is especially problematic. Feminism has confronted the fact that sisterhood is not always powerful. Thinking selectively can provide insight into the factors that facilitate and interfere with female solidarity. Darwinism has revealed some fundamental things about the male–female phenomenon, and it has the conceptual tools to direct the discovery of much more. Those interested in matters of gender—and who is not?—scorn the theory of evolution by selection to their own disadvantage.

Acknowledgments. Financial support for this research was provided by the Natural Sciences and Engineering Research Council of Canada, the Social Sciences and Humanities Research Council of Canada, the Harry Frank Guggenheim Foundation, and the Arts Research Board of McMaster University (Hamilton, Ontario, Canada). This chapter was written while the authors were scholars in residence at the Rockefeller Foundation's Bellagio Study Center (Bellagio, Italy). David Buss and Joanna Scheib provided useful criticism of an earlier version.

REFERENCES

Baker, R. R., & Bellis, M. A. (1989). Number of sperm in human ejaculates varies in accordance with sperm competition theory. *Animal Behaviour, 37,* 867–869.

Baker, R. R., & Bellis, M. A. (1994). *Human sperm competition: Copulation, masturbation and infidelity.* London: Chapman & Hall.

Becker, G. S., Landes, E. M., & Michael, R. T. (1977). An economic analysis of marital instability. *Journal of Political Economy, 85,* 1141–1187.

Betzig, L. (1986). *Despotism and differential reproduction: A Darwinian view of history.* Hawthorne, NY: Aldine de Gruyter.

Bryan, L. R., Coleman, M., Ganong, L., & Bryan, S. H. (1986). Person perception: Family structure as a cue for stereotyping. *Journal of Marriage and the Family, 48,* 169–174.

Buss, D. M., Larsen, R. J., Westen, D., & Semmelroth, J. (1992). Sex differences in jealousy: Evolution, physiology, and psychology. *Psychological Science, 3,* 251–255.

Buss, D. M., & Schmitt, D. P. (1993). Sexual strategies theory: An evolutionary perspective on human mating. *Psychological Review, 100,* 204–232.

Charnov, E. L. (1982). *The theory of sex allocation.* Princeton, NJ: Princeton University Press.

Cherlin, A. (1978). Remarriage as an incomplete institution. *American Journal of Sociology, 84,* 534–650.

Chimbos, P. D. (1978). *Marital violence: A study of interspouse homicide.* San Francisco: R & E Research Associates.

Creighton, S. J. (1985). An epidemiological study of abused children and their families in the United Kingdom between 1977 and 1982. *Child Abuse and Neglect, 9,* 441–448.

Daly, M., Singh, L., & Wilson, M. (1993). Children fathered by previous partners: A risk factor for violence against women. *Canadian Journal of Public Health, 84,* 209–210.

Daly, M., & Wilson, M. (1983). *Sex, evolution and behavior* (2nd ed.). Belmont, CA: Wadsworth.

Daly, M., & Wilson, M. (1985). Child abuse and other risks of not living with both parents. *Ethology and Sociobiology, 6,* 197–210.

Daly, M., & Wilson, M. (1988a). The Darwinian psychology of discriminative parental solicitude. *Nebraska Symposium on Motivation, 35,* 91–144.

Daly, M., & Wilson, M. (1988b). Evolutionary social psychology and family homicide. *Science, 242,* 519–524.

Daly, M., & Wilson, M. (1988c). *Homicide.* Hawthorne, NY: Aldine de Gruyter.

Daly, M., & Wilson, M. (1991). A reply to Gelles: Stepchildren *are* disproportionately abused, and diverse forms of violence can share causal factors. *Human Nature*, 2, 419–426.

Daly, M., & Wilson, M. (1994). Stepparenthood and the evolved psychology of discriminative parental solicitude. In S. Parmigiani & F. vom Saal (Eds.), *Infanticide and parental care*. Chur, Switzerland: Harwood Press, pp. 121–134.

Daly, M., & Wilson, M. (1995). Discriminative parental solicitude and the relevance of evolutionary models to the analysis of motivational systems. In M. Gazzaniga (Ed.), *The cognitive neurosciences*. Cambridge, MA: Massachusetts Institute of Technology Press, pp. 1269–1286.

Daly, M., Wilson, M., & Weghorst, S. J. (1982). Male sexual jealousy. *Ethology and Sociobiology*, 3, 11–17.

Darwin, C., & Wallace, A. R. (1858). On the tendency of species to form varieties; and on the perpetuation of varieties and species by natural means of selection. *Journal of the Linnaean Society of London (Zoology)*, 3, 45–62.

Dawkins, R. (1986). *The blind watchmaker*. Harlow, UK: Longmans.

Duberman, L. (1975). *The reconstituted family: A study of remarried couples and their children*. Chicago: Nelson-Hall.

Dupâquier, J., Hélin, E., Laslett, P., Livi-Bacci, M., & Segner, S. (Eds.). (1981). *Marriage and remarriage in populations of the past*. London: Academic Press.

Ferri, E. (1984). *Stepchildren: A national study*. Windsor, UK: NFER-Nelson.

Fine, M. A. (1986). Perceptions of stepparents: Variations in stereotypes as a function of current family structure. *Journal of Marriage and the Family*, 48, 537–543.

Fischer, E. A. (1988). Simultaneous hermaphroditism, tit-for-tat, and the evolutionary stability of social systems. *Ethology and Sociobiology*, 9, 119–136.

Flinn, M. V. (1988). Step- and genetic parent/offspring relationships in a Caribbean village. *Ethology and Sociobiology*, 9, 335–369.

Friedan, B. (1963). *The feminine mystique*. New York: Dell.

Gaulin, S. J. C., & Sailer, L. D. (1985). Are females the ecological sex? *American Anthropologist*, 87, 111–119.

Giles-Sims, J., & Crosbie-Burnett, M. (1989). Stepfamily research: Implications for policy, clinical interventions, and further research. *Family Relations*, 38, 19–23.

Gordon, M. (1989). The family environment of sexual abuse: A comparison of natal and stepfather abuse. *Child Abuse and Neglect*, 13, 121–130.

Gowaty, P. A. (1992). Evolutionary biology and feminism. *Human Nature*, 3, 217–249.

Haig, D. (1993). Maternal-fetal conflict in human pregnancy. *Quarterly Review of Biology*, 68, 495–532.

Hamilton, W. D. (1964). The genetical evolution of social behaviour. I and II. *Journal of Theoretical Biology*, 7, 1–52.

Hill, K., & Kaplan, H. (1988). Tradeoffs in male and female reproductive strategies among the Ache, part 2. In L. Betzig, M. Borgerhoff Mulder, & P. Turke (Eds.), *Human reproductive behavior*. Cambridge, UK: Cambridge University Press, pp. 291–305.

Hobart, C. (1991). Conflict in remarriages. *Journal of Divorce and Remarriage*, 15, 69–86.

Hotaling, G. T., & Sugarman, D. B. (1986). An analysis of risk markers in husband to wife violence: The current state of knowledge. *Violence and Victims*, 2, 101–124.

Ihinger-Tallman, M. (1988). Research on stepfamilies. *Annual Review of Sociology*, 14, 25–48.

Kempe, C. H., Silverman, F. S., Steele, B. F., Droegemuller, W., & Silver, H. K. (1962). The battered-child syndrome. *Journal of the American Medical Association, 181,* 105–112.

Low, B. S. (1978). Environmental uncertainty and the parental strategies of marsupials and placentals. *American Naturalist, 112,* 197–213.

Lundsgaarde, H. P. (1977). *Murder in space city.* New York: Oxford University Press.

Mayr, E. (1983). How to carry out the adaptationist program? *American Naturalist, 121,* 324–334.

Messinger, L. (1976). Remarriage between divorced people with children from previous marriages: A proposal for preparation for remarriage. *Journal of Marriage and the Family, 2,* 193–199.

Paley, W. (1802). *Natural theology; or evidences of the existence and attributes of the deity, collected from the appearances of nature.* London: Fauldner.

Pasley, K., & Ihinger-Tallman, M. (Eds.). (1987). *Remarriage and stepparenting: Current research and theory.* New York: Guilford Press.

Perkins, T. F., & Kahan, J. P. (1979). An empirical comparison of natural-father and stepfather family systems. *Family Process, 18,* 175–183.

Polk, K. (1994). *When men kill: Scenarios of masculine violence.* Cambridge, UK: Cambridge University Press.

Russell, D. E. H. (1984). The prevalence and seriousness of incestuous abuse: Stepfathers versus biological fathers. *Child Abuse and Neglect, 8,* 15–22.

Santrock, J. W., & Sitterle, K. A. (1987). Parent-child relationships in stepmother families. In K. Pasley & M. Ihinger-Tallman (Eds.), *Remarriage and stepparenting: Current research and theory.* New York: Guilford Press, pp. 273–299.

Symons, D. (1979). *The evolution of human sexuality.* New York: Oxford University Press.

Teismann, M. W., & Mosher, D. L. (1978). Jealous conflict in dating couples. *Psychological Reports, 42,* 1211–1216.

Thompson, S. (1955). *Motif-index of folk-literature* (Vols. 1–6). Bloomington, IN: Indiana University Press.

Tooby, J., & Cosmides, L. (1992). The psychological foundations of culture. In J. H. Barkow, L. Cosmides, & J. Tooby (Eds.), *The adapted mind: Evolutionary psychology and the generation of culture.* New York: Oxford University Press, pp. 19–136.

Trivers, R. L. (1972). Parental investment and sexual selection. In B. Campbell (Ed.), *Sexual selection and the descent of man 1871–1971.* Chicago: Aldine, pp. 136–179.

Trivers, R. L. (1974). Parent-offspring conflict. *American Zoologist, 14,* 249–264.

Voland, E. (1988). Differential infant and child mortality in evolutionary perspective: Data from late 17th to 19th century Ostfriesland. In L. Betzig, M. Borgerhoff Mulder, & P. Turke (Eds.), *Human reproductive behavior.* Cambridge, UK: Cambridge University Press, pp. 253–261.

White, L. K., & Booth, A. (1985). The quality and stability of remarriages: The role of stepchildren. *American Sociological Review, 50,* 689–698.

Wilson, M., & Daly, M. (1987). Risk of maltreatment of children living with stepparents. In R. J. Gelles & J. B. Lancaster (Eds.), *Child abuse and neglect: Biosocial dimensions.* New York: Aldine de Gruyter, pp. 215–232.

Wilson, M., & Daly, M. (1992a). The man who mistook his wife for a chattel. In J. H. Barkow, L. Cosmides, & J. Tooby (Eds.), *The adapted mind: Evolutionary psychology and the generation of culture.* New York: Oxford University Press, pp. 289–322.

Wilson, M., & Daly, M. (1992b). Who kills whom in spouse killings? On the exceptional sex ratio of spousal homicides in the United States. *Criminology, 30,* 189–215.

Wilson, M., & Daly, M. (1993). Spousal homicide risk and estrangement. *Violence and Victims, 8,* 3–15.

Wilson, M. I., Daly, M., & Weghorst, S. J. (1980). Household composition and the risk of child abuse and neglect. *Journal of Biosocial Science, 12,* 333–340.

Wilson, M., Daly, M., & Weghorst, S. J. (1981). Differential maltreatment of girls and boys. *Victimology, 6,* 249–261.

2

Power, Harassment, and Trophy Mates: The Feminist Advantages of an Evolutionary Perspective

DOUGLAS T. KENRICK, MELANIE R. TROST, AND VIRGIL L. SHEETS

When Darwin (1859) first proposed his theory of natural selection, it was regarded as a radical affront to the established order because it moved *Homo sapiens* from a special place at God's right hand to just another randomly selected spot on an ever-changing map. Ironically, some social scientists now seem to regard any application of Darwinian theory to human behavior as an attempt to bolster the established order, supposedly replacing cherished models of random cultural variation with a god-given and inviolable set of genetic blueprints. In particular, a number of social scientists believe that evolutionary theorists wish to lock men and women into rigid "genetically determined" sex roles that position men as omnipotent Gods and women as their humble handmaidens. This misperception is unfortunate for several reasons. To ignore the evolutionary history of any species is to blind oneself to some of the key pieces needed to explain the puzzle of why they do the things they do. This is as true of *Homo sapiens* as it is of any other living species. Another reason particularly relevant to the psychology of gender differences is that the alternative perspectives have often focused on narrow, male-oriented definitions of power and have failed to give females their due.

We begin by describing the phenomena of sexual harassment and so-called trophy wives. Prevailing sociocultural views have provided explanations for these phenomena that are not only incapable of explaining the available data, but that are also inadvertently sexist. These positions imply that females are helpless pawns and males are omnipotent despots in relationships. We explain how the gender differences linked with these phenomena are related to the general evolutionary principle of sexual selection, a concept that assumes female choice as its most powerful driving force. We also explain how evolutionary principles are linked to environmental regulation and not simply "genetic determinism." Rather than forcing women or men to throw up their hands in helpless despair, an evolutionary perspective provides a more powerful tool for effective action by replacing prejudice and superstition with basic knowledge of human nature.

ORGANIZATIONAL INTEGRATION AND SEXUAL HARASSMENT

Before World War II, the American workplace was much more sexually segregated than it is today. Subsequent increases in sexual integration have resulted in increases in sexual relationships within organizations (Dillard & Miller, 1988; Spruell, 1985). Several reviewers have suggested that attraction between coworkers may be an inevitable outcome of powerful social psychological processes (Colwill & Lips, 1988; Dillard & Miller, 1988). These processes include the tendency to become attracted to others who share similar interests (Byrne, 1971; Singh & Tan, 1992) and the tendency to become attracted to others to whom one is exposed frequently (Bornstein & D'Agostino, 1992; Festinger, Schachter, & Back, 1950). The similarity-attraction effect is likely to be enhanced as modern women and men take similar professional jobs based on personal interests.

It is probably uncontroversial to assume that the increasing integration of the workplace, accompanied by increases in personal freedom and opportunities for relationships with similar others, is a largely positive development. Yet this development has also precipitated some problems and controversies within organizations (Colwill & Lips, 1988; Ford & McLaughlin, 1987; Libbin & Stevens, 1988; Westhoff, 1986). For example, some have expressed concern that a personal relationship might disrupt the partners' work relationship. However, it has not been clearly established that productivity is hampered by intimate relationships with coworkers, and some evidence suggests positive effects in this domain (Dillard & Miller, 1988). Whereas affectionate relationships between mutually consenting coworkers can be a benefit, another outcome of increased relationship opportunities within organizations is an increase in sexual harassment (Ford & McLaughlin, 1987; Libbin & Stevens, 1988). This issue was brought to the forefront of the public's awareness during the congressional hearings for Supreme Court Justice Clarence Thomas, who was accused of having sexually harassed Anita Hill while she was working as a government employee under his supervision. Sexual harassment is not limited to corporations and government agencies; it is also a controversial issue on college and university campuses. In fact, several universities have banned all dating between students and faculty (Begley et al., 1993). The bans were adopted to alleviate the concern that female students feel pressured to become involved with male professors. In many cases, students who complain of "romantic feelers" from faculty worry that spurning the advances would endanger their grades (Begley et al., 1993).

A common thread uniting the university cases and the Thomas-Hill hearings is a stark sex difference—older, powerful males and younger females in subordinate roles. This gender difference is common in cases of sexual harassment. Studd and Gattiker (1991) report that, of 95 sexual harassment cases they found during one year in Canada, only 2 cases involved a male victim. It is interesting that both of those cases also involved a male perpetrator. One suggested solution to the problem of sexual harassment has been to define any sexual relations, or suggestion of such relations, between individuals at different power levels as sexual harassment. Such blanket rules have not been universally well received and have led to legal conflicts over their enforcement (Begley et al., 1993; Libbin & Stevens, 1988). Given that these rules are designed to protect women, it is interesting to note that not all of the voices objecting to these rules are men's; many women have rejected them as well (Begley et al., 1993). As we discuss below, an evolutionary perspective may help us to understand why women do not universally favor such sanctions.

TROPHY WIVES

A related controversy, also involving younger females and older males with organizational power, is the phenomenon of so-called trophy wives. In August 1989, an article in *Fortune* magazine provided the stimulus for this controversy (Connelly, 1989). A derivative article in our local paper was titled: "Many Women Not Amused—CEOs Collecting Trophies." That article described a

> growing trend among powerful chief executives who are discarding their long-standing spouses for "trophy wives"—women typically younger . . . beautiful and very often accomplished.

> The nine page cover story [in *Fortune*] has caused a late-summer sensation. [The editor of *Fortune* reportedly said] 80 percent of the mail—largely negative—has come from women. Many letter writers are first wives "outraged at the phenomenon." (Roel, 1989, pp. a1–a2)

Two points are important to note about these excerpts. First, the phenomenon of powerful chief executives remarrying younger, attractive women was described as a "growing trend"; second, men were given central responsibility for the "trophy hunting."

The purpose of this chapter is to examine some issues surrounding sex and power in organizations from an evolutionary perspective. Adopting an evolutionary perspective helps clarify the trophy wives phenomenon, as well as the reported sex difference in harassment. An understanding of the evolutionary bases of sex differences in sexual and power motives can also help to explain why blanket rules forbidding relationships between males and females in organizations are not always well received by women. Although such rules might serve to curb some of the more exploitative manifestations of male mating strategies, they also interfere with common female mating strategies. In fact, we argue that the very name given to the trophy wives phenomenon illustrates an unwitting sexist bias common in culturally based explanations of sex differences—the tendency to ignore the role of female choice in mating relationships.

We first summarize data that suggest that rules outlawing intimate relationships would affect a fairly large percentage of women and men in the workforce, many of whom may experience sexual attractions that cross power lines but who are innocent of harassment, favoritism, or unproductivity. Following this, we consider social scientists' explanations of the trophy wives phenomenon to illustrate how traditional, unquestioned assumptions about cultural determination can be quite misleading. We then discuss how findings related to sexual harassment and trophy wives can be understood in light of recent findings from evolutionary psychology.

THE PREVALENCE OF COWORKER RELATIONSHIPS

How many people have dated or been involved with others who work in the same organization? In a very informal study designed to get a feel for this, two of us asked our students in several large classes to survey people they knew who were over the age of 25. We used that age cutoff because we were interested in obtaining a sample of those who had worked long enough to have possibly dated a coworker. Figure 2.1 portrays the results of that informal survey.

As indicated in Figure 2.1, approximately 60% of both sexes in this sample had been involved with coworkers at least once. We also asked them to indicate their level of involvement with their coworkers and the relative status of the coworker with whom they were most recently involved. The results are depicted in Figure 2.2.

As Figure 2.2 indicates, a large percentage of relationships is between peers, as would be expected from both the similarity and interaction principles of attraction. However, there was a sex difference in involvement with a higher status versus a lower status coworker. Males were unlikely to have been involved with someone of higher status; conversely, females were unlikely to have been involved with someone of lower status. Other research reveals similar findings. For instance, Dillard and Miller (1988) collected more systematic data and found that 60% of females' relationships in organizations were with males of higher rank. There are several possible explanations for this discrepancy. One possibility is that coworkers may pair up randomly, but the sex discrepancy may be accounted for by the base rates of high- and low-status males and females in the workplace. A second explanation is that males may be using positions of power to influence females of lower status to

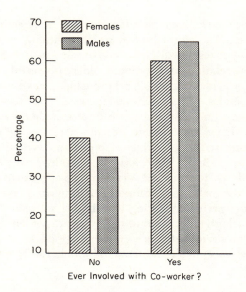

FIGURE 2.1. Percentage of respondents who have ever been involved with a coworker.

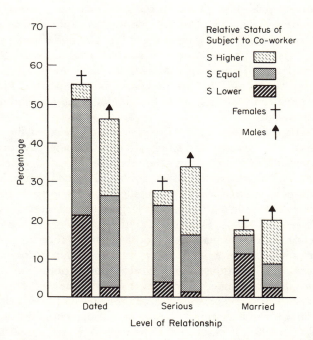

FIGURE 2.2. Relative status level of coworker involved with respondent as a function of sex and level of relationship.

date them. Another alternative is that females may be rejecting males who are below them in status. These possibilities are not mutually exclusive.

In the following pages, we discuss some of our research that deals with the general question of relationships between older, powerful men and younger women. We present evidence that (1) relationships between high-status males and lower status females, (2) greater male interest in initiating sexual relationships with colleagues, and (3) female selection of higher status males may all go hand in hand. These phenomena fit with a larger body of data on sex differences in mating strategies, which supports an evolutionary perspective on mate selection (e.g., Buss, 1989; Kenrick, Groth, Trost, & Sadalla, 1993; Mealey, 1985; Sadalla, Kenrick, & Vershure, 1987; Townsend, 1989). The evidence suggests that males may compete for status and power partly because our female ancestors preferred mating with higher status males. Evolutionary theorists are increasingly appreciating the extent to which differential female choice has been a powerful force in shaping many of the physical and behavioral differences between males and females (Small, 1992; Smuts, 1985).

GENERAL BACKGROUND ON THE
EVOLUTIONARY PERSPECTIVE

The notion that human social behavior can be explained in evolutionary terms has had a controversial history within the social sciences. In his 1908 book, *Social Psychology*, William McDougall adopted an explicitly Darwinian view of human social behavior. McDougall argued that an understanding of human nature is the "essential foundation" of all the social sciences. McDougall's predecessor at Harvard, William James, had likewise written his landmark *Principles of Psychology* (1890) from a Darwinian perspective. However, the evolutionary perspective of these early functionalists did not lead to a successful research paradigm.

After 1920, the evolutionary view was largely rejected by behaviorists who deemphasized phylogeny and emphasized ontogenetic environmental factors as determinants of behavior. In other areas of the social sciences, anthropologists such as Franz Boas and Margaret Mead argued that field studies of different cultures supported a view of human behavior in general, and of sex differences in behavior in particular, as largely unconstrained by biological influences (Freeman, 1983). Of course, neither behaviorists nor cultural anthropologists denied that humans evolved; they simply adopted a position that variations in adult behavior were more related to variations in the social environment than to variations in biological predisposition.

There have been a number of important advances in evolutionary research and theory since 1908, and recent research indicates that evolutionary models may be essential for understanding human social behavior (Buss, 1990; Daly & Wilson, 1983, 1988; Kenrick, 1993; Kenrick & Keefe, 1992; Lumsden & Wilson, 1981). The renewed excitement regarding evolutionary models of human behavior stems from several sources. Research on instinctive control of animal behavior has combined with research on artificial intelligence to suggest that it is hardly unreasonable to assume that animals could be "programmed" in ways that allow for a great deal of flexibility in dealing with a complex environment (Alcock, 1993; Barkow, Cosmides, & Tooby, 1992; Eibl-Eibesfeldt, 1975; Gardner, 1985; Lumsden & Wilson, 1981). At the same time, behavior genetic research has strongly supported the existence of heritable individual differences in human behavioral traits and has overturned the assumption that early family environment can easily account for differences in adult social behavior (Bouchard, 1993; Plomin & Daniels, 1987; Rowe, 1991). Finally, cross-cultural studies of social behavior have suggested that early interpretations of the anthropological literature were premature. The discoveries of a number of cross-cultural universals in human behavior suggest that at least some of human behavior is quite unaffected by chance variations in the cultural environment. For example, cross-cultural studies by Ekman and his colleagues have strongly supported Darwin's early speculations about the possible universality of emotional expressions (Ekman, 1992; Ekman & Friesen, 1971; Ekman et al., 1987). It appears that a smile and a scowl convey the same sentiment in Michigan, Mongolia, and Madagascar. In another domain, Daly and Wilson (1988) have reviewed homicide statistics to reveal a number of universalities in murderous violence across cultures. For example, males commit over 80% of the homicides in every human culture ever studied, contrary to the previous assumption of social scientists that this sex difference was attributable to some feature of modern Western society. Eibl-Eibesfeldt has uncovered universal flirtation gestures that involve subtle sequencing of micromovements that seem likely to occur outside of voluntary control or awareness. Along similar lines, recent studies by Buss (1989) and Kenrick and Keefe have unveiled cross-cultural sex differences in mate preferences that are unlikely to be explainable by common cultural experience; this is discussed below.

Is it necessary for social scientists typically interested in the proximate causes of behaviors such as mating choice and sexual coercion to consider evolution? We strongly believe the answer is yes. By ignoring the evolutionary context of ongoing human behavior, social scientists sometimes make serious blunders in their search for explanations of social phenomena. This is particularly true when discussing human courtship and mating behavior. Researchers in this area have often blindly assumed that certain patterns of mating behavior can be explained in terms of the norms of American culture, even without considering the evidence needed to support such an explanation. The trophy wives controversy provides an interesting illustration of the potential limitations of such explanations.

THE TROPHY WIVES PHENOMENON

As we noted above, the phenomenon of trophy wives was reported as a trend in which older male executives were divorcing their older wives and remarrying younger, attractive women. In the original article, several social science experts were called in to explain the so-called trend. Helen Singer Kaplan offered the following explanation:

> In some cases the man with the old nice matronly wife is looked down on. He's not seen as keeping up appearances. Why can't he do better for himself? (Connelly, 1989, p. 53)

Kaplan thus attributes the phenomenon to the powerful man's desire to present a successful public image. In the same article, psychologist Harry Levinson provides a more cultural explanation:

> The culture of self-indulgence has just crept up to the CEO level. Indulgence is an issue for people who have worked very hard to get where they are. They feel they've earned it, they're entitled to it. (Connelly, 1989, p. 53)

Two points are important to note about Levinson's explanation. First, the phenomenon is explained in terms of a "culture of self-indulgence"; second, Levinson assumes that this cultural influence has only recently begun to influence chief executive officers of large corporations.

In another article on the trend, sociologist Arthur Neal "attributes the trend to men's competitiveness and emotional immaturity" in combination with "longer lifespans and smaller family sizes." The article quotes Neal as saying that

> Our *cultural image* [italics added] of a mature man is typically in his late 40s or 50s, and has been successful in his career. . . . The *cultural image* [italics added] of the ideal female is someone in her 20s or early 30s. . . . This should be no surprise at all [says Neal since] we live in an advertising culture, and that is encouraged. It's also part of the insatiability built into modern culture. (Winegar, 1989, p. f2)

To summarize these explanations, the immediate causal emphasis is on the characteristics of the male, as opposed to the female. The ultimate source of the male's competitiveness, immaturity, and self-indulgence is traced to factors in the social environment—the "culture of self-indulgence" and the related "cultural images" in the advertising media.

Two features of these analyses are of interest. First, they are consistent with the tendency among social scientists to construct explanations based on norms of modern American society without ever documenting that the phenomenon in question is actually limited to our culture and to our time. A similar bias has been noted in explanations of homicide patterns in the United States (Daly & Wilson, 1988). Second, the cultural relativist assumption is accompanied by a tendency to view women as passive victims, pawns, and, in this case, trophies who are manipulated, controlled, and traded according to the whims and fancies of all-powerful and omniscient men.

Although some feminists have explicitly adopted an evolutionary perspective (e.g., Moore, 1985; Small, 1992; Smuts, 1985), the evolutionary viewpoint has often been rejected as politically unacceptable by many feminists, who have instead favored the view that sex roles are arbitrarily constructed by cultures. It is no doubt true that sex roles vary from culture to culture, in ways that sometimes seem arbitrary (men in Scotland wear skirts, their cousins in Montana do not). However, it is also true that a number of sex differences in human behavior are strongly linked to physiological variations that are best understood by looking further back in history than the beginning of American (or Athabascan or even aboriginal) culture. Even if the evolutionary model did have unprogressive implications in today's world, we cannot rewrite the evolutionary history of our species. In fact, we will suggest that it is instead the cultural explanations that have inadvertently adopted positions offensive and regressive in their depictions of women (and men alike). For example, Tangri, Burt, and Johnson (1982) outline a sociocultural model of sexual harassment that assumes that "sexual harassment is one manifestation of the larger patriarchal system in which men rule and social beliefs legitimize their rule," (p. 40) and that "society rewards . . . females for passivity and acquiescence . . . not to trust their own judgment about what happens to them, and to feel responsible for their own victimization" (p. 40).

Contrary to this widely accepted view of powerful males and helpless females, evolutionary approaches focus on female choice as one of the primary mechanisms driving gender differences (Moore, 1985; Small, 1992; Smuts, 1985). Thus, the evolutionary perspective, when accurately understood, is actually a more affirmative view of women than that of the sociocultural perspectives. We do not believe that scientific theories can be accepted or rejected out of considerations of sociopolitical popularity (otherwise Darwin's theory of natural selection and Galileo's view of the universe would not have won the day against the religious opposition). As we describe in the next section, however, the evolutionary perspective also offers a critical advantage from a scientific point of view — it more parsimoniously accounts for the available data.

TROPHY WIVES IN CROSS-CULTURAL PERSPECTIVE

Is the phenomenon of older powerful males marrying younger attractive females really a trend limited to chief executive officers (CEOs) of American corporations? To address this question, we compare the relative ages of trophy wives and their husbands to cross-cultural data on age preferences in mates (from Kenrick & Keefe, 1992). Following this comparison, we consider some recent data that reflect on the issue of female choice in determining these relationships. To presage one of our conclusions, we believe the data illustrate that females should get equal credit as trophy hunters; they are simply hunting for a different type of game.

The *Fortune* article on trophy wives actually provided an abundance of data in the form of ages for 53 remarried male CEOs and their wives. On average, the wives of these powerful men were 13.5 years younger than their husbands. Although there was less discussion of female chief executive officers (of whom there are presumably fewer representatives), 2 remarried female

CEOs were mentioned in the article. Unlike the case for the men, these women had remarried spouses who were older than themselves (averaging across the 2, the CEOs were 4.5 years younger than their most recent husbands).

By breaking the data on male CEOs down according to the decade of the man's age, we found that the older the male CEO was, the younger his wife (relative to him). Remarried CEOs in their forties married wives 9 years younger than themselves, remarried CEOs in their fifties married wives 12.6 years younger, and those above 60 married wives who were, on average, 15.4 years younger than themselves.

It may seem to fit with the sociocultural norms about sex and power that, as men move up in age (and presumably also in organizational status), they are able to obtain relatively younger (and presumably more desirable) wives. That explanation becomes less tenable, however, when the age discrepancies are considered alongside several other sources of data collected by Kenrick and Keefe (1992), including age discrepancies between husbands and wives, and between singles advertisers and their desired mates, across several cultures. Figure 2.3 places the age discrepancies between CEOs and their spouses in the context of singles advertisements from Phoenix, Arizona.

As illustrated in the right half of Figure 2.3, women of all ages tended to advertise for men slightly older than themselves. Kenrick and Keefe (1992) compared these advertisements to actual marriage ages for that year in Phoenix and found that marriage ages for both sexes were exactly as one would

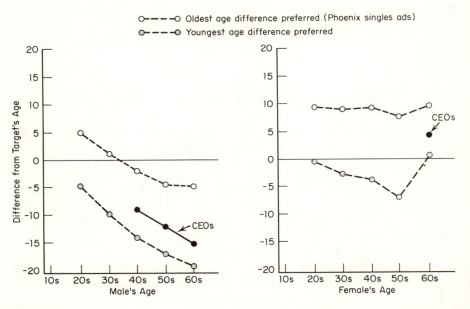

FIGURE 2.3.   A comparison of the age differences between chief executive officers (CEOs) and their spouses with age preferences expressed in singles advertisements.

expect from examining these preferences (the average of the high and low age difference lines). Note that the two female CEOs (both in their fifties) fall right at the expected place on this graph—they married men slightly older than themselves. The left half of the figure depicts age discrepancies sought by men. Note that the discrepancy between men and their desired partners changes with the man's age (as it did in actual marriages for the general population). Younger men sought (and married) women near their own age and were interested in older, as well as younger, partners. Older men sought (and married) women increasingly younger than themselves. Note also that the data for male CEOs fit right within the range of these preferences. Kenrick and Keefe found the same sex-differentiated pattern of age discrepancies in marriages in Seattle, Washington. These data suggest that the tendency of older men to marry women younger than themselves is not limited to CEOs.

It is possible that all modern Americans are influenced by similar cultural norms and related media influences. We noted the argument that the trophy mates phenomenon is a product of the "media images" projected in our modern advertising culture. If true, such images would be available to those of all classes and not simply high-level executives. One way to address the assumption that the pattern is due to a common feature of the modern American media culture is to examine marriage data from before the advent of television. Figure 2.4 depicts marriage data from Phoenix marriages for the year 1923 (the earliest year examined by Kenrick and Keefe, 1992).

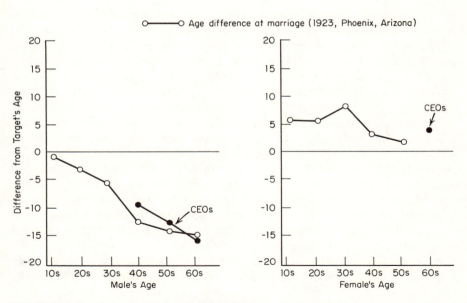

FIGURE 2.4. A comparison of age differences between chief executive officers (CEOs) and their spouses with average age discrepancies of Phoenix marriages in the year 1923.

The data in Figure 2.4 suggest that the tendency for older males to marry progressively younger females cannot be attributed to a recent trend caused by the images in the modern American media. Marriage patterns for 1923 show the same pattern as those found in the 1980s, and the CEO data map closely onto that pattern.

It is possible that the phenomenon might be linked to some other element of American culture. To examine the likelihood that some common American cultural element underlies this pattern of behavior, one can examine similar data from other societies. Kenrick and Keefe (1992) also examined singles advertisements from Dutch and German newspapers and found the exact same sex-differentiated pattern as shown in Figure 2.1. It could be argued that Holland, Germany, and the United States are all European-based cultures and might be subject to many of the same normative pressures. However, Kenrick and Keefe found the same sex-differentiated pattern in marital advertisements from East Indian newspapers. Those marital advertisements indeed indicated a very different set of cultural norms. The advertisements were commonly placed by family members acting on behalf of the single individual, and they specified characteristics related to caste and subcaste and subdenomination of the Hindu or Moslem faiths. They also requested horoscope information. These cultural differences argue against the possibility that the commonality in age preferences is due to the fact that Indian and American mating patterns are based in common European influences.

The clearest evidence against the argument of common cultural influences comes from the findings of similar age differences in mating patterns in widely diverse cultures, including African pastoralists and remote Pacific islanders who married between 1913 and 1939 (Harpending, 1992; Kenrick & Keefe, 1992). In fact, the sex-differentiated pattern shown by the CEOs and in Figures 2.3 through 2.5 was found to be universal in every culture examined by either Kenrick and Keefe (1992) or by anthropologists who considered cross-cultural data relevant to this issue (see also Broude, 1992; Symons, 1992; Thornhill & Thornhill, 1992). Figure 2.5 compares the CEO data to marriage ages recorded during 1913 to 1939 in a remote Philippine fishing village that had only minimal contact with outsiders and where a fair-skinned visitor is to this day regarded as a curiosity.

Thus, the phenomenon of older men marrying younger women does not appear to be limited to our culture. The same pattern appears in the marriage ages of famous historical figures and their partners (for whom knowledge of marriage ages is commonly still available). One amusing case is that of Henry VIII, who provided a single-case design with a relatively large number of longitudinal data points on marriage ages. When Henry married his first wife, Catherine of Aragon, he was in his late teens. She was older—in her early twenties. When he married his second wife, Anne Boleyn, he was 40 and she was 24 (16 years younger). At 52, he married his sixth and final wife, Catherine Parr; she was 31 (21 years younger). Henry VIII was born in 1492, the year Columbus sailed to the New World. The fact that his mate-seeking behavior fits so closely with that of American CEOs in the 1980s ought to be, at the

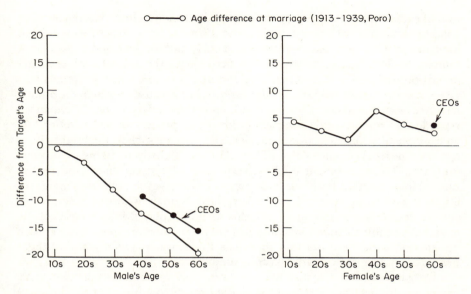

FIGURE 2.5. A comparison of age differences between chief executive officers (CEOs) and their spouses with average age discrepancies of marriages on a small, isolated island in the Philippines between 1913 and 1939.

least, a bit of a puzzle for those who favor the modern media images explanation. And Henry was not unique: Throughout history, powerful men in polygynous societies have married young, nubile women (Betzig, 1992).

OLDER, POWERFUL MALES AND YOUNGER, ATTRACTIVE FEMALES: THE EVOLUTIONARY PERSPECTIVE

Kenrick and Keefe (1992) argue that the gender-differentiated patterns of age preference are due not to cultural pressures, but to differential evolutionary forces acting on the two sexes. Stated very simply, males have been selected to place relatively greater value on signs of fertility in their female partners; females have been selected to place relatively greater value on signs of wealth and power in their male partners. The age differences in preference flow largely from these preferences in combination with sex-differentiated life histories. Males are most interested in women who are around their early twenties because female reproductive capacities peak in the twenties, then decline, and finally end with menopause. Females are interested in older males because males' material resources increase with age, and men do not undergo menopause—a man in his fifties or sixties or even seventies is still capable of fathering children (Nieschlag & Michel, 1986).

Several ideas advanced by Charles Darwin (1859) in his original formulation of evolutionary theory are helpful in understanding these differences. The concept of natural selection explains why a similar bone structure evolved to look like a wing in a bat, a flipper in a seal, and an arm and a hand in a human. Such structures evolved to fit better with the special ecological demands on each species. In short, they fostered survival. Some structures survive not because they help the animal survive, but because they help the animal compete with members of its own sex and ultimately pay off in enhanced reproductive opportunities. Darwin dubbed this process *sexual selection*. As an example of sexual selection, consider how features such as the bright plumage on a peacock might evolve. That plumage is costly in terms of survival pressures. To predators, it is like a neon sign advertising "fast food restaurant." However, that flashy decoration has advantages in attracting mates. In effect, it says to peahens: Here is a very healthy male who has been able to survive despite the enormous cost of this sort of display. Males whose genetic tendencies enable them to make displays are therefore more likely to be chosen by females, with the result that their genes increase, at the expense of those peacocks predisposed toward less colorful displays.

Darwin noted that female choice is generally more important than male choice in driving this sort of radical dimorphism within species. This sex difference in choosiness is currently explained in terms of *differential parental investment* (Trivers, 1972). Within a species, one sex, usually (but not always) the female, often has a higher investment in the offspring. That sex is well advised to do more comparison shopping before mating. Imagine that you knew you were going to pay a fixed price of $100 per person for a dinner that would take 3 hours to serve, as compared to stopping at a fast food restaurant with a sign that said "lunch special-$3.99 — quick service." Most people would probably think somewhat carefully about investing $100 and 3 hours, perhaps reading a review of the restaurant and comparing it to reviews of other fine restaurants in the vicinity. However, those same people would probably worry much less about dropping $3.99 and 20 minutes and might well take a chance on a randomly chosen restaurant under those circumstances.

For a female mammal, reproducing is considerably more costly than a fine restaurant meal. She might be able to produce a maximum of 10 offspring in her lifetime; these offspring must be carried within her body and nursed and protected for months afterward. Female elephant seals lose 2 kilograms for every kilogram gained by their pups, and the chance of a female red deer surviving from one season to the next goes down if she bears offspring (Clutton-Brock, 1984; Trivers, 1985). In some species, such as humans, the offspring must be fed and cared for even after they are weaned. Therefore, the minimum female parental investment is quite large. A male mammal, on the other hand, could father a child with a very low investment—the amount of energy required for one act of intercourse. In the theoretical minimum, this could require less investment than the 20 minutes and $3.99 for a fast lunch.

Consider how those differences in minimum parental investment apply to humans. The record number of legitimate children recorded for 1 man is 899 (Daly & Wilson, 1983), and the actual number could conceivably be higher than that. On the other hand, it is biologically difficult for a woman to have more than 24 children even if she had 899 husbands. For example, among the Xavante, a Brazilian hunter-gatherer group, the average number of offspring for males and females is 3.6 (logically, the mean has to be the same). However, the variance for women is 3.9, whereas for men it is 12.1. In other words, some Xavante men have quite a few offspring, some have very few. Only 1 of 195 Xavante women is childless at age 20, whereas 6% of men are still childless by age 40. One man in the group had 23 children, whereas the highest number of children for a woman was 8 (Daly & Wilson, 1983; Salzano, Neel, & Maybury-Lewis, 1967).

Evolutionary theorists sometimes overemphasize this difference in minimum parental investment and ignore the fact that, on average, the actual parental investment made by human males and females is much more equivalent. In species in which males invest heavily in their offspring, the sex differences in selectivity are less pronounced—males in such species are also selective, they just seek different characteristics than do females. Nevertheless, it is important to note that, despite the potential for high male investment, humans are still mammals. Given the possibility of mating with little or no investment, human males would still have less to lose than females, who would consequently be more selective.

SEX DIFFERENCES IN HUMAN RELATIONSHIPS

To elucidate the continuing mammalian sex differences in humans, consider one series of studies two of us conducted with Groth and Sadalla (Kenrick, Groth, Trost, & Sadalla, 1993; Kenrick, Sadalla, Groth, & Trost, 1990). We asked subjects to specify their minimum criteria for a partner on several qualities at several levels of involvement. In the first study, for instance, subjects reported the minimum percentile of traits they would accept in a date, a sexual partner, a steady date, or a marital partner. In the second pair of studies, subjects also rated their minimum criteria for partners for one-night encounters—someone with whom they would have sex once and would never see again. Figure 2.6 presents the results for the variable of intelligence from one of those studies (based on Kenrick et al., 1993).

Note that people of both sexes generally demanded higher levels of intelligence for higher levels of involvement, and that men and women were quite similar in their requirements. At the level of marriage or steady dating, in which both sexes have a high level of investment in the relationship, both sexes have similarly high criteria. For sexual relationships, however, for which the difference in potential investment is most discrepant, men and women had distinctly different criteria. When considering a sexual partner, particularly a short-term sexual partner, men were willing to settle for less intelligence than they desired in a date. These results were consistent across a number of dimensions—men were always willing to settle for less than women in a sexual partner. The variable of attractiveness is interesting because it is one on which

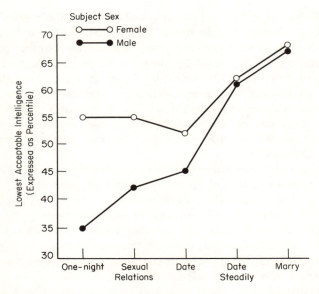

FIGURE 2.6.   Minimum percentile intelligence required by males and females at different levels of involvement.

men generally have slightly higher criteria than do women. For a one-night stand, however, this sex difference was reversed, with women demanding exceptionally attractive partners and men willing to settle for somewhat less attractiveness.

In a related series of studies, Buss and Schmitt (1993) recently reported a number of sex differences consistent with these findings. For instance, they found that men were willing to engage in sexual relations much earlier in a relationship than women. Likewise, in two field studies conducted across different decades, Clark and Hatfield (1989) found that most men, but almost no women, agreed to a sexual offer made by a complete stranger of the opposite sex. All of these studies support the evolutionary prediction that the sexes will differ most when considering low-investment relationships.

Kenrick et al. (1993) also asked subjects about their own standing on each of the dimensions. The results generally supported the social psychological principle of *matching*—there was a strong correlation between what a subject thought of himself or herself and what was demanded in a partner. The subjects who rated themselves more highly on a given dimension wanted more in a partner. Successful men and women demand successful partners, intelligent men and women demand intelligent partners, and so on. The exception to this matching rule was for males at the level of a one-night stand: Their self-ratings did not correlate strongly with their standards for a partner. Thus, men's standards for a one-night stand were not only relatively low, they were also uncorrelated with self-ratings. Despite these differences, however, males and females were quite similar when considering long-term partners—both men and women wanted someone well matched to them.

Such sex differences in potential investment help explain why men are so much more likely to be the perpetrators in sexual harassment cases, and why, even when a woman makes an advance, a male does not find it especially harassing (Studd & Gattiker, 1991). From an evolutionary perspective, indiscriminate pursuit of sexual relationships offers relatively little gain and great cost for a woman. It is important to note that, throughout most of human evolution, contraception was unavailable, and the cognitive mechanisms that led females to a more careful consideration of potential partners would be expected to persist even in the presence of birth-control technology. For women, the costs of chance pairings throughout virtually all of our evolutionary history included the loss of opportunities to pair with a higher quality male who could contribute to a more viable offspring, the potential loss of partners who would have been willing to invest in their limited number of offspring, as well as the danger of inciting jealousy in their current partners. For males, the costs are considerably less since a short-term pairing with one woman does not preclude the possibility of other partners. Partner jealousy is also a cost for males, but males stand somewhat less danger of losing their current partners or of being physically injured due to their partner's sexual jealousy (Buss, Larsen, Westen, & Semmelroth, 1992; Daly & Wilson, 1988).

DOMINANCE AND FEMALE CHOICE

One other reliable sex difference found in these studies is of central relevance to the issue of sex and power. On any dimension related to social dominance, status, or resources, females were more selective at all levels of involvement. The only variable on which men were more selective was the dimension of physical attractiveness, except at the level of a one-night stand as noted above. Why do men value physical attractiveness whereas women value social status? Evolutionary theorists explain these differences in terms of the different resources that each sex contributes to the offspring, which are then valued by the opposite-sex partner. Again, historically, ancestral females' contributions included carrying the offspring inside their bodies and nursing the young after they were born. Hence, males would have been selected to prefer features that were correlated with reproductive success, such as good physical health, clear skin, and a waist–hip ratio characteristic of a woman in her late teens or early twenties. Ancestral males, on the other hand, contributed indirect resources to their offspring in the form of material resources, protection, and so on. Hence, females would have been selected for preferring partners with characteristics that were correlated with likely social prowess and resource-generating potential.

These sex-differentiated contributions to offspring help explain the data on CEOs' marriage ages and their similarity to the patterns found around the world. As noted above, female fertility is highest during the twenties and gradually decreases until it ends with menopause, around age 50. Thus, it makes evolutionary sense that younger males should be interested in women their own age, whereas older males ought to seek relatively younger females. When females seek trophies, on the other hand, they seek social status, position in the dominance hierarchy, and resources rather than youth and physical attractiveness. This generalization has been well established—in laboratory experiments (e.g., Sadalla et al., 1987), in archival studies of personal advertisements (e.g., Rajecki, Bledsoe, & Rasmussen, 1991), in cross-cultural research (e.g., Buss, 1989; Mealey, 1985; Turke & Betzig, 1985), and in research across socioeconomic levels (e.g., Townsend, 1989; Townsend & Levy, 1990). A male's status and resources, on the other hand, do not peak in youth, but continue to accumulate with age. Note, for instance, that none of the chief executive officers of major corporations considered by *Fortune* magazine were below 40 years of age. Thus, our ancestral females would have gained advantages from seeking mates older than themselves, even as they aged (see also Leonard, 1989).

Evolutionary theorists do not assume that people or any other animals run around with the conscious goal of trying to optimize their reproductive choices. However, just as we have food preferences that would have optimized our ancestors' survival (bitter and rancid flavors are less preferred than sweet and fresh flavors, for instance), so we have evolved cognitive and affective mechanisms that influence mate choice. These mechanisms have direct and indirect effects on conscious thought and behavioral decisions and are discussed in the next section.

SEXUAL SELECTION AND ONGOING SOCIAL COGNITION

Evolutionary psychologists have become increasingly interested in the cognitive mechanisms that underlie the complex and flexible adaptations that humans make to changes in the environment. Rather than selecting a set of rigid instincts, human evolution obviously shaped a set of flexible information-processing adaptations. Hence, the study of social cognition is hardly at odds with the study of social evolution. On the contrary, the most interesting aspects of human evolution may be found not in fossil beds, but in the operation of ongoing cognitive processes. The gender differences we discussed above, though harbingers of the evolutionary past, ought to have implications for momentary changes in social cognition.

Consider one illustrative series of studies. Compared to men exposed to neutral stimuli, men exposed to beautiful female centerfolds later rated themselves as less attracted to the women with whom they were living (Kenrick, Gutierres, & Goldberg, 1989). This contrast effect was much less pronounced in women, however; women exposed to attractive male centerfolds did not reliably downgrade their feelings for their live-in partners. These findings could be understood in light of the sex differences in mate criteria discussed above. Exposure to attractive and sexy partners would affect men's estimates of the availability of partners with the features they seek in a mate. In other words, they might be attuned to the fact that there are available women who have more desirable qualities than their current partner. However, female judges would be less likely to focus on physical cues to sexual attractiveness. Alternatively, women's commitment to their mates might be more undermined by exposure to a series of highly socially dominant males given that dominance is a more relevant dimension for women's comparative assessments of a mate's worth.

To test the possibility of sex-differentiated contrast effects in mate assessment, Kenrick, Neuberg, Zierk, and Krones (1993) exposed students to members of the opposite sex who varied in both attractiveness and dominance. Subjects were exposed to members of the opposite sex who were presumably interested in a university singles service. Each subject viewed a series of profiles depicting people who were described as either highly dominant or nondominant in the context of other constant personality information. In addition, photos of either highly or moderately attractive people were attached to the profiles. Thus one subject might have viewed a series of dominant attractive members of the opposite sex, another might have viewed a series of nondominant members of the opposite sex of only average attractiveness, and so on. After viewing these profiles, subjects rated their commitment to their current relationship. The results again suggested a physical attractiveness contrast effect only for males. Men were less committed to their partners after exposure to good-looking women. Women's commitment, on other hand, showed no effect of exposure to physical attractiveness; they reported equal commitment to their partners after exposure either to highly physically attractive males or to less attractive males. However, women's commitment did show an effect of dominance. After exposure to a series of highly dominant males, women reported less commitment to their relationships.

These differential reproductive values of men and women can serve to bias cognitive processing in ways that lead to errors in interpreting the behaviors of the opposite sex. Those misperceptions can occasionally lead to both allegations and denials of sexual harassment. For instance, men have a lower threshold for perceiving flirtation in women's behavior. Even when observing the same interaction, behaviors that women see as nonsexual expressions of friendliness are perceived by men to be more sexual and flirtatious (Abbey, 1982, 1987; Abbey & Melby, 1986; Saal, Johnson, & Webber, 1989; Shotland & Craig, 1988).

If this lower threshold leads men to react with sexual interest when none is intended, their romantic come-ons would be perceived by women as uninvited and offensive. Typical power differences, such as male managers approaching female subordinates, may even make such advances threatening. It is interesting to note that research on perceptions of sexual harassment indicates that women are also biased in their perceptions of men's advances. Sheets (1993) found that men who occupy higher positions in the organizational hierarchy are not uniformly perceived to be more sexually harassing (see also Littler-Bishop, Seidler-Feller, & Opulach, 1982). Men's behavior was, however, more likely to be interpreted as sexual harassment when women judged the man to be either unattractive or unavailable (i.e., married). Furthermore, although harassers with higher organizational status were perceived to be more powerful, the tendency for power to enhance the threat of harassment was offset by the women's tendency to perceive a high-status harasser as also more socially dominant and hence more desirable.

So, cognitive biases that screen for valued characteristics in mates can color the perceptions of both sexes. Given that men and women are both faulty interpreters of behavior, it may be useful to question the validity of using definitions of sexual harassment that rely on the perception of the participants rather than on explicit behavioral criteria (Sheets, 1993).

CONCLUSIONS

An examination of the emerging findings on sex differences in mating strategies suggest one thought-provoking conclusion—the traditional culturally based views of gender differences in sex and power are often not only deficient in explaining much of the data, but they also often present a lopsided emphasis on male choice as the only relevant causal mechanism. As noted by the author of the original article on trophy wives:

> The part of the second wife's job that may require the most finesse . . . is convincing the chief executive that he targeted her rather than the other way around. . . . Esther Ferguson . . . brags "I'm the only woman in America to have been married to two CEOs of Fortune 500 companies."

> Georgette Mosbacher, 41, . . . has always been surprisingly frank about how she reeled in Robert, 62, the Houston Oilman [and later] Secretary of Commerce. . . . Having looked him up at the suggestion of a mutual friend, Georgette pursued him vigorously. When Bob tried to cancel dates, she told Texas Monthly magazine "I'd have to intimidate him." (Connelly, 1989, pp. 55, 57)

As another example from the academic arena, Rowland, Crisler, and Cox (1982) surveyed college women regarding their relationships and found that over one-third of the women in their sample had flirted with their male professors. Of these, 36% believed that such flirtations were typically initiated by the professor, whereas 52% believed that female students were more likely to initiate flirtation (the remainder assumed mutual initiation). Once again, these results indicate that courtship and quasi-courtship between powerful older males and younger females is not solely due to the operation of male choice, but is also driven by female choice. Such relationships are not simply a function of trophy-hunting males exploiting helpless young females. Females are seeking trophies as well. In contrast to males, however, females are hunting less for youth and attractiveness and more for relative power.

The data we discussed above suggest that a large percentage of the population become involved in romantic relationships at work. As we indicated, such relationships sometimes have negative consequences on performance at work, but they also sometimes have positive consequences, and they most often have no effect (Dillard & Miller, 1988). Whatever the consequences on work behavior, such relationships may be a natural consequence of the increasing sexual integration of the workplace (Colwill & Lips, 1988; Dillard & Miller, 1988). Put people of different sexes and similar interests together in high-interaction careers that often extend outside the office, and it is to be expected that attractions will develop. However, despite the millennia of differential selection pressures on men and women, we are also adapted for being sensitive to environmental contingencies. So, it might be possible to eradicate men's proclivity for making initial advances and for interpreting women's friendliness as flirtation. But, rules that preemptively forbid intimate relationships themselves, rather than forbidding abuses of those relationships, may violate basic civil rights, as well as the tendencies of human nature.

To say that relationships between older powerful males and younger females are a consequence of natural processes and that they involve female, as well as male, choices is not to argue that actual sexual harassment should be ignored. Such reasoning would be an example of the *naturalistic fallacy*—the assumption that because something is "natural" it is therefore good. The fallacy is seen most easily if we think about ulcers. Biologists who study ulcers assume they result from natural biological processes. However, they do not therefore assume that ulcers themselves ought to be encouraged. In the same way that ulcers can take the pleasure out of a good glass of wine, there are people (mostly males) who make persistent and obnoxious unwanted advances to others at work and who therefore make their coworkers' lives unpleasant. At the same time, to say that something is natural is not to say it is inevitable. Many men do learn to take no for an answer, even from a particularly attractive coworker; many women do learn how to say no comfortably, even to a powerful chief executive.

The most general conclusion we wish to make concerns the utility of an evolutionary framework in understanding a wide range of social issues, from relationships at work to domestic violence and even homicide (Daly & Wilson, 1988; Kenrick & Sheets, 1993). For some time, most psychologists have assumed that evolutionary theory is relevant only to paleontologists studying fossilized bones. On the contrary, an understanding of the ultimate background of human nature is essential for understanding how people think on a moment-to-moment basis in the laboratory, how people behave on a day-to-day basis at their jobs, and why some people "misbehave" on a regular basis. Darwin (1859) was right—there is a human nature, and McDougall (1908) was right—the understanding that nature is the essential basis of psychology and the other social sciences.

REFERENCES

Abbey, A. (1982). Sex differences in attributions for friendly behavior: Do males misperceive females' friendliness? *Journal of Personality and Social Psychology*, 42, 830–838.

Abbey, A. (1987). Misperceptions of friendly behavior as sexual interest: A survey of naturally occurring incidents. *Psychology of Women Quarterly, 11,* 173–194.

Abbey, A., & Melby, C. (1986). The effects of nonverbal cues on gender differences in perceptions of sexual intent. *Sex Roles, 15,* 283–298.

Alcock, J. (1993). *Animal behavior: An evolutionary approach.* Sunderland, MA: Sinauer Associates.

Barkow, J., Cosmides, L., & Tooby, J. (Eds.) (1992). *The adapted mind: Evolutionary psychology and the generation of culture.* New York: Oxford University Press.

Begley, S., Wingert, P., Chideya, F., Duffy, J., Rosenberg, D., & Hanna, D. (1993, May 3). Hands off, Mr. Chips! *Newsweek,* 58.

Betzig, L. (1992). Roman polygyny. *Ethology and Sociobiology, 13,* 309–329.

Bornstein, R. F., & D'Agostino, P. R. (1992). Stimulus recognition and the mere exposure effect. *Journal of Personality and Social Psychology, 63,* 545–552.

Bouchard, T. J., Jr. (1993). Genetic and environmental influences on adult personality: Evaluating the evidence. In J. Hettema & I. J. Deary (Eds.), *Foundations of personality.* Dordrecht, Netherlands: Kluwer Academic, pp. 15–44.

Broude, G. J. (1992). The May–September algorithm meets the 20th century actuarial table. *Behavioral and Brain Sciences, 15,* 94–95.

Buss, D. M. (1989). Sex differences in human mate preferences: Evolutionary hypotheses tested in 37 cultures. *Behavioral and Brain Sciences, 12,* 1–49.

Buss, D. M. (1990). Evolutionary social psychology: Prospects and pitfalls. *Motivation and Emotion, 14,* 265–286.

Buss, D. M., Larsen, R. J., Westen, D., & Semmelroth, J. (1992). Sex differences in jealousy: Evolution, physiology, and psychology. *Psychological Science, 3,* 251–255.

Buss, D. M., & Schmitt, D. P. (1993). Sexual strategies theory: An evolutionary perspective on human mating. *Psychological Review, 2,* 204–232.

Byrne, D. (1971). *The attraction paradigm.* New York: Academic Press.

Clark, R. D., & Hatfield, E. (1989). Gender differences in receptivity to sexual offers. *Journal of Psychology and Human Sexuality, 2,* 39–55.

Clutton-Brock, T. H. (1984). Reproductive effort and terminal investment in iteroparous animals. *American Naturalist, 123,* 212–229.

Colwill, N. L., & Lips, H. M. (1988). Corporate love: The pitfalls of workplace romance. *Business Quarterly, 53,* 89–91.

Connelly, J. (1989, August 28). The CEO's second wife. *Fortune,* 52–66.

Daly, M., & Wilson, M. (1983). *Sex, evolution, and behavior* (2nd ed.). Boston: Willard Grant Press.

Daly, M., & Wilson, M. (1988). *Homicide.* New York: Aldine de Gruyter.

Darwin, C. (1859). *On the origin of species.* London: Murray.

Dillard, J. P., & Miller, K. I. (1988). Intimate relationships in task environments. In S. W. Duck (Ed.), *Handbook of Personal Relationships.* New York: John Wiley & Sons, pp. 449–465.

Eibl-Eibesfeldt, I. (1975). *Ethology: The biology of behavior* (2nd ed.). New York: Holt, Rinehart, and Winston.

Ekman, P. (1992). An argument for basic emotions. *Cognition and Emotion, 6,* 169–200.

Ekman, P., & Friesen, W. V. (1971). Constants across cultures in the face and emotion. *Journal of Personality and Social Psychology, 17,* 124–129.

Ekman, P., Friesen, W. V., O'Sullivan, M., Chan, A., Diacoyanni-Tarlatzis, I.,

Heider, K., Krause, R., LeCompte, W. A., Pitcairn, T., Ricci-Bitti, P. E., Scherer, K., Tomita, M., & Tzavaras, A. (1987). Universals and cultural differences in the judgments of facial expressions of emotion. *Journal of Personality and Social Psychology, 53,* 712–717.

Festinger, L., Schachter, S., & Back, K. (1950). *Social pressures in informal groups: A study of human factors in housing.* New York: Harper and Bros.

Ford, R. C., & McLaughlin, F. S. (1987, October). Should cupid come to the workplace? *Personnel Administrator,* 100–109.

Freeman, D. (1983). *Margaret Mead and Samoa.* Cambridge, MA: Harvard University Press.

Gardner, H. (1985). *The mind's new science: A history of the cognitive revolution.* New York: Basic Books.

Harpending, H. (1992). Age differences between mates in southern African pastoralists. *Behavioral and Brain Sciences, 15,* 102–103.

James, W. (1890). *Principles of psychology.* New York: Holt.

Kenrick, D. T. (1994). Evolutionary social psychology: From sexual selection to social cognition. In M. P. Zanna (Ed.), *Advances in experimental social psychology* (Vol. 26). San Diego, CA: Academic Press, pp. 75–121.

Kenrick, D. T., Groth, G. R., Trost, M. R., & Sadalla, E. K. (1993). Integrating evolutionary and social exchange perspectives on relationships: Effects of gender, self-appraisal, and involvement level on mate selection criteria. *Journal of Personality and Social Psychology, 64,* 951–969.

Kenrick, D. T., Gutierres, S. E., & Goldberg, L. (1989). Influence of popular erotica on judgments of strangers and mates. *Journal of Experimental Social Psychology, 38,* 131–140.

Kenrick, D. T., & Keefe, R. C. (1992). Age preferences in mates reflect sex differences in human reproductive strategies. *Behavioral and Brain Sciences, 15,* 75–133.

Kenrick, D. T., Neuberg, S. L., Zierk, K., & Krones, J. (1993). Evolution and social cognition: Contrast effects as a function of sex, dominance, and physical attractiveness. *Personality and Social Psychology Bulletin, 20,* 210–217.

Kenrick, D. T., Sadalla, E. K., Groth, G., & Trost, M. R. (1990). Evolution, traits, and the stages of human courtship: Qualifying the parental investment model. *Journal of Personality, 58,* 147–117.

Kenrick, D. T., & Sheets, V. (1993). Homicidal fantasies. *Ethology and Sociobiology, 14,* 231–246.

Leonard, J. L. (1989). *Homo sapiens:* A good fit to theory, but posing some enigmas. *Behavioral and Brain Sciences, 12,* 26–27.

Libbin, A., & Stevens, J. C. (1988). Employee personal relationships. *Personnel, 65,* 56–60.

Littler-Bishop, S., Seidler-Feller, D., & Opulach, R. E. (1982). Sexual harassment in the workplace as a function of the initiator's status: The case of airline personnel. *Journal of Social Issues, 38,* 137–148.

Lumsden, C. J., & Wilson, E. O. (1981). *Genes, mind and culture: The coevolutionary process.* Cambridge, MA: Harvard University Press.

McDougall, W. (1908). *Social psychology: An introduction.* London: Methuen.

Mealey, L. (1985). The relationship between social status and biological success: A case study of the Mormon religious hierarchy. *Ethology and Sociobiology, 6,* 249–257.

Moore, M. M. (1985). Nonverbal courtship patterns in women: Context and consequences. *Ethology and Sociobiology, 6,* 237–247.

Nieschlag, E., & Michel, E. (1986). Reproductive functions in grandfathers. In L. Mastroianni, Jr. & C. A. Paulsen (Eds.), *Aging, reproduction, and the climacteric*, pp. 59–71. New York: Plenum Press.

Plomin, R., & Daniels, D. (1987). Why are children in the same family so different from one another? *Behavioral and Brain Sciences, 10*, 1–60.

Rajecki, D. W., Bledsoe, S. B., & Rasmussen, J. L. (1991). Successful personal ads: Gender differences and similarities in offers, stipulations, and outcomes. *Basic and Applied Social Psychology, 12*, 457–469.

Roel, R. E. (1989, August 26). Many women not amused: CEOs collecting "trophies." *Phoenix Gazette*, pp. al–a2.

Rowe, D. C. (1991). *Heredity*. In V. J. Derlega, B. A. Winstead, & W. H. Jones (Eds.), *Personality: Contemporary theory and research* (pp. 55–86). Chicago: Nelson-Hall.

Rowland, D. L., Crisler, L. J., & Cox, D. J. (1982). Flirting between college students and faculty. *Journal of Sex Research, 18*, 346–359.

Saal, F. E., Johnson, C. B., & Weber, N. (1989). Friendly or sexy? It may depend on whom you ask. *Psychology of Women Quarterly, 13*, 263–276.

Sadalla, E. K., Kenrick, D. T., & Vershure, B. (1987). Dominance and heterosexual attraction. *Journal of Personality and Social Psychology, 52*, 730–738.

Salzano, F. M., Neel, J. V., & Maybury-Lewis, D. (1967). Further studies on the Xavante Indians. I. Demographic data on two additional villages: Genetic structure of the tribe. *American Journal of Human Genetics, 19*, 463–489.

Sheets, V. L. (1993). *Organizational status and perceived sexual harassment: Detecting the mediators of a null effect*. Unpublished doctoral dissertation, Arizona State University, Tempe.

Shotland, R. L., & Craig, J. M. (1988). Can men and women differentiate between friendly and sexually interested behavior? *Social Psychology Quarterly, 51*, 66–73.

Singh, R., & Tan, L. S. C. (1992). Attitudes and attraction: A test of the similarity-attraction and dissimilarity-repulsion hypotheses. *British Journal of Social Psychology, 31*, 227–238.

Small, M. F. (1992). Female choice in mating. *American Scientist, 80*, 142–151.

Smuts, B. B. (1985). *Sex and friendship in baboons*. New York: Aldine de Gruyter.

Spruell, G. R. (1985). Love in the office. *Training and Development Journal, 39*, 20–23.

Studd, M. V., & Gattiker, U. E. (1991). The evolutionary psychology of sexual harassment in organizations. *Ethology and Sociobiology, 12*, 249–290.

Symons, D. (1979). *The evolution of human sexuality*. New York: Oxford University Press.

Symons, D. (1992). What do men want? *Behavioral and Brain Sciences, 15*, 113–114.

Tangri, S. S., Burt, M. R., & Johnson, L. B. (1982). Sexual harassment at work: Three explanatory models. *Journal of Social Issues, 38*, 33–54.

Thornhill, N. W., & Thornhill, P. A. A. (1992). The preferred age of a potential mate reflects evolved male sexual psychology. *Behavioral and Brain Sciences, 15*, 114–115.

Townsend, J. M. (1989). Mate selection criteria: A pilot study. *Ethology and Sociobiology, 10*, 241–253.

Townsend, J. M., & Levy, G. D. (1990). Effects of potential partners' physical attractiveness and socioeconomic status on sexuality and partner selection: Sex differences in reported preferences of university students. *Archives of Sexual Behavior, 19*, 149–164.

Trivers, R. L. (1972). Parental investment and sexual selection. In B. Campbell (Ed.), *Sexual selection and the descent of man*, Aldine de Gruyter, pp. 136–179.

Trivers, R. L. (1985). *Social evolution*. Menlo Park, CA: Benjamin/Cummings.

Turke, P. W., & Betzig, L. L. (1985). Those who can do: Wealth, status, and reproductive success on Ifaluk. *Ethology and Sociobiology, 6*, 79–87.

Westhoff, L. A. (1986). What to do about corporate romance. *Management Review, 75*, 50–55.

Winegar, K. (1989, September 30). Trophies on a pedestal: Younger mate seen as symbol of real success. *Arizona Republic*, pp. f1–f2.

3

Sexual Harassment

MICHAEL V. STUDD

Sexual harassment—unwanted and often persistent sexual attention most frequently involving male initiators and female victims—has recently emerged as a major issue in the management of organizations (e.g., Center for Women's Policy Studies, 1981; Farley, 1978; Gutek, 1985; Neugarten & Shafritz, 1980; Paludi, 1990; U.S. Merit Systems Protection Board, 1981). Sexual harassment in the workplace occurs within an environment in which issues associated with, and interactions among, sexual desire, individual power, and sociosexual conflict are especially pronounced and especially problematic (Studd & Gattiker, 1991). The personal and professional goals and desires of individuals in the workplace often conflict with those of other individuals with whom they interact. Moreover, individual and organizational objectives are often also in conflict. The problematic nature of these competing influences is in contrast to sexual motivation and sociosexual interactions in private life, in which incidents of unwanted sexual attention can at least potentially be resolved on a more individual and private basis. Such resolutions would generally lack implications for that individual's working or professional life and therefore would be unaffected by the confounding influence of organization-based power. The presence and use of this professional and organizational power greatly complicate sociosexual interactions between men and women in the workplace, especially with respect to unwanted sexual attention.

Thus, the study of sexual harassment in organizations has the potential to be particularly instructive for exploring the interaction among sex, power, and conflict and therefore for evaluating the relative merit of various theoretical perspectives on this element of human psychology and behavior. In this chapter, I explore and analyze the value of feminist and evolutionary perspectives for explaining and predicting the occurrence of, and factors affecting, unwanted sexual attention in organizations. To this end, I review prior research on sexual harassment, primarily within the context of providing and analyzing previously unpublished data on Canadian sexual harassment cases that have proceeded to settlement before legal tribunals. The reasons for this focus will be discussed in greater detail, but cases involving officially filed complaints of sexual harassment provide some of the clearest examples of cases in which issues of sex and power, individual and organizational objectives, and personal and professional desires compete and conflict.

Although this chapter focuses initially on a comparison of the two perspectives, it is important to note that neither the feminist nor the evolutionary perspective represent one unified theory on which all "feminist" and "evolutionary" researchers, respectively, agree. Each theoretical perspective does represent a fairly independent *metatheory*, or general framework for analysis. But, within each of these theoretical frameworks, there can be and are many competing *minitheories*, or specific hypotheses, that will often generate different predictions even though the same basic theoretical framework underlies each hypothesis. However, since one purpose of this chapter is to contrast these two general perspectives on sexual harassment, I initially simplify some of this complexity by using specific minitheories to represent each perspective. Although not necessarily mutually exclusive, it is clear that much of the feminist research on sexual harassment, as I discuss below, tends to focus on organizational and social "power" as the key independent variable of interest. Much less attention is paid to issues of sexual motivation and psychology. The opposite is true of the emerging evolutionary literature on sexual harassment, with its theoretical emphasis on evolved human nature, and evolved sexual psychology and motivation.

Thus, I initially compare and contrast the two perspectives by assuming that the *power hypothesis* and *sexual motivation hypothesis*, respectively, are fairly representative of the *feminist* and *evolutionary* frameworks. After I explore and evaluate these two hypotheses as distinct alternatives, I then argue in the last section of this chapter that this distinction is somewhat arbitrary. I propose that the two perspectives can be productively integrated into a more powerful explanatory framework for understanding sexual harassment in organizations than either perspective alone. Such a synthesis is not possible, however, without first establishing what is theoretically and empirically useful about each of the two specific hypotheses representing the two general perspectives.

FEMINIST PERSPECTIVE: POWER AND CONFLICT

Most of the existing research on sexual harassment in the management and organizational behavior (i.e., social science) literature does not *explicitly* invoke a feminist theoretical perspective (e.g., Gutek, 1985). This is in contrast to much of the published social science (i.e., nonbiological or non-evolutionary) research on rape (see reviews in Ellis, 1989; Palmer, 1988). However, a comparison of assumptions used in sexual harassment and rape research indicates that much of the social science literature on sexual harassment does at least *implicitly* adopt a feminist perspective. The key assumptions used implicitly or explicitly in both sets of social science literature are that (1) human minds are characterized (i.e., the evolution of the mind is not explicitly considered) by general, unspecialized, sexually monomorphic, and extremely labile psychological mechanisms; (2) socialization and enculturation are the major (if not the only) causal factors underlying human behavior; and (3) men are socialized in modern societies to seek to exercise patriarchal power, with the oppression of women through sexual aggression and violence as the desired goal of this exercise of power. The feminist perspective, particularly with respect to rape, goes one step further than this by generally denying that sexual motivation on the part of the perpetrator plays any important role in rape behavior (see Ellis, 1989; Palmer, 1988; see also Shields & Shields, 1983; Symons, 1979; R. Thornhill & N. W. Thornhill, 1983). This is also generally true of the management literature on sexual harassment (e.g., Tangri, Burt, & Johnson, 1982; also see Studd & Gattiker, 1991). Thus, it seems quite valid to characterize the social science literature on sexual harassment as essentially feminist in nature and perspective.

It is perhaps not surprising that much of the existing research on sexual harassment has been conducted from a feminist perspective. Feminism has traditionally been concerned primarily with improving the position of women in society, without explicit reference to the evolution of human nature or to what influence or practical significance evolved human nature might have on the achievement of this objective. With respect to the issue of sexual harassment, this has resulted in an academic and practical focus on the effect of proximate factors like the exercise of power, cultural and organizational pressures, and socialization (e.g., Fitzgerald et al., 1988; Fitzgerald & Hesson-McInnis, 1989; Gutek & Morasch, 1982; Jones, Remland, & Brunner, 1987; Konrad & Gutek, 1986; Lafontaine & Tredeau, 1986; Schneider, 1982; Tangri et al., 1982). In general, the feminist perspective on sexual harassment proposes that the exercise of power is the causal factor most responsible for the occurrence of unwanted sexual attention in the workplace (e.g., Paludi, 1990). Much like the feminist perspective on rape (see Palmer, 1988, for review), unwanted sexual attention is seen as a mechanism by which men achieve an arbitrarily socialized desire to maintain economic and professional power over women (Paludi, 1990). Simply stated, sexual harassment is viewed primarily as a direct consequence or function of differential social and organizational power between the sexes (e.g., Littler-Bishop, Seidler-Feller, & Opaluch, 1982; see also Studd & Gattiker, 1991, p. 275).

This exercise and maintenance of patriarchal power is seen as an end in itself, with the sexual aspects only a means to that end. There are, however, several problems with this proposition (Studd & Gattiker, 1991, p. 279). First, no research has conclusively shown that sexual attention is used as a means to achieve a power goal rather than, for example, power being used as a means to achieve a desired sexual goal. Nor is it likely that it would ever be easy to demonstrate empirically and unequivocally which aspect is motivation or goal and which aspect is the means to achieve that objective. Feminist writers are correct in pointing out that most unwanted sexual attention, especially rape, is not viewed or experienced by women as sexual in nature. However, this leads to a second problem: Just because women do not experience this as sexual does not logically and automatically mean that the motivation of the men involved is not sexual. Third, this power hypothesis, independent of any consideration of evolved differences in male and female psychological natures, would predict that women in power would also use sexual intimidation as a means to maintain and gain their own professional and economic power (i.e., not to satisfy any sexual motivation). That there is no evidence of this generally occurring suggests that the power hypothesis, in its simplest form, fails as a general explanation for the phenomenon of sexual harassment in the workplace.

On the positive side, however, the feminist movement has made some important contributions to the understanding and resolution of the social problems associated with unwanted sexual attention in the workplace. As a political movement, and as a scientific discipline, feminism has raised some important issues that, at the very least, have provided researchers with many basic questions about sexual conflict that need to be addressed by further research regardless of theoretical perspective. This contribution reflects both a concern with issues directly related to women's economic and professional positions in modern society and a justifiable (although usually unstated) appreciation that the workplace is an artificial (i.e., unnatural in an evolutionary or biological sense) social environment. Evolved human nature and other more ultimate influences on the phenomenon of sexual harassment need not be considered if the social and cultural challenges that women face today are assumed to be independent of any natural environment in which humans may have evolved. Although there are other reasons why feminism has in general rejected or ignored biological arguments, it is clear how feminism could come to view the evolution of human nature as irrelevant to areas of human experience that appear on the surface to involve only unusual social or cultural environments. In the next section, I discuss the potential benefit and value of considering the evolution of human nature for understanding sexual conflict both inside and outside organizations.

EVOLUTIONARY PERSPECTIVE: SEX AND CONFLICT

In contrast to the feminist perspective, the evolutionary perspective focuses primarily on identifying the ultimate biological and evolutionary bases of sexual motivation and behavior that lead to the sociosexual conflict observed in cases of sexual harassment (Studd & Gattiker, 1991). According to this perspective, evolved similarities and differences in the psychological natures of male and female sexuality lead to both sociosexual congruence and conflict between men and women (Buss, 1989a; Symons, 1979, 1987, 1989; Symons

& Ellis, 1989). Appreciated sexual attention (e.g., office romances) occurs when male and female motivations and desires are congruent, while unwanted sexual attention (e.g., sexual harassment) occurs in those contexts in which these motivations are not congruent. The evolutionary perspective predicts a common lack of congruence to be the inevitable outcome of the differences in male and female sexual psychology. The key underlying assumptions of this perspective are that (1) humans have evolved specific, specialized, sexually dimorphic, and environmentally mediated psychological mechanisms, particularly with respect to sexuality and reproduction; (2) these evolved psychological mechanisms are the major causal factor in human sexual behavior, albeit modified in biologically predictable ways by variation in environmental information processed through those psychological mechanisms; and (3) unwanted sexual attention from males is a direct consequence of differential sexual psychologies and motivations between the sexes (for a complete review of an evolutionary perspective on sociosexual interactions in the workplace, see Studd & Gattiker, 1991). Moreover, power is viewed from this perspective as simply a convenient means of accomplishing a desired sexual goal (Studd & Gattiker, 1991). In other words, an evolutionary perspective would also predict that evolved psychological mechanisms that process relevant environmental information about status and power could be quite relevant to a complete understanding of the causes of human sexual behavior and conflict. This potential for common ground between the feminist and evolutionary perspectives is discussed at the end of this chapter. However, evolved sexual motivation, not the independent exercise of power, is the critical component of this evolutionary framework.

Only recently has an effort has been made to systematically examine the possible biological or evolutionary influences affecting sociosexual behavior even within the artificial workplace environment (Studd & Gattiker, 1991). In our research, this has involved questioning the general assumption implicit in the feminist perspective that human experience in workplace environments is independent of any evolved or natural response to human experience in ancestral environments. The academic trigger for this research has been the growing literature on human "evolutionary psychology," which postulates that humans in ancestral environments evolved sex- and environment-specific psychological mechanisms that continue to react to relevant environmental information and result in predictable behavioral expression even within modern social environments (Cosmides & Tooby, 1987; Daly & Wilson, 1988a, 1988b; Tooby, 1988). It is not necessary that behavior in modern environments be currently adaptive in an evolutionary sense for an evolutionary perspective to be supported, but simply that psychological mechanisms and resulting behaviors adaptive in ancestral environments continue to be expressed in modern environments as predicted by a consideration of ecological forces acting on past human evolution. From this research, it has become clear that evolved human nature and ultimate biological factors could have a major influence on behavioral phenomena like sexual conflict even in modern organizational environments (Studd & Gattiker, 1991).

At the very least, this evolutionary perspective does lead to many research questions that differ from those generated by the feminist perspective. This has led in our research to a focus on factors and variables that the feminist perspective has implicitly and explicitly dismissed as irrelevant and unimportant (Studd, in press; Studd & Gattiker, 1991). Most important, this dismissal of the biological perspective has been done without any attempt to fully analyze evolutionary theory in this area and without any research actually being done to systematically test and disprove biological hypotheses. Thus the role of evolved human nature in sexual harassment is at least empirically an open question and a legitimate subject for further research. This chapter reviews what our research and theoretical development to date, conducted from an evolutionary perspective, has added to our understanding of sexual harassment. In addition, and with particular reference to the legal literature, I explore the role of both power and sexual motivation in sexual harassment situations as a basis for a more general evaluation of the feminist and evolutionary perspectives on sexual conflict in modern society.

LEGAL CASES: SEX, POWER, AND CONFLICT

Most researchers (e.g., Gutek, 1985) consider sexual harassment to be only one point along a continuum of sociosexual interaction between men and women, ranging from appreciated, mutual, and consensual sexual interest (e.g., romance) to unwanted, one-sided, and nonconsensual sexual advances (e.g., sexual assault). Moreover, much of the research to date has actually been one step removed from the issue of sexual harassment by focusing more on the entire spectrum of sociosexual behavior in the workplace (see Studd & Gattiker, 1991, for review). Such research approaches the study of sexual harassment by analyzing which aspects of this general pattern of behavior are unwanted and the factors that make some sexual advances appreciated and others not. This creates a potential problem in that the sexual attention explored in these studies, including our own, may not always represent sexual harassment. While sex is involved, power may not be, and conflict may often not even exist. This problem of defining and determining what is or is not sexual harassment (i.e., unwanted sexual attention) and the problem of defining exactly what constitutes power are recognized in both our studies (Studd, in press; Studd & Gattiker, 1991) and those in the more traditional literature (Gutek, 1985). While sociosexual behavior in general is in itself an interesting and relevant area of research and will be discussed as appropriate, this chapter focuses specifically on sex, power, and conflict through an analysis of legal cases involving officially filed complaints of sexual harassment and, therefore, explicit allegations of unwanted sexual attention.

Both the evolutionary and feminist perspectives on sociosexual behavior in the workplace tend to view situations involving convergent sexual interest as natural, essentially nonproblematic, outcomes of normal social interaction between coworkers (e.g., Gutek, 1985; Gutek & Dunwoody, 1987; Haavio-

Mannila, Kauppinen-Toropainen, & Kandolin, 1988; Quinn, 1977). It is in the area of divergent sexual interests (i.e., sexual harassment) that the feminist perspective, at least in the management literature, tends to interpret the interactions as understandable mostly, if not solely, in terms of social and cultural influences (e.g., differential power) and not, as the evolutionary perspective would suggest, in terms of evolved human nature (e.g., differential sexual attention). This is the critical assumption we have begun to question in our research (Studd & Gattiker, 1991); a review of the legal literature in this area is fundamental to a complete analysis of this problem. Exploring and analyzing the variables involved in the relatively clear but extreme cases involving official complaints of sexual harassment will either reinforce or bring into question some of the conclusions we have made in previous research using the evolutionary perspective and will assist in evaluating the relative merits of the feminist perspective. For example, it could be the case that, in more extreme cases of sexual harassment, evolved psychological mechanisms are overridden or obscured by the aberrant or pathological exercise of power or by the action of cultural or other proximate variables. This would support the feminist perspective and call into question the relative value of the evolutionary perspective. In any case, focusing on an analysis of legal cases allows us to better answer the question: Does the sexual motivation hypothesis (evolutionary perspective) provide a better theoretical framework than the power hypothesis (feminist perspective) for predicting and explaining sexual harassment and perhaps, therefore, a better basis for developing viable solutions to the problem of sexual conflict in modern society?

To this end, we reviewed the Canadian legal literature over a 10-year period (1980–1989) for published case reports involving sexual harassment complaints. These case reports were then analyzed for content, including variables examined in our previous research as well as other organizational and legal outcome variables. A total of 95 published case reports were found. Of these, 1 was removed from the sample because it involved a previously reported case on appeal. Male harassers and male victims were involved in 2 of the complaints and were also removed from the sample. The remaining 92 cases all involved male harassers and female victims and were used for the analyses presented below. Although this is a relatively limited and decidedly nonrandom sample of all sexual harassment situations, we were primarily interested in examining the relationship among variables within the sample and less interested in making inferences about the entire population of sexual harassment situations. Moreover, support for our general predictions even in this nonrandom sample would provide strong support for the evolutionary perspective, while lack of agreement would result in questioning its general applicability.

I discuss the details of the variables coded, the predictions tested, and previous research or results in the relevant sections below. I explore both the distributions of the individual variables and the relationships between variables. Following previous research, I have grouped these variables into broad categories we previously identified as important: type of harassment, harasser's profile, harasser's motivation, victim's profile, and victim's reaction (Studd, in press; Studd & Gattiker, 1991). Note that for purposes of clarity, only statistically significant relationships between variables are discussed in detail except if nonsignificant results are especially illuminating with respect to either of the two hypotheses being tested. For the most part, chi-square (x^2) tests of significance are used throughout, with degrees of freedom equal to 1 (i.e., 2×2 classification tables) unless otherwise noted. In addition, I also present an analysis of the employment consequences and legal outcomes of the sexual harassment cases and legal action taken. These organizational and social variables are of particular interest to the feminist perspective in existing research. At the end of each section below, I summarize the relative value of the power hypothesis and sexual motivation hypothesis in light of the data presented. This will lead to the conclusion that both the feminist and evolutionary perspectives have something to offer. However, the focus in the sections that follow is primarily on the evolutionary perspective since this perspective has only recently been introduced into the literature on sexual harassment (Studd & Gattiker, 1991) and must therefore, for purposes of clarity, be developed and discussed in some detail.

Type of Harassment

The sexual motivation hypothesis proposes that sexual harassment is a consequence of evolved psychological mechanisms that were naturally selected in ancestral environments. These mechanisms remain as part of human "minds," even if the consequences in today's environment are very different from the consequences in the environments of our ancestors. Specifically, sexual harassment is viewed as a behavioral consequence of evolved mechanisms that differ in the minds of men and women, due ultimately to the different reproductive consequences for each sex in past environments of engaging in relatively "nonselective" versus "selective" sexuality (see e.g., Buss & Schmitt, 1993; Gangestad & Simpson, 1990). Sexual harassment is therefore hypothesized to be the consequence of (1) evolved mechanisms guiding male motivation to strive for sexual access to females, which in ancestral environments had direct positive payoffs for male reproductive success in competition with other males, and (2) evolved mechanisms in females motivating negative responses to unwanted sexual attention, responses that in ancestral environments maximized the potential benefits from their "limited" reproductive opportunities and minimized the potential costs of reproductively disadvantageous sexual relationships (Studd & Gattiker, 1991). Moreover, the evolutionary perspective proposes that under some circumstances males may use coercive means to gain sexual access, even when females are nonconsenting, due to the reproductive payoffs in ancestral environments of sometimes resorting to such coercion (R. Thornhill & N. W. Thornhill, 1991, 1992; see also Pryor, 1987).

This leads to the prediction that sexual harassment will usually involve overt attempts by males to gain sexual access to unwilling females. In addition, since females are predicted to react more negatively to more sexually demanding uninvited advances due to the greater potential reproductive costs in ancestral environments (Studd & Gattiker, 1991), cases of explicit sexual harassment should involve more overtly sexually demanding forms of behavior than sexual advances in the workplace in general. This prediction is based on the assumption that taking legal action is an extreme behavioral consequence of an intensely negative reaction to unwanted sexual attention in the modern workplace environment. It follows then that this perspective would also predict relatively more persistent forms of harassment in official complaints of harassment. The threat and potential cost to a woman's reproductive choices would be increased by high degrees of persistence and by the implication that other means to discourage and end the continuing persistent attention have not been successful. While these predictions may seem, and probably are, intuitively obvious, it is important to note here that further predictions tested in this chapter follow directly from these more basic predictions. Of course, consistency with intuition and common sense should generally be considered a strength, and not a weakness, of a theoretical framework.

The power hypothesis, in contrast, makes no specific prediction about the type and persistence of harassment behavior. Since the power hypothesis proposes that the ultimate nature of sexual harassment is not sexual at all, this could lead to the prediction that all types of harassment behavior should be equally prevalent in legal cases (i.e., in proportion to their occurrence in the workplace). This prediction is based on the assumption inherent in the power hypothesis that women object primarily to the exercise of power and the attempts to intimidate them regardless of the type of harassment experienced. Similarly, the feminist perspective makes no clear prediction about the persistence of harassment likely to be observed before legal action is initiated.

Most of the sexual harassment cases in our sample involved multiple incidents of unwanted sexually oriented behavior. We therefore collected information from each case on the type of harassment behavior involved and the frequency of harassment incidents. Following previous research (e.g., Gutek, 1985), we coded the type of harassment along a scale of increasingly extreme or overtly sexually demanding forms of sexual harassment. One problem in coding was created by cases involving multiple incidents of various types of harassment. In these cases, we assigned a code appropriate to the most extreme form of harassment described in the case. This reflects our general finding and the finding of some other studies (e.g., Savoie & Larouche, 1990) that most sexual harassment involves a progression over time from less overt to more extreme forms of harassment. In addition, it is usually the last, most extreme form of harassment that immediately precedes the victim taking action. The frequency variable was an absolute count of the occurrence of all incidents of harassment described in the case, regardless of type. It should be noted that this frequency variable is very different from other studies in that we measured frequency within individual cases and not the frequency of harassment across all working women or as a function of the passage of time.

The classification of type of harassment behavior and percentage of cases falling into each class on our scale was as follows: offensive language and nonverbal/nonphysical harassment, 12.0%; sexual propositions or date requests without threats or promises, 16.3%; sexual propositions with job-related threats (i.e., negative consequences for not accepting the proposition) or promises (i.e., positive consequences for accepting the proposition), 18.5%; and physical contact of a sexual nature or sexual assault, 53.3% (note that only 2.2% of cases involved sexual assault or rape). Contrary to the power hypothesis, only 18.5% of these cases involved an overt threat of use of power, and only 2 cases involved outright sexual assault or rape. However, the prevalence of harassment cases involving physical contact of a sexual nature is in direct contrast to the findings of other, more general studies that less-extreme forms of sexual advances in the workplace are much more common than more overt forms (Burke & McKeen, 1992; Gutek, 1985). This result is, however, entirely consistent with the prediction above generated by the sexual motivation hypothesis. Moreover, our review of previous literature (Studd & Gattiker, 1991) also indicated that more overt forms of sexual advances lead to more extreme and negative reactions on the part of female recipients. More overt and sexually demanding advances are the greatest threat to a woman's ability to control and maximize her reproductive potential, and we have proposed that psychological mechanisms have evolved in women to motivate avoidance of coerced sexual access by males with whom they do not wish to mate. We suggest, therefore, that these evolved psychological mechanisms lead to the more extreme reactions observed in the legal cases than observed in response to sexual advances in general.

The frequency variable classification and percentage of cases were as follows: 1–4 incidents, 25.8%; 5–11, 31.5%; 15 or more, 42.7%. Clearly, the legal cases often involve highly persistent forms of sexual harassment behavior, even when lack of interest or annoyance is expressed early in the sequence of events. As R. Thornhill and N. W. Thornhill (1991) have pointed out, males appear to have evolved psychological mechanisms in competition with other males for mating opportunities that often treat female consent and interest as largely irrelevant. In ancestral environments, sexually persistent males likely had higher reproductive success than less persistent males, all else being equal. Although no comparative data on this measure of frequency exist, we were able to test for a relationship between type of harassment and frequency. To our surprise, we were unable to find evidence of any relationship; degree of persistence appears to vary independently of the most extreme type of harassment behavior ultimately leading to the complaint.

We conclude from this analysis (see Table 3.1, Section A for summary) that the predictions of the sexual motivation hypothesis are well supported but, with respect to type of harassment observed, there is limited support for the power hypothesis.

Harasser's Profile

We collected data, if specified in the case reports, on three variables related to the profile of the harasser: age, marital status, and occupational status. The

TABLE 3.1.   Summary of Major Findings with Respect to Type of Harassment, Harasser Profile, Harasser Motivation, Victim Profile, and Victim Reaction for the Legal Case Data Set

A. Type of harassment
- Extreme or more overtly sexually demanding forms of sexual advances more common in officially filed complaints of sexual harassment than in the workplace in general
- Cases generally involve a high degree of persistence by male harassers

B. Harasser's profile
- Harassers tend to be the same age as males making general sexual advances in the workplace, but more likely to be single and employed in supervisory positions over the victim
    1. Relationship to type of harassment
        - Some indication that younger males are more persistent
        - Single males more likely than married males to engage in extreme forms of sexual harassment and more likely to be highly persistent
        - Owners and owner/managers more likely to engage in extreme forms of sexual harassment than males in other occupational categories, while supervisors are more persistent than nonsupervisors

C. Harasser's motivation
- Male harassers almost always claimed some overt sexual or romantic motivation, while the overt use of power was limited to a minority of cases
    1. Relationship to type of harassment
        - Power most often invoked by males in cases involving sexual propositions with threats or promise: overall, however, we found no clear relationship here
    2. Relationship to harasser's profile
        - Single males more likely to invoke power or to claim only sexual motivation, with married males more likely to claim no overt sexual motivation or use of power
        - Supervisors more likely than nonsupervisors to invoke power but, within the subsample of supervisory males, occupational status is not related to the use of power

D. Victim's profile
- Female victims more likely to be younger and single than the population of women subject to sexual advances in the workplace and the population of women in the workforce
- Female victims are also almost exclusively from the lowest categories in the occupational hierarchy, and a large proportion of them are workers in the service sector
    1. Relationship to type of harassment
        - Younger women and service sector workers much more likely to be subject to the most extreme forms of harassment than older women or women working outside the service sector; no relationship between marital status and type of harassment
    2. Relationship to harasser's profile
        - Single male harassers more likely than married harassers to harass younger and single female victims rather than older and married victims
        - Owners and owner/managers more likely than other occupational categories of male harassers to harass young female victims and service sector workers rather than older victims or those working in organizations other than those in the service sector
    3. Relationship to harasser's motivation
        - The overt use of power is more prevalent in cases involving younger female victims and females working within office environments rather than other industry sectors

E. Victim's reaction
- Most victims of sexual harassment provide written notice to their employer before filing the official complaint with legal authorities
- Initial reactions of female victims appear to be carefully measured and cautious rather than the extreme reactions that might be expected in response to these clearly serious and overt cases of sexual harassment
    1. Relationship to type of harassment
        - No particular evidence in our legal case data of any relationship

TABLE 3.1. Continued

E. Victim's reaction (*continued*)
    2. Relationship to harasser's profile
        • Female victims more likely to use verbal confrontation in response to harassment by married males than by single males
        • Female victims tend to have less extreme initial reactions to owners and owner/managers than other categories of harasser's occupational status and are less likely to give prior notice of legal action if owners and owner/managers are involved
    3. Relationship to harasser's motivation
        • The initial reactions of female victims are less extreme when males make overt use of power in their sexual advances than when power is not invoked by the harassers
    4. Relationship to victim's profile
        • Younger female victims are less likely to give prior notice of legal action than are relatively older victims
F. Significant interactions among multiple variables
    Detailed analysis of interactions involving more than two variables revealed the following findings relevant to the results summarized above:
    1. Younger females more likely than older females to experience extreme forms of sexual harassment (see D.1) from males of any marital status and to experience more unwanted sexual attention in general from single males (D.2)
    2. No direct relationship between harasser's occupational status and type of harassment behavior: relationship found (B.1) is an incidental effect of owners and owner/managers more involved in cases involving service sector workers (D.2) and service sector workers subject to more extreme forms of harassment (D.1)
    3. Relationship between age of victim and use of power (D.3) is an incidental effect of single male harassers focusing their attention on younger females (D.2) and being more likely to use power as an accompaniment to their sexual advances (C.2)
    4. The fact that service workers are subject to less use of power (D.3) but are subject to harassment by higher status males (D.2) confirms that there is no direct relationship between harasser's motivation and harasser's occupational status (C.2); the finding above with respect to supervisory versus nonsupervisory males (C.2) likely due mostly to the fact that nonsupervisors engage in less-persistent harassment (B.1), and therefore have less opportunity for the use or exercise of power

sexual motivation hypothesis predicts that all of these variables are potentially relevant to understanding and explaining the phenomenon of sexual harassment (Studd & Gattiker, 1991). All three are reproductively relevant variables from both male and female perspectives in that each would affect the ultimate perceived costs and benefits (i.e., as perceived by evolved psychological mechanisms; Studd & Gattiker, 1991, p. 254) of pursuing sexual opportunities through social interactions in the workplace. Studd and Gattiker developed and tested predictions regarding age, marital status, and attractiveness of initiators of sexual advances in more detail than can be repeated here. Attractiveness is explored indirectly here through occupational status since there is much evidence consistent with an evolutionary perspective that women find higher status males, all else being equal, to be more sexually attractive (Buss, 1989b; Townsend, 1987, 1989, 1990). We predicted that harassers tend to be young, single, and attractive if their primary motivation is to establish long-term mating relationships and relatively old, married, and less attractive if short-

term exploitation of additional sexual opportunities is their primary motivation (Studd & Gattiker, 1991, pp. 264–265). A lack of difference between
harassers' profiles and the profiles of males in the workforce as a whole would
suggest a diversity or mixture of motivations (Buss & Schmitt, 1993) and
would suggest that a male of any given age, marital status, or occupational
status would have the same relative motivational potential to aggressively
and coercively pursue available sexual opportunities (R. Thornhill & N. W.
Thornhill, 1991, 1992; see also Studd & Gattiker, 1991).

The power hypothesis, in contrast, makes no specific predictions about
the age or marital status of the harasser since neither of these variables is
related directly or independently to the ability to exercise organizational
power. Hence, the feminist perspective would predict that occupational status,
a measure of an individual's organizational power, would be the key variable
of interest. This would lead to the prediction that men in positions of high
occupational status would be most likely to be involved in cases of sexual
harassment.

Age of the harasser was specified only in 11 of the 92 legal cases reviewed,
limiting our analysis in this area. Of the harassers, 5 were between the ages of
35 and 44, with the remaining 6 older than 45 years. Marital status was
specified in most of the cases, with 56% of the harassers single or divorced
and 44% married. The classification and frequency distribution of occupational status was as follows: owner, 23.9%; owner/manager, 38%; manager
or assistant manager, 10.9%; foreman or other direct supervisors, 15.2%;
other coworkers, 5.4%; other (e.g., customers or business representatives),
6.5%. Although the age information was limited, there were no particular
indications that the age distribution was different from that found in other
studies of initiators of sexual advances in the workplace or that this distribution was therefore significantly different from the age distribution of men in
the workforce (see Gutek, 1985; Studd & Gattiker, 1991). However, in our
sample, single males were more highly represented than in more general studies of sexual advances in the workplace (56% in our study compared to 34.7%
in Gutek's 1985 study) and therefore, relative to the workforce as a whole (see
Gutek, 1985; Studd & Gattiker, 1991). In addition, 88% of the harassment
cases involved males in all categories of supervisory positions (see above)
within the organization. This is much greater than the 44.8% of male initiators of sexual advances who were of higher occupational status than the female
recipient in Gutek's more-general study. It should be noted that we found no
significant, potentially confounding, correlations among these three variables
in our case sample.

In our previous review of the literature (Studd & Gattiker, 1991), we
found no indication that males of any given age or marital status were more
likely to initiate sexual advances in the workplace relative to their representation in the workforce. Our finding above with respect to marital status in the
legal cases contradicts this earlier finding. However, the fact that marital
status had any effect on patterns of harassment is still more consistent with the
sexual motivation hypothesis than the power hypothesis. We predicted above

that male harassers would be more likely to be single if sexual advances in the workplace are primarily motivated by a desire to establish long-term reproductive relationships (Studd & Gattiker, 1991). Although this prediction is supported by our case analysis, the preponderance of single males in the legal cases may also be due wholly or in part to the type of harassment behavior initiated by single males (see below). The preponderance of males in supervisory positions suggests an important role of organizational power in these severe cases of sexual harassment, a finding that clearly provides some support for the power hypothesis. It is also possible that men who are single or are in positions of power or both create more negative reactions (i.e., proportionally more complaints) in their victims regardless of type of harassment. The potential interaction among type of harassment behavior, harasser's profile, and victim's reaction is also explored in more detail in the relevant sections below.

Harasser's profile and type of harassment The sexual motivation hypothesis predicts that there will be a relationship between the reproductively relevant elements of the harasser's profile and the type of harassment behavior observed. We suggested that males would have evolved psychological mechanisms in ancestral environments sensitive to their own age and current mated status and, therefore, to the relative costs and benefits of coercive sexuality in competition for reproductive opportunities. We predicted that older males and single males would be more likely to initiate more severe and persistent forms of sexual harassment since older males of any given occupational status historically had fewer sexual opportunities than younger males and since single males are under more intense evolved psychological pressure than already mated males to gain sexual access to females (Studd & Gattiker, 1991). The power hypothesis only predicts that occupational status will be related to type of harassment: Higher status males have more power to exercise to achieve desired goals. This prediction, however, is also suggested by the evolutionary perspective since power may be used as a means to achieve sexual goals and since higher status males may also be more sexually attractive to women and therefore more psychologically encouraged to initiate overt sexual advances (Studd & Gattiker, 1991) whether apparently appreciated or not.

We found no significant relationship between age and type or frequency of harassment, possibly due to the limited data on harasser's age, although there is some indication that younger males may be the most persistent. Marital status was, however, clearly and significantly related to type and frequency of sexual harassment within our sample of harassment cases. Single males were much more likely than married males to be involved in cases involving more overt forms (physical contact and/or assault, $\chi^2 = 7.674$, $p = .0031$) and more persistent ($\chi^2 = 4.677$, $df = 2$, $p = .0482$) patterns of sexual harassment. This supports the prediction derived above. Unmated males ultimately have more to gain and less to lose (no current sexual relationship) than mated males in using coercive means to achieve sexual access. However, we also found that males of higher occupational status (owners and owner/managers) were significantly more likely to be involved in cases involving more severe forms of sexual harassment ($\chi^2 = 3.846, p = .0298$), and that men in supervisory positions were significantly more likely to be highly persistent than nonsupervisory males ($\chi^2 = 4.755, p = .0170$). This suggests that power may be used as a means to achieve sexual ends, and that the opportunity to exercise organization-based power is an important proximate variable in affecting the pattern of sexual harassment in organizations. This result is, therefore, consistent with both the sexual motivation and power hypotheses.

Thus, with respect to harasser's profile and its relationship to type of harassment (Table 3.1, Section B), we conclude that there is strong support for the sexual motivation hypothesis, but that there is also some support for the power hypothesis.

Harasser's Motivation

In our sample of legal cases, we also collected data on what we have loosely termed the *motivation of the harasser*. This variable is actually a summary combination of the stated goal of the harasser described in the legal testimony and the behavioral means used to achieve that goal. This variable was coded using information about the entire sequence of harassment incidents and not just the most extreme behavior (type of harassment variable). While all of the cases analyzed obviously involved unwanted sexual attention from a female perspective, this variable attempted to find whether the males involved perceived their actions to involve or be motivated by "simple" or "legitimate" sexual interest without overt coercion or whether their actions involved the exercise of power or coercion with or without apparent sexual or romantic motivation. It should be noted that, since this measure is more subjective than any of our other variables, the analyses and conclusions should be treated with caution. However, this is the closest we could get in this study to a direct test of the sexual motivation and power hypotheses. The sexual motivation hypothesis clearly predicts that sexual motivation is of foremost importance as an explanation, with power possibly used as a means to that end. The power hypothesis clearly predicts that the exercise of power is the key aspect underlying sexual harassment behavior.

The motivations were classified along the following scale: Category 1, cases involving claims that the harasser had no particular sexual intentions, was having "fun," or was simply asking the victim to date him (no overt sexual demands or use of power, 18.5% of cases); Category 2, cases that clearly involved attempts to initiate a sexual relationship or gain sexual access to the victim, but without any general or consistently overt attempt to use power or threats to achieve that end (overt sexual motivation but no overt use of power, 38.0%); and Category 3, sexually motivated advances that clearly and consistently involved the potential threat or actual exercise of power to achieve that end (overt sexual demands with overt exercise of power, 43.5%). It is clear from these data that many cases of sexual harassment do not involve the overt use of power (from a male perspective at least), yet almost all involve claims of sexual desire and unwanted sexual attention. This suggests that sexual access and not the exercise of power is the ultimate goal. Again, however, it is clear that power may often be used as a means to achieve sexual goals. Thus, the sexual motivation hypothesis is supported, but the power hypothesis is only partially supported and is perhaps refuted by the evidence that overt exercise of power does not play a major role in even the majority of sexual harassment cases and apparently never independently of perceived male sexual motivation.

Harasser's motivation and type of harassment We found no clear overall relationship between our harasser's motivation variable and type of harassment. This is contrary to the prediction from the power hypothesis that more overtly demanding sexual harassment would represent the greatest means by which to exercise and maintain power through sexual intimidation (Paludi, 1990). There was, however, a relationship between harassment cases classified as involving, at their most extreme, sexual propositions with threats or promises and our coding of the motivation as involving the threat of exercise of power ($\chi^2 = 9.237$, $p = .0013$). This is not surprising since one variable (type of harassment behavior) involves the threat of exercise of power given the most extreme form of harassment, while the other (motivation) involves coding for a general pattern of threat or actual exercise of power. There was, however, no indication that the general pattern of use of power was related to the degree of persistence involved in the harassment cases. This suggests that the exercise of power is not necessarily a significant component of highly persistent sexual harassment, with persistence equally likely in cases of harassment apparently motivated only by sexual desire. Thus, male harassers in cases involving high degrees of persistence may be as motivated by legitimate sexual interest, albeit involving some coercion of unwilling females, as they are by forcing sexual access through the overt use of power. This is consistent with our prediction from the sexual motivation hypothesis that men will use coercive or persistent means, with or without the overt use of power, to achieve either desired short-term sexual access or long-term relationships (Studd & Gattiker, 1991).

Harasser's motivation and harasser's profile We found no evidence of any relationship in the legal cases between the harasser's age and motivation. However, we did find that single males were more likely to invoke power (Category 3 of the motivation variable) or to be clearly sexually motivated (Category 2) than were married males ($\chi^2 = 8.048$; $p = .0025$). Married males were more likely than singles males to claim other motivations (Category 1). This is consistent with our earlier finding (Table 3.1, Section B) that single males are more likely to be involved in more severe forms of sexual harassment and suggests that the exercise of power is a common means by which single males attempt to overcome female resistance to coerced sexual access. Single males are clearly more likely to attempt to aggressively coerce sexual access to unwilling females than are married males. This is consistent with the sexual motivation hypothesis in that married males have more to lose (possible repercussions for existing sexual relationships) and less to gain (they already have success in the competition for sexual access) than single males. We also found occupational status to be closely related to motivation. Men in supervisory positions are more likely to use power than are men in nonsupervisory positions ($\chi^2 = 3.253$, $p = .0431$), likely because they alone have the organizational power to do so. However, it should be noted that, contrary to the power hypothesis, occupational status is not significantly related to motivation within the large subsample of cases involving only males in supervisory positions. This result will be of importance later in this analysis. In addition, the results here and above suggest that the prevalence of single and supervisory males in the legal cases is due more to their more overt use of power and more overt forms of sexual harassment than simply due to women reacting more negatively to single or supervisory males relative to married or nonsupervisory males.

We conclude that our analysis of harasser motivation and the interactions with the other two categories of variables (Table 3.1, Section C) discussed so far provides more support for the sexual motivation hypothesis than for the power hypothesis. The use of power is not closely related to type of harassment except in the most obvious sense, whereas reproductively relevant aspects of the harasser's profile are significantly related to motivation. Neither of these findings is predicted by the power hypothesis. However, the feminist perspective on the role of power is again partially supported by the relationship between supervisory status and harasser's motivation.

Victim's Profile

We also collected data on the age, marital status, and occupational status of the victims in the sexual harassment cases. The sexual motivation hypothesis makes specific predictions that the age and marital status of the female victim will be significantly related to the patterns of sexual harassment behavior (Studd & Gattiker, 1991). Both variables have ultimate reproductive significance. In demographic studies of human populations, youth has been found to be closely related to female fertility and reproductive value (see R. Thornhill & N. W. Thornhill, 1983). Evolutionary psychology predicts that males have evolved psychological mechanisms that are highly sensitive to this information in motivating sexual advances since access to females of high reproductive value or fertility would have, in past environments, increased reproductive success relative to males unable to gain such access (Buss, 1989b). Female marital status is also important in that, at least in ancestral environments, males would have been more successful in securing exclusive sexual access and the confidence of paternity that would result by focusing their sexual attentions, even if unappreciated, more on unmated than mated females (see Studd & Gattiker, 1991, pp. 261–263). The sexual motivation hypothesis further predicts that a female's social status is much less relevant, since in ancestral environments the relative status and resource-accrual ability of a female would be less important than her reproductive value, and less important than the ability of males themselves to accrue resources to exchange with females for sexual access in competition with other males. Males are predicted to compete more for the limited amount of reproductive opportunities that females offer, and females are assumed to compete for the otherwise limited resources that males can provide in support of those reproductive attempts (Studd & Gattiker, 1991; Trivers, 1972). In contrast, the power hypothesis makes no particular predictions about age and marital status since only occupational status can directly affect the imbalance in organizational power that this hypothesis proposes to be of fundamental importance.

Victim's age was specified in only 31 of the 92 cases. The distribution of ages was as follows: 16–19 years old, 38.7% of cases; 20–24, 29.0%; 25–29, 19.4%; 30–45, 12.9%. This distribution is clearly skewed toward younger women. Women in this sample are clearly much younger than the men by whom they have been harassed. This finding is also consistent with Terpstra and Cook's (1985) similar analysis of American sexual harassment complaints. Moreover, the age distribution here is even younger than the age distribution of recipients of general sexual advances in the workplace (Studd & Gattiker, 1991), which is in itself significantly younger than women in the workforce as a whole (see Gutek, 1985). With respect to marital status, we found 79.4% of the cases involved single, separated, and divorced women, with only 20.6% involving married or engaged victims. Women in these cases were more likely to be single than in Terpstra and Cook's study and much more likely to be single than recipients of sexual advances in the workplace in general (Gutek, 1985; Studd & Gattiker, 1991). Thus, younger, single women are either more likely to be subject to more severe forms of harassment or are more likely to respond more negatively to similar forms of harassment by filing complaints, a distinction also explored below.

It should be noted, however, that these results add powerful support to our above prediction derived from the sexual motivation hypothesis that younger, single women will be subject to more sexual harassment, especially of the more overt and extreme forms (Studd & Gattiker, 1991, p. 263). From a male evolutionary perspective, the potential reproductive benefit or value of securing sexual access to single, younger women is greater than for older, married women. Men are predicted to have evolved psychological mechanisms sensitive to this contextual information due to the higher potential reproductive payoffs from establishing sexual relationships with, or sexual access to, unmated women of high reproductive value. These ultimate benefits would offset the higher potential costs of using coercive means to achieve sexual access. We also predicted that sexual harassment would overall be directed toward women of reproductive age, a prediction strongly supported by the age distribution of victims. Clearly, the sexual motivation hypothesis is more strongly supported than the power hypothesis with respect to these two variables.

Our analysis of occupational status also yielded some interesting results. An unexpectedly large number of complaints involved women working as waitresses or cooks in the service sector (46.7% of cases). Of the cases, 25%

involve low-level office workers such as secretaries, with the remaining 28.3% involving women employed in a variety of positions (but, again, generally at low levels in occupational hierarchies; e.g., laborers). The relatively low occupational level of victims in this sample relative to the occupational status of the harassers and the distribution of women in the workforce by occupation again indicates, as the power hypothesis would predict, that differential occupational status or power is a key proximate variable underlying the occurrence of sexual harassment. However, the prevalence of service sector workers is also consistent with a social contact hypothesis we developed previously based on an evolutionary perspective and consistent with the sexual motivation hypothesis (see Studd & Gattiker, 1991, pp. 277–278). We predicted and found that one measure of the relative amount of social contact between men and women in various workplace settings, workplace sex ratios, was directly related to the incidence of sexual harassment in those situations. In the service sector, the degree of social contact between female workers and male owners, managers, and direct supervisors is likely to be at a maximum relative to other employment situations. The social contact hypothesis predicts that simple prolonged exposure to the stimulation provided by potentially sexually available women of reproductive age would motivate men to initiate sexual advances whether appreciated or not (Studd & Gattiker, 1991). Thus, the high degree of sexual harassment of service sector workers may at least in part be due to the action of evolved psychological mechanisms in males responding to the high degree of social contact and apparent opportunities for developing sexual relationships.

Before proceeding to a discussion of the relationship between the victim's profile and the other categories of variables discussed above, it is important to note that, unlike for the harasser's profile, the variables measured here are not independent. While there was no clear overall relationship between victim's age and occupational status, age and marital status (younger women more likely to be single) and marital status and occupational status (service sector workers more likely to be single) were closely related. This lack of independence of the last two pairs of variables could potentially confound some of the interpretations presented here and below. Nevertheless, the sexual motivation hypothesis predicts that significant relationships will be found between evolutionarily or reproductively relevant aspects of the victim's profile, harasser's profile, and the sexual aspects of the type of harassment. Again, the power hypothesis predicts that an analysis of occupational status and the use of power will provide the most significant relationships. These predictions are examined below.

Victim's profile and type of harassment   We found that frequency of harassment, or degree of persistence, was not correlated with any of the victim's profile variables. However, we did find the age of the victim to be significantly related to the type of harassment experienced. Younger women (under 25 years of age) were significantly more likely to be subject to the most overt and severe forms of sexual harassment (physical contact and sexual assault) than were older women (25 years or older) even within our sample of relatively young women ($\chi^2 = 4.775, p = .0168$). This provides additional strong support for the above prediction derived from the sexual motivation hypothesis that younger women will be subject to more severe forms of harassment. Men are predicted to have evolved psychological mechanisms that process information about a women's age, leading to different behavioral reactions depending on age. The increased potential reproductive benefit of sexual access to young, high-reproductive-value females likely offsets the perceived or potential costs of more coercive or overt sexual advances. There was, however, no relationship between a victim's marital status and the type of harassment experienced ($\chi^2 = 0.207$, $p = .7906$), suggesting that age is a more important proximate variable than its correlate, marital status. We also found a highly significant relationship between occupational status, which is not correlated with age in this sample, and type of harassment behavior. Service workers were most likely to be subject to severe sexual harassment, while office workers were least likely ($\chi^2 = 7.245$, $df = 2$, $p = .0134$). This result is consistent with the power hypothesis in that, as predicted above, occupational status is correlated with type of harassment behavior. However, this result is also consistent with the social contact hypothesis discussed above since there are more social opportunities for overt sexual advances in service sector settings and since men in those situations are more likely to have more direct and prolonged exposure to women's intended and unintended sexual signals.

Victim's profile and harasser's profile   We found no evidence of a relationship between age of the harasser and age of the victim. However, we did find that single males and owners and owner/managers were more likely than married males ($\chi^2 = 4.775, p = .0168$) and other occupational categories ($\chi^2 = 2.820$, $p = .0580$), respectively, to be involved in harassment cases involving younger female victims. The first result is consistent with the prediction based on the sexual motivation hypothesis that single males are motivated by the desire to maximize the potential for ultimate reproductive payoffs, while the second result again hints at an important proximate role of differential organizational power in affecting sexual harassment, as predicted by the power hypothesis. It should be noted that we found young women more likely to be victims of both single male harassers and of the most extreme types of harassment behavior (above). However, single males are also more likely to use more extreme forms of harassment (Table 3.1, Section B). Further analysis of the statistical interaction among these three variables (victim's age, harasser's marital status, and type of harassment behavior) revealed that younger women were more likely than older women to be subject to physical contact or sexual assault (rather than other types of harassment) by both single and married males and to all types of harassment behavior by single (rather than married) males. Only married males initiating types of harassment other than physical contact or assault were proportionally more likely than single males to focus their attention on relatively older females. Thus, younger females are more likely to experience more severe sexual harassment from all males, and more unwanted sexual attention in general from single males, than are older females (Table 3.1, Section F).

With respect to a victim's marital status, single women were more likely than married women to be harassed by single males than married males (χ^2 = 3.594, p = .0349). However, further analysis indicated that this effect was due more to the correlation between age and marital status of the victim than to any independent relationship between the victim's marital status and the harasser's marital status. This indicates again that the age of the victim is a more important proximate variable than the victim's marital status alone.

We found no relationship between the occupational status of the victim and the age and marital status of the harasser, suggesting again that the interactions between reproductively relevant variables are more important in shaping harassment behavior than those including organization-related variables. Not surprisingly, however, service workers are proportionally more likely to be harassed by owners and owner/managers than are women in other occupational fields (χ^2 = 13.917, df = 2, p = .0005). This likely reflects the predominant form of organizational hierarchy and social opportunity for interaction between owners and employees in the service sector as opposed to other industry sectors. Further analysis of the interaction between victim's occupational status, harasser's occupational status, and type of harassment behavior indicated that our earlier finding that service workers are more likely to be subject to more extreme forms of sexual harassment persisted even when we controlled for the influence of variation in the occupational status of the harasser. However, for any given victim's occupational status, there was no relationship between harasser's occupational status and type of harassment behavior. Thus, contrary to the power hypothesis, our earlier finding that, in general, males higher in the organizational hierarchy tend to commit the most extreme forms of sexual harassment (Table 3.1, Section B) has very little to do with the influence of organizational power per se. That relationship appears to be more an indirect consequence of the fact that owners and owner/managers are probably more involved in managing the day-to-day operations of service sector businesses, and that there is, therefore, simply more social contact with employees, which leads to more opportunity for aggressively pursuing sexual interests (see Table 3.1, Section F). Again, this result is consistent with the social contact hypothesis we developed earlier using an evolutionary perspective (Studd & Gattiker, 1991).

Victim's profile and harasser's motivation   We found no clear relationship between the overt use of power indicated by our motivation variable and the age and marital status of the victim. It appears that the sexual aspects of sexual harassment (e.g., type of harassment behavior, see above) are more affected by the victim's profile than are the power aspects, a finding consistent with the prediction that harassment is more sexually motivated than motivated by the desire simply to exercise power (sexual motivation hypothesis). However, when we limited our analysis of the victim's age and the harasser's motivation to power and sexual-only motivation (i.e., ignoring Category 1, or the other motivations, of our harasser's motivation variable), young women were proportionally more likely to be subject to the threat or use of power than older women (Fisher exact probability test, $p < .05$). Further analysis suggested that this was not due to a direct relationship between age of the victim and use of power, but due to an incidental effect of single male harassers concentrating on younger women and being more likely to use power as an accompaniment to their sexual harassment of younger women (see Table 3.1, Section F).

Surprisingly, the overt threat of the use of power (Category 3 of the motivation variable) was most common in cases involving office workers and least common in cases involving service sector and other workers ($\chi^2 = 10.804, df = 2, p = .0023$). Thus, the threat of use of power is less prevalent in service sector work environments, yet service workers are (as discussed above) subject to more severe sexual harassment involving relatively higher status males than are office workers. This result confirms that there is no direct relationship between the harasser's occupational status and the harasser's motivation, at least with respect to the larger subsample of cases involving males in supervisory positions (Table 3.1, Section C). In addition, further analysis indicated that the relationship we found between supervisory versus nonsupervisory status and the use of power (harasser's motivation) was due mostly to the mediating effects of nonsupervisors engaging in less-persistent sexual harassment and therefore having less opportunity to overtly exercise power in their sexual advances (see Table 3.1, Section F). The lack of a consistent relationship between harasser's occupational status and harasser's motivation is clearly contrary to the power hypothesis. We conclude, therefore, that power is less of a motivating factor in service sector harassment than the sexually motivating influence of opportunity and social contact alone (social contact hypothesis based on an evolutionary perspective).

We conclude that the analysis of the victim's profile and the interactions with other categories of variables discussed (Table 3.1, Sections D and F), although complex, provides much stronger support for the sexual motivation hypothesis than for the power hypothesis, although it is again clear that the role of power is of some proximate importance.

Victim's Reaction

The evolutionary and feminist perspectives both make predictions about the negative reaction of victims of sexual harassment. However, the sexual motivation hypothesis predicts that variation in reaction will be more related to sexual aspects of the harassment and to reproductively relevant profile variables than to organizational variables and the use of power. The power hypothesis makes the opposite prediction. In a vignette-based study (Studd, in press), we found that the emotional reaction of women to scenarios involving uninvited sexual attention was significantly affected by type of harassment, harasser's characteristics (age, marital status, attractiveness, occupational status), harasser's motivation (romantic, sexual only, annoyance only), and context variables (expected costs or benefits, personal or professional effects, long-term versus short-term effects). Hence, we were very interested in quantifying the responses of women described in the legal cases. Unfortunately, since emotional and psychological responses are very difficult to glean from the published case reports, we were forced to limit our analysis here to the more overt behavioral responses described in these cases. Thus, the responses measured here are more professional in nature than the personal or emotional reactions analyzed in our vignette study.

The two variables we looked at in the legal cases were whether written notice was given to the employer prior to filing the complaint (71.7% involved no prior notice, while 28.3% involved prior notice) and the general reaction to the ongoing harassment situation prior to filing a formal complaint. For the second variable (initial response or reaction), the classifications were organized and coded to roughly parallel a continuum of increasingly negative or extreme reaction: avoid, ignore, other, 32.6%; verbal confrontation with harasser, 40.2%; physical reaction, 14.1%; filing reports or other immediate employment-related reaction, 13.0%. It is interesting that, even in these legal cases involving severe sexual harassment, carefully measured responses appear to characterize female initial response more than immediate extreme reactions (the last two categories of the initial reaction variable). This may certainly reflect power differentials between harasser and victim, but may also reflect psychological mechanisms in women that evolved in response to the evolutionary reality of male sexual motivation and coercive sexuality. With the potential threat to a woman's reproductive potential and potential effects on existing relationships, women may have evolved psychological responses more simply to avoid the situations, to minimize signals of any sort to the male initiator if not interested, and not to exacerbate already potentially personally costly situations (Studd & Gattiker, 1991). The psychological pain experienced by victims of unwanted sexual attention may reflect the tenuous nature of these situations and the need for careful consideration of all aspects of the situation and options before reacting (Studd & Gattiker, 1991; N. W. Thornhill & R. Thornhill, 1990a, 1990b, 1990c, 1990d; R. Thornhill & N. W. Thornhill, 1989). If such situations can be handled without further escalation of the conflict, this would be of benefit to a woman's social and reproductive position in an ultimate or evolutionary sense.

Victim's reaction and type of harassment   In previous studies, we found that women react much more negatively to situations involving more overt or sexually demanding sexual advances (Studd, in press; Studd & Gattiker, 1991). These personal responses are not reflected in our analysis of professional responses detailed in the legal cases. There was no clear relationship between the two victims' reaction variables and the two harassment-type variables. This may reflect evolved psychological mechanisms more suited to personal or emotional responses functional in ancestral environments than to professional responses in artificial workplace environments, perhaps because only personal reactions could have been subject to evolutionary forces in ancestral environments. However, there was some indication that women may be more likely to try to avoid or ignore situations involving more frequent or persistent sexual harassment ($\chi^2 = 1.661$, $df = 1$, $p = 0.1349$). This attempt to avoid continuing situations involving prolonged unwanted sexual attention could be, as suggested above, a behavioral response motivated by evolved psychological mechanisms in women.

Victim's reaction and harasser's profile   Again, we found no clear relationship between the victim's reaction and harasser's profile variables, even though we were able to show in previous studies that male marital status, occupational status, and attractiveness did have significant effects on a woman's emotional response to otherwise similar sexual advances (Studd, in press). However, we did find in our analysis of the legal cases that women were more likely to attempt verbal confrontation as an initial response to harassment by married males than if single males were involved ($\chi^2 = 7.116$, $p = .0043$). This may reflect evolved female sexual psychology in that such confrontations may involve unequivocally notifying the male involved that she is simply not interested in even considering a sexual relationship in which she is unlikely to get the evolutionarily advantageous commitment of resources and attention to her in exchange for sexual access (Buss & Schmitt, 1993). Single males may also be more likely than married males to respond to this type of victim's reaction by conveying signals of potential commitment (whether honest or not) and therefore effectively misinterpret or ignore such attempts by the victim to end the unwanted sexual attention. Alternatively, a woman confronting a married male could threaten that male's existing relationship, an evolutionarily important potential cost that we predict would have a behavioral impact mediated by the evolved psychology of already-mated males. Thus, verbal confrontation may be sufficient to discourage a married man but not a single male harasser in both ancestral and current social environments.

With respect to the occupational status of the harasser, we found some indication of a relationship with victim's reaction. Prior notice is much less likely to be given if owners or owner/managers are the harassers than for other occupational categories ($\chi^2 = 14.956$, $p = .0000$). There is also some indication that the initial reaction of the victim is likely to be less extreme if the harassers are owners or owner/managers ($\chi^2 = 2.837$, $p = .0573$). This may reflect the negative effect of confronting harassers in positions of power and hence be consistent with the power hypothesis. However, this result is also consistent with our prediction (Studd & Gattiker, 1991) and Littler-Bishop et al.'s (1982) finding that initiators of sexual advances who have higher status than the recipients provoke less-negative reactions from the recipients of the advances than lower status males. A less-negative reaction would be predicted by the sexual motivation hypothesis since higher status males have more potential benefits to offer a woman in exchange for sexual access and women are predicted to have evolved sexual psychology sensitive to the potential availability of these short-term or long-term benefits (Buss & Schmitt, 1993; Studd & Gattiker, 1991).

Our vignette study also indicated an effect of occupational status on responses to uninvited sexual attention, but only in interaction with initiator's marital status (Studd, in press). Reaction to married nonpeers was more positive than for married peers, but more positive for single peers than for single nonpeers (and, overall, more positive for single initiators than married initiators). However, that same study clearly indicated that there was an effect of expected benefits versus costs from uninvited sexual attention on a victim's reaction. A significantly less-negative response was obtained when benefits were anticipated as a consequence of the sexual attention of the initiator, benefits that could certainly be provided by higher status initiators of sexual advances.

Victim's reaction and harasser's motivation In our vignette study, we found that women responded least negatively to scenarios involving romantically motivated males and most negatively to males motivated purely by sexual desire or the desire simply to annoy (Studd, in press). The legal case data do not allow us to explore this relationship since very few of the cases, if any, involve purely romantically motivated males. However, the absence of such cases itself suggests that it is sexual motivation alone (i.e., in isolation from romantic interest) that causes the most negative reaction among female victims. Within the legal case data, our motivation variable was unrelated to whether prior notice was given, but was related to initial response. When power was clearly used or threatened, the initial reaction tended to be milder or more carefully measured ($\chi^2 = 5.300$, $p = .0122$). This may reflect a relatively less-negative emotional response to sexual advances made by powerful males (sexual motivation hypothesis) or may simply reflect the discouraging effect of the exercise of power on female resistance tactics (power hypothesis).

Victim's reaction and victim's profile Previously, we predicted and found some support for the hypothesis that younger women and married women would respond more negatively to unwanted sexual attention due to the greater threat to reproductive potential and benefits than for older women and single women (Studd & Gattiker, 1991; see also N. W. Thornhill & R. Thornhill, 1990a). However, our analysis of professional response in the legal cases yields little support for this prediction. There was some indication that older women were more likely to give prior notice ($\chi^2 = 9.014$, $p = .0015$), but initial response was not related to the victim's age. Victim's occupational status and marital status were also not related to the victim's reaction. Again, this is not surprising given that evolved psychological mechanisms would be predicted to guide personal reactions more than professional responses to unwanted sexual attention.

It is worth noting, however, that the overrepresentation of younger women in the sexual harassment cases (Table 3.1, Section D) may indicate that younger women have more-negative emotional reactions. Perhaps not giving prior notice is part of a less-measured and more-extreme response to sexual harassment. This interpretation is, however, confounded by the fact that younger women are also subject to more severe sexual harassment (Table 3.1, Section D), leading to more-negative reactions. Since we lack appropriate data on personal or emotional responses, we were unable to explore any further this interaction among victim's reaction, victim's age, and type of harassment. We also found above, contrary to our prediction, that single women were not subject to more-extreme sexual harassment than married women, but were more highly represented in our legal case sample (Table 3.1, Section D). This overrepresentation could indicate that single women respond more negatively than married women to similar incidents of harassment. This would be contrary to the prediction above. Alternatively, the overrepresentation of single women could indicate that for married women the cost of unwanted sexual attention is more than offset by the potential cost to current relationships of extreme, public reactions, leading perhaps to more-negative personal reactions, but less overtly negative professional responses. Note that this interpretation could also be consistent with an evolutionary perspective if a different set of assumptions are made (i.e., used to develop a different hypothesis or evolutionary minitheory) about the relative costs and benefits of filing official complaints of sexual harassment as perceived by evolved female psychology.

The analysis above of the victim's reaction, although it is limited to professional responses in the legal cases, and the interaction of this category of variables with other previously explored variables (Table 3.1, Section E) provides more, albeit limited, support for the sexual motivation hypothesis than it does for the power hypothesis. Reproductively relevant aspects of victim's and harasser's profiles do have significant effects on victim's reaction. Moreover, the fact that higher harasser's occupational status and harasser's motivation involving more overt use of power lead to less-negative responses is in direct contradiction of the power hypothesis, which predicts more-negative responses to situations involving the threat or potential exercise of power (see Studd & Gattiker, 1991, p. 275). However, this finding, as discussed above, is quite consistent with the sexual motivation hypothesis concerning the role of male status and power in motivating sexual advances and female responses in the workplace.

Employment Consequences and Legal Outcomes

We also collected data on the employment consequences and legal outcomes involved in these cases of sexual harassment. Although perhaps less informative and more speculative from the viewpoint of an evolutionary perspective (since employment and legal consequences are modern social phenomena with little relevance to ancestral environments), these data could provide additional insight into the phenomenon of sexual harassment from either perspective. For example, it may be that evolved psychological mechanisms underlie some of these consequences more than the occupational variables the feminist perspective would predict to be important. With respect to employment consequences,

we found that the victims were discharged (i.e., fired) from employment in
40.2% of the cases, quit voluntarily in 47.8%, and experienced other employment consequences (e.g., not promoted) in 12.0% of cases. In 18.5% of the
cases, the legal complaint was dismissed, while in 81.5% of the cases judgment
was rendered in favor of the complainant. There was also an interesting relationship between these two variables: There was some indication that cases
were most likely to be dismissed if the employee victim had been fired than
if they suffered other employment consequences ($\chi^2 = 3.123$, $df = 2$, $p = .0490$). This suggests that legal judgments give some weight to the employer's
perspective, assuming that the employer has in some cases a valid reason to
discharge the employee. It could be, for example, that the victim made unfounded allegations, took inappropriate action in response, or conveyed intended or unintended sexual signals prior to (or in response to) initiation of
the unwanted sexual attention. All of these possibilities could be taken into
account by the employer or the legal tribunals before deciding on the appropriate action to take.

Employment consequences and other variables   We found that victims
were more likely to be fired or to quit than to experience other consequences if
single male harassers were involved ($\chi^2 = 4.204$, $p = .0238$), perhaps due to
the disruptive influence individually and organizationally of the more severe
harassment perpetrated by single males (Table 3.1, Section B). Power also
appears to have a role here in that there is some indication that victims were
more likely to be fired if owners and owner/managers were involved rather
than other occupational categories of male harassers ($\chi^2 = 2.523$, $p = .0711$). Not surprisingly, employment consequences were clearly related to
our motivation variable. Victims were more likely to be fired in harassment
cases in which the threat of exercise of power was present ($\chi^2 = 40.914$, $p = .0000$) and less likely to be fired if not. The exercise of power clearly does have
important consequences for female victims of sexual harassment. Employment
consequences were unaffected by the age and marital status of the victim.
However, there is some indication that office workers were more likely to be
fired than workers in other sectors ($\chi^2 = 3.391$, $p = .0398$), which is consistent with the fact that the threat of use of power is more common in cases
involving office workers than other workers (Table 3.1, Section D).

Legal outcomes and other variables   We found some indication that complaints were more likely to be allowed if they involved more-severe forms of
sexual harassment (physical contact or sexual assault, $\chi^2 = 2.704$, $p = .0628$). Jurisprudence in this area appears to give implicit recognition to the
extent to which a woman's sexual or reproductive interests are threatened
and to the resulting very negative emotional and psychological response. In
addition, it appears that, by giving weight to the type of harassment experienced, the legal rulings do leave room for what might be considered normal
social contact and misunderstanding of signals of sexual interest that likely
confound many cases of unwanted, less severe, sexual harassment (Abbey,

1982; Abbey & Melby, 1986; Saal, Johnson, & Walker, 1989; Studd & Gattiker, 1991). That persistence does not seem to affect legal outcomes suggests that it is the extent to which female interests are compromised by the type of harassment behavior experienced, not the persistence of the harassment itself, that is considered to be most important in rendering judgment.

There is also some indication that complaints are more likely to be dismissed if older males are involved (Fisher exact probability test, $p < .05$) and if supervisory males are involved ($\chi^2 = 2.832$, $p = .0576$). In fact, none (0) of the 11 cases involving nonsupervisory males were dismissed. The interpretation of these results is not clear, although, if women are attracted more to older and higher status males (as the sexual motivation hypothesis would predict), these cases may have involved some initial female interest or lack of initial negative response that has been taken into account by the judgments. Most judgments clearly specify as a guiding principle that normal social contact should not be punished. Some initial female sexual interest indicated to older or higher status male initiators could be a factor that would assign more social responsibility to the complainant for the resulting conflict and, therefore, lead to a higher probability of dismissal. However, we could find no relationship between legal outcomes and harasser's motivation. In judgments, it appears that the form of the harassment itself is more important than the motivational context in which the harassers claim to act. Legal outcomes were also not affected by any of the victim's profile characteristics, suggesting again that jurisprudence in this area implicitly considers only variables directly related to the form of, and response to, the actual incidents involved.

We did find that, in cases involving relatively more extreme initial reactions, the victim was more likely to quit (or other action) than to be discharged ($\chi^2 = 5.836$, $p = .0089$). In addition, there is some indication that more-extreme initial reactions increase the likelihood that a complaint will be allowed ($\chi^2 = 2.502$, $p = .0722$). This appears to confirm that the judgments do implicitly consider a victim's reaction as a relevant variable, with less-extreme initial reactions and failure to quit employment perhaps assumed to represent some evidence that the harassment was not completely unappreciated or considered that serious by the victim herself. In contrast, a more-extreme or immediate response by the victim may be an indication that the victim clearly expressed her lack of sexual interest in the harasser and that the harassment was a serious compromise to her emotional, psychological, and professional health. Thus, judgements appear to be most affected by the type of harassment behavior initiated and the general pattern of victim response. This suggests that both the perspective of the reasonable male initiator interested in sexual access within the realm of normal social contact and the perspective of the reasonable female response (given the possibility of initial female sexual interest and the variation in response to uninvited sexual advances across women; Studd & Gattiker, 1991) are considered in determining whether legal punishment is warranted in these cases.

In summary, the analysis in this section provides some additional indirect support for the evolutionary perspective in that variables found to be related to patterns of sexual harassment also appear to have effects on employment consequences and legal outcomes. Moreover, legal judgments seem to be most affected by biologically significant aspects of the harassment cases: type of harassment and victim's reaction. This may be due to the fact that the people who shape jurisprudence and decide these cases are guided by the same evolved psychological mechanisms for evaluating information and guiding resulting behavior as the harasser and the victim. The finding that harasser's motivation does not affect legal judgments suggests that the role of power is not as important as the feminist perspective predicts. The feminist perspective would also have trouble explaining why cases involving supervisors are more likely to be dismissed that those involving nonsupervisors if the effect of power on women is supposed to be so negative. The sexual motivation hypothesis, in contrast, would predict that cases involving higher status males do often involve some initial female interest. This would complicate the legal task of assigning responsibility for the sexual harassment situation since women are predicted to be more sexually attracted to higher status males and to respond less negatively to the initial advances from those males (Studd & Gattiker, 1991).

EVOLUTIONARY AND FEMINIST THEORY: A SYNTHESIS

Our analysis of officially filed complaints of sexual harassment indicates that the incidence and pattern of sexual harassment is consistent with previous research conducted from an evolutionary perspective (Studd, in press; Studd & Gattiker, 1991) and with predictions derived from that perspective. Variables predicted to be important, based on a consideration of the evolved psychological mechanisms postulated to underlie sociosexual motivation and interactions between men and women, were found to have a significant effect on the pattern of sexual harassment in the legal cases. Type of harassment, harasser's and victim's profile, harasser's motivation, and victim's reaction are all variables that influence the pattern of sexual harassment and interact with each other in predictable fashion given the evolutionary perspective (see also Studd, in press; Studd & Gattiker, 1991). In contrast, the feminist perspective makes few, if any, specific predictions about the influence of these variables. Moreover, our analysis of variables related to differential organizational or social power, such as harasser's and victim's occupational status, indicates that these variables are not as useful in predicting and explaining sexual harassment as the more reproductively relevant personal and psychological variables predicted to be important under the evolutionary perspective. While victim's and harasser's occupational status do have some significant effects, this may be, as discussed above, due more to the influence of the amount of social contact, rather than to unequal power relationships per se, and to some influence of a greater degree of evolved sexual attraction in women to high-status relative to low-status males.

However, power does have an important role as at least a proximate variable. The exercise of power is often one component of the package of behavioral actions taken by a harasser. This is reflected in our analysis of the motivation variable, in the types of sexual harassment seen, and in the employment consequences for the victims of sexual harassment. However, there is no compelling evidence that the exercise of power is an end itself or that the overt use of power is always involved in cases of unwanted sexual attention. Sexual harassment is better explained as one outcome of conflicting sexual desires and interests among men and women interacting in the workplace. For example, men have a greater interest than women in nonselective sexuality (i.e., short-term, low-cost, and potentially coercive sexual opportunities), while women have a greater desire than men to engage in selective sexuality (i.e., long-term sexual relationships with greater investment and commitment by partners; Buss & Schmitt, 1993).

While a theoretical perspective rooted in the perspective of evolved sexual psychology can predict and explain the broad continuum of sociosexual interaction and conflict, the feminist perspective (with its focus on power and its general denial of evolved sex differences in sexual psychology) does not provide a coherent theory for this entire continuum of behavior (see also Studd & Gattiker, 1991). The feminist power hypothesis even has difficulty predicting and explaining key aspects of our analysis of the legal cases of sexual harassment in which there clearly are sexual conflict. However, the role of power, and other social and cultural factors, must be included in the development of the evolutionary perspective given its obvious role in many harassment cases. This is not a problem for the evolutionary perspective since evolutionary psychology does not consider ultimate (evolved) and proximate (environmental) influences on behavioral phenomena to be mutually exclusive, but rather sees both sets of influences interacting through the action of relevant environmental information on evolved psychological mechanisms leading to overt human behavior (Cosmides & Tooby, 1989; N. W. Thornhill & R. Thornhill, 1990a, 1990b, 1990c, 1990d; Tooby, 1988). For example, the use of social power to achieve desired sexual goals may be a major component of the psychological mechanisms that have evolved in the male mind to facilitate the achievement of more mating opportunities in competition with other males.

Given all of the above, we would argue for an integration or synthesis of the evolutionary and feminist perspectives (see also Kenrick & Keefe, 1989). There are at least a couple of reasonable grounds for making this proposal. First, the two perspectives offer different levels or types of explanation for the same phenomena. As behavioral ecologists and ethologists have long pointed out, different levels of explanation are not necessarily incompatible and usually support and reinforce one another (Daly & Wilson, 1983). Second, the feminist perspective has traditionally had an applied or practical focus (e.g., what are the immediate or proximate causes of the phenomena, and what can be done to solve the problem?), whereas the evolutionary perspective has had more of an academic or theoretical focus (e.g., ultimately, why does the behavioral phenomenon exist, and what does this say about existing theory rather than the problem itself?). A more complete and integrated model of human behavior would be achieved with the evolutionary perspective providing a better theoretical grounding for the feminist perspective and the feminist perspective adding to the evolutionary perspective a greater concern for and focus on the practical applications and issues surrounding sexual harassment and sexual conflict in general. Such a theoretical and practical integration can only enhance our understanding of sexual conflict in modern society and the possible steps that could be taken to alleviate or minimize the consequences of this conflict. We would argue that it is no longer appropriate or necessary to think of these perspectives as entirely mutually exclusive alternatives. The evolutionary perspective should be more open to the important issues that feminism is attempting to address, but the feminist perspective itself must be more open to the importance of evolved human nature in affecting sociosexual behavior and conflict even within modern social environments.

This would, however, mean that the feminist perspective would have to give explicit recognition to the realities of evolved psychological mechanisms in both women and men and to the fact that continuing sexual misunderstanding, miscommunication, and conflict are inevitable consequences of sexual differences in evolved human nature and sexual psychology. As academic researchers, this would entail dropping the empirically invalid assumption of general, unspecialized, and sexually monomorphic psychological mechanisms in humans (see also Studd & Gattiker, 1991, p. 279). With this assumption dropped, the evolutionary and feminist perspectives will be theoretically quite compatible partners in a synthesized, but evolutionarily grounded, research framework. It is important to note, however, that the feminist perspective already makes implicit assumptions about what women desire and feel in these situations (i.e., about female sexual nature). For example, none of the social science or feminist literature on sexual harassment to date have even suggested that a woman's negative response to unwanted sexual attention is simply the result of social and cultural conditioning and that the problem of sexual conflict could therefore be easily resolved simply by socializing women to respond positively to all sexual attention from males. In contrast, this is exactly the argument that has been applied to the behavior of male harassers: Sexual conflict could be eliminated by simply conditioning or socializing men to behave differently. This clearly begs the question of why male sexual psychology and behavior can and must be changed, but female sexual psychology and response cannot and must not be changed. Why, as the feminist perspective implies, should female sexuality be considered, a priori, more "natural" and "right" than male sexual expression in modern society?

What is needed to resolve this inconsistency in the feminist perspective is an explicit recognition (already inherent in the evolutionary perspective) that the forces of "nature" and "nurture" are inseparably and intimately linked (see, e.g., N. W. Thornhill & R. Thornhill, 1990a, 1990b, 1990c, 1990d) and are not, as has been traditionally believed in the social science literature, mutually exclusive and competing hypotheses. The details of much of the interaction between "genes" and "environment" remains to be studied, but sexual dimorphism in evolved psychological mechanisms is the constraint within which the influence of more immediate or proximate environmental variables such as differential power are mediated leading to the expression of human sexual behavior. Such recognition that male, as well as female, sexual motivation and response is not simply an arbitrary and capricious outcome of socialization and cultural pressures, and that women should therefore assume some responsibility to deal realistically and sensibly with all sociosexual interactions with men, is a concept that feminism has been very reluctant to accept. However, a better understanding of evolved human nature and its role in sexual conflict may actually assist the feminist agenda for change, rather than impede it, by producing a theoretical framework that is internally and externally more valid than most, if not all, existing feminist frameworks.

It is worth noting that legal jurisprudence in this area already appears to recognize implicitly and explicitly the role of human nature in sexual harassment situations. The written judgments we reviewed consistently noted that it should not be the function of the law to interfere with normal or natural social interactions between men and women. In addition, the judgments clearly relied at least in part on a consideration of the initial response of the women involved to the sexual attention directed at them and their responsibility to communicate sexual interest or lack of interest clearly. This indicates that the legal perspective has already implicitly adopted a perspective rooted in the realities of human sexual nature. This is further confirmed by the relationship we found among type of harassment behavior, victim's reaction, and legal outcome of the complaint. Clearly, it would not be equitable in a legal sense to punish harassers arbitrarily without considering the inevitable and complex interaction between male and female sexual nature and the trade-offs between male and female interests and motivation. Feminism, in its quest for equity in sexual harassment cases, would likely be more successful in achieving its political agenda by employing the perspective and insights of evolutionary psychology, following legal precedent, and considering equity and fairness in sociosexual behavior and consequences from the perspective of both evolved female and male nature. For example, an appreciation that (1) women do have an evolved motivation under appropriate circumstances to seek out and initiate sexual and romantic relationships with target males even in the workplace, as well as evolved psychological reasons to respond negatively to unwanted sexual attention, and (2) men have likely evolved sexual motivation and behavioral responses that may lead to overreaction to (or misperception of) female sexual signals would go a long way toward contributing positively to the development and implementation of effective solutions to the problem of sexual conflict in modern society.

Feminism has justifiably succeeded in making organizations and the legal system aware of the professional and personal challenges working women face today and in making the viewpoints of women involved in these cases of sexual conflict an important part of their resolution. Current jurisprudence is quite clearly and rightly concerned with the rights of women to full employment opportunity and to work free from discrimination on the basis of sex and from the inappropriate use of power to achieve this discrimination. However, even in this case, the feminist political and social agendas would be strengthened immeasurably by attention to the evolution of female, as well as male, sexuality. Alexander (1979) has suggested that legal systems evolve primarily to regulate the reproductive strivings of individuals in complex societies. If this is accurate, feminism could do worse than to recognize and use our knowledge of evolved sexual psychology, which is ultimately rooted in theories related to the reproductive striving of both sexes, to develop and achieve sexually equitable and fair solutions (whether legal, organizational, or other) to the problem of sociosexual conflict in all areas of modern society. At the same time, evolutionary researchers should also recognize the legitimate concerns of feminist scholars and activists and use their growing knowledge of the evolution of human sexual psychology to participate directly with feminists and to help contribute to a better understanding of, and the development of more effective solutions to, the problem of sexual conflict. Such a theoretical synthesis and practical partnership would, presumably, lead only to the betterment of society for men and women alike.

REFERENCES

Abbey, A. (1982). Sex differences in attribution for friendly behavior: Do males misperceive females' friendliness? *Journal of Personality and Social Psychology, 42,* 830–838.

Abbey, A., & Melby, C. (1986). The effects of nonverbal cues on gender differences in perceptions of sexual intent. *Sex Roles, 15,* 283–298.

Alexander, R. D. (1979). *Darwinism and human affairs.* Seattle: University of Washington Press.

Burke, R. J., & McKeen, C. A. (1992). Social-sexual behaviors at work: Experiences of managerial and professional women. *Women in Management Review, 7,* 22–30.

Buss, D. M. (1989a). Conflict between the sexes: Strategic interference and the evocation of anger and upset. *Journal of Personality and Social Psychology, 56,* 735–747.

Buss, D. M. (1989b). Sexual differences in human mate preferences: Evolutionary hypotheses tested in 37 cultures. *Behavioral and Brain Sciences, 12,* 1–49.

Buss, D. M., & Schmitt, D. P. (1993). Sexual strategies theory: An evolutionary perspective on human mating. *Psychological Review, 100,* 204–232.

Center for Women's Policy Studies. (1981). *Harassment and discrimination in employment.* Washington, DC: Center for Women's Policy Studies.

Cosmides, L., & Tooby, J. (1987). From evolution to behavior: Evolutionary psychology as the missing link. In J. Dupre (Ed.), *The latest on the best: Essays on evolution and optimality* (pp. 277–306). Cambridge, MA: Massachusetts Institute of Technology Press.

Cosmides, L., & Tooby, J. (1989). Evolutionary psychology and the generation of culture. Part II. Case study: A computational theory of social exchange. *Ethology and Sociobiology, 10,* 51–97.

Daly, M., & Wilson, M. (1983). *Sex, evolution and behavior.* North Scituate, MA: Duxbury Press.

Daly, &., & Wilson, M. (1988a). Evolutionary social psychology and family homicide. *Science, 242*, 519–524.

Daly, M., & Wilson, M. (1988b). *Homicide*. Hawthorne, NY: Aldine de Gruyter.

Ellis, L. (1989). *Theories of rape: Inquiries into the causes of sexual aggression*. New York: Hemisphere.

Farley, L. (1978). *Sexual shakedown: The sexual harassment of women on the job*. New York: McGraw-Hill.

Fitzgerald, L. F., & Hesson-McInnis, M. (1989). The dimensions of sexual harassment: A structural analysis. *Journal of Vocational Behavior, 35*, 309–326.

Fitzgerald, L. F., Shulman, S. L., Bailey, N., Richards, M., Swecker, J., Gold, Y., Ormerod, M., & Weitzman, L. (1988). The incidence and dimensions of sexual harassment in academia and the workplace. *Journal of Vocational Behavior, 32*, 152–175.

Gangestad, S. W., & Simpson, J. A. (1990). Toward an evolutionary history of female sociosexual variation. *Journal of Personality, 58*, 69–96.

Gutek, B. A. (1985). *Sex and the workplace: The impact of sexual behavior and harassment on women, men, and organizations*. San Francisco: Jossey-Bass.

Gutek, B. A., & Dunwoody, V. (1987). Understanding sex in the workplace. In A. H. Stromberg, L. Larwood, & B. A. Gutek (Eds.), *Women and work: An annual review, Volume 2* (pp. 249–269). Newbury Park, CA: Sage.

Gutek, B. A., & Morasch, B. (1982). Sex-ratios, sex-role spillover, and sexual harassment of women at work. *Journal of Social Issues, 38*, 55–74.

Haavio-Mannila, E., Kauppinen-Toropainen, K., & Kandolin, I. (1988). The effect of sex composition of the workplace on friendship, romance, and sex at work. In B. A. Gutek, A. H. Stromberg, & L. Larwood (Eds.), *Women and work: An annual review, Volume 3* (pp. 123–137). Newbury Park, CA: Sage.

Jones, T. S., Remland, M. S., & Brunner, C. C. (1987). Effects of employment relationship, response of recipient and sex of rater on perceptions of sexual harassment. *Perceptual and Motor Skills, 65*, 55–63.

Kenrick, D. T., & Keefe, R. C. (1989). Time to integrate sociobiology and social psychology. *Behavioral and Brain Sciences, 12*, 24–26.

Konrad, A. M., & Gutek, B. A. (1986). Impact of work experiences on attitudes toward sexual harassment. *Administrative Science Quarterly, 31*, 422–438.

Lafontaine, E., & Tredeau, L. (1986). The frequency, sources, and correlates of sexual harassment among women in traditional male occupations. *Sex Roles, 15*, 433–442.

Littler-Bishop, S., Seidler-Feller, D., & Opaluch, R. E. (1982). Sexual harassment in the workplace as a function of initiator's status: The case of airline personnel. *Journal of Social Issues, 38*, 137–148.

Neugarten, D. A., & Shafritz, J. M. (1980). *Sexuality in organizations: Romantic and coercive behaviors at work*. Oak Park, IL: Moore.

Palmer, C. T. (1988). Twelve reasons why rape is not sexually motivated: A skeptical examination. *Journal of Sex Research, 25*, 512–530.

Paludi, M. (Ed.) (1990). *Ivory power: Sex and gender harassment in the academy*. New York: State University of New York Press.

Pryor, J. B. (1987). Sexual harassment proclivities in men. *Sex Roles, 17*, 269–290.

Quinn, R. E. (1977). Coping with cupid: The formation, impact, and management of romantic relationships in organizations. *Administrative Science Quarterly, 22*, 30–45.

Saal, F. E., Johnson, C. B., & Walker, N. (1989). Friendly or sexy? It may depend on whom you ask. *Psychology of Women Quarterly, 13*, 263–276.

Savoie, D., & Larouche, V. (1990). Le harcelement sexuel au travail: Resultats de deux etudes quebecoises [Sexual harassment in the workplace: Results of two Quebec studies]. *Relations Industrielles, 45*, 38–62.

Schneider, B. E. (1982). Consciousness about sexual harassment among heterosexual and lesbian women workers. *Journal of Social Issues, 38*, 75–98.

Shields, W. M., & Shields, L. M. (1983). Forcible rape: An evolutionary perspective. *Ethology and Sociobiology, 4*, 115–136.

Studd, M. V. (in press). Evolutionary psychology of sexual harassment: Initiator profile, social context, and victim reactions. *Ethology and Sociobiology*.

Studd, M. V., & Gattiker, U. E. (1991). The evolutionary psychology of sexual harassment in organizations. *Ethology and Sociobiology, 12*, 249–290.

Symons, D. (1979). *The evolution of human sexuality*. Oxford, England: Oxford University Press.

Symons, D. (1987). An evolutionary approach: Can Darwin's view of life shed light on human sexuality. In J. H. Geer & W. T. O'Donohue (Eds.), *Theories of human sexuality* (pp. 91–125). New York: Plenum Press.

Symons, D. (1989). A critique of Darwinian anthropology. *Ethology and Sociobiology, 10*, 131–144.

Symons, D., & Ellis, B. (1989). Human male-female differences in sexual desire. In A. E. Rasa, C. Vogel, & E. Voland (Eds.), *The sociobiology of sexual and reproductive strategies* (pp. 131–146). London: Chapman and Hall.

Tangri, S. S., Burt, M. R., & Johnson, L. B. (1982). Sexual harassment at work: Three explanatory models. *Journal of Social Issues, 38*, 33–54.

Terpstra, D. E., & Cook, S. E. (1985). Complainant characteristics and reported behaviors and consequences associated with formal sexual harassment charges. *Personnel Psychology, 38*, 559–574.

Thornhill, N. W., & Thornhill, R. (1990a). An evolutionary analysis of psychological pain following rape I: The effects of victim's age and marital status. *Ethology and Sociobiology, 11*, 155–176.

Thornhill, N. W., & Thornhill, R. (1990b). An evolutionary analysis of psychological pain following rape II: the effects of stranger, friend and family-member offenders. *Ethology and Sociobiology, 11*, 177–193.

Thornhill, N. W., & Thornhill, R. (1990c). An evolutionary analysis of psychological pain following rape III: The effects of force and violence. *Aggressive Behavior, 16*, 297–320.

Thornhill, N. W., & Thornhill, R. (1990d). An evolutionary analysis of psychological pain following rape IV: The effect of the nature of the sexual act. *Journal of Comparative Psychology, 105*, 243–252.

Thornhill, R., & Thornhill, N. W. (1983). Human rape: An evolutionary analysis. *Ethology and Sociobiology, 4*, 137–173.

Thornhill, R., & Thornhill, N. W. (1989). The evolution of psychological pain. In R. Bell (Ed.), *Sociobiology and the social sciences* (pp. 73–103). Lubbock, TX: Texas Tech University Press.

Thornhill, R., & Thornhill, N. W. (1991). Coercive sexuality of men: Is there psychological adaptation to rape? In E. Grauerholz & M. Koralewski (Eds.), *Sexual coercion: Its nature, causes and prevention* (pp. 91–107). Toronto: D. C. Heath.

Thornhill, R., & Thornhill, N. W. (1992). The evolutionary psychology of men's coercive sexuality. *Behavioral and Brain Sciences, 15*, 363–375.

Tooby, J. (1988). The emergence of evolutionary psychology. In D. Pines (Ed.), *Emerging syntheses in science* (pp. 67–76). Redwood Park, CA: Addison-Wesley.

Townsend, J. M. (1987). Sex differences in sexuality among medical students: Effects of increasing socioeconomic status. *Archives of Sexual Behavior, 16*, 425–444.

Townsend, J. M. (1989). Mate selection criteria: A pilot study. *Ethology and Sociobiology, 10*, 241–253.

Townsend, J. M. (1990). Effects of potential partners' physical attractiveness and socioeconomic status on sexuality and partner selection. *Archives of Sexual Behavior, 19*, 149–164.

Trivers, R. L. (1972). Parental investment and sexual selection. In B. Campbell (Ed.), *Sexual selection and the descent of man 1871–1971* (pp. 136–179). Chicago: Aldine.

U.S. Merit Systems Protection Board. (1981). *Sexual harassment in the federal workplace*. Washington, DC: U.S. Government Printing Office.

4

Psychological Adaptation to Sexual Coercion in Victims and Offenders

NANCY WILMSEN THORNHILL

ADAPTATIONIST APPROACH

Controversy and misunderstanding often surround studies of human behavior that utilize the modern adaptationist approach (e.g., see Scarr's [1989] view of evolutionary psychology; but also see Crawford et al., 1990). Some of the misunderstanding stems from a lapse in recognition of the importance of both proximate and ultimate causes and explanations for adaptations, the complexly integrated, purposeful traits of individual organisms. Proximate explanations for the existence of adaptations focus on genetic, biochemical, physiological, developmental, social, and all other immediate causes leading to the expression of adaptations. Ultimate explanations of adaptation have their theoretical foundation in causes that operated during evolutionary history to lead to adaptation. Because selection is the only agent of evolution that can produce phenotypic design/adaptation, the ultimate approach's theoretical foundation is the relationship between adaptation and the nature of the selection that produced adaptation—that is, how an adaptation of interest allowed its bearers to outreproduce others in the environments of evolutionary history. The ultimate causal theoretical framework is also used in the study of proximate causation. Proximate and evolutionary explanations of causation do not conflict. Both proximate and ultimate explanations are needed for complete understanding of adaptations. By understanding the evolutionary purpose of an adaptation, one should be able successfully to predict and understand the proximate causes that affect the expression of the adaptation.

It is generally accepted by evolutionary theorists that adaptations are consequences of selection that is only effective at the level of individuals. This theory argues than an organism's adaptations are designed ultimately for perpetuation of its own genes, because selection is always for Hamiltonian inclusive fitness. It is at the level of inclusive fitness differentials among individuals that selection is most effective in bringing about evolutionary change (Alcock, 1984; Alexander, 1975, 1979, 1987; Daly & Wilson, 1983; Dawkins, 1976, 1982, 1986; Hamilton, 1964; Mayr, 1983; Rubenstein & Wrangham, 1986; R. Thornhill & Alcock, 1983; Trivers, 1985; Williams, 1985).

From the general theory, hypotheses are derived by investigators in an attempt to understand the evolutionary function of an adaptation of interest. The hypotheses so derived are then tested against nature in a specific empirical way. Since prediction is a logical consequence of a hypothesis, hypotheses may be tested by attempts to falsify their predictions. An adaptation's functional design or evolutionary function identifies the type of selection that designed it (e.g., selection in the context of avoiding a type of predator). A hypothesis about the evolutionary function of an adaptation is tested by examining its predictions about the functional design of the adaptation. If the hypothesis identifies relevant selective history, design features should be predictably revealed.

PSYCHOLOGICAL PAIN

This chapter is divided into two sections. The first addresses psychological pain, particularly in one manifestation, that experienced by rape victims. The question at hand is: Does psychological trauma following rape implicate adaptation to the circumstances surrounding coerced sex? The second section of this chapter addresses questions about male sexual psychology. Does male sexual behavior implicate adaptation to the situation of coerced sex? This question can be restated in the form of a hypothesis that mental pain is a manifestation of psychological adaptation designed for dealing with social circumstances that would have reduced inclusive fitness in human evolutionary history. This hypothesis views the evolutionary significance of mental pain as analogous to the evolutionary importance of physical pain (R. Thornhill & N. W. Thornhill, 1989; also Alexander, 1986; R. Thornhill & N. W. Thornhill, 1983, 1987; R. Thornhill, N. W. Thornhill, & Dizinno, 1986). Physical pain serves to draw an individual's attention to some aspect of anatomy that needs tending and can be fixed by the individual's attention. Mental pain seems to focus an individual's attention on the significant social events surrounding the pain and promotes correction of the events causing the pain and avoidance of these events in the future. Like physical pain, it may be associated with a social display of need. Psychological pain is distinguished from emotion in that it does not itself involve display. Psychological pain is exemplified in things like depression, anxiety, recurrent and intrusive distressing recollections of a traumatic event, recurrent and distressing dreams, and the like.

Psychological adaptations are information-processing mechanisms that are phenotypic solutions to information-processing problems that influenced inclusive fitness during evolutionary history. A psychological adaptation's evolutionary purpose is precisely identified by the kind of information that the adaptation is designed to process (for detailed discussion of modern adaptationism applied to psychological analysis, see Cosmides & Tooby, 1987, 1989; Symons, 1987, 1989; Tooby & Cosmides, 1989). If psychological pain reflects a psychological adaptation that is designed for the purpose of correcting and preventing problems stemming from social interactions, mental pain will show patterns indicative of this design.

The hypothesis of psychological pain makes the following two general predictions about the kinds of environmental information that will result in psychological pain. First, it predicts that the proximate ecological causes of mental pain will be circumstances that affected inclusive fitness of individuals in social circumstances. Second, the hypothesis predicts that the more an event potentially or actually negatively affects the evolved social tendencies, desires, and aspirations of humans, the more psychological pain will occur surrounding the event. Furthermore, the hypothesis makes many specific predictions about social proximate events that are expected to lead to psychological distress. These predictions are explained in detail elsewhere (R. Thornhill & N. W. Thornhill, 1989).

Psychological Trauma of Rape Victims

Copulation without implicit or explicit consent distinguishes rape from other kinds of sexual behavior. It is assumed that rape, unlike consensual sex, reduced the inclusive fitness or potential for genetic propagation of women during evolutionary history (R. Thornhill & N. W. Thornhill, 1983).

In human evolutionary history, rape may have resulted in a reduction in female fitness in the following six ways.

1. Rape may lead to the victim's injury.
2. Rape may reduce a woman's ability to choose the timing and circumstances for reproduction, as well as choice of the man who fathers her offspring. When rape leads to conception and gestation of a zygote, a woman may expend her limited reproductive effort in the wrong (for successful reproduction) circumstances and with the wrong man.
3. Rape also circumvents a woman's ability to trade sex for material benefits.
4. Rape of a mated woman may adversely influence protection of her by her mate or the quantity and quality of parental care her offspring receives.
5. Rape may damage the social reputation of a woman, reducing her potential mate value.
6. Rape may damage the status of a woman's kingroup by causing the appearance of failure on their part to protect her.

Human males are one of the most parentally investing of male mammals, and parental care from both sexes has been critical to the fitness of each sex during our evolutionary history (see Alexander & Noonan, 1979; Benshoof & Thornhill, 1979). Human paternal care is discriminative in terms of genetic overlap between men and offspring; men care more for their genetic offspring (Daly & Wilson, 1988). Actual or suspected rape would reduce reliability of male parentage. In human evolutionary history, this could have negatively influenced a man's behavior toward a woman and the offspring she produced, thereby damaging a raped woman's potential reproduction. Even attempted rape may be of great concern to men from the standpoint of paternity reliability. In the male mind, a woman placing herself in a situation conducive to a rape attempt may fail to avoid similar situations in the future (or have failed to avoid them in the past). Any copulation by a pair-bonded woman with someone other than her mate reduces his reliability of parentage.

Rape is thus expected to upset mates of victims. However, the probability of conception (and thus for compromised paternity) is much lower for a single rape event than it is for the multiple sexual interactions of a love affair. Mates of rape victims might be quite suspicious of an alleged rape, preferring to view the sexual assault of their wives/girlfriends as simply adulterous liaisons. The doubt that mates of rape victims seem to exhibit about the victim's credibility is expected as a paternity protection mechanism. Requiring proof of actual victimization might be one outcome (see R. Thornhill & N. W. Thornhill, 1983).

Rape, from the woman's perspective, can be understood by considering the negative influences it has had on women. If rape were a fitness-reducing social event for women in human evolutionary history, the evolutionary perspective on mental pain should apply to psychological changes experienced by rape victims. The mental pain hypothesis applied to rape victims assumes that in human evolutionary history raped women had increased fitness as a result of mental pain because the pain forced them to focus attention on the evaluation of the above-outlined fitness-reducing circumstances surrounding rape, including the evaluation of the social circumstances that resulted in the sexual assault. Just as physical pain prompts an individual to avoid situations that may lead to similar injury, mental pain may cause individuals to consider circumstances that resulted in the pain more carefully and to avoid them in the future.

The evolutionary perspective on psychological pain requires that, in general, mental pain will be manifested in women who are victims of rape. Indeed, social scientists have documented that, following rape, victims do experience psychological distress due to the rape and circumstances precipitated by the rape (R. Thornhill & N. W. Thornhill, 1989).

This perspective makes certain specific predictions about the characteristics of rape victims that will influence the degree of mental pain experienced by victims. Many of these predictions have been tested on a population of 790 rape victims who were treated at the Philadelphia General Hospital between 1973 and 1975. The data taken on these victims comprise 265 variables ranging from their age and marital status to psychiatric profiles. It is important that measures of immediately evident anxiety and psychological distress were assessed within five days following the rape and then reassessed in two long-term follow-up studies (see N. W. Thornhill & R. Thornhill, 1990a, for methods). The psychological distress variables were scored as chance variables, each victim reporting her self-assessed chance since the rape in such things as eating and sleeping patterns, fears of strange men and known men, being home alone, heterosexual relationships, and so on. Using each victim as her own control, this design allowed evaluation of victim's psychological trauma.

One of the most critical predictions depended on the victim's age and reflected expected patterns of psychological trauma following rape. The expectation that victim's age should be an important predictor of psychological trauma following rape stems from the hypothesized fitness consequences of rape for our female ancestors. The consequences were likely to have been most severe for women of reproductive age because these women have an increased probability that any sexual interaction will result in conception. Reproductive-age victims were significantly more psychologically traumatized by rape than were pre-reproductive-age girls (0–11) or post-reproductive-age women (45+), as measured by all psychological distress variables in this sample of victims (N. W. Thornhill & R. Thornhill, 1990a).

Another important prediction pertains to married rape victims. It was expected that married victims would experience greater psychological distress than would unmarried victims. Husbands and boyfriends of rape victims often find the rape allegations not credible. Husbands and boyfriends are often inclined to think of rapes simply as consensual sex about which their wives and girlfriends are lying. Consequently, rape can have a severe negative impact on a woman's relationship with her mate. Married victims, especially married reproductive-age victims, were significantly more traumatized than were unmarried victims in this sample (N. W. Thornhill & R. Thornhill, 1990a).

The data supporting the two predictions about age and marital status could easily be confounded by any number of other causal factors. For example, in the sample of victims studied, stranger rape was most common for each of the three age categories of victims. Reproductive-age and post-reproductive-age women were more likely to be victims of rape by a stranger than were pre-reproductive girls. Post-reproductive-age women were less likely to be raped by a friend than were either reproductive- or pre-reproductive-age victims. Pre-reproductive girls were the most likely victims of family member rape. Married women were more likely to be raped by a stranger than were unmarried women, but unmarried women were not significantly more likely to be raped by a friend than were married women.

When the variables pertaining to psychological pain following rape were analyzed by stranger, friend, or family member rape, the results indicated clearly that, for this sample, stranger rape is by far the most psychologically traumatizing and rape by a family member is the least psychologically traumatizing. However, this pattern is not confounded by victim age (N. W. Thornhill & R. Thornhill, 1990b). Stranger rapes were found to be more violent than either friend or family member rapes, but it appears that increased violence is not the factor influencing the greater psychological traumas of victims of stranger rape. Rape by strangers actually may be more psychologically traumatizing than rape by nonstrangers (N. W. Thornhill & R. Thornhill, 1990b).

Recently, Shields and Hanneke (1987) conducted a study comparing victims of stranger rape with those of marital rape. They concluded that marital rape is far more psychologically traumatizing than is stranger rape. The situational dynamics of rape in mateships are likely to be much different from rape perpetrated by other acquaintances. Furthermore, the victims of marital rape in the Shields and Hanneke study were likely to have been severely physically abused, as well as raped, to have been victims for some length of time, and to be living in women's shelters, all of which alone could lead to psychological distress, as Shields and Hanneke acknowledge.

These results suggest that the psychology that regulates mental pain processes information about age and mateship status in the event of a woman's rape. If age and mateship status are shown to be actual causes of the mental pain of the rape victim, then these two factors identify design features—evolved information-processing procedures—of the psychological adaptation involved.

As suggested above, husbands and boyfriends of rape victims are often disbelieving, even to the extent of requiring evidence of rape (physical evidence of violence or force) before believing their mates to be victims. The occurrence of violence and concomitant physical evidence of rape should moderate psychological trauma for reproductive-age, and especially married, victims. The data set included variables that allowed analysis of the extent of psychological trauma dependent on the severity of physical violence (other than the rape) experienced by victims. Violence during the rape was coded as a variable including verbal threats, pushing or holding the victim, or the use of weapons (knives, guns, etc.). Married reproductive-age rape victims in the sample did seem to be less psychologically traumatized when the rape included violence (N. W. Thornhill & R. Thornhill, 1990c). This result for married victims supports the finding that mateship status is a proximate cause of the psychological trauma in the event of a woman's rape.

Some of the analyses of this data set did not support this prediction. For example, it was predicted that physical evidence of resistance by the victims would alleviate psychological pain experienced. This was predicted for the same reason that violence during the rape was predicted to reduce psychological trauma. However, even though physical evidence of resistance (bruises, lacerations, broken bones, etc.) was more marked in reproductive-age and married victims, it had no moderating effect on the psychological pain they experienced. Even more surprising is the finding that unmarried reproductive-age victims experienced greater trauma when they manifested physical evidence of resistance, particularly as reflected in areas of social life that involved meeting and interacting with potential mates. When they are physically traumatized, unmarried reproductive-age rape victims were more psychologically distressed in interactions with known and unknown men, in heterosexual relationships, in fear of being in the street, in social activities, and in insecurities about their sexual attractiveness. This surprising result may be taken into account by considering the way in which men and women interact in mating contexts. Men tend to evaluate women as potential mates based on their physical attractiveness. Over the course of evolutionary time, this has resulted in women competing with one another in the realm of attractiveness. Women who are beaten, bruised, and lacerated may have lowered self-perceptions of attractiveness than other women and consequently think of themselves as less competitive (less attractive compared to other women). This might be reflected in their dealings with unknown women and known men and in their heterosexual relationships in general.

The nature of sexual activity that occurs during a rape has some surprising moderating effects on a victim's psychological trauma. In this sample of victims, the greatest psychological trauma was seen in those who experienced penile-vaginal intercourse. This was true when victims of penile-vaginal rape were compared with victims who experienced any other form of sexual assault (including forced fellatio, anal intercourse, etc.) (N. W. Thornhill & R. Thornhill, 1990c). Reproductive-age victims were overwhelmingly more often victims of penile-vaginal intercourse than were victims in the other age categories (N. W. Thornhill & R. Thornhill, 1990c).

Pre-reproductive-age girls and post-reproductive-age women in this sample were less psychologically traumatized by rape than were reproductive-age women (N. W. Thornhill & Thornhill, 1990a). But, since the non-reproductive-age rape victims (especially the pre-reproductive-age victims) were less often victims of penile-vaginal intercourse, the apparent age effect might be confounded. However, this potential confound may have no effect because pre-reproductive-age girls who were victims of penile-vaginal intercourse were no more psychologically traumatized than were pre-reproductive-age girls who were not. The same is true for post-reproductive-age women. However, reproductive-age women who were victims of penile-vaginal intercourse were more psychologically traumatized than those who were victims of other forms of sexual assault, not including penile-vaginal intercourse.

Conclusion

The results indicate that the psychology that regulates mental pain processes information about age in the event of a woman's rape: Reproductive-age victims have the most psychological pain. Moreover, the results have indicated that both mateship status (married vs. unmarried) and the credibility of rape are significant proximate causes of psychological pain after rape, with married victims and victims of less-violent rapes having more mental trauma. However, physical evidence of the occurrence of rape had no moderating effect and even exacerbated psychological trauma in some cases. Another proximate factor—the nature of the sex act during rape—may be another piece of information processed by the psychological machinery that affects mental pain in the event of a woman's rape (N. W. Thornhill & R. Thornhill, 1990a, 1990b, 1990c, 1990d).

If age, mateship status, rape credibility, and the nature of the sex act during rape are actual causes affecting the mental pain of rape victims, then these four factors are actual design features of the psychological adaptation involved. The causes identified in this chapter do indeed suggest that the psychological trauma suffered by rape victims is specific to the rape experience.

The finding that age is a significant causal factor in the expression of psychological trauma following rape is important. However, that reproductive-age women are more psychologically traumatized by rape is, by itself, not evidence of mechanistic design. It could be that, reproductive-age women are more traumatized by any social event that has a potential negative impact on fitness. There are some data that deny this possibility. For example, when psychological trauma experienced by women victims of robbery is analyzed by victim's age, it turns out that older victims are more traumatized than are younger victims (N. W. Thornhill, in preparation). Similarly, psychological trauma is much greater when older mothers suffer the death of a child than when younger mothers do. This is true even when the age of the child is controlled (R. Thornhill & N. W. Thornhill, 1989). Studies designed to test the age effect in experience of psychological trauma relative to various crimes are needed to test fully the possibility that young women are simply more easily traumatized than are older women.

More important, though, it may be that the age (and marital status) effects that are seen in psychological trauma following rape are general to any fitness-reducing event that occurs in the domain of sexuality. If this is true, then the proposed design features of the rape response mechanism are not specific to rape. Psychological trauma might, for example, be more extreme in young women than in older women who are voluntarily involved in a sexual encounter of short duration, in unprotected sex, in a sexual relationship simply because they are lonely or bored, and so on. In order to fully implicate a rape-specific response mechanism, studies must be designed to test whether the age, marital status, and other suggested design features are sexuality specific or only confined to rape.

MALE SEXUAL PSYCHOLOGY

As indicated in this chapter, since women seem to have evolved specific psychological adaptations to rape circumstances, the question of men's psychological adaptation to the perpetration of rape becomes important. The remainder of this chapter addresses that question.

Is rape just a side effect of psychological adaptations to circumstances other than rape, such as a desire for sex coupled with a general coercive tendency, or does it come directly from an evolutionary adaptation to sexual coercion itself? Men's mating repertoire consists of three tactics: honest advertisement and courtship, deceptive advertisement and courtship, and coercion. Coerced matings are those achieved by physical force by explicit or implicit threat of physical or social malice. The hypothesis that there is adaptation to rape implies that rape is a sex-specific, specieswide aspect of the evolved mating strategy of men (Shields & Shields, 1983; R. Thornhill & N. W. Thornhill, 1983).

The sex difference in mating strategy (women reluctant, men eager) can lead to disparity in the evolved self-interests of men and women about whether mating should occur and its timing and frequency of occurrence. Because women are more selective of mates and more interested in evaluating mates and delaying sexual congress than men, in order to achieve sexual access men often must break through feminine barriers of sexual hesitation, equivocation, and resistance (see Kirkendall, 1961, for a review of human heterosexual sexual interactions). Men get women to comply with their wishes by using all three tactics of their mating strategy. These tactics can be used singly in pursuit of single matings or together in pursuit of single matings. Men sometimes include coercion in their repertoire of sexual behavior, and some men's sexual repertoire is a mix of noncoercive and coercive, including physically coercive, approaches.

In addition, men often pursue single matings by using a mix of tactics. It is erroneous in general to dichotomize copulations into those resulting from honest versus deceptive courtship or from force versus nonforce tactics. Courtship and the interactions associated with maintenance of pair bonds include explicit and implicit promises about commitment that are not always realized, in part because of lack of positive intention (Kirkendall, 1961). The three tactics grade into each other to the extent that there are sometimes seemingly arbitrary boundaries between them. Viewing the three tactics as objective and distinct categories does not describe the entirety of sexual behavior in humans. Sexual coercion or noncoercion is a continuum. The literature dealing with rape by husbands, boyfriends, and dates (Kirkendall, 1961; Russell, 1984; see review in R. Thornhill & N. W. Thornhill, 1990a) leaves the impression that there is often no distinct objective boundary between coerced and noncoerced sex. However, sexual coercion is a real event. When it occurs, the participants know it. It, like all forms of coercion, leaves one party suffering uncompensated cost and the other enjoying undeserved benefit.

Men's Sexual Motivation

The view that men's sexual psychology contains adaptation to coercive sexual interaction predicts that their use of noncoercive and coercive mating tactics will be associated with high levels of sexual arousal and competence. However, if men are sexually aroused only or primarily when they perceive that a potential mate is interested in coitus or if significant sexual arousal in men requires perception of nonresistance in a potential mate, the psychology of sexual motivation is not designed by selection to achieve copulations with women who are sexually uninterested or actively resistant; that is, the idea that men have psychological adaptation to rape is false.

There is extensive literature on men's sexual arousal to audio and visual sexual stimuli in the laboratory setting (Malamuth, 1991; Malamuth & Donnerstein, 1984; R. Thornhill & N. W. Thornhill, 1992). The studies generally take one of two forms. Either the research design includes men incarcerated for sex crimes (typically rape) and compares their sexual responses with those of male volunteers from the general population in an effort to determine rapists' sexual arousal patterns (or compares rapists' sexual arousal to rape versus nonrape scenarios) or the studies utilize male student populations and measure their sexual responses to coercive and noncoercive sexual scenarios in an effort to measure propensity to rape. Sexual response in the studies is measured by self-reported arousal, by a phallometric device, or by both. The studies manipulate not only sexual and noncoerciveness apparent in the video or audio stimuli, but, in various combinations, violence, depicted female sexual arousal, and sex of the person reading the stimulus story (in the case of audio tapes). Other factors are manipulated as well, depending on the study, including the type of instructions given to participants (e.g., the instructions might include a statement indicating that response to unusual sexual stimuli is nominal) and alcohol consumption or belief of alcohol consumption by participants.

The laboratory studies were used to examine six predictions about a rape-specific sexual psychology (R. Thornhill & N. W. Thornhill, 1992). The predictions were

1. Men will exhibit high levels of sexual motivation and performance in both coercive and noncoercive mating situations.
2. Gaining physical control over an unwilling sexual partner by force should be sexually arousing to men because it facilitates forced sexual interaction.
3. A man's age should affect his willingness to use sexual coercion.
4. Men's willingness to use sexual coercion should be negatively related to their social status.
5. Sexual coerciveness will be very sensitive to the probability of detection and negative social consequences or punishment to a pair-bonded mate when he suspects or discovers infidelity.

The data reported by R. Thornhill and N. W. Thornhill (1992) supported all six predictions, inspiring the following conclusion:

The hypothesis that men have psychological traits that are designed for the specific purpose of rape has survived the following tests: It is consistent with (a) what is known of the natural history of men's sexual coerciveness; (b) the results of laboratory studies of arousal to depictions of sexual coercion; (c) the results of laboratory studies and other evidence indicating that men are sexually aroused by physical control of an unwilling mate through force; (d) data suggesting that men's desire to give the appearance of having a moral sexuality is an important condition regulating men's use of sexual coercion, and (e) information on rape in mateships. In addition, there is reason to infer that our male evolutionary ancestors sometimes enhanced their reproductive success through rape. (R. Thornhill & N. W. Thornhill, 1992, p. 347)

This conclusion, however, seems premature. A reevaluation of the data indicates that they do not support so confident a conclusion. The laboratory studies used to test Prediction 1, for example, may have been misinterpreted or misunderstood. Most of the lab studies cited utilize various manipulations (as discussed above). Here, I discuss disinhibiting manipulations and contextual manipulations of stimulus materials.

Malamuth (1992) suggests that disinhibiting devices such as alcohol consumption by subjects and permissive instructions given to subjects may have large effects on men's sexual response.

> Quinsey et al. (1981) focused on the effect of telling men that sexual responsiveness to unusual themes was expected in the testing situation. The Thornhills believe that this study indicates that the "community men who have received permissive instructions showed a significantly greater response to rape narratives than the community men with regular instructions." Also, the former community men "did not differ significantly from the rapists in their response to the rape narratives." This community sample did show more sexual arousal to both rape and consenting depictions than those without permissive instructions, however. There was no differential effect of the instructions on responsiveness to rape themes. These data appear to be inconsistent with the "adaptation to rape" interaction effects described earlier in target article. Moreover, even for these community subjects with permissive instructions, the overall pattern indicated that they were less aroused in response to the rape depictions than the mutually consenting ones. (Malamuth, 1992, p. 395)

In other words, in laboratory studies in which sexual arousal responses are measured, subjects given permissive instructions respond more to both rape and nonrape themes. Furthermore, the overall response to rape themes was lower, no matter what the instruction, than it was to depictions of mutually consenting sex.

An important aspect of lab depictions of rapes involves portrayal of the woman victim. Largely overlooked by R. Thornhill and N. W. Thornhill (1992) are the visual and verbal cues to which men respond with respect to the woman. Malamuth and Linz (1993) report data from a study in which men responded to depictions of sexual coercion in which the victim's sexual arousal is manipulated. When the victim is shown to be continually abhorrent, showing no sexual arousal, men have far less of a sexual response than when she is shown to become sexually aroused.

In addition to victim response, some research has focused on realism in laboratory rape depictions (Malamuth & Donnerstein, 1984; Stock, 1982). Many alleged rape depictions are more involved with erotic aspects of the sexual situation or with the perpetrator's apparent pleasure than they are on the negative response of the victim (Stock, 1983). Content analyses of rape descriptions used by three researchers disclosed that in all of them less than 20% of dialogue is devoted to the victim's pain or resistance and is focused instead on the visual appearance of the woman (her body or parts of it), the perpetrator's sexual arousal, and descriptions of the sexual acts being performed (Allgeier & Weiderman, 1991).

These results suggest that lab studies meant to separate coerced and noncoerced sexual situations and to measure male sexual response to them might actually be measuring something else. The cues to which men are responding are, at least potentially, not the ones the researchers intend to manipulate and likely not the ones R. Thornhill and N. W. Thornhill (1992) impute to sexual response.

In light of the above discussion, it seems that Prediction 1 (and perhaps Prediction 2) of the rape adaptation hypothesis may not be as secure as proposed in R. Thornhill and N. W. Thornhill (1992). Whether there are psychological adaptations designed for sexual coercion or whether the adaptations involved are more generally involved in sexual motivation combined with adaptations motivating coercion is still an open question. In future research, it will be critical to isolate the causes of male sexual arousal in laboratory settings. By simply asking the subjects, following the experiment, what aspect of the scenario was most exciting or that they paid most attention to, information about cause could be gleaned. Furthermore, the nonconsent scenarios should be written or directed by women. A woman's perspective on what constitutes sexual nonconsent, sexual coercion, and sexual violence is likely vastly different from that of a man.

It is also necessary to determine men's responses to coercion in general. If it is shown that realistic depictions of coerced appropriation of desired commodities (other than women) causes heightened physiological arousal (heart rate, galvanic skin response, etc.), the hypothesis that men's physiological responses are rape specific is without basis.

Conclusion

Behavior provides a window to psychological adaptive design because it is a manifestation of psychological adaptations. Adaptations are solutions to environmental problems that have consistently impinged on human endeavors to survive and reproduce. The suggestion that male sexual psychology is a coercive one (i.e., envelops rape adaptations) and that women's minds include adaptations for response to rape assumes that rape has been one of the consistent and recurrent problems of human evolutionary time. It suggests that rape, like finding a mate, protecting offspring, and finding food and shelter, has been an integral part of the human adaptive environment. The general mating strategy of men sometimes includes sexual coercion, and sexual coercion of one form or another may be involved in many matings in humans. It might be that obtaining sexual intercourse by coercion is as much a part of men's sexual behavior as men's use of noncoercive sexual approaches. However, current knowledge of men's sexual behavior does not provide evidence of psychological adaptation to rape itself. It seems likely that the occurrence of coercive sexual behavior by men could as easily be the combined effect of species-typical adaptation to coerce desired rewards and sex-specific adaptation for sexual behavior.

Acknowledgments.   Many thanks go to David Buss and Neil Malamuth for their critical comments on this chapter. Their close attention vastly improved it. Conversations with Martin Daly, Donald Symons, Margo Wilson, and particularly with my husband, Mark Ingram, caused me to reevaluate much of my earlier work on rape psychology, leading to the expression of the more realistic view disclosed herein.

REFERENCES

Alcock, J. (1984). *Animal behavior: An evolutionary approach* (1st Ed., 1975). Sunderland, MA: Sinauer.

Alexander, R. D. (1975). The search for general theory of behavior. *Behavior Science*, 20, 77–100.

Alexander, R. D. (1979). *Darwinism and human affairs*. Seattle, WA: University of Washington Press.

Alexander, R. D. (1986). Ostracism and indirect reciprocity: The reproductive significance of humor. *Ethology and Sociobiology*, 7, 105–122.

Alexander, R. D. (1987). *The biology of moral systems*. Hawthorne, NY: Aldine de Gruyter.

Alexander, R. D., & Noonan, K. M. (1979). Concealment of ovulation, parental care, and human social evolution. In N. A. Chagnon & W. G. Irons (Eds.), *Evolutionary biology and human social behavior: An anthropological perspective* (pp. 436–453). North Scituate, MA: Duxbury Press.

Allgeier, E. R., & Wiederman, M. W. (1991). Evidence for an evolved adaptation to rape? Not yet. *Behavioral and Brain Sciences*, 15, 377–379.

Benshoof, L., & Thornhill, R. (1979). The evolution of monogamy and concealed ovulation in humans. *Journal of Social and Biological Structures*, 2, 95–106.

Cosmides, L., & Tooby, J. (1987). From evolution to behavior: Evolutionary psychology as the missing link. In J. Dupré (Ed.), *The latest on the best: Essays on evolution and optimality* (pp. 247–306). Cambridge, MA: Massachusetts Institute of Technology Press.

Cosmides, L., & Tooby, J. (1989). Evolutionary psychology and the generation of culture, Part II: Case study: A computational theory of social exchange. *Ethology and Sociobiology*, 10, 51–98.

Crawford, C. B. (1989). The theory of evolution: Of what value to psychology? *Journal of Comparative Psychology*, 103, 4–22.

Daly, M., & Wilson, M. (1983). *Sex, evolution and behavior* (1st Ed., 1978). Boston, MA: Willard Grant Press.

Daly, M., & Wilson, M. (1988). *Homicide*. New York: Aldine de Gruyter.

Dawkins, R. (1976). *The selfish gene*. Oxford, UK: Oxford University Press.

Dawkins, R. (1982). *The extended phenotype: The gene as the unit of selection*. San Francisco: W. H. Freeman.

Dawkins, R. (1986). *The blind watchmaker*. New York: Norton.

Hamilton, W. D. (1964). The genetical evolution of social behavior. I and II. *Journal of Theoretical Biology, 12,* 12–45.

Malamuth, N. M. (1992). Evolution and laboratory research on men's sexual arousal. What do the data show and how can we explain them? *Behavioral and Brain Sciences, 15,* 394–396.

Malamuth, N. M., & Donnerstein, E. (1984). *Pornography and sexual aggression.* New York: Academic Press.

Malamuth, N. M., & Linz, D. (1993). *Pornography: Social Aspects.* Beverly Hills, CA: Sage.

Mayr, E. (1983). How to carry out the adaptationist program? *American Naturalist, 121,* 324–334.

Rubenstein, D. I., & Wrangham, R. W. (1986). *Ecological aspects of social evolution: Birds and mammals.* Princeton, NJ: Princeton University Press.

Russell, D. (1984). *Sexual exploitation: Rape, child sexual abuse and sexual harassment.* Beverly Hills, CA: Sage.

Scarr, S. (1989). Sociobiology: The psychology of sex, violence and oppression? *Contemporary Psychology, 34,* 440–443.

Shields, N., & Hanneke, L. (1987). Rape and wife battery: a comparison. *Aggressive Behavior, 12,* 27–51.

Shields, W. M., & Shields, L. M. (1983). Forceable rape: An evolutionary perspective. *Ethology and Sociobiology, 4,* 115–136.

Stock, W. (1982). The effect of violent pornography on women. In E. Allgeier & A. Allgeier (Eds.), *Sexual interactions* (pp. 128–142). New York: D. C. Heath.

Symons, P. (1987). If we're all Darwinians, what's the fuss about? In C. Crawford, M. Smith, & D. Krebs (Eds.), *Sociobiology and psychology* (pp. 121–146). Hillsdale, NJ: Erlbaum.

Symons, D. (1989). A critique of Darwinian anthropology. *Ethology and Sociobiology, 10,* 131–144.

Thornhill, N. W., & Thornhill, R. (1990a). An evolutionary analysis of psychological pain following rape: 1990. I. The effects of age and marital status. *Ethology and Sociobiology, 11,* 155–176.

Thornhill, N. W., & Thornhill, R. (1990b). An evolutionary analysis of psychological pain following rape: II. The effects of stranger, friend and family member rape. *Ethology and Sociobiology, 11,* 177–193.

Thornhill, N. W., & Thornhill, R. (1990c). An evolutionary analysis of psychological following rape III: The effects of force and violence. *Aggressive Behavior, 16,* 297–320.

Thornhill, N. W., & Thornhill, R. (1991). An evolutionary analysis of psychological pain following rape V: The effects of the nature of the sexual assault. *Journal of Comparative Psychology, 103,* 243–252.

Thornhill, R., & Alcock, J. (1983). *The evolution of insect mating systems.* Cambridge, MA: Harvard University Press.

Thornhill, R., & Thornhill, N. W. (1983). Human rape. An evolutionary analysis. *Ethology and Sociobiology, 4,* 63–99.

Thornhill, R., & Thornhill, N. W. (1987). Human rape: The strengths of the evolutionary perspective. In C. Crawford, C. Krebs, & M. Smith (Eds.), *Psychology and sociobiology: Ideas, issues and applications* (pp. 269–291). Hillsdale, NJ: Erlbaum.

Thornhill, R., & Thornhill, N. W. (1989). The evolution of psychological pain. In R.

Bell & N. Bell (Eds.), *Sociobiology and the social sciences* (pp. 73–103). Lubbock, TX: Texas Tech University Press.

Thornhill, R., & Thornhill, N. W. (1992). The evolutionary psychology of men's coercive sexuality. *Behavioral and Brain Sciences, 15*, 363–421.

Thornhill, R., Thornhill, N. W., & Dizinno, G. (1986). The biology of rape. In S. Tomaselli & R. Porter (Eds.), *Rape* (pp. 102–121). Oxford, UK: Blackwell.

Trivers, R. L. (1985). *Social evolution*. Menlo Park, CA: Benjamin Cummings.

Williams, G. C. (1985). A defence of reductionism in evolutionary biology. In R. Dawkins & M. Ridley (Eds.), *Oxford surveys in evolutionary biology* (pp. 1–27). Oxford, UK: Oxford University Press.

II

Feminist Perspectives

5

Where Are the Gender Differences?
Where Are the Gender Similarities?

JANET SHIBLEY HYDE

In this chapter, I discuss what psychologists consider to be basic phenomena or "facts" about gender differences. I use the term *facts* in quotation marks because we do not have facts in psychology—rather, we have theories and scientific data, but we sometimes start thinking that we have facts. My analyses, then, emanate from a social constructionist epistemology (e.g., Gergen, 1985; Hare-Mustin & Marecek, 1988) and a feminist theoretical perspective.

Social constructionism stands in opposition to positivism, the latter having been the epistemology of most psychological scientists until recently. *Positivism* assumes that we can know reality, facts, or phenomena directly and objectively. *Constructionism*, in contrast, argues that people—including scientists—do not discover reality; instead, they construct or invent it based in part on prior experiences and predispositions. Constructionism, then, questions whether science and scientists can be completely objective.

Feminist theory is not a single, unified theory created by a single theorist. Many persons have contributed to feminist theory, and there is a spectrum of feminist theoretical perspectives, including liberal feminism, Marxist feminism, and radical feminism. Some are even attempting to develop feminist sociobiology (e.g., Smuts, 1992). Nonetheless, there is a central core to most of feminist theory that emphasizes the importance of gender roles and socialization as powerful forces on human behavior (Hyde, 1991). It is this aspect of feminist theory that is emphasized in this chapter.

I first go back approximately 100 years ago to see how the earliest psychologists portrayed gender differences. Next I skip to 1974 and the publication of Maccoby and Jacklin's influential book on gender differences, *The Psychology of Sex Differences*.

My contention is that, over the last 15 years, meta-analysis has caused a revolution in scientific understanding of the nature of psychological gender differences. Therefore, I present a user-friendly introduction to meta-analysis for the beginner. I then review a number of important meta-analyses of psychological gender differences that provide this new evidence and new view.

THE PSYCHOLOGY OF GENDER A CENTURY AGO

Formal psychology began just over a century ago. Stephanie Shields (1975) has provided a fascinating view of the intellectual climate of the time. Darwinism dominated intellectual thought in the sciences. The theory of evolution, because it highlighted the importance of variability or individual differences, made it legitimate to study variations in behavior, including gender differences. Thus, psychology grew from fledgling status with gender differences as one of its topics, and evolutionary theory helped legitimize the research area.

The relation between gender and intelligence was first investigated by phrenologists and neuroanatomists. The belief at the time was that male and female brains must be as different in their gross appearance as are male and female bodies in the areas that are called into service during sex. An argument that gained great popularity was that females had smaller brains than males, that brain size was a direct indicator of intelligence, and that women must therefore be less intelligent than men (Bain, 1875). Indeed, George Romanes considered brain size and its correlate, intelligence, to be among the secondary sex characteristics (Romanes, 1887).

Later theorizing was based on the notion of localization of function. For a time it was thought that the frontal lobes were the site of the highest mental abilities; quickly, researchers claimed that males possessed larger frontal lobes (Mobius, 1901). Next, the parietal lobes were thought to be the location of intelligence, and the parietal lobes of females were found sadly wanting (Ellis, 1934).

Helen Thompson Woolley, one of the fine early women psychologists, provided the first review of psychological research on gender differences in 1910. She reviewed studies that measured rate and endurance in tapping a telegraph key, handwriting (women's was judged colorless, conventional, neat, and small, whereas men's was bold, careless, experienced, and individual), and tests of association. For this last variable, participants were required to write a series of associations to a given word. The investigator interpreted the results as indicating that women showed abnormality of reaction, meager presentations, a less active flow of ideas, less variety in ideas, more concrete forms of response, a more subjective attitude, and more indecision. Woolley wrote a devastating methodological critique of the research. She concluded: "There is perhaps no field aspiring to be scientific where flagrant personal bias, logic martyred in the cause of supporting a prejudice, unfounded assertions, and even sentimental rot and drivel have run riot to such an extent as here" (Woolley, 1910, p. 340).

CURRENT TEXTBOOK "FACTS"

I move quickly from 1910 to 1974 (thereby skipping the emergence of the mental testing movement, which in many ways was interesting in its commitment to gender equity). The year 1974 saw the publication of a book that had a remarkable impact on the field, Eleanor Maccoby and Carol Jacklin's *The Psychology of Sex Differences*. By that time, literally thousands of studies had been done on psychological gender differences. In a heroic effort, Maccoby and Jacklin reviewed over 2,000 studies on gender differences in psychological characteristics ranging from abilities to personality, social behaviors, and memory. They organized the data and conceptualized the questions well, and were able to bring large quantities of empirical evidence to bear in assessing a number of widely held beliefs about gender differences. They dismissed many common beliefs in gender differences: that girls are more social than boys, that girls are more suggestible than boys, that girls have lower self-esteem, that girls are better at rote learning and simple tasks whereas boys are better at high-level cognitive processing, and that girls lack achievement motivation.

Maccoby and Jacklin concluded that the evidence did not support the existence of these gender differences. In so doing, they took a *gender similarities* position. On the other hand, they concluded that four gender differences were "well established": female superiority in verbal ability, male superiority in mathematical and spatial ability, and the greater aggressiveness of males. Their conclusions about these four well-established differences were tremendously influential and have become the "facts" put in textbooks. Textbook authors, by and large, ignored all the evidence Maccoby and Jacklin had for gender similarities.

The textbook facts over the last 20 or more years have been that there are gender differences in aggression and in verbal, mathematical, and spatial abilities, and even the most recent textbooks (with only a couple of exceptions) do not stray much from that orthodox position. In so doing, they teach a *differences model*.

Now let us turn to meta-analysis, which gives us a considerably improved scientific method for determining whether there is good evidence for these gender differences.

INTRODUCTION TO META-ANALYSIS

Meta-analysis can be thought of as a statistical method that allows the researcher to quantitatively combine the results from many different studies of the same question (e.g., Cook et al., 1992; Hedges & Olkin, 1985; Hyde & Linn, 1986). Essentially, it is a quantitative or statistical method for doing a literature review.

A meta-analysis proceeds in several stages. First, the researchers collect as many studies as possible that report data on the question of interest (e.g., gender differences in sexuality). Computerized literature searches (e.g., of PSYCLIT or ERIC) are a wonderful asset in this process, helping to ensure that there is a complete sampling of studies, including unpublished ones that may have gone unpublished because of a failure to find significant differences. On questions of gender differences, one can often obtain large numbers of relevant studies. For example, for gender differences in sexuality we found 177 usable studies that yielded 239 independent samples (Oliver & Hyde, 1993).

Second, the researchers perform a statistical analysis of the statistics reported in each article. For each study, an effect size d is computed,

$$d = (M_M - M_F)/s$$

where M_M is the mean score for males, M_F is the mean score for females, and s is the average within-sex standard deviation. Essentially, then, d indicates how far apart the means for males and females are in standard deviation units. Positive values of d mean that males scored higher than females, and negative values mean that females scored higher. One of the virtues of d as a statistic is that it is independent of n (the number of subjects)—unlike t or F, which are highly dependent on n so that a tiny effect can be significant if the n is large enough. The statistic d simply measures effect size. It is a statistic much like the familiar z score: It can take on positive or negative values, has a mean of 0, and is probabilistically very unlikely to take on values very far from 0, such as 5.2. Unlike z, however, d does not have a normal distribution, so statisticians have worked out the appropriate formulas for doing further computations with d (e.g., Hedges & Olkin, 1985).

In the third stage of the meta-analysis, the researchers average the d values obtained from all studies, which allows them to draw conclusions based on the average of the results of all of the studies. For example, the mean value of d averaged over 100 studies of gender differences in verbal ability might be $d = -0.18$. At this stage, the researcher can tell whether there is a gender difference, whether it is in the hypothesized direction, and how large the difference is. For those who are not experienced with d statistics, the following guidelines may be helpful in knowing how to evaluate the size of d. According to Cohen (1969), a d of 0.20 is small, $d = 0.50$ is moderate, and $d = 0.80$ is large. Some disagree and say that these guidelines are arbitrary, but at least they provide a guide for the beginner; in my own work, I have found them to be sensible.

RESULTS OF META-ANALYSES OF GENDER DIFFERENCES

Cognitive Differences

We have available three comprehensive meta-analyses that look at the issue of cognitive gender differences. They treat the questions of gender differences in verbal ability, spatial ability, and mathematical ability.

The textbook fact is that females outscore males on measures of verbal ability. Yet, in a meta-analysis based on 165 studies reporting the testing of

1.4 million people, we found that $d = -0.11$ (Hyde & Linn, 1988). This indicates that, on the average, females did score higher than males, but the difference is tiny. If we return to the Cohen rule that a d of 0.20 is small, 0.50 moderate, and so on, this is approximately half the magnitude of a small effect size. As a general rule, I suggest that d values of 0.10 or less (in absolute value) be considered to be 0—that is, that meta-analysis allows us to take the revolutionary step of accepting the null hypothesis. I would argue, therefore, that there are no longer any gender differences in verbal ability.

Textbook facts hold that males outscore females on measures of visual-spatial ability. Marcia Linn and Anne Petersen (1985) conducted the major meta-analysis of gender differences in spatial ability. They concluded that there are three distinct types of spatial ability, each measured by different types of items tapping spatial ability: spatial perception, mental rotation, and spatial visualization measured by instruments such as the Embedded Figures Test. The magnitude of the gender difference was considerably different depending on the type of measure. For spatial perception, based on data from 62 samples, $d = 0.44$. For mental rotation, based on data from 29 samples, $d = 0.73$. For spatial visualization, based on data from 81 samples, $d = 0.13$. The results indicate that, depending on the type of spatial ability being measured, gender differences can be large (mental rotations) or nonexistent (spatial visualization). A global generalization such as "males are superior in spatial ability" is simply unwarranted. The only large difference is in mental rotation (see also Masters & Sanders, 1993).

It also has been part of conventional wisdom in psychology that the gender difference in spatial ability does not emerge until adolescence, say around age 13. Indeed, whole theories of sex differences in brain lateralization have been built on the assumption that gender differences in spatial ability emerge at puberty (e.g., Waber, 1977). Linn and Petersen (1985) tested this hypothesis and found that there was no evidence of age trends in gender differences in spatial ability. That is, there was no evidence to support the hypothesis that a large gender difference in spatial ability emerges at puberty.

Another textbook fact is that "boys are better than girls at math," based on the conclusions of Maccoby and Jacklin (1974) and many other reviews. Here, too, meta-analysis changes the prevailing view. Based on 254 samples and the testing of over 3 million subjects (so that we can have a lot of confidence in the results), $d = 0.15$ (Hyde et al., 1990). That is, males scored higher, but the difference is less than Cohen's small effect size of 0.20. Moreover, there were many peculiar samples included in this overall result, such as samples of mathematically precocious youth. If we look just at studies based on reasonably good samples of the general population, then $d = -0.05$. That is, overall girls actually outperform boys slightly.

Several other widely held beliefs about gender and math were also exploded by this meta-analysis. One belief is that girls and boys are equal in math performance through elementary school, and that the superior performance of males emerges around the beginning of adolescence, say age 12 (e.g., Maccoby & Jacklin, 1974). Another belief is that, although girls may be as good as boys at simple computation, boys excel particularly at complex math problem solving such as one finds in story problems. We looked at these questions in an analysis of Age × Cognitive Level of Test. Females do better at computation, but the difference is small. There are no gender differences in understanding mathematical concepts at any age. The gender difference in problem solving does not emerge until the high school years, when it is of small-to-moderate size. This last finding is important because it is just in the last few years of high school when mathematics courses become elective and girls choose not to take math much more frequently than boys do. To me, the real issue in gender and math is not whether males and females differ in abilities — the evidence indicates that they do not — but rather why girls stop taking math courses in high school and college (e.g., Eccles, 1987) and how we can encourage them to pursue math with enthusiasm.

One other interesting finding emerged in this meta-analysis. If we separate studies according to year of publication, we find that older studies, published in 1973 or earlier, had an average $d = 0.31$, whereas studies published since 1973 find an average $d = 0.14$. In other words, in the last two decades the magnitude of the gender difference has dropped to about half of what it was previously. This trend toward a narrowing of the gender gap in abilities was also found in the meta-analysis of verbal ability, for which the value of d declined from -0.23 to -0.10 across those two time periods (Hyde & Linn, 1988).

To address this volume's theme of sex and conflict, in all the major research universities there is a serious underrepresentation of women among the faculty in engineering and the hard sciences. This underrepresentation has caused much debate and conflict, both social conflict and scholarly conflict. Some want to dismiss the issue of the dearth of female faculty in these areas by saying that women lack the mathematical and spatial ability to perform at the exceptional level that is required.

How can meta-analyses inform this argument? First, in regard to mathematical performance, the findings indicate that the differences are negligible, with the exception of mathematical problem solving, which of course is critical to being a faculty member in the sciences. But the issue seems to be the courses taken, and we can work to change that pattern. Even for the value of $d = 0.29$ for mathematical problem solving in high school populations (Hyde et al., 1990), the difference is not large enough to account for the tiny percentage of women faculty. If we assume that faculty would have to have mathematical ability in the top 1% of the distribution, that would place 1.38% of males above the cutoff and 0.7% of females above the cutoff, a ratio of approximately 2 males for each 1 female. That ratio is quite far from the finding that only about 12% of tenured science faculty are women (Matyas & Malcom, 1992). That would lead us to seek additional explanations such as sex discrimination and an unfriendly climate for women in the sciences. Insofar as some men scientists, whether consciously or unconsciously, create an unfriendly climate for women in the sciences, these men exert power and control over women, keeping them out of certain departments, causing them to leave a particular university, and so on. We need many more analyses of this kind of gender-related power and control.

Aggression

A number of meta-analyses are available in the social–personality realm, including reviews of gender differences in aggression, helping behavior, nonverbal behavior, leadership, and psychological well-being (Eagly & Crowley, 1986; Eagly & Johnson, 1990; Eagly & Karau, 1991; Eagly, Makhijani, & Klonsky, 1992; Eagly & Steffen, 1986; Hall, 1984; Hyde, 1984, 1986; Wood, Rhodes, & Whelan, 1989). In order to address the theme of this volume, I consider only one of them here, aggression.

When Maccoby and Jacklin concluded that four gender differences were well established, the fourth—in addition to verbal, spatial, and mathematical abilities—was in aggression. Two meta-analyses have examined gender differences in aggression, one from a developmental perspective (Hyde, 1984, 1986) and the other from a social perspective (Eagly & Steffen, 1986). In my developmental meta-analysis, I found overall that $d = 0.50$. That is, males are more aggressive, and the difference is moderate in size (and certainly larger than gender differences in verbal ability or mathematical ability). Eagly and Steffen's social psychological meta-analysis found $d = 0.40$ averaged over all studies. The results also supported Eagly and Steffen's social role analysis of the socialization of gender differences in aggression. For example, gender differences in aggression were larger for those aggressive behaviors or situations in which women, more than men, perceived that the behavior would harm someone or that the behavior could bring danger to oneself. The social context in which the behavior occurs has a profound effect on the pattern of gender differences.

Again returning to the theme of gender and conflict, the gender difference in aggression—which is moderate in magnitude based on the meta-analyses—is an obvious source of conflict between males and females and of violence toward women. Surely the greater aggressiveness of males is important in explaining phenomena such as rape and woman battering.

Both biological–evolutionary (e.g., Barash, 1977) and feminist (e.g., Eagly, 1987; Matlin, 1993) explanations for the greater aggressiveness of males have been offered. Feminist theories generally reject explanations that rest on biological factors such as sex hormones. A feminist explanation holds that gender roles and socialization are key factors (e.g., Hyde, 1991). Research on gender stereotypes shows consistently that aggressiveness is a key part of the male role in the United States (Eagly, 1987). Additional roles, such as military roles and competitive athletics, also foster heightened levels of aggressiveness in males (Arkin & Dobrofsky, 1978; Stein & Hoffman, 1978). The female role, in contrast, places little or no emphasis on aggression and encourages other behaviors such as nurturance that are incompatible with aggression (Eagly, 1987). The gender difference in aggression then, according to the feminist view, is a direct result of males being socialized into the male role and females being socialized into the female role. Apparently this social-ization is successful because females experience more guilt and anxiety about being aggressive (Eagly & Steffen, 1986); thus, internalized cognitions and affect act to place controls on females' aggressive behavior.

In an elegant demonstration of the power of gender roles on aggressive behavior, Lightdale and Prentice (1994) used the technique of deindividuation, in which individuals are made to feel anonymous and thereby lose their sense of responsibility and feel little or no need to conform to social norms such as gender roles. Although in the normal, individuated condition there were gen-der differences in aggressive behavior, this gender difference was eliminated in the deindividuation condition. This study found, then, that when gender-role norms are removed, there are no gender differences in aggression.

Sexuality

Mary Beth Oliver and I conducted a meta-analysis of gender differences in sexuality (Oliver & Hyde, 1993). We found 177 usable sources reporting data on 239 separate samples representing the testing of 128,363 respondents. We examined gender differences on 21 different measures of sexual attitudes and sexual behaviors: attitudes about premarital sex; attitudes about premarital sex in a casual relationship; attitudes about premarital intercourse in a com-mitted relationship; attitudes about premarital intercourse when the couple are engaged; attitudes about homosexuality; attitudes about civil liberties for homosexuals; attitudes about extramarital sex; sexual permissiveness; sex guilt or anxiety; sexual satisfaction; double-standard attitudes; attitudes about masturbation; the incidence of the following behaviors—kissing, petting, in-tercourse, masturbation, homosexual behavior, oral sex; age at first inter-course; number of sexual partners; and frequency of intercourse.

Here, I present some highlights from that study—findings that I thought were particularly interesting or striking. The largest gender difference was in the incidence of masturbation, $d = 0.96$. The second-largest gender differ-ence was in attitudes about casual sex, $d = 0.81$. Notice that these differences are enormous compared with the ones discussed above for gender differences in mathematics ability and verbal ability. We need much more attention in theory and research to these very large differences.

I do not want to be guilty of focusing only on the differences model, however. There were many variables that showed no gender difference. Exam-ples are attitudes about civil liberties for homosexuals ($d = 0.00$), attitudes about masturbation ($d = 0.09$), and attitudes of sexual satisfaction ($d = -0.06$).

Other gender differences were moderate in magnitude: attitudes about intercourse in a committed relationship such as being married or engaged ($d = 0.49$) and anxiety or guilt about sex ($d = -0.35$).

Regarding gender and conflict, let me consider the implications of the two big gender differences: masturbation and attitudes about casual sex. It might seem a bit odd to think of gender differences in masturbation creating male–

female conflict, but I want to argue that there is a connection. *Anorgasmia* — specifically, having difficulty having an orgasm during sex with a partner — is common among women and rare among men (Hyde, 1994). Sex therapists believe that orgasm problems in women are often a result of lack of experience with masturbation, and, indeed, directed masturbation therapy is a standard form of sex therapy for anorgasmia (Andersen, 1981; LoPiccolo & Stock, 1986). Sex therapists and marital therapists also tell us that anorgasmia is a source of marital or relationship conflict between men and women. The wife is upset with the husband for not being skillful in bringing her to orgasm, and at the same time the husband feels inadequate. So, in short, the gender difference in masturbation may indeed be related to male–female conflict in close relationships. There is a rather simple — although controversial — solution to this problem. It is to have mandatory sex education in the schools and to include information about female masturbation as part of the curriculum.

The other large gender difference, in attitudes about casual sex, seems to be fairly directly related to male–female conflicts. This robust gender difference means that, in many male–female interactions, sexual intercourse seems to the male to be a perfectly good outcome, whereas for the female it seems to be the wrong outcome. The stage is set for male–female conflict. To illustrate how salient male–female differences are in this area, consider some direct quotations from college students in a study in which they were asked, "What would be your motives for having sexual intercourse?" The following are typical answers from females:

- My motives for sexual intercourse would all be due to the love and commitment I feel for my partner.
- To show my love for my partner and to feel loved and needed.
- Love, to feel loved, to express love to someone.

The following are typical answers from males to the same question:

- Need it.
- To gratify myself.
- When I'm tired of masturbation. (Carroll, Volk, & Hyde, 1985, pp. 137–138)

Coming to a sexual encounter with such different attitudes and motivations, it is not surprising that there is male–female conflict. In extreme cases, date rape is the result.

We must also be concerned with an explanation for the phenomenon: Why do males and females hold such different attitudes about casual sex? Sociobiology, social learning theory, social role theory, and script theory all predict this gender difference (Oliver & Hyde, 1993). Arguing from an evolutionary perspective, Buss and Schmitt (1993) proposed the sexual strategies theory. It holds that men and women have different sexual strategies and that the strategies differ for each, depending on the context. Buss and Schmitt argued that short-term mating (what I have termed *casual sex*) will constitute a larger component of men's sexual strategy than women's, and that women generally will require reliable signs that a man is committed to them for the long term as a prerequisite for sexual intercourse.

A feminist analysis would cast the matter quite differently. It would see this gender difference as the outcome of gender-role socialization. In particular, the sexual double standard is critical in defining norms for male and female sexuality. Evidence indicates that the old double standard—in which sexual intercourse outside marriage was acceptable for men but not women—has been replaced by a conditional double standard in which sex outside marriage is tolerated for both men and women, but under more restrictive circumstances—such as love or engagement—for women (Sprecher, McKinney, & Orbuch, 1987). This corresponds precisely to our finding of females disapproving of casual sex much more than males. Moreover, males are socialized to have callous attitudes toward sex (Mosher & Tomkins, 1988), leading them to be more approving of casual sex.

How does this gender difference in attitudes toward casual sex relate to male–female conflicts? I contend that this gender difference contributes to a number of aspects of conflict—in some cases, violence—directed by men toward women. Consider the case of men's sexual harassment of women at work. The data indicate that, on the average, casual sex is more acceptable and satisfying to men. Moreover, the male role defines expressions of sexual interest as always appropriate. Sexual propositions at work involve precisely those two components: casual sex and an inappropriate (on the job) expression of sexual interest.

Moreover, a feminist analysis sees this gender difference in attitudes embedded in a social context in which men have more power—both institutional power and physical power—than women. Institutional power is critical in the issue of sexual harassment at work because the situation in which the supervisor is male and the worker female is much more common than the reverse. Insofar as sexual harassment involves the "unwanted imposition of sexual requirements in the context of a relationship of unequal power" (MacKinnon, 1979, p. 1), the institutional work setting carries with it the power imbalance that contributes to sexual harassment. The greater physical strength of males, when combined with the gender difference in attitudes toward casual sex, contributes powerfully to the phenomenon of date rape.

CONCLUSION

In conclusion, meta-analyses have founded that gender differences in abilities are small or nonexistent, with a couple of exceptions, particularly the gender difference in the ability to perform three-dimensional mental rotation. To advance our understanding of male–female conflict, research should focus on the moderately large gender difference in aggression and on the large gender difference in attitudes toward casual sex.

REFERENCES

Andersen, B. L. (1981). A comparison of systematic desensitization and directed masturbation in the treatment of primary orgasmic dysfunction in females. *Journal of Consulting and Clinical Psychology, 49,* 568–570.

Arkin, W., & Dobrofsky, L. R. (1978). Military socialization and masculinity. *Journal of Social Issues, 34*(1), 151–168.

Bain, A. (1875). *Mental science.* New York: Appleton.

Barash, D. P. (1977). *Sociobiology and behavior.* New York: Elsevier.

Buss, D. M., & Schmitt, D. P. (1993). Sexual strategies theory: An evolutionary perspective on human mating. *Psychological Review, 100,* 204–232.

Carroll, J., Volk, K., & Hyde, J. S. (1984). Differences between males and females in motives for engaging in sexual intercourse. *Archives of Sexual Behavior, 14,* 131–139.

Cohen, J. (1969). *Statistical power analysis for the behavioral sciences.* New York: Academic Press.

Cook, T. D., Cooper, H., Cordray, D. S., Hartmann, H., Hedges, L. V., Light, R. J., Louis, T. A., & Mosteller, F. (1992). *Meta-analysis for explanation: A casebook.* New York: Russell Sage Foundation.

Eagly, A. H. (1987). *Sex differences in social behavior: A social-role interpretation.* Hillsdale, NJ: Erlbaum.

Eagly, A. H., & Crowley, M. (1986). Gender and helping behavior: A meta-analytic review of the social psychological literature. *Psychological Bulletin, 100,* 283–308.

Eagly, A. H., & Johnson, B. T. (1990). Gender and leadership style: A meta-analysis. *Psychological Bulletin, 108,* 233–256.

Eagly, A. H., & Karau, S. J. (1991). Gender and the emergence of leaders: A meta-analysis. *Journal of Personality and Social Psychology, 60,* 685–710.

Eagly, A. H., Makhijani, M. G., & Klonsky, B. G. (1992). Gender and the evaluation of leaders: A meta-analysis. *Psychological Bulletin, 111,* 3–22.

Eagly, A. H., & Steffen, V. (1986). Gender and aggressive behavior: A meta-analytic review of the social psychological literature. *Psychological Bulletin, 100,* 309–330.

Eccles, J. S. (1987). Gender roles and women's achievement-related decisions. *Psychology of Women Quarterly, 11,* 135–172.

Ellis, H. H. (1934). *Man and Woman: A study of secondary and tertiary sexual characteristics* (8th ed.). London: Heinemann.

Gergen, K. J. (1985). The social constructionist movement in modern psychology. *American Psychologist, 40,* 266–275.

Hall, J. A. (1984). *Nonverbal sex differences: Communication accuracy and expressive style.* Baltimore, MD: Johns Hopkins University Press.

Hare-Mustin, R. T., & Marecek, J. (1988). The meaning of difference: Gender theory, post-modernism, and psychology. *American Psychologist, 43,* 455–464.

Hedges, L. V., & Olkin, I. (1985). *Statistical methods for meta-analysis.* New York: Academic Press.

Hyde, J. S. (1984). How large are gender differences in aggression? A developmental meta-analysis. *Developmental Psychology, 20,* 722–736.

Hyde, J. S. (1986). Gender differences in aggression. In J. S. Hyde & M. C. Linn (Eds.), *The psychology of gender: Advances through meta-analysis* (pp. 51–66). Baltimore, MD: Johns Hopkins University Press.

Hyde, J. S. (1991). *Half the human experience: The psychology of women* (4th ed.). Lexington, MA: D. C. Heath.

Hyde, J. S. (1994). *Understanding human sexuality* (5th ed.). New York: McGraw-Hill.

Hyde, J. S., Fennema, E., & Lamon, S. J. (1990). Gender differences in mathematics performance: A meta-analysis. *Psychological Bulletin, 107,* 139–155.

Hyde, J. S., & Linn, M. C. (1986). *The psychology of gender: Advances through meta-analysis.* Baltimore, MD: Johns Hopkins University Press.

Hyde, J. S., & Linn, M. C. (1988). Gender differences in verbal ability: A meta-analysis. *Psychological Bulletin, 104,* 53–69.

Lightdale, J. R., & Prentice, D. A. (1994). Rethinking sex differences in aggression: Aggressive behavior in the absence of social roles. *Personality and Social Psychology Bulletin, 20,* 34–44.

Linn, M. C., & Petersen, A. C. (1985). Emergence and characterization of sex differences in spatial ability: A meta-analysis. *Child Development, 56,* 1479–1498.

LoPiccolo, J., & Stock, W. (1986). Treatment of sexual dysfunction. *Journal of Consulting and Clinical Psychology, 54,* 158–167.

Maccoby, E. E., & Jacklin, C. N. (1974). *The psychology of sex differences.* Stanford, CA: Stanford University Press.

MacKinnon, C. A. (1979). *Sexual harassment of working women.* New Haven, CT: Yale University Press.

Masters, M. S., & Sanders, B. (1993). Is the gender difference in mental rotation disappearing? *Behavior Genetics, 23,* 337–341.

Matlin, M. W. (1993). *The psychology of women* (2nd ed.). Fort Worth, TX: Harcourt Brace Jovanovich.

Matyas, M. L., & Malcom, S. M. (1992). *Investing in human potential: Science and engineering at the crossroads.* Washington, DC: American Association for the Advancement of Science.

Mobius, P. J. (1901). The physiological mental weakness of woman. *Alienist and Neurologist, 22,* 624–642.

Mosher, D. L., & Tomkins, S. S. (1988). Scripting the macho man: Hypermasculine socialization and enculturation. *Journal of Sex Research, 25,* 60–84.

Oliver, M. B., & Hyde, J. S. (1993). Gender differences in sexuality: A meta-analysis. *Psychological Bulletin, 114,* 29–51.

Romanes, G. J. (1887). Mental differences between men and women. *Nineteenth Century, 21*(123), 654–672.

Shields, S. (1975). Functionalism, Darwinism, and the psychology of women: A study in social myth. *American Psychologist, 30,* 739–754.

Smuts, B. (1992). Male aggression against women: An evolutionary perspective. *Human Nature, 3,* 1–44.

Sprecher, S., McKinney, K., & Orbuch, T. L. (1987). Has the double standard disappeared? An experimental test. *Social Psychology Quarterly, 50,* 24–31.

Stein, P. J., & Hoffman, S. (1978). Sports and male role strain. *Journal of Social Issues, 34*(1), 136–150.

Waber, D. P. (1977). Sex differences in mental abilities, hemispheric lateralization, and rate of physical growth at adolescence. *Developmental Psychology, 13,* 29–38.

Woolley, H. T. (1910). A review of the recent literature on the psychology of sex. *Psychological Bulletin, 7,* 335–342.

Wood, W., Rhodes, N., & Whelan, M. (1989). Sex differences in positive well-being: A consideration of emotional style and marital status. *Psychological Bulletin, 106,* 249–264.

6

Is Rape Sex or Violence?
Conceptual Issues and Implications

CHARLENE L. MUEHLENHARD,
SHARON DANOFF-BURG, AND IRENE G. POWCH

Say you have a man who believes a woman is attractive. He feels encouraged by her and he's so motivated by that encouragement that he rips her clothes off and has sex with her against her will. Now let's say you have another man who grabs a woman off some lonely road and in the process of raping her says words like, "You're wearing a skirt! You're a woman! I hate women! I'm going to show you, you woman!" Now, the first one's terrible. But the other's much worse. If a man rapes a woman while telling her he loves her, that's a far cry from saying he hates her. A lust factor does not spring from animus.
Orrin Hatch, U.S. Senate (quoted by Shalit, 1993, p. 7B)

Rape is never an act of lust. Mr. Hatch just doesn't get it.
Eleanor Smeal, Fund for a Feminist Majority
(quoted by Shalit, 1993, p. 7B)

The above debate regarding the Violence Against Women Act of 1993 focused on how rape is to be conceptualized: Is rape sex, motivated by lust, or is rape violence? This question has emerged in numerous contexts, including political, scientific, clinical, and interpersonal contexts.

A simplistic answer to the question—Is rape sex or violence?—would be that nonfeminists view rape as sex, whereas feminists[1] view rape as violence.

As we show, however, this simplistic answer is incorrect. Both feminists and nonfeminists have taken a variety of positions on this question. Furthermore, neither a "rape is sex" nor a "rape is violence" position has solely positive or negative implications for rape victims or for all women.

The purpose of this chapter is not to answer the question, "Is rape sex or violence?" Rather, our purpose is to examine thoughtfully the conceptual issues behind this question. These conceptual issues include the following: Is rape sex or violence from whose perspective? From the perspective of the victim? The perpetrator? All women and men in our society?

What is rape? That is, what is it that we are characterizing as sex or violence? What is sex? That is, what characteristics would rape need to have before we could say that rape "was" sex? Similarly, what is violence? What characteristics would rape need to have before we could say that rape "was" violence?

Finally, what are the implications of different positions on this debate? What are the social, scientific, and legal implications for rape victims and perpetrators, as well as for all women and men?

FROM WHOSE PERSPECTIVE?

The question—"Is rape sex or violence?—implies that rape is a monolithic entity, similar from any perspective. Rape, however, is experienced from numerous perspectives. In fact, Spender (1980) suggested that the experience of rape from the victim's perspective is so different from the perpetrator's experience that we need two different words to describe these totally different experiences.

In this section, we discuss rape from the perspectives of victims, perpetrators, and all women and men in this culture.[2] Paradoxically, however, when we turn to the literature for insights, what we find are the perspectives of various writers about the perspectives of victims, perpetrators, and all women and men. Historically, many of these writers have expressed views consistent with the interests of those in power, such as those scientists who attempted to justify or trivialize rape by writing that rape was unconsciously desired by female victims. Before we conclude that the least biased approach is for persons involved to speak for themselves, however, we should ask ourselves if we would take perpetrators' accounts at face value, knowing that even incarcerated perpetrators often deny engaging in sexual coercion (Wolfe & Baker, 1980).

Furthermore, as we discuss this question from different perspectives, it will become clear that the meaning of the question—"Is rape sex or violence?"—is ambiguous. It could refer to motivation, to consequences, or to how one experiences, conceptualizes, and labels the experience. Thus, when someone says, "Rape is sex to the rapist and violence to the victim," they often are referring to the motivation and experience of the rapist but to the experience of and consequences for the victim.

With these complexities in mind, we now discuss the perspectives of victims, perpetrators, and all women and men.

The Victim's Perspective

In the scientific literature published through the mid-1970s, experts' conceptualizations of victims' perspectives could be characterized as follows: To the extent that these experts regarded rape as a "real" phenomenon rather than as false charges made up by hysterical women (e.g., Deutsch, 1944), they frequently viewed rape as a sexual experience that the victim unconsciously desired (e.g., Factor, 1954; Wille, 1961) and that the victim invited by being unconsciously seductive (e.g., Blanchard, 1959) or blatantly provocative to the rapist (e.g., Amir, 1971; MacDonald, 1971; see Muehlenhard, Harney, & Jones, 1992, for further discussion).

Beginning in the 1970s this scientific analysis of rape as sexually desirable for victims was challenged by feminist writers. These feminists focused an unprecedented amount of attention on rape, engaging in political activism and advocating new theoretical perspectives. Although the grassroots nature of feminist activism makes a complete record impossible to compile, existent records indicate that feminist activists held the first speak-outs on rape and organized the first rape crisis centers in the early 1970s (Deckard, 1983; Rape Victim Support Service, n.d.). Feminist theorists such as Brownmiller (1975), Greer (1970), Griffin (1971), and Millett (1969) emphasized the violent nature of rape and conceptualized rape as a form of social control of women. For example, in her classic article, "Rape: The All-American Crime," Susan Griffin (1971) wrote,

> Rape is an act of aggression in which the victim is denied her self-determination. It is an act of violence which, if not actually followed by beatings or murder, nevertheless always carries with it the threat of death. And finally, rape is a form of mass terrorism, for the victims of rape are chosen indiscriminately. (p. 35)

Since the 1970s, research has documented the devastating consequences experienced by rape victims. Currently, even persons who argue that rape is sex from the perpetrator's perspective often say that rape is violence from the victim's perspective. For example, Palmer (1988), in an article arguing that rapists are frequently motivated by sexual desire, wrote, "Thanks to the feminist movement, no one any longer defends the dangerous claim that rape is a sexually arousing or sought-after experience on the part of the *victim*" (p. 514, italics in original). Symons (1979), who also argued that sexual desire motivates rapists, commented, "What has, of course, been shown is that rape very rarely is a sexual experience for the victim" (p. 284).

It would be overly simplistic, however, to say that rape is never sex from the victim's perspective. The definition of rape and who labels the act become an issue here. For example, Koss, Dinero, Seibel, and Cox (1988) used a definition of rape based on a legal definition. They found that women who had been raped (based on Koss et al.'s definition) did not always consider themselves to have been raped. This was especially likely in the context of a dating relationship: Women labeled the incident rape in 55.0% of cases involving strangers, in 27.7% of cases involving nonromantic acquaintances, and in 18.3% of cases involving steady dating partners. Some of the women viewed the incident as a crime other than rape (this was the case for 15.6% of the incidents involving strangers and 15.0% of the incidents involving acquaintances). Other women viewed the incident as miscommunication (this was the case for 21.5% of the incidents involving strangers and 50.9% of the incidents involving acquaintances). Still other women reported not feeling victimized (this was the case for 7.9% of the incidents involving strangers and 11.1% of the incidents involving acquaintances). Although Koss et al. did not specifically ask women if they viewed the incident as violence or sex, it seems probable that women who viewed the incident as rape or some other crime probably regarded it as violence (they may or may not also have viewed the incident as sex). Conversely, it seems likely that women who viewed the incident as miscommunication and women who did not feel victimized probably were more likely to have viewed the incident as sex and less likely to have viewed it as violence.

Victims' conceptualizations of their experiences are influenced by what they learn from the popular culture. The law, depictions of rape in the media, and what others say about rape influence victims' ideas of what events constitute rape and how they should interpret these events. The dominant culture sends us powerful messages about rape, sex, and violence: that "real rape" is a narrowly defined set of events (e.g., a stranger with a weapon forcing a woman to have penile-vaginal intercourse); that men cannot control their sexual urges if women "get them" aroused; that "real men" may use force to get what they want; and that, under certain circumstances, one is obligated to have sex whether one wants to or not (Beneke, 1982; Estrich, 1987; Reinholtz, Muehlenhard, Phelps, & Satterfield, 1995). To the extent that rape victims (as defined by researchers, the law, etc.) have internalized these messages, they may or may not interpret their experiences as rape, sex, or violence. How victims label an incident is not necessarily related to the seriousness of the consequences, however. For example, Koss et al. (1988) found that, although victims of acquaintance rape (as the researchers defined it) were less likely than victims of stranger rape to label their experience as rape, the two groups did not differ significantly in their subsequent depression, anxiety, problems with relationships, problems with sex, or thoughts of suicide (over one-fourth of both groups reported considering suicide).

The Perpetrator's Perspective

Cultural messages that influence how victims label their experiences also influence how perpetrators experience and conceptualize their behavior. The question of whether rape is sex or violence to a perpetrator, however, frequently refers to motivation. Motivational questions could be addressed by investigating what perpetrators say about their motivation; however, this approach is likely to be complicated by perpetrators' desire to view their behavior in a positive light, as well as by the illegality of rape and the possibility (albeit a minute possibility) of criminal sanctions. Motivational questions could also be addressed by investigating perpetrators' underlying motivations—unconscious motivations (from a psychodynamic perspective) or behavioral contingencies (from an operant perspective). An observer's conclusions about such underlying motivations may be very different from perpetrators' explanations of their own behavior.

In asking about perpetrators' motivations, we also must keep in mind that different rapists have different motivations (Groth, 1979; Hall & Hirschman, 1991; Prentky & Knight, 1991; Russell, 1990); in fact, even the same rapist may be motivated by different factors at different times. Thus to say that rape is motivated by sex or violence or by any other single factor is likely to be overly simplistic.

The Perspectives of All Women and Men

One feature that distinguished feminists' analyses of rape from previous scientific accounts was feminists' focus on the perspectives of all women and all men. Recall Griffin's (1971) statement, quoted above, that "rape is a form of mass terrorism, for the victims of rape are chosen indiscriminately" (p. 35). Brownmiller (1975) also considered the perspective of all women and men: "From prehistoric times to the present, I believe, rape has played a critical function. It is nothing more or less than a conscious process of intimidation by which *all men* keep *all women* in a state of fear" (p. 5, italics in original).

Feminist theorists noted similarities in the impact of rape and other forms of violence: similarities in consequences for victims and similarities in producing fear that forces potential victims to alter their behavior. Thus they argued for the utility of conceptualizing rape as violence. In such an analysis, one could ask about "society's"[3] motives for perpetuating rape myths that blame women for rape, for advocating rape prevention strategies that limit women's freedom, and for establishing a legal system that shields rapists by making a charge of rape almost impossible to prove. This system benefits men at the expense of women.

People who do not rape are likely to have different motives for perpetuating this system than do rapists. For example, even men who do not rape might benefit by having access to occupational, educational, leisure, and other opportunities that women are afraid to pursue (Brownmiller, 1975; Green, Hebron, & Woodward, 1987; Griffin, 1971). "Any one man might not rape to preserve the patriarchy" (Muehlenhard, Harney, & Jones, 1992, p. 240), but preserving the patriarchy might well be the motivation of those who benefit from a system that forces women to restrict their sexual behavior, their dress, their mobility—in short, their freedom.

THE IMPACT OF DEFINITIONS

The question—"Is rape sex or violence?"—depends on how rape, sex, and violence are defined and conceptualized. Often, these terms are used as if their definitions were obvious, and most English-speaking people would report knowing the definitions of these terms. Beneath the surface understandings of these terms, however, the boundaries of people's definitions are fuzzy. Although people often can provide examples of acts that would definitely be construed as rape or sex or violence, they often have difficulty giving precise definitions or saying whether certain acts would or would not fit into these categories. Different people also disagree about how these terms should be defined.

We do not intend to provide the "true" or "accurate" definitions of these terms; in fact, we regard a true definition as a meaningless concept. Instead, we approach these definitional issues from a social constructionist perspective. "Social constructionism is principally concerned with elucidating the processes by which people come to describe, explain or otherwise account for the world in which they live" (Gergen, 1985, pp. 3–4). Of primary interest to us here is to note that the words that we use are created by people: "The terms in which the world is understood are social artifacts, products of historically situated interchanges among people" (Gergen, 1985, p. 5). The meanings that we assign to words are made up by people and change over time and place. The meanings of words reflect the power relations among people; people dominant in the culture define words from their perspective, usually in ways that benefit themselves (Lerner, 1986; Spender, 1980). Because language does not merely name reality but actually shapes reality, it can be an act of resistance for less-powerful groups to point out who benefits and who loses from commonly accepted definitions and conceptualizations and to develop their own definitions and conceptualizations.

What Is Rape?

There is no single correct definition of *rape*. Commonly used definitions of rape all include the notion of nonconsensual sexual behavior, but definitions differ dramatically along several dimensions (see Muehlenhard, Powch, Phelps, & Giusti, 1992, for a further discussion). Depending on how sex and violence are conceptualized, the differences in various definitions may influence our thinking about whether rape is sex or violence.

In the stereotypic rape, the rapist is either threatening the victim with a weapon or hitting her with his fists; the victim is crying, pleading, and perhaps struggling. Consistent with this stereotype, some definitions of rape—for example, some legal definitions—require a great deal of force by the perpetrator (Estrich, 1987). Similarly, some definitions require that the victim fight, cry, scream, or plead (e.g., Alder, 1985; Kanin, 1967).

Other definitions do not require force; the fact that the perpetrator initiated sexual behavior without the victim's consent makes the act rape. Consent, however, is itself a complicated concept. Sometimes consent occurs in the context of limited options. For example, if a woman consents to sex because the alternative is to be physically beaten, most people would regard her consent as meaningless and would regard the sex as rape even though she "consented." What if she consents to sex with her husband because the alternative is divorce and poverty, perhaps even homelessness, for herself and her children? In this case, would her consent be regarded as meaningless and would sex with her husband be regarded as rape? In this society and others, sex within marriage is regarded as the norm—a spouse's entitlement (Finkelhor & Yllo, 1985; Russell, 1990). A husband who expects sex in his marriage is likely to be motivated by sex, as he understands it, rather than by violence.

Some feminist theorists' definitions of rape are much broader than traditional definitions. For example, MacKinnon (1987) wrote, "Politically, I call it rape whenever a woman has sex and feels violated" (p. 82). This would include situations in which women have sex due to economic pressure, fear of being raped if they refuse, or other sorts of pressure. Robin Morgan (1974/ 1992) wrote, "*I would claim that rape exists any time sexual intercourse occurs when it has not been initiated by the woman, out of her own genuine affection and desire*" (p. 84, italics in original). Robin Morgan's definition would even include some situations in which the woman herself initiated sex, given the pressures on women to initiate sex out of "fear of losing the guy, fear of being thought a prude, fear of hurting his fragile feelings, *fear*" (R. Morgan, 1974/1992, p. 84, italics in original). Gavey (1992) wrote that

> Dominant discourses on heterosexuality position women as relatively passive subjects who are encouraged to comply with sex with men, irrespective of their own sexual desire. Through the operation of disciplinary power, male dominance can be maintained in heterosexual practice often in the absence of direct force or violence. The discursive processes that maintain these sets of power relationships can be thought of as "technologies of heterosexual coercion." (p. 325)

Such technologies include the tyranny of normality, which dictates how often and under what circumstances "normal" women must engage in sex; the ideology of permissive, meaningless sex, which deprives women of reasons to refuse; and negative labeling, such as a woman's being taunted as "sexually uptight" (p. 340) or "a ball-breaking feminist" (p. 347) if she refuses. Thus, these technologies of heterosexual coercion can hide sexual coercion from both those who coerce and those who are coerced.

Some writers contend that in our patriarchal culture women can never truly consent to sex (A Southern Women's Writing Collective, 1990). They argue that, in a patriarchal culture, even if women desire sex, this desire is likely to have been constructed by the patriarchal culture. Furthermore, A Southern Women's Writing Collective argued that in this culture sex is part of a package that includes love, security, and emotional support; giving up sex would result in giving up all this. For these reasons, they argued, women in this culture can never freely consent to sex.

Levine (1959) highlighted the culturally constructed nature of rape when he defined rape as the "*culturally disvalued* [italics added] use of coercion by a male to achieve the submission of a female to sexual intercourse" (p. 965). If the cultural norm is to regard certain types of coercion as appropriate, then those behaviors, however unwanted, will not be considered rape. Thus rape generally is not defined as broadly as the definitions just discussed; it has been in the interest of people with power to define rape as requiring blatant acts of force rather than subtle uses of power. As we move away from definitions requiring blatant force by the perpetrator and vehement reactions by the victim to more subtle uses of power, however, the distinction between rape and "normal sex" becomes blurred. Motivations for rape can become indistinguishable from motivations for sex.

What Is Sex?

In order to address the question—"Is rape sex or violence?"—we need to consider the definition of *sex*. That is, what criteria would rape need to meet to be considered sex?

In his article arguing that rape is sexually motivated, Palmer (1988) criticized the following argument:

Sex includes tenderness, affection, and joy.
Rape does not include these qualities.
Therefore, rape is not sex.

Palmer argued that "the validity of this argument depends on the accuracy of its definition of 'sex,' and there appears to be considerable evidence that this definition of sex is unduly limiting" (p. 516). Apparently Palmer meant unduly limiting to men, for he proceeded to give examples of how men can divorce sex from love. Palmer's statement about the "accuracy" of a definition suggests that he believes that there is an accurate definition of sex. We, on the other hand, take the position that there is no accurate definition of sex. Using a social constructionist perspective, we view sex as a fluid, socially negotiated concept.

Although conceptualizing sex as "tenderness, affection, and joy" differentiates sex from rape, other conceptualizations of sex make sex and rape indistinguishable and thus make rape appear normal, invisible as rape and visible only as sex. For instance, psychoanalytic theorists traditionally have conceptualized women's sexuality as inextricably linked to pain and violence (see Muehlenhard, Harney, & Jones, 1992, for a further discussion). Deutsch (1944) described masochism as a fundamental trait of femininity and a component of mature sexual intercourse. She wrote that, because women's vaginas are "passive," women need to be overpowered by men in order to experience sexual pleasure. Bonaparte (1953/1965) wrote that "In coitus, the woman, in effect, is subjected to a sort of beating by the man's penis. She receives its blows and often, even, loves their violence" (p. 87). Some, though not all, contemporary psychoanalysts have similar attitudes. Adams-Silvan (1986) discussed her patient's wish to be raped and "her wish for sexually gratifying masochistic submission" (p. 470). If one conceptualizes women as masochistic and violence as a necessary component of women's sexuality, then one might conclude that women could experience rape as sex or perhaps as both sex and violence.

Feminist writers also have discussed links between sex and violence. Rather than viewing these links as essential components of femininity or female sexuality, however, feminists have emphasized the dominant culture's construction of sex as violence and the role of this construction in perpetuating male dominance. In her article emphasizing the violent nature of rape, Griffin (1971) described rape as "the perfect combination of sex and violence" (p. 109). She wrote that "erotic pleasure cannot be separated from culture, and in our culture male eroticism is wedded to power. . . . For in our culture heterosexual love finds an erotic expression through male dominance and female submission" (pp. 29–30). Dworkin (1988) also wrote about the merging of sex and violence for men:

> When feminists say *rape is violence, not sex*, we mean to say that from our perspective as victims of forced sex, we do not get sexual pleasure from rape; contrary to the rapist's view, the pornographer's view, and the law's view, rape is not a good time for us. This is a valiant effort at crosscultural communication, but it is only half the story: because for men, rape and sex are not different species of event. Domination is sexual for most men, and rape, battery, incest, use of prostitutes and pornography, and sexual harassment are modes of domination imbued with sexual meaning. (pp. 179–180, italics in original)

Beneke (1982) discussed parallels between rape and sex as conceptualized by "ordinary men." He analyzed metaphors that men use to discuss sex: sex as a hunt or conquest (e.g., "I'm going *to go out and get a piece of ass tonight*," p. 13); sex as war (e.g., "I tried to get her into bed but *got shot down*. . . . He's always *hitting on* women," p. 13); sex as hitting women's genitals (e.g., "I'd like to *bang* her *box*," p. 14); the penis as a gun and sperm as ammunition (e.g., "*He shot his load* into her," p. 14); impregnation as violence (e.g., "He *knocked her up*," p. 14); sex as aggressive degradation (e.g., "I'd like to *screw* her. I want to *fuck* her," p. 17) (italics in original). Beneke concluded that, for many men, seeking sex has more to do with status, hostility, control, and dominance than with sensual pleasure or sexual satisfaction. He drew parallels between these motivations of normal men for normal sex and Groth's (1979) discussion of rapists' motivations:

> Rape, then, is a pseudosexual act, a pattern of sexual behavior that is concerned much more with *status, hostility, control, and dominance* [italics added] than with sensual pleasure or sexual satisfaction. It is sexual behavior in the primary service of non-sexual needs. (Groth, 1979, p. 13)

Beneke concluded,

> If we are going to say that, for a man, rape has little to do with sex, we may as well add that sex itself often has little to do with sex, or, if you like, that rape has plenty to do with sex as it is often understood and spoken about by men. (p. 16)

What Is Violence?

In order to consider whether rape is sex or violence, we need to consider how violence is conceptualized. D. H. J. Morgan (1987) discussed the process by which acts are labeled as violence. Generally, he argued, acts of "legitimated" violence are labeled *force* or *restraint* rather than violence (he preferred to discuss legitimated violence rather than "legitimate" violence because the former term emphasizes the legitimation process rather than implying "fixed structures or uncontested essences," p. 182). In some cases (e.g., corporal punishment), the legitimation process is so effective that the violence almost disappears.

Along these lines, Greenblatt (1982) discussed two kinds of cultural rules: (1) prescriptive and proscriptive rules, which tell members of a society what they should and should not do, and (2) interpretive rules, which "tell societal members how to interpret and make sense of what someone (oneself or another) has done" (p. 235). These two kinds of rules are related in that interpretive rules determine which prescriptive and proscriptive rules apply in a given situation. Some people have more power than others to influence society's interpretive rules, including rules about whether a behavior should be considered sex or violence. "The fact is, anything that anybody with power experiences as sex is considered ipso facto not violence, because someone who matters enjoyed it" (MacKinnon, 1987, p. 233).

Violence can be understood in many ways. Theorists writing about aggression, a concept closely related to violence, have found it useful to distinguish between hostile, angry, or affective aggression and instrumental aggression (Buss, 1971; Geen, 1990; Jones, Hendrick, & Epstein, 1979; Myers, 1983). In this conceptualization, *hostile aggression* arises from anger; the goal is to injure. *Instrumental aggression*, on the other hand, is aggression employed as a means to attain some goal; injury may occur, but it is not the goal in and of itself.

This distinction is important when we think about rape and violence. Sometimes when rape is conceptualized as violence, hostile aggression is implicit, such as in the statement, "Rape is about power and anger. Often, a man rapes to overpower or express anger at a woman—to get back at her" (American College Health Association, 1992). Campbell (1993), however, argued that, for men, aggression is usually instrumental. "Men see aggression as a means of exerting control over other people when they feel the need to reclaim power and self-esteem" (Campbell, 1993, p. viii).

The point of men's instrumental aggression is not to signal emotional upset or to let off steam but to control the behavior of another person, and this can be done as effectively, if not more effectively, when anger does not get in the way. . . . Such cold and calculated aggression finds its most sinister expressions in the exclusively male crime of rape and the predominantly male crime of robbery, both of which nearly always demand an aggressor who feels no anger toward the target of his violence. (Campbell, 1993, p. 72)

Thus, we could conceptualize rape as instrumental aggression regardless of the rapists' level of anger as long as we could show that violence or force is being used as a means of obtaining some goal.

Within this framework of instrumental aggression, the goal to be obtained through the act of rape varies according to different theorists and according to one's perspective. One could conceptualize rape as instrumental aggression in which a rapist uses force to achieve the goal of sex, in which a rapist uses sex to achieve the goal of dominating the victim, or in which powerful people perpetuate rape myths and the legal system to achieve the goal of controlling women, keeping women locked in their homes, afraid, dependent on men for protection.

In general, nonfeminist theorists have emphasized the goal of sex, and feminist theorists have emphasized the goals of dominating and controlling rape victims and women in general. It would be inaccurate, however, to say that feminists claim that sex is never the goal of rape. In Diana Russell's (1990) classic book on marital rape, she outlined several reasons why a husband might rape his wife. She regarded marital rape as most frequently motivated by a husband's desire to dominate his wife—that is, as instrumental aggression in which he uses rape to achieve the goal of dominance. She regarded some cases of marital rape as motivated by sex, however—instrumental aggression in which a husband uses force to achieve the goal of sex:

Implicit in my typology, particularly the . . . category of husbands who prefer consensual sex with their wives but who have raped them when their sexual advances are refused, is the notion that rape in marriage can be sexually motivated. . . . Some husbands have sex whenever and however they wish, regardless of whether or not their wives are willing, since, they, like the law, see this as their right. They are *exercising* power when they do this, but they are not necessarily *motivated* by the desire for power. (p. 142, italics in original)

So far, our discussion of violence has been consistent with the *American Heritage Dictionary* definition, "physical force exerted for the purpose of violating, damaging, or abusing" (Morris, 1975, p. 1431). This dictionary also defines violence as "the abusive or unjust exercise of power" (p. 1431). Using this definition, what counts as violence broadens considerably. Theorists in the field of domestic violence have identified a variety of forms of violence that a batterer can use, including not only physical abuse but also emotional abuse, economic abuse, sexual abuse, isolating the victim from friends and family, and intimidating the victim (Domestic Abuse Intervention Project, n.d.). Pinthus (1982, as quoted in Ramazanoglu, 1987) also defined violence broadly in terms of its function: "Violence should be understood as any action or structure that diminishes another human being" (p. 64). Such definitions come more from the perspective of victims than of perpetrators. They highlight the fact that both blatant physical force and more subtle acts that do not appear brutal on the surface all may be equally devastating in their effects on victims.

IMPLICATIONS

The question of how to conceptualize rape has important legal, scientific, clinical, and interpersonal implications. It has sometimes been assumed that conceptualizing rape as sex has solely negative implications for women, whereas conceptualizing rape as violence has solely positive implications. We believe, however, that the situation is considerably more complex.

Rape as Sex Rather Than Violence

Prior to the feminist reanalysis of rape beginning in the 1970s, influential segments of both the scientific community and the public conceptualized all but the most narrowly defined acts of rape as sex that was desired by female victims (Muehlenhard, Harney, & Jones, 1992). This led to blaming rape victims for inviting rape, either unconsciously or consciously, and it led to solutions that entailed restricting women's freedom.

The feminist reanalysis has certainly had an impact, and today it is less acceptable than before to state publicly that women enjoy or invite rape. Such beliefs still exist, however. For example, in a March 24, 1990, speech, Texas Republican gubernatorial nominee Clayton Williams compared foul weather to rape, saying, "If it's inevitable, just relax and enjoy it" ("Victim says," 1990, p. 1a). The idea that women "ask for" or "invite" rape by getting men sexually aroused also still persists. Advice columnist Ann Landers, for example, wrote that "the woman who 'repairs to some private place for a few drinks and a little shared affection' has, by her acceptance of such a cozy invitation, given the man reason to believe that she is a candidate for whatever he might have in mind" (1985a, sec. 4, p. 2). She also agreed with a reader who argued that women "invite trouble" by "telling raw jokes and using street language. Bouncing around (no bra) in low-cut sweaters and see-through blouses. Wearing skirts slit to the city limits up the sides, back or front" (Landers, 1985b, p. B6). Such attitudes serve as a form of social control of women, dictating that women refrain from any behavior that might sexually arouse men. Furthermore, such attitudes suggest that if a women is raped, she is likely to have enjoyed it, and, in any case, she is to blame for the rape.

Clearly, then, conceptualizing rape as sex can have negative consequences for rape victims and for all women. There can also be positive consequences, however. To the extent that men's sexual arousal to rape cues precipitates rape, assessment and treatment of such sexual arousal may help prevent rape

(Barbaree & Marshall, 1991). Furthermore, analyses of the similarities between rape and normal sex have highlighted the coercive nature of many socially acceptable forms of sex (Gavey, 1992; MacKinnon, 1987; Muehlenhard & Schrag, 1991; Russell, 1990). Such analyses have led to a critique of how sex is constructed in our society and how such constructions serve to make sexual coercion invisible or to make it appear to be trivial or the fault of the victim (Beneke, 1982; Reinholtz et al., 1995; Russell, 1982/1990). Challenges to normal forms of coercive sexuality will ultimately benefit rape victims and all women.

Rape as Violence Rather Than Sex

Five years after Brownmiller's 1975 publication of *Against Our Will,* Warner (1980) wrote, "It is now generally accepted by criminologists, psychologists, and other professionals working with rapists and rape victims that rape is not primarily a sexual crime, it is a crime of violence" (p. 94). The implications of this reconceptualization were profound. Rape crisis centers, rape law reform, and a new courage of rape victims to speak out were among the positive effects of this change in how rape was conceptualized. The lives of many rape victims were improved because, when rape is regarded primarily as violence rather than as sex "invited" by the victim, a rape victim is less likely to be retraumatized by victim-blaming questions and attitudes from family, friends, and the legal system. The blame is more clearly placed where it belongs — on the perpetrator. When rape is regarded as primarily an act of violence, rape victims are granted a framework for understanding feelings of rage, fear, and depression as normal reactions. For example, rape victims' reactions can be conceptualized as posttraumatic stress disorder, similar to reactions of others who have experienced violence (e.g., Vietnam veterans), rather than as signs of being "crazy." Rape victims are empowered to work through their anger in constructive ways through counseling and activism. All this would help a person to move through recovery stages from victim to survivor.

Viewing rape as an act of violence also allows for a recognition of the fear of rape that is pervasive among women as a group and hence allows for the recognition that the ever-present threat of rape serves as a powerful social control of women's behavior, restricting women and keeping women in the home, which was supposed to be safe (Gordon & Riger, 1989; Stanko, 1988). This, in turn, highlights the sociopolitical conditions that create a rape-prone culture, which connects the problem of rape with the more general problem of the subjugation of women (Sanday, 1981). In other words, conceptualizing rape as violence contributes to an understanding of rape within its social context. This conceptualization has had heuristic value, suggesting new sets of variables to be investigated.

In some cases, however, conceptualizing rape as violence rather than sex has shortcomings that may fail rape victims. Estrich (1987) argued that, if rape is understood as violence rather than sex, it is difficult to convince a jury that coercive sex is rape if it did not involve a great deal of extrinsic violence.

Even if the prosecutor can prove that sex was nonconsensual, the jury may be unlikely to convict if the case did not include a great deal of violence as the jury understands it. If a jury is unlikely to convict, a prosecutor may be dissuaded from prosecuting. Equating rape with violence could lead to policies exemplified by the advice a detective sergeant gave to fellow officers in a 1975 issue of *Police Review* (cited in Temkin, 1986):

> It should be borne in mind that except in the case of a very young child, the offence of rape is extremely unlikely to have been committed against a woman who does not immediately show signs of *extreme violence* [italics added]. If a woman walks into a police station and complains of rape with no such signs of violence she must be closely interrogated. Allow her to make her statement to a policewoman and then drive a horse and cart through it. It is always advisable if there is any doubt of the truthfulness of her allegations to call her an outright liar. (p. 12)

Not only are juries and judges subject to this difficulty, victims themselves may not define what was done to them as violence and hence may not define it as rape. Rapists frequently use intimidation or the weight of their bodies; they take advantage of the victim's confusion, shock, fear, or intoxication; they ignore the victim's refusal; or they act without the victims' consent. Many rapists do not use weapons, punches, or other actions that people readily identify as violence. Thus, rape victims who understand rape as violence, not sex, might not think of their experience as rape. They might feel out of place going to a rape crisis center and thus never seek help. Or, if they seek help and are told that rape is "not sex," they might not feel understood if to them the act seemed like sex. This might cause problems especially for rape victims who experienced a physiological sexual response during the rape. Not conceptualizing what was done to them as rape may result in the victim becoming stuck in a cycle of desperately trying to make something tolerable out of a horrible experience, especially if this is a first sexual experience for a young person (Bass & Davis, 1988).

Regarding rape as violence, not sex, was "a breakthrough at a time when labeling virtually any act sex was considered exonerating" (MacKinnon, 1987, p. 233). When we say that sex is separate from rape and violence, however, "we fail to criticize what has been made of *sex,* what has been done to us *through* sex, because we leave the line between rape and intercourse . . . right where it is" (MacKinnon, 1987, pp. 86–87, italics in original). We now turn to another conceptualization that views rape as both sex and violence and that critiques how sex, as well as rape and violence, has been constructed in our culture.

Rape as Sex and Violence

Rather than regarding rape as sex *or* violence, rape can be conceptualized as sex *and* violence, with an understanding that these concepts are socially constructed rather than essential and that in this culture violence against women is eroticized (Beneke, 1982; Dworkin, 1988; Griffin, 1971; Russell, 1993). Such a conceptualization could make it easier for rape victims to identify their experience as rape, even if it felt like sex, albeit unwanted sex, and even if they experienced a sexual response. This conceptualization might make it easier for them to seek the support they need.

A conceptualization of rape as sex and violence could also be useful for rape prevention programs, such as programs sponsored by junior high schools, high schools, and universities. Students could be told that even if behavior feels like sex to them, it could still be rape; sex and rape are not mutually exclusive. The current emphasis on sexual harassment in the schools (Barringer, 1993) is fertile ground for a discussion of the links between violence and sexuality.

Such a conceptualization also highlights the links between sex and violence found not only in pornography, but also in mainstream narratives ranging from fairy tales to beer commercials to romance novels in which "a brutal male sexuality is magically converted to romance" (Snitow, 1983, p. 253). Thus, conceptualizing rape as both sex and violence has positive implications not only for understanding rape, but also for critiquing the socially constructed links between sex and violence.

Control: Beyond Sex and Violence

Ultimately, we would like to see this discussion move beyond sex versus violence to one of control. Control is a broader, more encompassing concept than violence; if someone is powerful enough, they can control others without having to resort to violence as it is commonly understood. A focus on control would lead us to ask questions such as, Who controls women's sexuality? Who controls men's sexuality? How free are women and men to control their own sexuality? How free are women and men to refuse to engage in unwanted sex, to engage in sex with the partner of their choice, or to engage in the type of consensual sexuality that they would like?

Using such a conceptualization, the criterion for sexual coercion would not be whether someone had experienced violence, it would be whether someone had freely consented to the sexual activity. Rape prevention programs would not merely tell students to avoid violence; they would tell students to refrain from sexual behavior with anyone who had not freely consented. Jurors would not focus on whether an incident involved violence; they would ask themselves whether the victim had freely consented.

Such a conceptualization would ultimately need to move beyond the level of individual behavior to the level of constraints that inhibit people's ability to consent or refuse freely. This would include critiquing economic disadvantages that make women as a group dependent on men. It would include critiquing the "technologies of heterosexual coercion" (Gavey, 1992, p. 325), such as the tyranny of normality, ideologies that deprive women and men of reasons to refuse, and negative labeling of women and men who refuse sex. It would include critiquing laws, such as sodomy laws, that restrict consenting adults from freely consenting to the kind of consensual sex they want and thus force them to choose between sex that they do not want and no sex at all. Until women and men have the ability and the resources to freely refuse or consent to have sex, no one—especially the less-powerful people in our society—can truly control their own sexuality.

NOTES

1. There is no one definition of feminism; in fact, diversity is inherent in feminism. Our view of feminism includes the beliefs "that women are valuable and that social change to benefit women is needed" (Unger & Crawford, 1992, p. 9; see Tong, 1989, for further discussion).

2. We acknowledge that it is problematic to presume to speak for "all women and men" in this culture. When we refer to the perspectives of all women and men regarding rape, we are referring to the impact of rape on how gender is constructed in this society.

3. We are using the term *society* to refer to the entire social system that affects us. This includes our customs, governments, laws, religions, and sciences; our conversations and media depictions; our mutually accepted ways of understanding the world; and so forth. We have some reservations about using this term. It is convenient, but it also renders individuals' actions and responsibilities invisible. It becomes too easy to say that rape is no one's fault; society is to blame (see Pope, 1992, for further discussion).

REFERENCES

Adams-Silvan, A. (1986). The active and passive fantasy of rape as a specific determinant in a case of acrophobia. *International Journal of Psycho-Analysis*, 67, 467–473.

Alder, C. (1985). An exploration of self-reported sexually aggressive behavior. *Crime and Delinquency*, 31, 306–331.

American College Health Association. (1992). *Acquaintance rape*. [Brochure]. Baltimore, MD: Author.

Amir, M. (1971). *Patterns in forcible rape*. Chicago: University of Chicago Press.

Barbaree, H. E., & Marshall, W. L. (1991). The role of male sexual arousal in rape: Six models. *Journal of Consulting and Clinical Psychology*, 59, 621–630.

Barringer, F. (1993, June 2). School hallways as a gantlet of sexual taunts. *New York Times*, education sec., p. 7.

Bass, E., & Davis, L. (1988). *The courage to heal: A guide for women survivors of child sexual abuse*. New York: Harper and Row.

Beneke, T. (1982). *Men on rape*. New York: St. Martin's Press.

Blanchard, W. H. (1959). The group process in gang rape. *Journal of Social Psychology*, 49, 259–266.

Bonaparte, M. (1965). *Female sexuality*. New York: Grove Press. (Original work published 1953)

Brownmiller, S. (1975). *Against our will: Men, women, and rape*. New York: Bantam.

Buss, A. H. (1971). Aggression pays. In J. L. Singer (Ed.), *The control of aggression and violence: Cognitive and physiological factors* (pp. 7–18). New York: Academic Press.

Campbell, A. (1993). *Women, men, and aggression.* New York: Basic Books.

Deckard, B. S. (1983). *The women's movement: Political, socioeconomic, and psychological issues* (3rd ed.). New York: Harper and Row.

Deutsch, H. (1944). *The psychology of women.* New York: Grune and Stratton.

Domestic Abuse Intervention Project. (n.d.). *Power and control.* (Poster available from Domestic Abuse Intervention Project, 206 West Fourth Street, Duluth, MN 55806.)

Dworkin, A. (1988). *Letters from a war zone.* London: Secker and Warburg.

Estrich, S. (1987). *Real rape: How the legal system victimizes women who say no.* Cambridge, MA: Harvard University Press.

Factor, M. (1954). A woman's psychological reaction to attempted rape. *Psychoanalytic Quarterly, 23,* 243–244.

Finkelhor, D., & Yllo, K. (1985). *License to rape: Sexual abuse of wives.* New York: Holt, Rhinehart and Winston.

Gavey, N. (1992). Technologies and effects of heterosexual coercion. *Feminism and Psychology, 2,* 325–351.

Geen, R. G. (1990). *Human aggression.* Pacific Grove, CA: Brooks/Cole.

Gergen, K. G. (1985). Social constructionist inquiry: Context and implications. In K. J. Gergen & K. E. Davis (Eds.), *The social construction of the person* (pp. 3–18). New York: Springer-Verlag.

Gordon, M. T., & Riger, S. (1989). *The female fear.* New York: Free Press.

Green, E., Hebron, S., & Woodward, D. (1987). Women, leisure, and social control. In J. Hanmer & M. Maynard (Eds.), *Women, violence, and social control* (pp. 75–92). Atlantic Heights, NJ: Humanities Press International.

Greenblatt, C. S. (1982). A hit is a hit is a hit . . . or is it? Approval and tolerance of the use of physical force by spouses. In D. Finkelhor, R. J. Gelles, G. T. Hotaling, & M. A. Straus (Eds.), *The dark side of families: Current family violence research* (pp. 235–260). Beverly Hills, CA: Sage.

Greer, G. (1970). *The female eunuch.* New York: McGraw-Hill.

Griffin, S. (1971). Rape: The all-American crime. *Ramparts, 10,* 26–35.

Groth, A. N. (1979). *Men who rape: The psychology of the offender.* New York: Plenum.

Hall, G. C. N., & Hirschman, R. (1991). Toward a theory of sexual aggression: A quadripartite model. *Journal of Consulting and Clinical Psychology, 59,* 662–669.

Jones, R. A., Hendrick, C., & Epstein, Y. M. (1979). *Introduction to social psychology.* Sunderland, MA: Sinauer Associates.

Kanin, E. J. (1967). An examination of sexual aggression as a response to sexual frustration. *Journal of Marriage and the Family, 29,* 428–433.

Koss, M. P., Dinero, T. E., Seibel, C. A., & Cox, S. L. (1988). Stranger and acquaintance rape: Are there differences in the victim's experience? *Psychology of Women Quarterly, 12,* 1–23.

Landers, A. (1985a, July 29). "Date rape" not always clear-cut. *Houston Chronicle,* sec. 4, p. 2.

Landers, A. (1985b, August 12). Many actions tend to invite trouble: Women should convey right messages to their dates. *Houston Chronicle,* p. B6.

Lerner, G. (1986). *The creation of patriarchy.* New York: Oxford University Press.

Levine, R. A. (1959). Gusii sex offenses: A study in social control. *American Anthropologist, 61,* 965–990.

MacDonald, J. M. (1971). *Rape offenders and their victims*. Springfield, IL: Thomas.

MacKinnon, C. (1987). *Feminism unmodified: Discourses on life and law*. Cambridge, MA: Harvard University Press.

Millett, K. (1969). *Sexual politics*. New York: Ballantine.

Morgan, D. H. J. (1987). Masculinity and violence. In J. Hanmer & M. Maynard (Eds.), *Women, violence, and social control* (pp. 180–192). Atlantic Highlands, NJ: Humanities Press International.

Morgan, R. (1992). Theory and practice: Pornography and rape. In R. Morgan, *The word of a woman: Feminist dispatches, 1968–1992*. (Original work published 1974)

Morris, W. (Ed.). (1975). *American Heritage dictionary of the English language*. Boston: American Heritage/Houghton Mifflin.

Muehlenhard, C. L., Harney, P. A., & Jones, J. M. (1992). From "victim-precipitated rape" to "date rape": How far have we come? *Annual Review of Sex Research*, 3, 219–253.

Muehlenhard, C. L., Powch, I. G., Phelps, J. L., & Giusti, L. M. (1992). Definitions of rape: Scientific and political implications. *Journal of Social Issues*, 48, 23–44.

Muehlenhard, C. L., & Schrag, J. (1991). Nonviolent sexual coercion. In A. Parrot & L. Bechhofer (Eds.), *Acquaintance rape: The hidden crime* (pp. 115–128). New York: John Wiley and Sons.

Myers, D. G. (1983). *Social psychology*. New York: McGraw-Hill.

Palmer, C. T. (1988). Twelve reasons why rape is not sexually motivated: A skeptical examination. *Journal of Sex Research*, 25, 512–530.

Pope, B. (1992). Agency—Who is to blame? In C. Kramarae & D. Spender (Eds.), *The knowledge explosion* (pp. 413–422). New York: Teacher's College Press.

Prentky, R. A., & Knight, R. A. (1991). Identifying critical dimensions for discriminating among rapists. *Journal of Consulting and Clinical Psychology*, 59, 643–661.

Ramazanoglu, C. (1987). Sex and violence in academic life or you can keep a good woman down. In J. Hanmer & M. Maynard (Eds.), *Women, violence, and social control* (pp. 61–74). Atlantic Highlands, NJ: Humanities Press International.

Rape Victim Support Service. (n.d.). *History*. [Unpublished manuscript]. Lawrence, KS: Author.

Reinholtz, R. K., Muehlenhard, C. L., Phelps, J. L., & Satterfield, A. T. (1995). Sexual discourse and sexual intercourse: How the way we communicate affects the way we think about sexual coercion. In P. J. Kalbfleisch & M. J. Cody (Eds.), *Gender, power, and communication in human relationships* (pp. 141–162). Hillsdale, NJ: Lawrence Erlbaum Associates.

Russell, D. E. H. (1990). *Rape in marriage* (Rev. ed.). Bloomington, IN: Indiana University Press.

Russell, D. E. H. (Ed.). (1993). *Making violence sexy: Feminist views on pornography*. New York: Teachers College Press.

Sanday, P. R. (1981). The socio-cultural context of rape: A cross-cultural study. *Journal of Social Issues*, 37, 5–27.

Shalit, R. (1993, June 28). Is rape a hate crime? *San Jose Mercury News*, p. 7B.

Snitow, A. B. (1983). Mass market romance: Pornography for women is different. In A. Snitow, C. Stansell, & S. Thompson (Eds.), *Powers of desire: The politics of sexuality* (pp. 245–263). New York: Monthly Review Press.

A Southern Women's Writing Collective. (1990). Sex resistance in heterosexual arrangements. In D. Leidholdt & J. Raymond (Eds.), *The sexual liberals and the attack on feminism* (pp. 140–147). New York: Pergamon.

Spender, D. (1980). *Man made language*. London: Routledge and Kegan Paul.

Stanko, E. A. (1988). Fear of crime and the myth of the safe home: A feminist critique of criminology. In K. Yllo & M. Bograd (Eds.), *Feminist perspectives on wife abuse* (pp. 75–88). Newbury Park, CA: Sage.

Symons, D. (1979). *The evolution of human sexuality*. New York: Oxford University Press.

Temkin, J. (1986). Women, rape, and law reform. In S. Tomaselli & R. Porter (Eds.), *Rape: An historical and social enquiry*. New York: Basil Blackwell.

Tong, R. (1989). *Feminist thought: A comprehensive introduction*. Boulder: Westview Press.

Unger, R., & Crawford, M. (1992). *Women and gender: A feminist psychology*. New York: McGraw-Hill.

Victim says rapist quoted Williams. (1990, April 2). *Bryan-College Station Eagle*, p. 1a.

Warner, C. G. (Ed.). (1980). *Rape and sexual assault: Management and intervention*. Germantown, MD: Aspen Systems.

Wille, W. S. (1961). Case study of a rapist: An analysis of the causation of criminal behavior. *Journal of Social Therapy, 7*, 10–21.

Wolfe, J., & Baker, V. (1980). Characteristics of imprisoned rapists and circumstances of the rape. In C. G. Warner (Ed.), *Rape and sexual assault: Management and intervention* (pp. 265–278). Germantown, MD: Aspen Systems.

7

Alcohol, Misperception, and Sexual Assault: How and Why Are They Linked?

ANTONIA ABBEY, LISA THOMSON ROSS,
DONNA MCDUFFIE, AND PAM MCAUSLAN

In our studies of sexual assault, both perpetrators and victims have described alcohol's role in what occurred. One man justified forcing sex on his date by saying, "I was very drunk and upset by the fact that it was our prom night and she spent most of it helping someone throw up while I sat by myself." Another man thought the assault occurred "because I was a little drunk and so was she. She wanted only to kiss and I misinterpreted this." One young woman told of how she "wasn't able to respond soon enough to his advances. Maybe I wasn't aware of his serious intentions soon enough because of my drinking." Another woman wrote, "I was very drunk and could not drive or get away from him even though we were in my car. He took me to a motel and carried me inside." One man felt that the assault was due to his date's drinking: "She asked for it [by being drunk] and she got it." A woman explained her assault by writing, "because I allowed myself to drink beyond what I could handle and I trusted the man too much."

These quotes illustrate some of the main themes of this chapter: that alcohol facilitates males' aggression, that alcohol enhances misperception of sexual intent, that alcohol makes it harder for women to resist an attack, and that alcohol tends to make men feel less responsible and women feel more responsible for what happened. Although many researchers and practitioners have described the co-occurrence of alcohol consumption and sexual assault, few have carefully examined the reasons for this relationship. When two variables are related, there are three possible explanations: the first causes the second, the second causes the first, or a third variable causes both of them.

There has been a great deal of discussion as to whether alcohol consumption causes aggressive behavior or merely provides a post hoc justification for aggression. It is also possible that third variables such as personality styles associated with impulsivity and sensation seeking, may partially explain this relationship. It is our sense that all of these explanations are true; different individuals can have different motives, individuals' motives can change over time, and feedback loops can develop so that what was originally an effect becomes a predictor of later behavior. The purpose of this chapter is not to address all causal pathways, but to provide several explanations for how and why alcohol and sexual assault are linked.

The theoretical model reviewed in this chapter focuses on gender differences in beliefs about sexuality and alcohol, misperception of sexual intent, and alcohol consumption as facilitators of sexual assault among heterosexual acquaintances. This model does not address sexual assault between strangers or same-sex individuals; it also is not relevant to childhood or incestuous incidents. This model focuses on the most common type of sexual assault in which a man forces sex on a woman he knows (Bureau of Justice Statistics, 1991; Koss, 1988). Some important predictors of sexual assault are not covered in this model, such as family dynamics, the experience of childhood sexual abuse, perpetrator's personality traits, peer group characteristics, and exposure to media depictions of heterosexual relations in stereotypic or sexually violent ways or both (see Ageton, 1983; Berkowitz, 1992; Hall & Flannery, 1984; Koss, Gidycz, & Wisniewski, 1987; Malamuth & Briere, 1986; Malamuth, Sockloskie, Koss, & Tanaka, 1991; Scully, 1991, for discussions of these factors). This model is designed to explain some, but not all, types and causes of sexual assault (earlier versions of this model were presented in Abbey, 1991, and Abbey, Ross, & McDuffie, 1993). Much of the data presented are cross-sectional, which makes it difficult to establish causal direction. Also, other theoretical perspectives (e.g., evolutionary) could be used to interpret the existing evidence. We want to acknowledge from the outset that our interpretation of the available literature is guided by our theoretical perspective as described below.

The hypotheses and model described in this chapter are embedded within the context of general theories of socialization and feminist psychology. "Is it a boy or a girl?" is the first question a new parent is asked. From birth, girls and boys are frequently treated differently by parents, peers, and teachers, thus shaping their responses in gender-specific ways (Rubin, Provenzano, & Luria, 1974). Through direct reinforcement and vicarious learning through modeling, members of a culture learn to behave in ways viewed as appropriate for their gender and to internalize gender-consistent self-schemas (Bandura, 1977; Eagly, 1987; Maccoby & Jacklin, 1974). Although there is no single feminist perspective on gender roles, many feminists emphasize the role of social norms in the creation and maintenance of gender differences.

Feminist approaches to sexual assault focus on several factors: that rape is a crime of aggression, that rape is not an isolated act but part of a continuum of sexually assaultive behaviors, and that the causes of rape are to be found within the perpetrators and society rather than within the victims (Donat & D'Emilio, 1992). This chapter's examination of alcohol's role in sexual assault includes a discussion of the ways in which alcohol increases women's risk of being sexually assaulted. This is not meant as victim blaming. As one rape victim shared with the first author, she could have avoided being raped by not going out with a man she did not know well; she knew he was "weird" but was "obsessed with meeting someone and not wanting to stay at home." But, she felt in no way responsible for the assault because "no matter what I did, he still had no right to do what he did to me" (Abbey, 1987b, p. 14). Lay people, as well as theoreticians, can distinguish among risk, avoidability, responsibility, and blame (for a discussion of the different meanings of these terms, see Abbey, 1987b, and Shaver, 1987). Identifying risk factors does not reduce the responsibility of perpetrators of sexual assault, or any other crime, for their actions. Information about ways to decrease the probability of being sexually assaulted is intended to increase women's sense of personal control and empowerment (Bechhofer & Parrot, 1991).

Throughout the chapter, studies that relate to the theoretical model are reviewed. No one study addresses all the elements of the model, but across many different studies supportive data can be found. Several unpublished data analyses and illustrative quotations are presented from a study recently completed by the authors. Abbey, Ross, McDuffie, and McAuslan (in press) and Abbey, Ross, and McAuslan (in preparation, 1995) surveyed 1,160 women and 814 men from 94 undergraduate courses representing 27 different majors at a large, urban, commuter university. Sexual assault experiences were measured using a slightly modified version of Koss et al.'s (1987) Sexual Experience Survey. Attitudes toward rape and violence against women were measured with a reduced set of items from Burt's (1980) Rape Myth Acceptance questionnaire. Alcohol expectancies in the domains of sexuality and aggression were assessed using an expanded version of Brown, Goldman, Inn, and Anderson's (1980) items. Alcohol consumption during the sexual assault, attributions about the assault, current alcohol consumption, and misperception of sexual intent were also measured. Some of the data from this study is described elsewhere (Abbey et al., in press; in preparation, 1995); some is only reported in this chapter.

Of the women, 59% had experienced some level of sexual assault since age 14. The highest level of sexual assault experienced by 2% of the women was forced sexual contact (e.g., kissing, petting), 26% experienced sexual coercion (e.g., verbally pressured into sexual intercourse), 8% experienced attempted rape, and 23% experienced completed rape. If women had experienced multiple sexual assaults, they provided detailed information on whichever one they felt was most serious. Of the self-reported most serious sexual assaults, 95% were committed by someone the woman knew; 55% occurred with a date. Prior to 28% of these sexual assaults, the woman and perpetrator were drinking alcohol, in 16% only the perpetrator was drinking, in 2% only the woman was drinking, and in 54% neither was drinking alcohol.

Of the men, 26% acknowledged committing sexual assault. The highest level of sexual assault committed by 2% of these men was forced sexual contact, 14% committed sexual coercion, 1% committed attempted rape, and 9% committed rape. In 94% of the self-reported most serious sexual assaults, men knew the women they assaulted; 58% occurred with dates. Prior to 38% of these sexual assaults, the perpetrator and woman were drinking alcohol, in 4% only the perpetrator was drinking, in 4% only the woman was drinking, and in 54% neither was drinking alcohol.

PREEXISTING BELIEF SYSTEMS

Individuals' stereotypes and expectancies influence how they perceive others and how they behave in social interactions. As can be seen in Figure 7.1, men's and women's beliefs about gender roles, alcohol's effects on sexual and aggressive behavior, and women who drink alcohol are hypothesized to increase the probability of sexual assault through two different pathways. These beliefs can directly encourage sexual assault (through self-fulfilling prophecies) and indirectly encourage sexual assault by increasing men's misperception of women's sexual intent. In the next sections, the role of each of these preexisting beliefs is described.

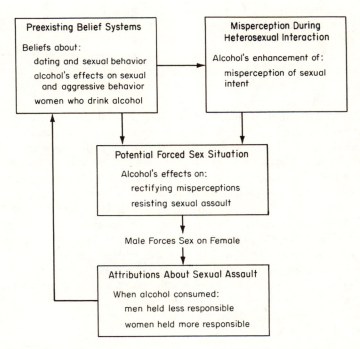

FIGURE 7.1. The role of alcohol and misperception in sexual assault. (*Source*: Adapted from Abbey, Ross, & McDuffie, 1993.)

Beliefs about Dating and Sexual Behavior

Gender-role norms are implicit and explicit rules about how males and females should behave. Most members of a society learn common gender-role stereotypes and scripts, although people vary in their exposure to them. Also, people in different roles (e.g., parents vs. date) may emphasize different aspects of gender-role stereotypes. In general, however, from a variety of sources, American women learn that on dates they should avoid acting too interested in sex and that they should not take the initiative in sexual activities. A woman's reputation can be damaged if she is perceived by others as being sexually loose or available (Berger, Searles, Salem, & Pierce, 1986). Women are expected to be sexual gatekeepers; it is their responsibility to establish the limits on sexual activities and to convince their partner to uphold them (Grauerholz & Serpe, 1985; LaPlante, McCormick, & Brannigan, 1980; Zellman & Goodchilds, 1983).

Although women are socialized to hide or repress their sexual desires, men are often socialized to flaunt theirs. About half of the teenage men and women interviewed for one study agreed that "guys have a greater physical need for sex than girls do" (Zellman & Goodchilds, 1983, p. 55). Many American men learn to initiate sexual encounters and to believe that women want their dates to be forceful and persistent about sex (Muehlenhard, 1988). There are countless media portrayals of women who initially resist their partner's sexual advances, but gradually, after he forcefully persists, begin to show enjoyment and reciprocate (e.g., "Moonlighting," *Straw Dogs*). Numerous exposures to this image may encourage men to think that "no" means "convince me" (Muehlenhard, 1988). For example, a convicted rapist interviewed by Scully (1991) stated that when "she says 'no, I'm a nice girl,' you have to use force. All men do this. She said 'no' but it was a societal 'no,' she wanted to be coaxed" (p. 104).

Despite the gradual erosion of some occupational gender-role stereotypes, those in the sexual and dating domains remain firmly entrenched. For example, Grauerholz and Serpe (1985) found that male college students felt more comfortable than females did in initiating sexual intercourse, while female college students felt more comfortable than males did in refusing sexual intercourse. When presented with scenarios in which someone tries to get their partner to have sex with them, both male and female college students found it most credible that a man would engage in such behaviors. In contrast, when presented with scenarios in which someone tries to keep their partner from having sex with them, both male and female college students found it most likely that a woman would engage in such behaviors (LaPlante et al., 1980). In another study, many high school youths could not imagine a situation in which a man would try to avoid having sex with a woman. They told the interviewer "that's not possible; guys always want sex" (Zellman & Goodchilds, 1983, p. 56).

Beliefs about the Acceptability of Men Forcing Sex on Women Part of

the message about gender differences in sexual desires and behavior is that men's strong sexual needs sometimes make it acceptable for a man to force sex on a woman. Kikuchi (1988, reported in Bechhofer & Parrot, 1991) surveyed 1,700 middle school youths about the conditions under which it was acceptable for a man to force sex on a date against her consent. Forced sex was considered acceptable by more than half of these youths if "she gets him sexually excited" or "if they have been dating a long time." Approximately one-third of these students felt that forced sex was acceptable if "she has had sexual intercourse with other men" or "if he is so turned on he can't stop."

Similar results have been found with high school youths. Zellman, Good-childs, and their colleagues (Goodchilds, Zellman, Johnson, & Giarrusso, 1988; Zellman & Goodchilds, 1983) asked 432 adolescents, "under what circumstances is it OK for a guy to hold a girl down and force her to have sexual intercourse?" (pp. 59–60). More than half the young men and more than a quarter of the young women believed that forced sex was acceptable if she "led him on," if she changed her mind, or if she got him sexually excited. More than a third of the men and a fifth of the women thought that forced sex was acceptable if she let him touch her above the waist or if he was so aroused he could not stop.

Data from college students show a similar pattern. Craig and Kalichman (in Koss & Harvey, 1991) found that 13% of college students reported that forced sex was acceptable when a woman agreed to sex but then changed her mind, 24% when the couple had been dating exclusively, 29% when she had touched her partner's genitals, and 35% said forced sex was acceptable when a man and a woman had both taken their clothes off. Of the college men studied by Check and Malamuth (1983), 30% stated that there was some likelihood that they would commit a rape if no one would know. These studies with individuals of different ages demonstrate that both men and women have internalized the message that it is sometimes acceptable for a man to force sex on a woman. These beliefs can set the stage for men to feel justified forcing sex and for women to feel responsible for failing in the gatekeeping role.

Alcohol and Gender-Role Norms   As described in detail in the section, "Alcohol's Enhancement of Misperceptions of Friendliness as Sexual Intent," alcohol encourages people to focus on the most salient cues in a setting. Gender-role stereotypes are well learned; consequently, they are likely to be highly salient to members of drinking couples. Men who have been drinking alcohol may focus on gender-role stereotypes regarding female coyness and male persistence to justify forcing sex on their companions. In our study we measured rape-supportive beliefs (Burt, 1980), which include items such as "if a woman engages in necking or petting and she lets things get out of hand, it is her own fault if her partner forces sex on her" and "many times a woman will pretend she doesn't want to have intercourse because she doesn't want to seem loose, but she's really hoping that the man will force her." It was hypothesized that the combination of rape-supportive beliefs and alcohol consumption would be positively related to the likelihood of committing sexual assault.

A preliminary examination of this hypothesis was conducted using hierarchical multiple regression analyses to determine if the interaction of rape-supportive beliefs and alcohol consumption would predict men's assault group status (nonassaulter, sexual coercer, rapist). As expected, in Step 1 both rape-supportive beliefs ($\beta = .17$) and usual social alcohol consumption ($\beta = .22$) were significant predictors of assault group status. In the second step, the interaction term was also significant ($\beta = .08$; 1% additional variance explained), providing modest support for the hypothesis that the combination of rape-supportive beliefs and frequent drinking increase men's likelihood of committing sexual assault.

Beliefs about Alcohol's Effects on Behavior

Just as people have gender-role beliefs, they also have beliefs about alcohol's effects on behavior. As can be seen in Figure 7.1, alcohol expectancies are hypothesized to encourage misperception of sexual intent and sexual assault. Research using the balanced placebo design has demonstrated that many of the effects of alcohol, particularly in the sexual domain, are psychological rather than pharmacological in nature (see George & Marlatt, 1986; Lang, 1985; Leonard, 1989; and Steele & Southwick, 1985, for reviews of this literature). Men who believe they have consumed alcohol experience greater physiological and subjective sexual arousal than do men who believe they have consumed a nonalcoholic beverage (Lang, 1985; Wilson, 1981). Except at very low doses, actual alcohol consumption typically decreases men's physiological and subjective sexual arousal (see Crowe & George, 1989, for a review of this literature). Results for women are mixed (McCarty, Diamond, & Kaye, 1982; Wilsnack, 1984; Wilson & Lawson, 1976), perhaps because there are more negative social sanctions associated with women's sexual behavior compared to men's (Robbins, 1989).

Several authors have examined the effects of alcohol on men's arousal to sexually violent stimuli (Briddell et al., 1978; George & Marlatt, 1986; Lang, Searles, Lauerman, & Adesso, 1980). For example, Briddell et al. found that men who thought they had consumed alcohol were more sexually aroused by recordings of forcible rape and sadistic aggression than were men who did not think they had consumed alcohol. Actual alcohol consumption did not affect sexual arousal. (These results were not replicated by Barbaree, Marshall, Yates, & Lightfoot, 1983.)

There is a second line of alcohol expectancy research in which self-reports of alcohol expectancies are examined. Men report expecting to feel less inhibited and more powerful, aggressive, and sexual after drinking alcohol than do women (Brown et al., 1980; Crawford, 1984; Leigh, 1987; Ratliff & Burkhart, 1984; Rohsenow, 1983). By fourth grade, many youths have developed expectancies that associate alcohol with sexuality and aggression (Miller, Smith, & Goldman, 1990). Abbey, McDuffie, and Ross (1993) compared college women's and men's alcohol expectancies regarding both male and female drinkers in the domains of aggression, sexuality, and sexual vulnerability. For each alcohol expectancy, there was a main effect of target gender:

Male drinkers were expected to be more aggressive and female drinkers were expected to be more sexual and more sexually vulnerable. These stereotypes correspond to the typical rape in which a male aggressor forces sex on a vulnerable woman.

People tend to act in ways that confirm their original expectancies, thus expectancies can become self-fulfilling prophecies (Darley & Fazio, 1980; Neuberg, 1989). If a man believes that alcohol makes people more sexual and aggressive, then he is likely to act sexual and aggressive when drinking alcohol. His alcohol-enhanced feelings of power and sexual desire may make him more willing to use physical force to obtain sex. A man who participated in one of our focus groups described to the facilitator how alcohol affected sexual interactions: "You might have a strong conviction against . . . being pushy, but if you have enough alcohol, you might go . . . farther than you should." Another member of this group said, "It's like you don't care anymore. After a couple of beers you say, 'well maybe' and then after some more you're not going to care. . . . You'll try to force her to have sex."

Based on this theorized (and anecdotally supported) relationship between alcohol expectancies and sexual assault, we proposed two hypotheses. The first was that men who committed sexual assault would more strongly endorse alcohol expectancies in the domains of sexuality and aggression than would men who had not committed sexual assault. As can be seen in Table 7.1, this hypothesis was partially supported. Men who had forced sexual intercourse on women either through verbally coercive means (coercers) or through physical force or lack of consent (rapists) held stronger alcohol expectancies regarding male and female sexuality than did men who had not committed sexual assault.

The second hypothesis was that, among men who had committed sexual assault, those who consumed alcohol during the assault would have stronger sexual and aggressive alcohol expectancies than men who did not consume alcohol. As can be seen in Table 7.2, men who drank alcohol while perpetrating sexual assault more strongly believed that alcohol increased male and

TABLE 7.1.   Mean Differences in Alcohol Expectancies Between Rapists, Coercers, and Nonassaultive Men

Alcohol Expectancy Scale	Rapists $(n = 75)$	Coercers $(n = 116)$	Nonassaulters $(n = 608)$	F Value
Domain				
Male sexuality	2.72[a]	2.60	2.48[b]	4.86*
Female sexuality	3.08[a]	2.97[a]	2.79[b]	9.00*
Male aggression	3.74	3.66	3.59	n.s.
Female aggression	3.00	2.96	2.89	n.s.

Note: Means with different superscripts were significantly different from each other using follow-up Newman-Keuls tests, $p < .05$.
n.s. = not significant
*$p < .01$

TABLE 7.2.   Mean Differences in Alcohol Expectancies
Between Sexually Assaultive Men Who Did and Did Not
Consume Alcohol During the Assault

Alcohol Expectancy Scale	No Alcohol Consumed ($n = 106$)	Alcohol Consumed ($n = 85$)	F Value
Domain			
Male sexuality	2.45	2.80	11.55**
Female sexuality	2.82	3.17	12.87**
Male aggression	3.67	3.75	n.s.
Female aggression	2.90	3.09	4.56*

n.s. = not significant
*$p < .05$
**$p < .01$

female sexuality and female aggression than men who did not drink while perpetrating sexual assault. It is interesting that men who had committed sexual assault while under the influence of alcohol were no more likely than those who had not to believe that alcohol increases male aggression. These findings support the proposition that beliefs about alcohol can contribute to sexual assault by encouraging men to focus on their own sexual desires and any potentially sexual cues displayed by their companion. Alcohol expectancies regarding aggression seemed less relevant to these perpetrators.

Beliefs about Women Who Drink Alcohol

Although the image of a drinking man may be positive, stereotypes of drinking women are not (Crowe & George, 1989). For example, George, Gournic, and McAfee (1988) asked 176 college undergraduates to read a vignette about a couple on a date. The man always drank alcohol; the woman drank either alcohol (beer, wine, or whiskey) or a soft drink. Male and female college students rated the woman who had a few drinks of alcohol (any type) as being easier and more willing to be seduced, more responsive to a sexual advance, and more willing to engage in foreplay and sexual intercourse. The drinking woman was also perceived as being less socially skilled and more aggressive.

In a related study (Corcoran & Thomas, 1991), 195 college students read vignettes about a couple on a first date. One of the two (the female or the male target) always drank alcohol and the other drank either soda pop or alcohol. Overall, men were perceived as being more likely than women to initiate sexual intercourse. However, alcohol consumption by men and women was associated with perceptions of being more likely to initiate sexual intercourse.

Abbey and Harnish (1995) extended these studies by having 422 college students rate vignettes in which female and male targets' alcohol consumption was fully crossed. The female target's alcohol consumption was perceived as being most appropriate, and she was rated as being most sexual when both she and her companion drank alcohol.

The studies described above assessed alcohol's effects on perceptions of sexuality in dating scenarios. Norris and Cubbins (1992) extended this line of research by examining the role of alcohol in perceptions of date rape scenarios. In their study, college students ($N = 132$) were least likely to label what happened as rape and to perceive the assailant as most romantic and likable when the victim and assailant had been drinking alcohol together. Students were most likely to label what happened as rape and to view the assailant as least romantic and likable when only the victim had been drinking. The authors summarize their results by stating that, "Acquaintance rape is not judged as severely when both members of a dating couple have been consuming alcohol. . . . The implication is that a woman and man drinking together may signify an expectation that sexual activity will occur" (pp. 188–89).

Norris and Cubbins' (1992) results suggest that college students may consider it inappropriate for a man to take advantage of a woman drinking alone. This finding contradicts other research. Surveys of high school and college students suggest that a sizable percentage of young men feel that it is acceptable to use physical force on an intoxicated date. Of high school males in one study, 40% approved of physically forcing sex on an intoxicated date (Goodchilds & Zellman, 1984). More than half of the college men interviewed by Kanin (1985) who had committed date rape reported that their status with their peers would be enhanced if they picked up a woman in a bar and forced sex on her. In their large, national college study, Koss et al. (1987) found that more women were raped because of their alcohol-induced inability to give consent than because of physical force. These findings indicate that, in many situations, drinking women are perceived as appropriate targets for sexual assault. More research is needed to determine under what circumstances men who take sexual advantage of intoxicated women are villified and under what circumstances they are admired.

MISPERCEPTION DURING HETEROSEXUAL INTERACTIONS

The beliefs described in the section above increase the likelihood that misperception of sexual intent will occur during heterosexual interactions. In this section of the chapter, the general misperception process is described, and then alcohol's role is outlined (see Figure 7.1).

Verbal and nonverbal cues intended to convey platonic friendliness are frequently perceived by the recipient as a sign of sexual interest. In a survey of 598 college undergraduates, Abbey (1987a, Study 1) found that approximately two-thirds of them reported that their friendliness toward a member of the opposite sex had been misperceived as sexual interest. Significantly more women (72%) than men (60%) reported being been misperceived. In the survey of sexual assault that we conducted, 65% of the women surveyed stated that they had been sexually misperceived; in 66% of these incidents the man had been drinking alcohol and in 49% the woman had been drinking alcohol. Of the men in this survey, 48% stated that they had misperceived a woman's sexual intent; in 61% of these incidents the man had been drinking alcohol and in 63% the woman had been drinking alcohol.

Men are more likely than women to perceive verbal and nonverbal stimuli as signaling a woman's interest in having sexual intercourse with her male companion. In a series of studies, Abbey and her colleagues have consistently found that men perceive women as behaving more sexually and as being more interested in having sex than do women. Cues such as eye contact, physical closeness, touch, and revealing clothing are perceived by both women and men as potential signs of sexual interest. However, regardless of the type of cue, men perceive women to be more sexy, seductive, promiscuous, and sexually available than do women (Abbey, 1982; Abbey, Cozzarelli, McLaughlin, & Harnish, 1987; Abbey & Harnish, 1995; Abbey & Melby, 1986; Harnish, Abbey, & DeBono, 1990). These results have been replicated with materials that simulate dating, employment (female cashier and male manager), and educational (female student and male professor) settings (Saal, Johnson, & Weber, 1989).

Similar results have also been found with high school students. Goodchilds and Zellman (1984) asked males and females to rate a variety of different verbal, behavioral, clothing, and situational cues in terms of how strongly they conveyed an interest in having sexual intercourse with one's date. As compared to females, males rated verbal comments (complimenting partner's appearance), specific behaviors (tickling, playing with partner's hair), revealing clothing worn by either a male (open shirt) or a female (low-cut top, shorts, tight jeans), and specific date locations (his home, the beach) as stronger signals of willingness to have sexual intercourse. Males and females agreed that some of these cues were more sexual than others (e.g., being alone at the guy's house vs. being at a party), but males' sexuality ratings were always higher than females'.

These results suggest that men perceive situations in a more sexualized manner than women do and are more likely than women to interpret friendliness as evidence of sexual attraction. Men's schemas regarding sex appear to be more central and more salient (Abbey, 1982). Given men's traditional responsibility for initiating dates and sexual behavior, it can be helpful for them to focus on their female companion's potentially sexual cues. This focus on the implicit sexual meaning of women's actions, however, can also lead men to make errors when women are only trying to convey friendliness.

Alcohol's Enhancement of Misperceptions of Friendliness as Sexual Intent

According to our hypothesized model, alcohol consumption increases the likelihood that a man will mistake his female companion's friendly cues as a sexual invitation (see Figure 7.1). Drinking alcohol also makes a man less able to recognize a woman's attempts to rectify his misperception of her. As noted above, friendly and sexual cues are often ambiguous and easy to confuse. The likelihood of misinterpreting an ambiguous cue is hypothesized to be increased by the cognitive impairments produced by alcohol consumption. Higher-order cognitive processes such as abstraction and conceptualization are disrupted by alcohol, making it difficult to interpret complex stimuli (Berkow, 1982; Leonard, 1989; Ryan & Butters, 1983; Steele & Southwick, 1985). Under the influence of alcohol, people have a narrower perceptual field and consequently are less able to attend to multiple cues (Hull & Van Treuren, 1986; Taylor & Leonard, 1983). Steele and Josephs (1988) describe this state as "alcohol myopia" and suggest that when intoxicated "our emotions and behaviors are based on only a superficial grasp of the more salient, immediate aspects of experience" (p. 197).

By focusing only on the most salient cues, ambiguous information is more likely to be interpreted in a way that confirms one's initial hypothesis. For many men, their date's behaviors are ambiguous and their initial hypothesis is that they will have sex (Gross, 1978). One man in our study said, "We were drinking and she acted like she wanted to fool around so I thought she wanted to. I just misinterpreted her actions." As one woman in our study stated "[alcohol] may have put me in the mood for petting, kissing, holding, and hugging and he may have interpreted that as going further with sexual activity."

Many verbal and nonverbal aspects of dating behavior are ambiguous. If a young man suggests to his date that they leave a noisy bar to go back to his apartment to talk, he could mean exactly that—he wants to talk in a comfortable, private place. He could also mean "let's go there so we can have sexual intercourse." People often feel awkward about explicitly stating their sexual desires. Consequently, they may express them in an ambiguous fashion so that they will not be embarrassed if their companion does not share their interest. Alcohol makes it even more difficult for people to communicate their sexual desires accurately, thus increasing the likelihood that a man will interpret his companion's "no" as a "yes" and feel comfortable forcing sex.

As described above, many men expect alcohol to increase their sexual arousal and aggressiveness (Brown et al., 1980; Lang, 1985). Alcohol consumption leads some men to miss implicit situational cues inhibiting violent behavior (Leonard, 1989; Steele & Southwick, 1985; Taylor & Leonard, 1983), making it easier to force sex on their female companion. One of the incarcerated rapists interviewed by Scully (1991) stated that "Straight, I don't have the guts to rape. I could fight a man but not that" (p. 124). Richardson (1981) conducted a study in which male study participants had the opportunity to deliver shock to a female confederate as part of a competition paradigm. Intoxicated men delivered larger shocks than did nonintoxicated men when the female target was behaving nonaggressively. Richardson concluded that the cognitive impairments associated with alcohol consumption caused these men to miss the female target's nonaggressive cues.

POTENTIAL FORCED SEX SITUATION

If a man and woman find themselves in a situation that has the potential for forced sex, alcohol and earlier misperception can increase the likelihood that forced sex will occur (see Figure 7.1). Alcohol makes it more difficult to rectify misperceptions of sexual intent and to resist physical force effectively.

Alcohol's Effects on Rectifying Misperceptions of Sexual Intent

Women who have been drinking alcohol may disregard their companion's cues that suggest their degree of sexual interest is being misperceived. The narrowing of attention and reduction in inferential processing associated with alcohol consumption (Berkow, 1982; Ryan & Butters, 1983) can keep a woman from realizing that her partner is perceiving her friendly behavior as a sexual invitation. Because women tend to code ambiguous cues as being friendly rather than sexual (Shotland & Craig, 1988), when women focus on the most salient aspects of the situation they are likely to focus on friendliness rather than sexuality.

If and when a woman realizes that she is being misperceived, she must decide how to handle the situation. Norms of female politeness and indirectness regarding sexual topics are so well internalized that some women feel uncomfortable mentioning them. Often the woman is attracted to the man and is afraid that he will lose interest in her if she is too direct and forceful in her rebuff of his sexual advances. Consequently, she may use an indirect strategy such as moving a little further away from him or trying to change the topic. Her companion is likely to perceive this as flirtation or coyness rather than as a refusal. Thus, the misperceiver continues to interpret her ambiguous words and actions as evidence of sexual interest. As one man wrote in our survey, "The fact that she couldn't say no was interpreted by me as a yes. I often pushed sex. . . . Anything other than a firm 'no' was interpreted as a 'yes' or a 'maybe.'" The longer a man continues to think that consensual sex will occur without having his misperception corrected, the more likely it is that he will feel justified forcing sex because he feels that he has been "led on." As noted in the section on beliefs about forced sex, a sizable percentage of men and women feel that forced sex is acceptable if the man has been sexually provoked (Goodchilds & Zellman, 1984).

In our survey we asked women who had been the victims of sexual assault to rate the extent to which a number of factors contributed to the occurrence of the assault. One question focused on the male's misperception of her friendly cues as sexual interest. Women whose perpetrators had consumed alcohol felt that misperception played a stronger role in the sexual assault ($M = 3.13$) than did women whose perpetrators had not consumed alcohol ($M = 2.71$), $F(1, 387) = 6.08$, $p < .01$. Similarly, women who consumed alcohol during the sexual assault ($M = 3.01$) felt that misperception played a stronger role in the assault than did women who had not consumed alcohol ($M = 2.71$), $F(1, 387) = 3.62$, $p < .06$. This kind of data cannot demonstrate causality; however, these results indicate that women perceive a link among alcohol consumption, misperception, and sexual assault. As one of the women we interviewed who had been drinking with her date stated, "I wasn't aware of his serious intentions soon enough because of my drinking. . . . Had I been sober, I think I would have seen his intentions sooner and been able to change the situation."

Alcohol's Effects on Resisting Sexual Assault

Alcohol has physical, as well as cognitive, effects. The physical effects of alcohol can make it more difficult to engage in either verbal or physical resistance to a sexual assault. Attempted and completed rapes have been distinguished by the more frequent use of prompt verbal and physical resistance in attempted rapes (Koss & Dinero, 1989; Seigel, Sorenson, Golding, Burnam, & Stein, 1989). Data also suggest that women who physically resist experience less-severe types of sexual assault (Ullman & Knight, 1991).

Alcohol's negative effects on cognitive and motor functioning should diminish the effectiveness of a woman's response to being attacked. Hawks and Welch (1991) compared the responses of 25 college women raped as a result of alcohol or drug intoxication as compared to 41 college women raped through the use or threat of force. Intoxicated victims were less likely than other rape victims to scream for help, run away, or physically struggle with their assailant. We examined in our survey the relationship between alcohol consumption and the occurrence of attempted and completed rape. Although completed rape was more common than attempted rape for drinkers and nondrinkers, women who consumed alcohol were more likely to be victims of completed rape than attempted rape (88% v. 12%) as compared to women who did not drink alcohol (64% v. 36%), $\chi^2 (1) = 27.54, p < .001$. One of the women in this study stated that "You don't have a lot of strength [when drunk]. . . . If I hadn't have been drunk, it probably wouldn't have happened because I could have gotten up and ran out." Another intoxicated woman wrote, "I was unable to stand up. . . . I was easily taken over."

Kanin (1985) interviewed 71 college men who had committed date rape. Extensive interviews were conducted with these men both to confirm an act that met the legal definition of rape had been perpetrated and to learn more about their attitudes and behaviors regarding heterosexual interactions. Of these men, three-quarters reported purposely getting a date intoxicated with alcohol or marijuana in order to have sexual intercourse with her. According to Kanin, these men viewed dating as a "no-holds-barred contest" (p. 223) in which any strategy was acceptable for procuring sex.

Mosher and Anderson (1986) surveyed 175 male college sophomores about their use of force or exploitation to have sexual intercourse with their dates. Alcohol and illegal drugs or both had been used by 75% of these men to obtain sex. Some men reported using substances to make the woman less able to resist, while others shared expensive drugs in order to make their date feel obligated to perform a sexual favor. Traditional gender-role beliefs were positively related to using alcohol or other drugs to obtain sex.

To summarize this section on potential forced sex situations, theory and data suggest that alcohol augments the link between misperception and sexual assault through several pathways. Alcohol can make misperceptions more likely to occur and less likely to be promptly rectified. Alcohol can also provide men with additional self-justification for forcing sex on women whose sexual intentions they misperceived and can make women less able to resist attacks effectively. Although the available data support this argument, additional research is needed, particularly to address causal questions.

ATTRIBUTIONS ABOUT SEXUAL ASSAULT

A variety of different attitudes, beliefs, personality characteristics, and aspects of the preassault interaction influence how men and women perceive sexual assault after it has happened. This chapter focuses on alcohol's effects on perceptions of sexual assault. Recent theory and research indicate that alcohol consumption decreases men's, but increases women's, sense of responsibility for sexual assault.

Alcohol's Effects on Attributions About Perpetrators of Sexual Assault

Participants in laboratory studies consistently hold men who consumed alcohol less responsible than men who did not consume alcohol for a variety of crimes including robbery, spouse abuse, and rape (Carducci & McNeely, 1981; Critchlow, 1985; Hammock & Richardson, 1989, reported in Richardson & Hammock, 1991; Richardson & Campbell, 1982). Court transcripts and interviews with convicted rapists suggest that alcohol is sometimes used by judges and rapists to partially exonerate rapists' behavior (Harrell, 1981; Scully & Marolla, 1984).

Many men acknowledge that they get drunk in order to experience disinhibition, power, and heightened sexuality (Berkowitz & Perkins, 1987). Some men admit to drinking alcohol in order to feel more comfortable about forcing sex on their female companions (Scully & Marolla, 1984). Of the date rapists interviewed by Kanin (1984), 62% attributed the rape completely or partially to their alcohol consumption. These men felt that alcohol initially led them to misperceive their partner's degree of sexual interest and then allowed them to feel comfortable using force to obtain sex when the woman's lack of consent became clear to them. These date rapists saw themselves as "technical" criminals not "real criminals" (p. 97). According to these men, real criminals used weapons to assault strangers and what they did warranted only minor punishment. These comments do not exonerate these men, and it is not clear if they were using alcohol post hoc to justify their behavior or if they intentionally or unintentionally drank in order to experience disinhibition. Although these comments do not prove causal relationships, they do illustrate how alcohol is perceived by assaulters.

MacAndrew and Edgerton (1969) conducted extensive cross-cultural research on beliefs about alcohol. They found that drunkenness is treated in many cultures as a "time-out" during which men are not held to their usual behavioral standards. The time-out provided by alcohol allows men to attribute any violations of personal or social norms to the alcohol rather than to themselves (Wilson, 1981). Bandura (1977) argued that if the link between a desirable yet inappropriate behavior and self-evaluation can be broken, then people are more likely to engage in the inappropriate behavior. Thus, alcohol is a convenient external factor that can be blamed without harm to one's self-image. A date rapist need not make a negative internal attribution such as "I took advantage of a defenseless woman" if he can say to himself, "I was really blasted last night." Such attributions are obviously convenient for the perpetrator. However, as can be seen by the feedback loop in Figure 7.1, if men are not held responsible, by themselves or society, for sexual assaults committed while intoxicated, then societal norms tolerant of sexual assault are reinforced, ultimately encouraging future sexual assaults.

Alcohol's Effects of Attributions about Victims of Sexual Assault

Alcohol consumption has very different effects on attributions about victims as compared to perpetrators of sexual assault. Men are much more likely than women to use intoxication to justify socially inappropriate or morally reprehensible behavior (Berglas, 1987; Schwartz, Burkhart, & Green, 1982). Because societal norms do not treat women's intoxication as appropriate, drunkenness cannot typically be used by women to justify errors of judgment or socially inappropriate behavior (Berglas, 1987; Robbins, 1989).

We examined the attributions made by sexual assault victims as a function of alcohol consumption. Overall, women tended to attribute most of the responsibility to their assailant. However, when the perpetrator drank alcohol, women rated him as marginally less responsible ($M = 3.82$) than when he did not drink alcohol ($M = 4.07$), $F (1, 382) = 3.68$, $p < .06$. Thus, some of these women accepted the idea that drinking makes men less responsible for their actions. In contrast, when the woman drank alcohol she rated herself as being significantly more responsible ($M = 2.61$) than when she did not drink alcohol ($M = 2.12$), $F = 11.15$, $p < .001$. This finding demonstrates that, for some women, drinking alcohol increases their sense of responsibility; they do not allow alcohol to excuse their errors of judgment. One woman wrote about how she agreed to go back to her date's house after a party: "We played quarter bounce (a drinking game). I got sick drunk. I was slumped over the toilet vomiting. He grabbed me and dragged me into his room and raped me. I had been a virgin and felt it was all my fault for going back to his house when no one else was home." Rather than telling herself, "I couldn't help it because I was drunk," this woman felt more responsible because her drinking clouded her judgment.

Other people tend to view women who were under the influence of alcohol when sexually assaulted as partially responsible for what happened (Aramburu & Leigh, 1991; Richardson & Campbell, 1982). For example, Richardson and Campbell asked 187 college students to read a vignette about a college woman raped by a guest while cleaning up after a party. The perpetrator, the victim, both, or neither was intoxicated. Male and female students considered the male perpetrator to be less responsible when he was intoxicated rather than sober, but the female victim was rated as more responsible when she was intoxicated. The woman was also perceived as less moral and likable when she was drunk; this was not true for the man. These findings indicate that negative stereotypes about drinking women are still commonly endorsed by college students; women are derogated while men are exonerated for drinking. Because both women and men share these stereotypes, a woman who was drinking alcohol prior to being sexually assaulted may believe that a "drunken woman is fair game" and consequently feel responsible. As one woman who participated in our research wrote, "For years I believed it was my fault for being too drunk. I never called it 'rape' until much more recently, even though I repeatedly told him 'no.'" As shown by the feedback loop in Figure 7.1, this double standard regarding perceptions of men's and women's responsibility for their behavior when intoxicated strengthens societal norms that encourage sexual assault.

CONCLUSIONS AND SUGGESTIONS FOR
FUTURE RESEARCH AND INTERVENTION

This chapter has considered several pathways through which alcohol consumption contributes to sexual assault. A number of studies have been reviewed that support the model; however, none of these studies are appropriate for testing the entire model. One obvious problem with attempts to fully evaluate hypotheses about alcohol and sexual assault concerns the inability to conduct randomized experiments on this topic. The typical sexual assault study involves conducting interviews with individuals who acknowledge being victims or perpetrators. Any retrospective survey presents a number of internal validity issues, including establishing causal direction (e.g., did the perpetrator have high sexual alcohol expectancies prior to the assault or develop them afterward?) and ruling out alternative explanations (e.g., does a third variable such as sensation seeking explain the link between alcohol and sexual assault?). There are also concerns about individuals' ability and willingness to recall their past beliefs and behaviors accurately. Given the sensitive nature of the topic and the need for individuals to volunteer for these studies, there are potential problems associated with self-presentational biases and the representativeness of the sample.

Although it is easy to point out the flaws in past research, it is more difficult to provide good, realistic alternative designs. White (in preparation, 1995) conducted a multiyear prospective study of sexual assault and has included measures of alcohol consumption. By interviewing students at the beginning of college and following them through their college career, one can determine if specific beliefs, attitudes, and experiences predict future commission of sexual assault.

Another exciting approach involves conducting experimental analog studies. In the laboratory, participants can be randomly assigned to conditions that systematically vary factors such as alcohol consumption, alcohol expectancies, and a female confederate's behavior. Outcomes such as men's sexual arousal and sexual attraction and willingness to hurt the confederate can be assessed with physiological, observational, and self-report measures (George & Marlatt, 1986; Lang et al., 1980; Malamuth, 1988). This approach maximizes internal validity in situations that are conceptually relevant to sexual assault. In our own laboratory, we are currently conducing a balanced placebo study examining alcohol's role in misperceptions of sexual intent.

More can be learned from cross-sectional surveys of sexual assault. Although many have been conducted, few have carefully examined the role of alcohol before, during, and after the assault from both the victim's and perpetrator's perspectives. Scully's (1991) interviews with incarcerated rapists provide a wealth of qualitative information that is extremely useful for hypothesis generation and elaboration. Similar interviews are needed with perpetrators of unreported sexual assaults and with rape survivors.

It is unlikely that any one of these methodologies used in isolation will address all the questions about alcohol's role in sexual assault. But, through a combination of methods, each most effective at obtaining certain types of information, many of these questions can be answered and more complex hypotheses can be developed and evaluated. There is no single cause of sexual assault and no single mechanism of alcohol involvement. Additional research is needed to clarify further how, when, and why alcohol contributes to sexual assault.

Implications for Prevention

Despite the gaps in existing knowledge, this information about the links among alcohol, misperception of sexual intent, and sexual assault has exciting implications for sexual assault prevention programming. Many of the victims of campus rapes are first- and second-year college students who do not have much experience with alcohol and get very drunk at a social gathering. They also report taking risks, such as going up to a man's room during a party or drinking several glasses of punch (without knowing how much alcohol was added), that more experienced women may avoid. This illustrates the need to provide information about alcohol and sexual assault to new students. Not only do women need to be warned about the risks associated with heavy drinking, but men need to be taught that alcohol consumption, by themselves or their partner, does not justify forced sex.

Programs are also needed that teach women and men to communicate their sexual desires clearly. Men need to accept that no really means no. For this to occur, women must say no only when that is what they really mean.

Men and women need to feel comfortable saying maybe if they are genuinely unsure about their sexual intentions. Open communication about sex is unlikely to occur in an environment in which women are penalized for acknowledging their sexual drives and men are penalized for acknowledging their sexual naiveté or conservatism. In a related vein, Lloyd (1991) emphasizes the need for programs that teach students how to manage dating conflict without engaging in physical or sexual abuse.

Programs are also needed to address the peer pressure many students feel regarding sexual behavior and alcohol consumption. Many men feel pressured by their friends to demonstrate their sexual prowess. One college man who participated in our study justified physically forcing his date to have sexual intercourse by writing, "All my friends had engaged in sex with a girl that night and I hadn't. So I resorted to this not to be ridiculed by them." Small-group exercises in all-male groups led by male facilitators might lead some men to question a "sex at all costs" philosophy. Many male and female college students also experience peer pressure to drink alcohol. Sharing pitchers; drinking sweet, spiked punch; taking turns buying rounds; drinking games; feeling the need to indulge oneself after a week of work; and taking pride in one's ability to "drink others under the table" all contribute to heavy drinking.

A number of excellent sexual assault prevention programs have been developed on college campuses. Although this is an appropriate target audience, many sexual assaults occur in high school (Koss, 1988); consequently, programs are needed for younger students. Research cited above indicates that, by sixth grade, many youths believe that there are circumstances that justify forced sex. These findings highlight the need to begin counteracting sexual stereotypes about male assertiveness and female passivity in elementary school. These stereotypes are unlikely to change unless media, parental, and peer messages also convey egalitarian gender-role beliefs. For example, many alcohol advertisements emphasize the connections among drinking, sexuality, and disinhibition. Coordinated efforts at the individual, dyadic, small-group, institutional, and societal level are needed to eliminate the links among alcohol, misperception, and sexual assault.

Acknowledgments.   This work was partially funded by grants from the National Institute on Alcohol Abuse and Alcoholism and the U.S. Department of Education's Fund for the Improvement of Secondary Education.

REFERENCES

Abbey, A. (1982). Sex differences in attributions for friendly behavior: Do males misperceive females' friendliness? *Journal of Personality and Social Psychology, 42,* 830–838.

Abbey, A. (1987a). Misperceptions of friendly behavior as sexual interest: A survey of naturally occurring incidents. *Psychology of Women Quarterly, 11,* 173–194.

Abbey, A. (1987b). Perceptions of personal avoidability versus responsibility: How do they differ? *Basic and Applied Social Psychology, 8*, 3–20.

Abbey, A. (1991). Acquaintance rape and alcohol consumption on college campuses: How are they linked? *Journal of American College Health, 39*, 165–169.

Abbey, A., Cozzarelli, C., McLaughlin, K., & Harnish, R. J. (1987). The effects of clothing and dyad sex composition on perceptions of sexual intent: Do women and men evaluate these cues differently? *Journal of Applied Social Psychology, 17*, 108–126.

Abbey, A., & Harnish, R. J. (1995). Perception of sexual intent: The role of gender, alcohol consumption and rape supportive attitudes. *Sex Roles, 32*, 297–313.

Abbey, A., McDuffie, D. M., & Ross, L. T. (1993, June). *Effect of raters' gender and targets' gender on alcohol expectancies.* Paper presented it the annual meeting of the American Psychological Society, Chicago.

Abbey, A., & Melby, C. (1986). The effects of nonverbal cues on gender differences in perceptions of sexual intent. *Sex Roles, 15*, 283–298.

Abbey, A., Ross, L. T., & McAuslan, P. (in preparation, 1995). Alcohol, misperception of sexual intent, and gender role beliefs as predictors of sexual assault perpetration.

Abbey, A., Ross, L. T., & McDuffie, D. (1993). Alcohol's role in sexual assault. In R. R. Watson (Ed.), *Drug and alcohol abuse reviews: Addictive behaviors in women* (Vol. 5, pp. 1–27). Totowa, NJ: Humana.

Abbey, A., Ross, L. T., McDuffie, D., & McAuslan, P. (in press). Alcohol and dating risk factors for sexual assault among college women. *Psychology of Women Quarterly.*

Ageton, S. S. (1983). *Sexual assault among adolescents.* Lexington, MA: Lexington Books.

Aramburu, B., & Leigh, B. C. (1991). For better or for worse: Attributions about drunken aggression toward male and female victims. *Violence and Victims, 6*, 31–41.

Barbaree, H. E., Marshall, W. L., Yates, E., & Lightfoot, L. O. (1983). Alcohol intoxication and deviant sexual arousal in male social drinkers. *Behaviour Research and Therapy, 21*, 365–373.

Bandura, A. (1977). *Social learning theory.* Englewood Cliffs, NJ: Prentice-Hall.

Bechhofer, L., & Parrot, A. (1991). What is acquaintance rape? In A. Parrot & L. Bechhofer (Eds.), *Acquaintance rape: The hidden crime* (pp. 9–25). New York: John Wiley and Sons.

Berger, R. J., Searles, P., Salem, R. G., & Pierce, B. A. (1986). Sexual assault in a college community. *Sociological Focus, 19*, 1–26.

Berglas, S. (1987). Self-handicapping model. In H. T. Blane & K. E. Leonard (Eds.), *Psychological theories of drinking and alcoholism* (pp. 305–345). New York: Guilford Press.

Berkow, R. (1982). *Merck manual of diagnosis and therapy* (14th ed.). Rahway, NJ: Merck and Company.

Berkowitz, A. D. (1992). College men as perpetrators of acquaintance rape and sexual assault: A review of recent research. *Journal of American College Health, 40*, 175–181.

Berkowitz, A. D., & Perkins, H. W. (1987). Recent research on gender differences in collegiate alcohol use. *Journal of American College Health, 36*, 123–129.

Briddell, D., Rimm, D., Caddy, G., Krawitz, G., Sholis, D., & Wunderlin, R. (1978).

The effects of alcohol and cognitive set on sexual arousal to deviant stimuli. *Journal of Abnormal Psychology, 87*, 418–430.

Brown, S. A., Goldman, M. S., Inn, A., & Anderson, L. R. (1980). Expectations of reinforcement from alcohol: Their domain and relation to drinking patterns. *Journal of Consulting and Clinical Psychology, 48*, 419–426.

Bureau of Justice Statistics. (1991). *Criminal victimization in the United States.* Washington, DC: U.S. Department of Justice.

Burt, M. R. (1980). Cultural myths and supports for rape. *Journal of Personality and Social Psychology, 38*, 217–230.

Carducci, B. J., & McNeely, J. A. (1981, August). *Attribution of blame for wife abuse by alcoholics and nonalcoholics.* Paper presented at the annual meeting of the American Psychological Association, Los Angeles.

Check, J. V. P., & Malamuth, N. M. (1983). Sex role stereotyping and reactions to depictions of stranger versus acquaintance rape. *Journal of Personality and Social Psychology, 45*, 344–356.

Corcoran, K. J., & Thomas, L. R. (1991). The influence of observed alcohol consumption on perceptions of initiation of sexual activity in a college dating situation. *Journal of Applied Social Psychology, 21*, 500–507.

Crawford, A. (1984). Alcohol and expectancy—I. Perceived sex differences in the effects of drinking. *Alcohol and Alcoholism, 19*, 63–69.

Critchlow, B. (1985). The blame in the bottle: Attributions about drunken behavior. *Personality and Social Psychology Bulletin, 11*, 258–274.

Crowe, L. C., & George, W. H. (1989). Alcohol and human sexuality: Review and integration. *Psychological Bulletin, 105*, 374–386.

Darley, J. M., & Fazio, R. H. (1980). Expectancy confirmation processes arising in the social interaction sequence. *American Psychologist, 35*, 867–881.

Donat, P. L. N., & D'Emilio, J. (1992). A feminist redefinition of rape and sexual assault. *Journal of Social Issues, 41*, 9–22.

Eagly, A. H. (1987). *Sex differences in social behavior: A social-role interpretation.* Hillsdale, NJ: Lawrence Erlbaum.

George, W. H., & Marlatt, G. A. (1986). The effects of alcohol and anger on interest in violence, erotica, and deviance. *Journal of Abnormal Psychology, 95*, 150–158.

George, W. H., Gournic, S. J., & McAfee, M. P. (1988). Perceptions of post drinking female sexuality: Effects of gender, beverage choice, and drink payment. *Journal of Applied Social Psychology, 18*, 1295–1317.

Goodchilds, J. D., & Zellman, G. L. (1984). Sexual signaling and sexual aggression in adolescent relationships. In N. M. Malamuth & E. Donnerstein (Eds.), *Pornography and sexual aggression* (pp. 233–243). Orlando, FL: Academic Press.

Goodchilds, J. D., Zellman, G. L., Johnson, P. B., & Giarrusso, R. (1988). Adolescents and their perceptions of sexual interactions. In A. W. Burgess (Ed.), *Rape and sexual assault* (Vol. 2, pp. 245–270). New York: Garland.

Grauerholz, E., & Serpe, R. T. (1985). Initiation and response: The dynamics of sexual interaction. *Sex Roles, 12*, 1041–1059.

Gross, A. E. (1978). The male role and heterosexual behavior. *Journal of Social Issues, 34*, 87–107.

Hall, E. R., & Flannery, P. J. (1984). Prevalence and correlates of sexual assault experiences in adolescents. *Victimology: An International Journal, 9*, 398–406.

Harnish, R. J., Abbey, A., & DeBono, K. G. (1990). Toward an understanding of "the sex game." *Journal of Applied Social Psychology, 20*, 1333–1344.

Harrell, W. A. (1981). The effects of alcohol use and offender remorsefulness on sentencing decisions. *Journal of Applied Social Psychology, 11,* 83–91.

Hawks, B. K., & Welch, C. D. (1991, August). *Alcohol and the experience of rape.* Paper presented at the meeting of the American Psychological Association, San Francisco.

Hull, J. G., & Van Treuren, R. R. (1986). Experimental social psychology and the causes and effects of alcohol consumption. In H. D. Cappell (Ed.), *Research advances in alcohol and drug problems* (pp. 211–244). New York: Plenum Press.

Kanin, E. J. (1984) Date rape: Unofficial criminals and victims. *Victimology, 9,* 95–108.

Kanin, E. J. (1985). Date rapists: Differential sexual socialization and relative deprivation. *Archives of Sexual Behavior, 14,* 219–231.

Koss, M. P. (1988). Hidden rape: Sexual aggression and victimization in a national sample of students in higher education. In A. W. Burgess (Ed.), *Rape and sexual assault* (Vol. 2, pp. 3–25). New York: Garland.

Koss, M. P., & Dinero, T. E. (1989). Discriminant analysis of risk factors for sexual victimization among a national sample of college women. *Journal of Consulting and Clinical Psychology, 57,* 242–250.

Koss, M. P., Gidycz, C. A., & Wisniewski, N. (1987). The scope of rape: Incidence and prevalence of sexual aggression and victimization in a national sample of higher education students. *Journal of Consulting and Clinical Psychology, 55,* 162–170.

Koss, M. P., & Harvey, M. R. (1991). *The rape victim: Clinical and community interventions* (2nd ed.). Newbury Park, CA: Sage.

Lang, A. R. (1985). The social psychology of drinking and human sexuality. *Journal of Drug Issues, 2,* 273–289.

Lang, A., Searles, J., Lauerman, R., & Adesso, V. (1980). Expectancy, alcohol and sex guilt as determinants of interest in and reaction to sexual stimuli. *Journal of Abnormal Psychology, 89,* 644–653.

LaPlante, M. N., McCormick, N., & Brannigan, G. G. (1980). Living the sexual script: College students' views of influence in sexual encounters. *Journal of Sex Research, 16,* 338–355.

Leigh, B. C. (1987). Beliefs about the effects of alcohol on self and others. *Journal of Studies on Alcohol, 48,* 467–475.

Leonard, K. E. (1989). The impact of explicit aggressive and implicit nonaggressive cues on aggression in intoxicated and sober males. *Personality and Social Psychology Bulletin, 15,* 390–400.

Lloyd, S. A. (1991). The darkside of courtship: Violence and sexual exploitation. *Family Relations, 40,* 14–40.

MacAndrew, C., & Edgerton, R. B. (1969). *Drunken comportment: A social explanation.* Chicago: Aldine.

Maccoby, E. E., & Jacklin, C. N. (1974). *The psychology of sex differences.* Stanford, CA: Stanford University Press.

Malamuth, N. M. (1988). Predicting laboratory aggression against female and male targets: Implications for sexual aggression. *Journal of Research in Personality, 22,* 474–495.

Malamuth, N. M., & Briere, J. (1986). Sexual violence in the media: Indirect effects on aggression against women. *Journal of Social Issues, 42,* 75–92.

Malamuth, N. M., Sockloskie, R. J., Koss, M. P., & Tanaka, J. S. (1991). Characteristics of aggressors against women: Testing a model using a national sample of college students. *Journal of Consulting and Clinical Psychology, 59,* 670–681.

McCarty, D., Diamond, W., & Kaye, M. (1982). Alcohol, sexual arousal, and the transfer of excitation. *Journal of Personality and Social Psychology, 42,* 977–988.

Miller, P. M., Smith, G. T., & Goldman, M. S. (1990). Emergence of alcohol expectancies in childhood: A possible critical period. *Journal of Studies on Alcohol, 51,* 343–349.

Mosher, D. L., & Anderson, R. D. (1986). Macho personality, sexual aggression, and reactions to guided imagery of realistic rape. *Journal of Research in Personality, 20,* 77–94.

Muehlenhard, C. L. (1988). "Nice women" don't say yes and "real men" don't say no: How miscommunication and the double standard can cause sexual problems. *Women and Therapy, 7,* 95–108.

Neuberg, S. L. (1989). The goal of forming accurate impressions during social interactions: Attenuating the impact of negative expectancies. *Journal of Personality and Psychology, 8,* 374–386.

Norris, J., & Cubbins, L. A. (1992). Dating, drinking and rape. *Psychology of Women Quarterly, 16,* 179–191.

Ratliff, K. G., & Burkhart, B. R. (1984). Sex differences in motivations for and effects of drinking among college students. *Journal of Studies on Alcohol, 45,* 26–32.

Richardson, D. (1981). The effect of alcohol on male aggression toward female targets. *Motivation and Emotion, 5,* 333–344.

Richardson, D., & Campbell, J. L. (1982). Alcohol and rape: The effect of alcohol on attributions of blame for rape. *Personality and Social Psychology Bulletin, 8,* 468–476.

Richardson, D. R., & Hammock, G. S. (1991). Alcohol and acquaintance rape. In A. Parrot & L. Bechhofer (Eds.), *Acquaintance rape: The hidden crime* (pp. 83–95). New York: John Wiley and Sons.

Robbins, C. (1989). Sex differences in psychosocial consequences of alcohol and drug use. *Journal of Health and Social Behavior, 30,* 117–130.

Rohsenow, D. J. (1983). Drinking habits and expectancies about alcohol's effects for self versus others. *Journal of Consulting and Clinical Psychology, 51,* 752–756.

Rubin, J. Z., Provenzano, F. J., & Luria, Z. (1974). The eye of the beholder: Parents' views on sex of newborns. *American Journal of Orthopsychiatry, 44,* 512–519.

Ryan, C., & Butters, N. (1983). Cognitive deficits in alcoholics. In B. Kissin & H. Begleiter (Eds.), *The pathogenesis of alcoholism: Biological factors* (Vol. 7, pp. 485–538). New York: Plenum Press.

Saal, F. E., Johnson, C. B., & Weber, N. (1989). Friendly or sexy? It may depend on whom you ask. *Psychology of Women Quarterly, 13,* 263–276.

Schwartz, R. M., Burkhart, B. R., & Green, S. B. (1982). Sensation seeking and anxiety as factors in social drinking by men. *Journal of Studies on Alcohol, 43,* 1108–1114.

Scully, D. (1991). *Understanding sexual violence: A study of convicted rapists.* Boston: Unwin Hyman.

Scully, D., & Marolla, J. (1984). Convicted rapists' vocabulary of motive: Excuses and justifications. *Social Problems, 31,* 530–544.

Seigel, J. M., Sorenson, S. B., Golding, J. M., Burnam, M. A., & Stein, J. A. (1989). Resistance to sexual assault: Who resists and what happens? *American Journal of Public Health, 12,* 27–31.

Shaver, K. G. (1987). *The attribution of blame.* New York: Springer-Verlag.

Shotland, R. L., & Craig, J. M. (1988). Can men and women differentiate between friendly and sexually interested behavior? *Social Psychology Quarterly, 51,* 66–73.

Steele, C. M., & Josephs, R. A. (1988). Drinking your troubles away II: An attention-allocation model of alcohol's effect on psychological stress. *Journal of Abnormal Psychology, 97,* 196–205.

Steele, C. M., & Southwick, L. (1985). Alcohol and social behavior I: The psychology of drunken excess. *Journal of Personality and Social Psychology, 48,* 18–34.

Taylor, S. P., & Leonard, K. E. (1983). Alcohol and human physical aggression. In R. G. Green & E. I. Donnerstein (Eds.), *Aggression: Theoretical and empirical reviews* (Vol. 2, pp. 77–101). New York: Academic Press.

Ullman, S. E., & Knight, R. A. (1991). A multivariate model for predicting rape and physical injury outcomes during sexual assaults. *Journal of Consulting and Clinical Psychology, 59,* 724–731.

Wilsnack, S. C. (1984). Drinking, sexuality, and sexual dysfunction in women. In S. C. Wilsnack & L. J. Beckman (Eds.), *Alcohol problems in women* (pp. 189–227). New York: Guilford Press.

Wilson, G. T. (1981). The effects of alcohol on human sexual behavior. In N. Mello (Ed.), *Advances in substance abuse* (Vol. 2, pp. 1–40). Greenwich, CT: JAI Press.

Wilson, G. T., & Lawson, D. M. (1976). Expectancies, alcohol and sexual arousal in male social drinkers. *Journal of Abnormal Psychology, 85,* 587–594.

Zellman, G. L., & Goodchilds, J. D. (1983). Becoming sexual in adolescence. In E. R. Allgeier & N. B. McCormick (Eds.), *Changing boundaries: Gender roles and sexual behavior* (pp. 49–63). Palo Alto, CA: Mayfield.

8

The Threat of Rape: Its Psychological Impact on Nonvictimized Women

GERD BOHNER AND NORBERT SCHWARZ

One of the most controversial hypotheses about rape and sexual violence holds that rape serves to show women their place in society and hence contributes to the preservation of the societal status quo of male dominance (e.g., Brownmiller, 1975; Griffin, 1979). In what is probably the most widely known statement of this hypothesis, Susan Brownmiller suggested that rape "is nothing more or less than a conscious process of intimidation by which *all men* keep *all women* in a state of fear" (Brownmiller, 1975, p. 15 [italics added]). Whereas it is difficult to assess the assumed conscious nature of this assumed process of intimidation, the hypothesis that the threat of rape has an intimidating effect on women in general is amenable to empirical research.

Several bodies of research bear on this hypothesis, although often indirectly. At the societal level, it has been observed that societies with a high prevalence of rape are characterized by higher gender inequality in terms of legal status, power, and access to resources (Baron & Straus, 1987; Sanday, 1981a, 1981b). At the individual level, fear of rape has been found to be associated with self-imposed behavioral restrictions among women (Riger & Gordon, 1981), bearing on personal freedom as another aspect of gender inequality. Although compatible with Brownmiller's (1975) hypothesis, this correlational research does not establish a causal impact of rape. To provide a more direct test, we conducted a series of experiments, using experimental procedures borrowed from social cognition research, in which we assessed the impact of the threat of rape on women's self-esteem, their trust in others, and their perception of personal control. Before we turn to this experimental work,

162

however, we provide a short summary of correlational evidence bearing on rape and different aspects of gender inequality.

CORRELATIONAL EVIDENCE: RAPE PREVALENCE AND GENDER INEQUALITY

At the societal level, several studies demonstrated that a higher prevalence of rape is associated with a higher degree of gender inequality in traditional, as well as, modern societies. In a cross-cultural examination of 156 traditional societies, Sanday (1981a, 1981b) found that the incidence of rape varied widely. More important, societies classified as "rape prone" were characterized by a pattern of male dominance that manifested itself in male–female differences in political and economical power. Moreover, these societies were characterized by sexual separation and males tended to express disregard for women's contributions to the culture. In contrast, men in "rape-free" societies tended to treat women with respect and showed a higher appreciation of their productive and reproductive roles.

Similar results were obtained by Baron and Straus (1987) for the United States. These researchers compared the 50 states of the United States with respect to rape prevalence and a number of conditions potentially facilitating or inhibiting rape. As expected, states with higher rape rates were likely to exhibit greater gender inequality to the disadvantage of women, as reflected by an index that combined economic, political, and legal aspects of social status. Whereas Baron and Straus conceptualized gender inequality as an antecedent rather than a consequence of rape, it is conceivable that the threat of rape may contribute to the preservation of gender inequality, as the Brownmiller hypothesis suggests.

This relationship between gender inequality and rape prevalence at the societal level is paralleled at the individual level by a reliable relationship between individuals' attitudes toward women's rights and their endorsement of beliefs about rape that put women at a disadvantage (e.g., Burt, 1980; Costin & Schwarz, 1987). These beliefs, often referred to as *rape myths*, attribute a high degree of responsibility to the victim, as indicated by pronouncements such as, "Women who are raped asked for it," or "Women often provoke rape by their appearance or behavior." Moreover, these beliefs serve to exonerate the rapist by portraying rape as the act of oversexed males who can not control their behavior when confronted with female "sexual provocation." These beliefs are likely to contribute to a social climate permissive of rape and to require women to restrict their behavior in order to avoid rape, thus contributing to gender inequality regarding the range of behavioral options.

In a survey of 598 Minnesota adults, Burt (1980) observed that acceptance of rape myths is a rather common phenomenon in U.S. society, and that these beliefs are meaningfully correlated with a number of attitudinal variables, including gender-role stereotyping, adversarial sexual beliefs (e.g., "A lot of women seem to get pleasure in putting men down"), and acceptance of interpersonal violence.

A close relationship between rape myth acceptance (RMA) and restrictive attitudes toward women's rights has also been confirmed in a number of intercultural studies, including countries as different as the United States, England, Israel, West Germany (Costin, 1985; Costin & Schwarz, 1987), and Turkey (Costin & Kaptanoglu, 1993).

In combination, these studies indicate that the acceptance of beliefs about rape that put women at a disadvantage is closely associated with the endorsement of traditional gender-role prescriptions that imply the approval of male dominance and female subordination. Thus, these findings at the individual level parallel findings at the societal level that indicate a close relationship between rape prevalence and gender inequality.

Finally, the threat of rape has been assumed to impose severe restrictions on women's behaviors. Consistent with this hypothesis, Riger and Gordon (1981) found a strong relationship between women's fear of rape (and other violent crimes) and the extent to which these women used precautionary behavioral strategies in a survey study conducted in three U.S. cities. These precautionary strategies included self-imposed "isolation" (e.g., not going out alone for entertainment) and "street savvy" (e.g., "wearing shoes that permit one to run"; p. 83). Furthermore, fear of crime in general was much higher among female than among male respondents. Specifically, 43.6% of females, but only 17.9% of males, reported being "very" or "somewhat afraid" when out alone at night, despite the fact that females are objectively less likely than males to become victims of violent crimes, with the exception of rape. Accordingly, Riger and Gordon proposed that "the original feminist formulation of rape as a means of controlling women may need to be expanded to include other crimes of violence" (p. 86). We return to this proposition when presenting our own experimental data.

In summary, the results of Sanday (1981a, 1981b) and Baron and Straus (1987) show that societies characterized by a high prevalence of rape are also characterized by a high degree of gender inequality, to the disadvantage of women. This relationship is paralleled at the individual level by a close association between traditional gender-role attitudes and the acceptance of beliefs about rape that put women at a disadvantage (e.g., Burt, 1980; Costin & Schwarz, 1987). Moreover, the subjective feeling of being threatened by rape is associated with behavioral restrictions that limit women's participation in social life (e.g., Riger & Gordon, 1981).

LIMITATIONS OF CORRELATIONAL RESEARCH AND AN EXPERIMENTAL ALTERNATIVE

Although the reviewed findings are suggestive, their correlational nature does not allow unequivocal conclusions about the hypothesized causal links among the various aspects of gender inequality, rape prevalence, and women's self-perceptions and behavior. The data permit at least three different interpretations. First, one may assume that there is a causal influence of gender inequality on rape prevalence. Thus, a high degree of gender inequality may increase the incidence of rape in a society, and the acceptance of gender inequality, as implied by traditional gender-role beliefs, may foster the development of antivictim attitudes, as illustrated by findings at the individual level. Alternatively, one may assume that rape exerts a causal influence on gender inequality, both at the societal and individual levels, as implied by Brownmiller's (1975) hypothesis. Finally, third variable(s) may determine both the incidence of rape and gender inequality, with no direct causal link between these variables. Moreover, the first two possibilities are not mutually exclusive, and the relationship between rape and gender inequality could be bidirectional (see Schwarz, 1987, for a more detailed discussion).

The primary methodological tool to clarify the causal pathways among a set of variables would be an experiment in which one variable is systematically varied as the independent variable and variations in the other variables are observed (e.g., Rosenthal & Rosnow, 1984). For obvious reasons, direct experimental tests are impossible with respect to our research question. However, research in cognitive psychology suggests an alternative experimental procedure "for identifying causal effects when it is impossible to manipulate the independent variable of interest" (Schwarz & Strack, 1981, p. 554). This approach, which is discussed in more detail by Schwarz and Strack, takes advantage of the fact that individuals rarely retrieve all information that might be relevant to form a judgment on a given topic. Rather, they truncate the search process as soon as enough information has come to mind to form a judgment with sufficient subjective certainty. Hence, the judgment depends on the information that is most accessible at the time (see Bodenhausen & Wyer, 1987, for a review). Accordingly, we may test the hypothesized causal influence of a variable by increasing its cognitive accessibility at the time at which the individual is asked to form a judgment or to make a behavioral decision. This can be accomplished by randomly assigning subjects to conditions in which they either are, or are not, induced to think about the hypothesized causal variable prior to assessment of the dependent variable of interest (see Schwarz & Strack, 1981, for a more detailed discussion). If the hypothesized causal variable does indeed affect the dependent variable, its impact should be more pronounced when its cognitive accessibility has been increased.

This strategy allows us to address the hypothesized causal impact of rape on women's attitudes, self-perceptions, and behavior. If the social reality of rape has a causal influence on women's self-evaluations, women who were recently induced to think about rape should report less-favorable self-judgments than women who were not induced to think about rape. We employed this research strategy in three different studies conducted in Germany and the United States. We exposed women and men to descriptions of a case of rape or assault to increase the cognitive accessibility of rape or other forms of violence and assessed their impact on a variety of self-related judgments.

EXPERIMENTAL EVIDENCE

The Impact of Rape on Women's Self-Perceptions: Initial Evidence

The first of these experiments was conducted by Schwarz and Brand (1983) with female college students at a U.S. university. The women who participated in this study completed a personality questionnaire either before or after they were exposed to a realistic description of a rape, which had ostensibly occurred on their campus. This description read:

> The police reported a rape case early this semester. Further inquiries with their source yielded this story. The young woman, a sophomore at U. of I., was riding her bicycle home from campus around 10:30 that evening. Ahead of her, on an otherwise deserted street a man started to cross, so she slowed down. As she got closer she found she had to stop because the man was now in her way. While asking her "Hey baby, how you doing?" his friend came out of the bushes holding a small silver handgun. They ordered her off her bike, which they threw aside. Both were tall and young, so when each grabbed an arm firmly and they jammed the gun in her back, she knew it would be difficult to escape. She could only protest by dragging her feet as they led her into the nearby park. Her verbal protests were only answered with "Shut up" or "Don't look at us or you'll get it!" accompanied with nudges of the gun into her back.
>
> When they got to the dark pavilion in the park, they ripped off her clothes. They each raped her on the rough picnic table, holding her down and covering her face with a sweatshirt. They left her with threats of shooting her if she tried to leave the pavilion too soon after they did. (Schwarz & Brand, 1983, pp. 72–73).

As shown in Figure 8.1, women who had been exposed to the description of a rape incident subsequently reported more traditional gender-role attitudes than women in the control group, who had not read the rape description. Thus, these college women were more likely to agree, for example, that "women should worry less about their rights and more about becoming good wives and mothers", or that "sons in a family should be given more encouragement to go to college than daughters." Moreover, exposure to the rape description resulted in reports of lower self-esteem, as reflected in agreement with items such as, "I often wish I were someone else." Finally, and least surprisingly, reading about rape decreased women's trust in others, making them less likely to agree with items such as, "Most people can be trusted."

In combination, these findings indicate that the threat of rape has a negative impact on women's self-perceptions. In the present study, exposure to a single reminder of this threat resulted in a temporary decrease in reported self-esteem and trust in others, as well as an increased acceptance of traditional gender-role propositions. These reports reflect self-perceptions that are incompatible with gender equality and support the assumption that the threat of rape has an intimidating effect on women in general, not only those immediately victimized. However, this initial study left a number of important questions

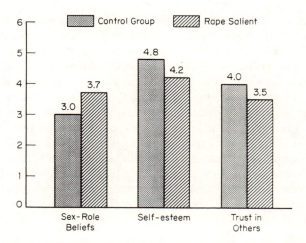

FIGURE 8.1.   Sex role beliefs, self-esteem, and trust as a function of salience of rape. Scale range is 1 to 7; higher values indicate more-conservative sex-role beliefs, higher self-esteem, and higher trust. (*Source:* Adapted from Schwarz & Brand, 1983.)

unanswered; these were addressed in subsequent experiments by Bohner, Weisbrod, Raymond, Barzvi, and Schwarz (1993).

How Specific Is the Impact of Rape?

One of the open questions concerns the specificity of the observed impact of the threat of rape: Is the impact of the threat of rape limited to women, or are men also affected by this threat, and, if so, how? Moreover, are the observed effects specific to rape, or do they reflect a more general impact of the threat of violent crime?

According to feminist theory, some of the adverse effects of rape accessibility observed by Schwarz and Brand (1983) should be gender specific. This is primarily the case for the impact of rape on self-esteem: If rape is operational in "showing women their place in society," one should expect that women, but not men, exhibit lower self-esteem after exposure to a rape description. A strong version of Brownmiller's (1975) argument would even imply that men might present a more-positive view of themselves when rape is salient than when it is not, as rape serves to confirm male dominance. The observed effects of rape on interpersonal trust and gender-role attitudes, on the other hand, are less likely to be gender specific. One may assume that low interpersonal trust and traditional gender roles are part of the value system of a male-dominated society and are therefore affected similarly in both women and men as a function of exposure to rape. To determine whether the effects of rape are gender specific, Bohner and collaborators (1993) included both women and men as subjects in their studies.

Furthermore, they examined if the results of Schwarz and Brand (1983) reflected a response that is specific to rape rather than a general reaction to interpersonal violence. Recall that Riger and Gordon (1981) proposed that the threat of criminal violence in general may serve a similar function as the threat of rape in intimidating women. There is also empirical evidence that exposure to a variety of negative events (like crime, accidents, or natural disasters) may result in generally amplified judgments of risk across different domains (Johnson & Tversky, 1983). Moreover, exposure to rape reports and other negative material may temporarily impair a person's mood, which may in turn lead to more negative evaluative judgments about the self (Levine, Wyer, & Schwarz, 1994; Schwarz, 1990; Schwarz & Clore, 1988). Therefore, Bohner et al. (1993) contrasted the influence of rape descriptions with the influence of descriptions of a violent assault against a male victim that were comparably negative in tone, but unlikely to induce specific thoughts about rape.

The Moderating Role of Rape Myths

Another open question concerns the possibility that the impact of the threat of rape may be moderated by subjects' beliefs about rape. As many researchers observed, beliefs about rape that put women at a disadvantage, often referred to as rape myths, are widespread (e.g., Burt, 1980; Costin & Schwarz, 1987). As discussed above, these beliefs imply a high degree of responsibility of the victim and serve to exonerate the rapist. Accordingly, individuals with a high acceptance of rape myth have been found to assign more responsibility to the victim, and less to the rapist, than individuals low in rape myth acceptance (e.g., Giesecke, Schlupp, & Schwarz, 1986).

How might these beliefs influence the impact of the threat of rape on women's self-perceptions? On one hand, we may assume that women high in rape myth acceptance may be more strongly affected by the threat of rape than women who do not accept rape myths, because the former attribute greater responsibility to the raped woman. In fact, high acceptance of rape myths has been found to be directly related to lower self-esteem, lower trust in others, and more traditional gender-role beliefs (e.g., Burt, 1980; Costin & Schwarz, 1987), even in the absence of any temporary increase in the accessibility of the threat of rape.

On the other hand, however, a high acceptance of rape myths implies the belief that rape can be avoided if women follow certain rules, such as dressing in a "decent" and "nonprovoking" way or not going out alone. Moreover, rape myths encompass a stereotypical representation of the "typical rape victim," which may suggest that only women who conform to this stereotype are vulnerable to rape. If so, a woman who believes in rape myths may exclude herself from the social category of potential rape victims and may assume that she can personally avoid rape by following certain rules. Accordingly, high rape myth acceptance may actually reduce the impact of the threat of rape by fostering a perception of control over the threat. By the same token, women who are low in rape myth acceptance may be likely to think of rape as a threat to all women, including themselves, and may hence be less likely to perceive individual control over the threat (see Tabone, Pardine, & Salzano, 1992). Accordingly, they may be particularly vulnerable to the adverse impact of the threat of rape. If so, attempts to reduce the acceptance of rape myths would, ironically, render women more vulnerable to the adverse psychological effects of the threat of rape.

To explore the potentially moderating role of individuals' persistent beliefs about rape, subjects' rape myth acceptance was included as a factor in Bohner et al.'s (1993) studies, which we now describe in more detail.

Procedures

To replicate the initial findings and to address the open questions discussed above, two follow-up experiments were conducted (see Bohner et al., 1993, for details). These experiments included both men and women as subjects, compared the effects of rape to those of a violent assault, and explored the potentially moderating role of individuals' persistent beliefs about rape. The first experiment was conducted with German trade school students and the second experiment with U.S. college students. Both studies followed the same design and employed similar measures. They are therefore discussed together.

In both studies, subjects first read a paragraph (presented as a "newspaper article") designed to manipulate the salience of crime. This paragraph either described a no-crime topic, a rape, or a violent assault. The paragraphs for the last two conditions were very similar and varied only with respect to the type of crime described and the victim's gender. In the U.S. study, they read:

Rape: On Thursday, March 16, 1991, at approximately 3:20 p.m., Alicia B., twenty years old, was raped in her own building at 42 Jones Street between Bleecker and West 4th Street. A junior at Hunter College, she worked at Henry & Davidson's as a paralegal. Hoping to acquire some experience before applying for law school, she worked diligently and was given a number of important responsibilities. On the day of March 16, Alicia walked the seven blocks from her work place to her apartment in order to gather some case files that her supervisor had requested. Upon turning the key and entering through the first doorway of the small brownstone building, she was grabbed immediately by a man who had been hiding behind the door. He threatened her with a knife and forced her down the flight of stairs that led to the basement. He raped her and immediately fled. The police are currently investigating a suspect, but decline to reveal details.

Assault: On Thursday, March 16, 1991, at approximately 3:20 p.m., Andrew B., twenty years old, was assaulted in his own building at 42 Jones Street between Bleecker and West 4th Street. A junior at Hunter College, he worked at Henry & Davidson's as a paralegal. Hoping to acquire some experience before applying to law school, he worked diligently and was given a number of important responsibilities. On the day of March 16, Andrew walked the seven blocks from his work place to his apartment in order to gather some case files that his supervisor had requested. He noticed two men loitering and drinking on the sidewalk in front of his small brownstone building. Upon turning the key and entering through the first doorway, he was grabbed immediately by the two men, who had followed him to the door. One threatened him with a knife and the other forced him down the flight of stairs that led to the basement. Although they did not rob him, they beat him up until he lost consciousness. The police are currently investigating suspects, but decline to reveal details.

Subjects were randomly assigned to one of the three salience conditions. In addition, groups high and low in rape myth acceptance were formed on the basis of responses to rape myth items taken from Burt (1980) and Costin and Schwarz (1987). This resulted in a 3 (salience of crime) × 2 (sex of subject) × 2 (rape myth acceptance) factorial design.

The major dependent variables in both studies were scales assessing subjects' self-esteem (items selected from scales by Hormuth & Lalli, 1988, e.g., "I can be proud of myself"; and by Fleming & Watts, 1980, e.g., "I often worry about whether other people like to be with me"), their gender-role attitudes (Costin 1985; Costin & Schwarz, 1987 e.g., "A woman's social status should be determined by the status of her husband"), their trust in other people (Amelang, Gold, & Külbel, 1984, e.g., "There are only few people one can rely on"), and their momentary general affect (Abele-Brehm & Brehm, 1986, e.g., "carefree," "depressed"). In the U.S. experiment, the data of women who reported prior experiences of sexual aggression were excluded from the analyses to provide an explicit test of the impact of rape on nonraped women.

Although conducted in different countries and with different subject populations, both experiments yielded very similar results; these results are therefore discussed together.

Results

Self-esteem   The impact of thinking about rape or a violent assault on reported self-esteem was gender, as well as crime, specific and was moderated by rape myth acceptance (see Figure 8.2). Specifically, women who did not endorse rape myths (low RMA) reported lower self-esteem when they had read about a case of rape than when they had not. In contrast, reading about rape had no negative impact on self-esteem for women high in rape myth acceptance or for men. These groups, especially men high in rape myth acceptance, even tended to report higher self-esteem when they had been exposed to a rape report than when they had not. Thus, the self-esteem results replicated the initial findings of Schwarz and Brand (1983) and supported Brownmiller's (1975) key hypothesis, but only with respect to women who did not endorse rape myths and hence conceived of rape as a threat to all women, including themselves.

Finally, thinking about a case of assault did not reliably affect reported self-esteem for either women or men. Hence, we conclude that the observed

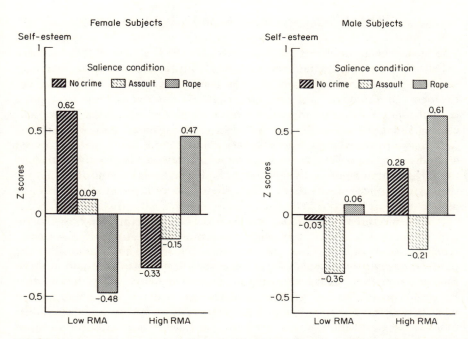

FIGURE 8.2. Self-esteem as a function of salience condition (NO CRIME = no-crime salient; ASSAULT = assault salient; RAPE = rape salient), gender, and rape myth acceptance [RMA]). Data represent means of *z* scores combining general self-esteem and social confidence and are combined across Experiments 1 and 2 of Bohner et al., 1993.

negative impact on self-esteem is specific to rape and does not reflect a general impact of the threat of violent crime.

Affective state The impact of the experimental manipulations on subjects' self-reported momentary affective states paralleled the effects on self-esteem. Again, only women low in rape myth acceptance were negatively affected by reading about a case of rape. In contrast, women high in rape myth acceptance reported feeling better when they had been confronted with rape, as did men, independently of their beliefs about rape.

Gender-role attitudes and trust in others Finally, Bohner et al. (1993) did not detect any effects of salience of rape or assault on interpersonal trust or on attitudes toward women in either study, although a high correlation between gender-role attitudes and acceptance of rape myths was again observed. Thus, the specific effects of rape salience on affect and self-evaluations may be more pervasive and reliable than the effects on attitudinal variables.

The Moderating Role of Rape Myth Acceptance

The most crucial finding of the Bohner et al. (1993) studies is that women's beliefs about rape moderate the impact of the threat of rape on women's self-perceptions. Ironically, women who endorse beliefs about rape that put the victim at a disadvantage were not negatively affected by thinking about a case of rape. To the contrary, these women reported somewhat higher self-esteem and more-positive affect when rape was salient than when it was not. In contrast, women whose beliefs about rape did not put the victim at a disadvantage were most vulnerable psychologically to the threat of rape. How can we explain this pattern of findings? More specifically, what are the cognitive mechanisms that mediate the effects of rape on self-esteem and affect?

We conjecture that a person's enduring beliefs about rape serve as a cognitive schema to interpret incoming information about rape. If a woman's schema consists of beliefs like "any woman can be raped" (which is indicative of low rape myth acceptance), she is more likely to interpret information about rape as a potential threat to herself and is negatively affected. If, on the other hand, a woman's schema embodies beliefs like "women who are raped get what they deserve" (indicative of high rape myth acceptance), she should be more likely to exclude herself from the category of potential rape victims (cf. Schwarz & Bless, 1992, for a more detailed discussion of the role of categorization processes in social judgment). She may thus comprehend information about rape as a potential threat to other women, but not herself, which may even result in a contrast effect, as reflected in more-positive judgments of self-esteem.[1] This analysis is in line with the correlational observation that women who accept rape myths perceive their own risk of victimization to be lower (Tabone et al., 1992).

Turning to the findings for men, both studies indicated that men were not negatively affected by the salience of rape. Because men are generally likely to exclude themselves from the category of potential victims because of their gender regardless of their enduring belief in rape myths, this finding is not surprising. However, men reported somewhat higher self-esteem and more-positive affect when rape was salient than when it was not, in particular when they had a high rape myth acceptance. This finding may reflect different processes that cannot be distinguished on the basis of the present data. On one hand, men high in rape myth acceptance may be less likely to conceive of rape as an outrageous crime, but may see rape as a "rightful" act of male dominance, as reflected in a positive correlation of self-reported rape proclivity and rape myth acceptance in "normal" men (Malamuth, 1981). Thus, identification with the rapist may have potentially resulted in more-positive affect and self-esteem. On the other hand, men high in rape myth acceptance may well have seen the rape they read about as an outrageous crime. Based on their beliefs about rape, however, these men may be particularly likely to categorize the rapist as an abnormal individual. If so, perceiving themselves in contrast to "the abnormal rapist" would also be likely to result in more-positive judgments of self-esteem. A clarification of these divergent process assumptions awaits further research.

CONCLUSIONS

Taken together, the correlational and experimental studies we reviewed yielded converging evidence in support of feminist researchers' claim that the social reality of rape, in combination with cultural myths about rape, contributes to gender inequality in various respects (Brownmiller, 1975). At the societal level, a high rape prevalence is correlated with disadvantages of women regarding societal power, status, and authority (e.g., Sanday, 1981a, 1981b). At the individual level, beliefs about rape that put the victim at a disadvantage are associated with negative attitudes toward women's rights (e.g., Costin & Schwarz, 1987) and more traditional gender-role attitudes (e.g., Burt, 1980). Moreover, fear of rape is associated with preventive behavioral restrictions that limit women's participation in social life (e.g., Riger & Gordon, 1981).

Whereas correlational findings of this type do not speak to the causal direction of the relationship between rape and gender inequality, using an experimental approach based on research procedures developed in social cognition allowed us to demonstrate that the threat of rape has a causal impact on women's self-perceptions. Obviously, the demonstration of this causal link does not preclude the existence of other causal relationships, and it seems highly plausible to assume that gender inequality, in turn, contributes to rape prevalence (e.g., Baron & Straus, 1987). As the present results indicate, however, this relationship is likely to be bidirectional (Schwarz, 1987), with rape, in turn, contributing to gender inequality at the individual level through an intimidating impact on women who have themselves not been raped.

In addition to bearing on the hypothesized causal impact of rape, our results illuminate the mediating role of beliefs about rape and draw attention to the possible impact of media accounts of rape. If exposure to just one relatively pallid description of a rape incident of the type used in our studies (Bohner et al., 1993; Schwarz & Brand, 1983) has a profound influence on women's self-esteem, the multiple exposure to rape accounts in television and newspapers, which are often quite graphic, should have even more detrimental effects. As the findings about the mediating role of beliefs about rape indicate, it is likely that the women who are most affected by the threat of rape conveyed by these reports are women who maintain what may be considered a realistic view of the nature of rape (as evidenced by affirmation of items such as "any woman can be raped") and who do not hold antivictim attitudes (such as "women who were raped got what they deserved"). In contrast, the self-perceptions of women who hold beliefs that put the victim at a disadvantage seem invulnerable to the threat of rape. Ironically, beliefs that foster the tendency to blame the victim (e.g., Giesecke et al., 1986), and hence put the victim at a disadvantage, may prove beneficial to women who are themselves not victimized. This leaves us with the unsettling conclusion that women are facing the choice of either blaming the victim to maintain an "illusion of control" (Langer, 1975) over the threat of rape or of living in constant fear.

NOTE

1. In general, however, rape myth acceptance seems to be negatively correlated with self-esteem (Burt, 1980), which is also reflected in the results of control subjects, who were not exposed to information about crime, in the studies of Bohner et al. (1993).

Acknowledgments. The reported research was supported by grants from the Deutsche Forschungsgemeinschaft (Schw278/1) and the Bundesminster für Forschung und Technologie of the Federal Republic of Germany (SWF0044-6) to Norbert Schwarz, and by a Feodor Lynen research fellowship from the Alexander von Humboldt Foundation to Gerd Bohner. We thank David Buss, Dorothee Dickenberger, Carla Grayson, and Michaela Wänke for helpful comments on a previous draft. Address correspondence to Gerd Bohner, University of Mannheim, Social Psychology, D-68131 Mannheim, Germany (E-mail: GBOHNER@MLSOWI.SOWI.UNI-MANNHEIM.DE), or to Norbert Schwarz, Institute for Social Research, University of Michigan, Ann Arbor, MI 48106-1248 (E-mail: NORBERT.SCHWARZ@UMICH.EDU).

REFERENCES

Abele-Brehm, A., & Brehm, W. (1986). Zur Konzeptualisierung und Messung voh Befindlichkeit: Die Entwicklung der Befindlickeitsskalen (BFS) [The conceptualization and measurement of affect]. *Diagnostica, 32,* 209–228.

Amelang, M., Gold, A., & Külbel, E. (1984). Über einige Erfahrungen mit einer deutschsprachigen Skala zur Erfassung zwischenmenschlichen Vertrauens [Some results gathered with a German scale assessing interpersonal trust]. *Diagnostica, 30,* 198–215.

Baron, L., & Straus, M. A. (1987). Four theories of rape: A macrosociological analysis. *Social Problems, 34,* 467–488.

Bodenhausen, G. V., & Wyer, R. S. (1987). Social cognition and social reality: Information acquisition and use in the laboratory and the real world. In H. J. Hippler, N. Schwarz, & S. Sudman (Eds.), *Social information processing and survey methodology* (pp. 6–41). New York: Springer-Verlag.

Bohner, G., Weisbrod, C., Raymond, P., Barzvi, A., & Schwarz, N. (1993). Salience of rape affects self-esteem: The moderating role of gender and rape myth acceptance. *European Journal of Social Psychology, 23,* 561–579.

Brownmiller, S. (1975). *Against our will.* New York: Simon and Schuster.

Burt, M. (1980). Cultural myths and supports of rape. *Journal of Personality and Social Psychology, 38,* 217–230.

Costin, F. (1985). Beliefs about rape and women's social roles. *Archives of Sexual Behavior, 14,* 319–325.

Costin, F., & Kaptanoglu, C. (1993). Beliefs about rape and women's social roles: A Turkish replication. *European Journal of Social Psychology, 23,* 327–330.

Costin, F., & Schwarz, N. (1987). Beliefs about rape and women's social roles: A four-nation study. *Journal of Interpersonal Violence, 2,* 46–56.

Fleming, J. S., & Watts, W. A. (1980). The dimensionality of self-esteem: Some results for a college sample. *Journal of Personality and Social Psychology*, 39, 921–929.

Giesecke, H., Schlupp, M., & Schwarz, N. (1986). Schuldzuschreibung nach Verge- waltigung: Traditionelle Geschlechtsrollenorientierung und die Akzeptanz von Vergewaltigungsmythen [Attribution of responsibility for rape]. In A. Schorr (Ed.), *Bericht über den 13. Kongreß für Angewandte Psychologie* (Vol. 2, pp. 182–193). Bonn: Deutscher Psychologenverlag.

Griffin, S. (1979). *Rape: The power of consciousness*. New York: Harper and Row.

Hormuth, S. E., & Lalli, M. (1988). Eine Skala zur Erfassung der bereichsspezifischen Selbstzufriedenheit [A scale assessing domain-specific self-satisfaction]. *Diag- nostica*, 34, 148–166.

Johnson, E. J., & Tversky, A. (1983). Affect generalization and the perception of risk. *Journal of Personality and Social Psychology*, 45, 20–31.

Langer, E. J. (1975). The illusion of control. *Journal of Personality and Social Psychol- ogy*, 32, 311–328.

Levine, S., Wyer, R. S. Jr., & Schwarz, N. (1994). Are you what you feel? The affective and cognitive determinants of self-esteem. *European Journal of Social Psychology*, 24, 63–77.

Malamuth, N. M. (1981). Rape proclivity among males. *Journal of Social Issues*, 37(4), 138–157.

Riger, S., & Gordon, M. T. (1981). The fear of rape: A study in social control. *Journal of Social Issues*, 37(4), 71–89.

Rosenthal, R., & Rosnow, R. L. (1984). *Essentials of behavioral research*. New York: McGraw-Hill.

Sanday, P. R. (1981a). *Female power and male dominance: On the origins of sexual inequality*. New York: Cambridge University Press.

Sanday, P. R. (1981b). The socio-cultural context of rape: A cross-cultural study. *Journal of Social Issues*, 37(4), 5–27.

Schwarz, N. (1987). Geschlechtsrollenorientierung und die Einstellung zu Gewalt gegen Frauen: Informationsaktivierung als Alternative zu ex post facto- Versuchsplänen [Sex role orientation and attitudes toward violence against women: Priming of information as an alternative to ex post facto designs]. *Psychologische Rundschau*, 38, 137–144.

Schwarz, N. (1990). Feelings as information: Informational and motivational functions of affective states. In E. T. Higgins & R. Sorrentino (Eds.), *Handbook of motivation and cognition: Foundations of social behavior* (Vol. 2, pp. 527– 561). New York: Guilford.

Schwarz, N., & Bless, H. (1992). Constructing reality and its alternatives: Assimilation and contrast effects in social judgment. In L. L. Martin & A. Tesser (Eds.), *The construction of social judgment* (pp. 217–245). Hillsdale, NJ: Erlbaum.

Schwarz, N., & Brand, J. F. (1983). Effects of salience of rape on sex-role attitudes, trust and self-esteem in non-raped women. *European Journal of Social Psychol- ogy*, 13, 71–76.

Schwarz, N., & Clore, G. L. (1988). How do I feel about it? Informative functions of affective states. In K. Fiedler & J. Forgas (Eds.), *Affect, cognition, and social behavior* (pp. 44–62). Toronto: Hogrefe International.

Schwarz, N., & Strack, F. (1981). Manipulating salience: Causal assessment in natural settings. *Personality and Social Psychology Bulletin*, 6, 554–558.

Tabone, C., Pardine, P., & Salzano, J. (1992, April). *Why do women accept the rape myth?* Poster presented at the Annual Meeting of the Eastern Psychological Association, Boston.

III

Integrating Evolutionary and Feminist Perspectives

9

Sexual Politics: The Gender Gap in the Bedroom, the Cupboard, and the Cabinet

FELICIA PRATTO

There are no human societies in which women dominate men. Instead, societies in which men dominate women are so common that male dominance has been considered a human universal (e.g., Goldberg, 1973; Millet, 1970; Rosaldo, 1974; but see Eisler, 1987; Leacock, 1981; Lepowsky, 1990; Sacks, 1979; Sanday, 1981; Schlegel, 1990; Schwendinger & Schwendinger, 1983). This makes the question of sexual dominance special in intergroup relations for there is no other "grouping" besides sex in which, when there is inequality, one group is always subordinate. Yet, the variability that exists from society to society in the means and degree of sexual inequality indicates that simplistic explanations of male dominance will not suffice.

Theorizing about sexual politics presents a number of special problems. First, although sex appears to be an inherent biological basis for social groups, the meaning of sex is social and cultural (e.g., Schlegel, 1990). As such, we would not want to build a theory based primarily on the examples of only a few similar societies (cf. Leacock, 1981) nor would we want to gloss over variance within societies. D. E. Brown (1991) recently attempted to document patterns of human behavior cross-culturally (see also Williams & Best, 1982, on cross-culturally consistent elements of sex stereotypes; see Murdock, 1949, for an early worldwide survey of nonindustrialized societies). Such work, along with careful study of any exceptions, provides one part of the data to which a theory must be fit; a survey of systematic variations from society to society must constitute the other part. Ethnographic surveys such as the Human Relations Area File do this, but usually only for nonindustrial societies. It seems to me that all human societies should be included in such a corpus because we cannot consider people in either "primitive" or "modern" (both problematic terms) societies to be more human. Second, the social grouping "sex" occurs within other stratified social groups such as classes, races, and castes. The third difficulty, as the anthropologist's notion of ethnocentrism, the feminist critique of science, and modern cognitive psychology tell us, is that our perceptions are very likely to be biased by what we have seen (or not seen). Again, knowledge about several different human societies should help get us past this problem. In addition, we must be open-minded about the kinds of explanations or variables we accept. One of the simplest reasons for rejecting a theory is that it uses a different explanatory style than that one favors. If one insists on one variable, process, or explanatory style, one argues about what my computer science friends call "religious issues": deeply held preferences about what is true that cannot be argued. Religious stances about theories essentially concern what one accepts as an ultimate cause (e.g., nature, God, socialization). To the detriment of the development of integrative or "ecumenical" theories, humans are famous both for religious division and for not accepting the ultimate causes of alien cultures (or disciplines), as the following parable illustrates.

An anthropologist interviews a young informant about what holds the earth in the heavens. The informant explains that the earth rests on the back of an elephant. Having gotten a proximal explanation, the anthropologist asks the informant what holds up the elephant, and is told, "Giant turtles." The informant, when asked what holds up the turtles, replies, "It's turtles all the way down from there." At this point, the story is supposed to evoke laughter because no one in our culture accepts turtles as an ultimate cause.

One can easily imagine less mirthful responses to the story. A person could argue that the explanation is absurd because the informant had neglected to mention that it is eagles that the earth or turtles really rest on, so the other does not matter. That argument, in essence, is that only proximate or only distal causes matter. Such a narrow-minded view seems likely to produce a stunted theory. Another response would be that the whole story is wrong because, in actuality, the earth rests on wolves and then bears. If we have empirical evidence pointing to the presence of elephants and turtles *and* wolves and bears, then I think it behooves theorists to acknowledge this and to specify how all the causes coexist, rather than to argue that one ultimate cause is sufficient or superior. In this chapter, I outline a theory of human dominance, including male dominance, that includes sexual and other cultural factors and attempt to explain their interrelation.

To specify some other standards for the development of a theory of sexual politics, we can examine the reasons that several theories have been rejected. For brevity's sake, I will describe the theories in charicatured terms. Some functional theories (e.g., women are barred from "dangerous" politics to insure that children are nurtured) have been rejected because they have presumed that serving certain people's functions (e.g., children's, men's) is more important than serving other people's (e.g., women's). Such an argument could be made if it could be shown that everyone benefited by such priority, but otherwise it seems more sensible to avoid postulating theories that presume that a system or outcome that is clearly better for some people is equally good for everyone.

Psychologists, humanists, and, now, evolutionists tend to reject theories that posit societal functions; to them, the idea that societies are rational organisms who can identify and solve functional problems, or are the organisms upon which selection acts, makes no sense. Theoretical specificity could remedy either of these problems. If one's view suggests that cultures can be thought of metaphorically as organisms, one could say why by specifying the processes that link individuals with societies (e.g., how shared ideas coordinate action among members of a society, how individual survival is predicated on cultural survival, or how the less powerful have to conform to the standards enforced by the more powerful in order to survive). This has the additional advantage of specifying who the actors are and whether different people within the society behave similarly for the same or different reasons. The "history repeats itself" thesis that "we've always had male dominance so we'll always have male dominance" is unsatisfactory because it provides no process explanation and needlessly invokes inevitability. One fairly common version of this thesis, that patriarchy is ubiquitous, also ignores research on several societies organized in other ways. The "nature" explanations (e.g., "It is human nature to have male domination" or "Women, naturally, would rather play with children than engage in politics") make the same mistakes and thus are as meaningful (or meaningless) in answering the question of sexual politics as turtles.

ECUMENISM FOR FEMINIST AND EVOLUTIONARY THEORIES

What we need instead are *process models*: theories that specify a process by which predictor variables influence outcome variables that contribute to the degree of sexual inequality. Both feminist (sociocultural and socioeconomic) and evolutionary theories have produced process explanations of aspects of the gender gap in social power that are empirically testable. Contrary to popular belief, these paradigms are not necessarily at odds with one another. The two approaches share a special interest in individual variability, choice, gender differences, and family relationships. The main type of process that concerns each theory is interactions between persons and social environments that differentially influence the distribution of characteristics (e.g., body size, self-concepts, occupational roles) among individuals or subgroups. For example, role socialization and natural selection are both instances of this general process.

The feminist and evolutionary paradigms seem to differ most with respect to the "deepest" and most charicatured cause of the gender gap: nature versus nurture or culture. In my view, this is a false dichotomy. Humans are, and always have been, cultural creatures; culture is part of our nature. It is thus pointless to build theories that refuse to examine either nature or culture as having influence on the gender gap. A common reconciliation of this dilemma is to posit that "first we evolved biologically" and later "cultural evolution" became more important (e.g., see D. E. Brown, 1991, for a discussion). Not only does this view omit what more and more researchers suspect are very significant social-cultural influences on human evolution, but because we are still a sexually reproducing organism and exhibit a species-specific psychology (some of which is contingent on the kind of brains we have), biological factors cannot be relegated to ancient history. The view I take is that nature and culture cannot be meaningfully separated: they are mutually influential on each other and jointly influential on the nature of the gender gap. Another way to put this is that humans largely construct their own societies, which constitute the bulk of their selection environments.

The feminist and evolutionary paradigms also both emphasize history: in particular, elements of the past environment (including cultural norms, economy, etc.) influence the present and future. This approach suggests that we cannot simply specify that one kind of variable influences another in a linear fashion (e.g., cultural stereotypes cause gender differences in personality traits), but that dynamic influences are possible (e.g., not only do sex stereotypes influence gender differences, but people perceive men and women to be different and so form sex stereotypes). Specifying dynamic relationships may seem unparsimonious, but they are the only way to bring history, and therefore something other than proximal causes, into models. They also free us from the deterministic orientation that has sometimes been assumed about cultural and biological evolution.

Popular thinking has assumed that evolution and human cultural change are linear processes beginning with less development and accumulating more "progress" with time. This view implies two pernicious assumptions: (1) that there is essentially one dimension along which progress can be judged, and (2) that the status quo is the best "solution" available so far or, equivalently, that there is a grand design or best solution toward which we are heading. Both these stances seem to put the theory in the position of justifying what is, instead of explaining how it got that way, and again these stances are unnecessarily deterministic.

In this chapter, I begin to outline a dynamic theory that integrates social, political, economic, reproductive, cultural, and psychological factors into a model of sexual politics. I try to specify proximal and distal influences on the degree of sexual inequality, that is, what is elephant and what is turtle, but even more importantly, I do not assume that all patterns of causation must be strictly unidirectional. For reasons that become clear as the model is explicated, the model includes other forms of intergroup politics as well. The work presented here is a further development of social dominance theory (see Sidanius, 1993; Sidanius & Pratto, 1993a), which is illuminated as the chapter progresses.

ARENAS OF MALE DOMINANCE

A remarkable number of human societies share features of sexual politics (for similar descriptions, see Friedl, 1975; Sacks, 1979; and Sanday, 1981). The first arena of male dominance is society at large. In sexually unegalitarian societies, men more than women enjoy social status or prestige, the social currency associated with more social attention, resources, safety, positive self-regard, respect, and well-being (e.g., Rosaldo, 1974). The second arena is the elite. In political and other leadership positions, men predominate (e.g., D. E. Brown, 1991, p. 137). It is instructive to note that this has occurred in societies as small as that of the ancient Hebrews and as large as modern democracies, none of which even approach gender parity in their national legislatures, administrations, or party leadership (see Norris, 1987). The third arena of male dominance is social roles that maintain or enforce order within society, such as adjudicators, religious authorities, prosecutors, and police (e.g., Tiger, 1970; Vianello & Siemienska, 1990). Not all societies have such authorities, but, in those that do, women are not only rare or absent in such roles, but the ordering belief systems, exemplified in laws, religious canon, and professional regulations, often prohibit women from performing these roles. The fourth arena is those roles that maintain each society's dominance position with respect to other societies. In these roles governing intergroup relations, such as the military and the diplomatic corp, men also predominate. This male predomination occurs in some tribal societies such as the Yanomamö (e.g., Chagnon, 1992, p. 184), in democratic states such as the United States and France, and in dictatorships such as Iraq. Although occasionally women serve as soldiers and less often as military leaders, on the whole, war making is a male activity (Harris, 1993; Keegan, 1993, pp. 75–76).

In short, in male-dominant societies, men have more status, power, and authority within the society, and more coercive power toward outsiders, than women. Because of the exercise of differential authority, power, and force within the society, many male dominance societies are also internally stratified, often based on nonsexual groups such as class, ethnicity, nation, or the like. This means that some of the men in such societies may suffer from low status, low political power, and so forth, as well, and such men may be considered to be lower in the social hierarchy than upper-strata women. Social dominance theory analyzes the dominance relationships among social groups, and so the bulk of this chapter is devoted to stratified societies. At the end of the chapter, I discuss sexual politics in nonstratified societies.

GENDER DIFFERENCES AND POLITICS

Perhaps the simplest explanation one could provide for the gender gap in power, status, and roles is that men and women differ in their political-psychological characteristics. Before we discuss how this might happen, let us start with the question of whether such a gender difference exists, at least in the context of male dominance societies.

Bakan (1966) described the feminine orientation toward social relationships as *communal*, characterized as emotionally close, caring, and interconnected, and the masculine orientation as *agentic*, characterized as efficacious and powerful; similar distinctions have been made by many researchers of gender-linked personality differences (e.g., Bem, 1974; Block, 1984; Eagly, 1987; Eaton & Enns, 1983; Feshbach, 1982; Spence, Helmreich, & Stapp, 1975). In the political domain, Eisler and Loye (1983) characterized the two approaches as linking and ranking, suggesting that these approaches apply to intergroup, as well as to interpersonal, relationships. Sidanius, Cling, and Pratto's (1991) cross-national[1] review of the empirical literature on social and political attitudes showed that more women favor the establishment of equal status and wealth relationships between groups of people (*linking*) and more men favored the establishment of group-based hierarchies (*ranking*)—a gender difference in political orientation that also appears in political party affiliation.

For example, in a random sample of Swedish adolescents, Sidanius and Ekehammar (1980) found females to be less racist, more supportive of social equality, and lower in political-economic conservatism than males (see also Ekehammar & Sidanius, 1982). Furnham (1985) found the same gender differences in samples of middle-class British and English-speaking white South African adolescents. In a review of the major U.S. national opinion surveys from the 1950's to the early 1980's, Shapiro and Mahajan (1986) found substantial gender gaps (differences in proportion of support) for policies of violence and force. Men were more supportive than women of the use of troops in foreign countries, providing arms to foreign countries, defense spending, and the death penalty and were more opposed to gun control (see also Smith, 1984). The policies that women supported more than men were essentially redistributive (e.g., more spending on social welfare, education, health, and programs for the poor, black, and elderly, equalizing wealth, student loans, wage and price controls, and minimum incomes). Similarly, in a 1979 random sample of nearly 2,000 Canadian adults, Kopinak (1987) found that women supported the government welfare effort and organized labor more than men did.

CAUSES OF THE GENDER GAP IN
SOCIAL AND POLITICAL ATTITUDES

The ranking-versus-linking distinction might then be described as differing orientations toward social dominance or social inequality. My colleagues and I postulate that many attitudes pertaining to prejudice against outgroups and to policies that maintain unequal group relations are accounted for by a general individual difference variable called *social dominance orientation* (SDO), the degree of preference for one's own group to dominate other groups (e.g., Pratto, Sidanius, Stallworth, & Malle, 1994). People can desire or oppose group dominance without wanting to be leaders or to dominate other individuals themselves. In fact, social dominance orientation is uncorrelated with personality measures of interpersonal or task dominance (see Pratto et al., 1994). Social dominance oriented people favor group inequality in general, and so they also support ideologies that justify group inequality and policies that enforce or maintain group inequality. Reflective of the gender gaps in political attitudes noted above, people who are higher on social dominance orientation tend to support social policies that maintain unequal relationships among groups and to oppose social policies that would equalize resource distribution among groups. So, for example, SDO is positively related to support for the military (Pratto et al., 1994; Sidanius & Pratto, 1993b), police (Pratto et al., 1994; Sidanius, Liu, Pratto, & Shaw, 1994) and the police beating of Rodney King (Sidanius & Liu, 1992), going to war (Pratto et al., 1994; Sidanius & Liu, 1992), the death penalty (Mitchell, 1993; Pratto et al., 1994), and capitalism (Sidanius & Pratto, 1993b) and is negatively related to support for affirmative action (Pratto et al., 1994; Sidanius, Devereux, & Pratto, 1992), social programs, women's rights, and gay and lesbian rights (Pratto et al., 1994). In male dominance societies, we postulate that men are more social dominance oriented than women, and that the gender difference on SDO underlies the gender gap in political attitudes.

Let us examine the evidence for this hypothesis. Although the average gender difference on social dominance orientation is not large, it is quite robust. Among California college students, the gender difference on social dominance orientation was reliable in 10 of 12 samples, with an average effect size d of .54 (Pratto et al., 1994). In a random survey of about 1,000 Los Angeles area adults, social dominance orientation showed a reliable gender difference that was constant across culture of origin, income level, educational level, political ideology, and a number of other variables that influence social dominance orientation (Sidanius, Pratto, & Bobo, 1994). In every study in the United States and Sweden in which we have measured social dominance orientation or similar constructs, we have found that men are more oriented to social dominance than women (see also Sidanius, Cling, & Pratto, 1991; Sidanius et al., 1992; Sidanius, Pratto, & Brief, 1995; Sidanius & Pratto 1993a, 1993b).

If gender differences on SDO underlie the attitudinal gender gap, then the gender gap should disappear once individual differences in SDO are controlled. Pratto, Stallworth, and Sidanius (1995) tested this hypothesis in two surveys in which adults' attitudes toward a number of public policies were assessed along with SDO and gender. Sample 1 consisted of 478 San Francisco Bay area voters surveyed at the election polls on November 3, 1992. Sample 2 consisted of 463 undergraduates at San Jose State University (San Jose, CA) who completed an attitude and SDO survey during the fall or winter, 1990–1991. Despite our efforts, we did not obtain very large numbers of Hispanic and African-American voters, but all the other samples discussed in this chapter included substantial ethnic and income heterogeneity and approximately equal proportions of men and women (see description of samples in Table 9.1).

The voter sample was verbally administered an eight-item balanced SDO scale interspersed with nine policy attitude statements. The voters were told that their responses would be anonymous and to indicate whether they felt very negative, somewhat negative, neutral, somewhat positive, or very positive

TABLE 9.1.   Frequencies of Sex, Ethnicity, and Income Level in Samples

	Voters Sample 1		SJSU Sample 2		Stanford and SJSU Sample 3		UCLA Sample 4		SJSU Sample 5	
	N	%	N	%	N	%	N	%	N	%
Total	478	100	463	100	474	100	723	100	118	100
Sex										
Men	214	45	217	47	225	47	310	43	68	58
Women	258	54	245	53	246	52	402	56	50	42
Missing	6	1	1	0	3	1	11	1	0	0
Ethnicity										
Euro-American	336	70	175	38	179	38	234	32	18	15
Asian-American	31	7	186	40	168	35	167	23	77	65
Hispanic	18	4	36	8	57	12	145	20	14	12
African-American	55	12	21	5	32	7	63	9	1	1
Native American	4	1	34	7	5	1	29	4	0	0
Other	22	4	10	2	15	3	76	11	7	6
Missing	12	2	1	0	18	4	9	1	1	1
Yearly family income										
Under $20,000	28	6	57	12	32	7	69	10		
$20,000–$30,000	64	13	42	9	25	5	78	11		
$30,000–$40,000	40	8	51	11	21	4	70	10		
$40,000–$55,000	46	10	78	17	17	4	75	10		
$55,000–$70,000	75	16	91	20	30	6	79	11		
$70,000–$100,000	73	15	66	14	28	6	154	21		
$100,000–$150,000	73	15	35	8	18	4	45	6		
$150,000–$200,000	52	11	21	4	9	2	18	2		
over $200,000	—	—	22	5	6	1	27	4		
Missing	27	6	0	0	288	61	108	15		

SJSU = San Jose State University; UCLA = University of California at Los Angeles

about each statement. Sample 2 read similar instructions, but used seven-point evaluative scales. The SDO scales had adequate internal reliability (α = .71 for the smallest scale in Sample 1, above .81 in other samples; see items in Table 9.2). Men had higher SDO scores than women in Samples 1 and 2 ($p < .001$).

We tested whether a gender gap on preference for dominance policies was attributable to gender differences on SDO by testing for gender differences on the attitudinal variables before and after covarying SDO. On seven of the nine issues in Sample 1, there was a main effect for gender on the attitude ratings obtained (see Table 9.3). All of these were in directions consistent with previous research, with men preferring dominance policies and women egalitarian policies. SDO was a significant covariate at $p < .001$ for all items except "government support for business" ($p < .02$). After SDO was covaried, there

TABLE 9.2.   Social Dominance Orientation Items

Increased economic equality.* (1,2,3,4,5)
Inferior groups should stay in their place. (1,2,3,5)
In an ideal world, all nations would be equal.* (1,2,3,5)
Social charities just create dependency. (1,2,3,5)
Some groups of people are simply not the equals of others. (1,2,3,5)
Sometimes war is necessary to put other countries in their place. (1,2,3,5)
If people were treated more equally, we would have fewer problems in this country.* (1,2,3,4,5)
Increased social equality.* (1,2,3,4,5)
This country would be better off if we cared less about how equal all people were. (2,3,5)
Equality.* (2,3,4,5)
It is not a problem if some people have more of a chance in life than others. (2,3,4,5)
Too much effort at equality hurts a society. (2,3,5)
As a country's wealth increases, more of its resources should be channeled to the poor.* (2,3,5)
Those who are well-off can't be expected to take care of everyone else. (2,3,5)
Some people are just more deserving than others. (2,3,5)
All humans should be treated equally.* (2,3,5)
This country would be better off if inferior groups stayed in their place. (2,3,5)
The country that spends all its time trying to end poverty will never get ahead. (2,3,5)
Winning is more important than how the game is played. (4)
Getting ahead in life by almost any means necessary. (4)
Some people are just more worthy than others. (4)

Note: The asterisk indicates item was reverse coded. Subjects rated how negative to positive they felt about each item on either 1–5 (Sample 1) or 1–7 (Samples 2 to 5) scales. The samples in which each item was employed are indicated by number after each item.

were reliable gender differences only on government support for business and "public day care", and the residual effect sizes for gender were extremely small for all issues (under 1% of the variance). Thus, individual variability on SDO accounted for the variability in policy attitudes associated with gender and more; the effect sizes for SDO were all one or two orders of magnitude larger than the effect sizes for gender (see Table 9.3).

The more extensive survey in Sample 2 allowed us to construct policy scales for racial policies, gay/lesbian rights, social welfare programs, and military programs (see items and reliabilities in Table 9.4). Attitudes toward these four policy areas showed the predicted gender differences; women more supported gay/lesbian rights, racial policies, and social welfare programs, and men more supported military programs (see Table 9.5). Social dominance orientation was a reliable covariate on each attitude scale ($p < .001$), but after SDO was covaried from the attitudinal measures, a reliable gender difference remained only on the gay/lesbian rights scale ($p < .001$). As in Sample 1, SDO accounted for a much larger proportion of variance in policy attitudes than gender did (see effect sizes in Table 9.5).[2] Analyses of Samples 1 and 2 showed that, although a gender gap on policy attitudes exists, it is mainly attributable to individual differences on SDO that are gender linked.

We have also begun to study whether social dominance orientation underlies candidate preference and voting behavior. In Sample 1, the gender gap the United States has seen since 1980 (e.g., see Wirls, 1986)—women voting

TABLE 9.3.   Gender Differences and Social Dominance Orientation Effects
on Sociopolitical Attitudes, Sample 1

Issue	Mean Attitude, Women	Mean Attitude, Men	Sex Effect, $F(1, 414)$	Sex Effect Size, η^2	SDO Effect Size, η^2	Residual Sex Effect Size, η^2
Equal rights for women	4.84	4.69	5.2**	.012	.11	.004
Less aid to the poor	2.03	2.33	6.8**	.016	.24	.003
The U.S. military	3.14	3.46	7.1***	.017	.10	.007
Higher taxes on the rich	2.61	2.39	2.6	.006	.18	.000
Gay and lesbian rights	2.89	2.49	8.9**	.021	.25	.005
Government support for business	3.52	3.69	2.8	.006	.009	.009
Death penalty	2.94	3.30	5.5*	.010	.18	.003
Affirmative action	2.80	2.44	8.6**	.020	.16	.007
Public day care	3.23	2.91	8.3*	.020	.17	.007

Note: Sex effect and effect size show gender differences without including SDO in the analysis. SDO was then covaried and its effect size and the residual sex effect size reported.

*$p < .05$, **$p < .01$, ***$p < .001$. Voters indicated how they felt about each item by giving a number from 1 (very negative) to 5 (very positive).

for the Democratic presidential candidate in higher proportions than men—obtained $\chi^2(1) = 7.15$, $p < .007$, despite this sample's overwhelming vote for Bill Clinton (72% among women, 59% among men). Social dominance theory would expect this gender gap to be mediated by social dominance orientation and SDO-linked ideological beliefs. In particular, social dominance theory postulates that people who are higher on social dominance orientation support ideologies that legitimize group inequality and that people who support such ideologies support discriminatory policies and engage in discriminatory personal behavior (i.e., different behavior toward different groups).

We tested a path model derived from social dominance theory in which gender "predicted" SDO and SDO predicted policy attitudes, political ideology, and political party, which in turn predicted voting. The results showed that the gender gap in voting can be entirely accounted for by gender-linked differences on SDO that drive the other variables (Pratto, Stallworth, & Sidanius, 1995).

As shown by the paths in Figure 9.1, men were higher on social dominance orientation, which was positively related to Republican party identification, political conservatism, and support for the policies described above (coded so that they would all correlate positively with conservatism and SDO

TABLE 9.4.   Items on the Policy Scales and Internal Reliabilities, Sample 2

Racial policy (α = .71)
    Racial quotas to achieve integration
    Affirmative action
    School busing
    Civil rights
    Helping minorities get a better education
    Government helping minorities get better housing
    Government has no business helping any particular ethnic group in the job market.*

Gay/lesbian rights (α = .82)
    Gay or lesbian marriage
    Gay/lesbian rights

Social welfare programs (α = .78)
    Government-sponsored health care
    More support for early education
    Better support for the homeless
    Greater aid to poor children
    Reduced benefits for the unemployed*
    Low-income housing
    Free school lunches
    Arresting the homeless for sleeping in public places*
    Guaranteed jobs for all
    Increased taxation of the rich

Military programs (α = .67)
    Decreased defense spending
    The Strategic Defense Initiative (SDI)
    The B2 bomber (Stealth)

Note: Items with an * were reverse coded.

TABLE 9.5.   Gender Differences and Social Dominance Orientation Effects on Policy Attitudes, Sample 2

Attitude Scale	Female Mean, N = 245	Male Mean, N = 216	Sex Effect, $F(1, 459)$	Sex Effect Size, η^2	SDO Effect Size, η^2	Residual Sex Effect Size, η^2
Racial policy	5.15	4.83	16.4***	.035	.213	.005
Gay and lesbian rights	3.92	3.11	27.7***	.057	.106	.025
Social welfare programs	5.33	5.14	6.6**	.014	.307	.000
Military programs	3.24	3.54	7.2**	.016	.102	.002

Note: Items comprising scales are shown in Table 9.4. Respondents indicated how they felt about items by rating their responses from 1 (very negative) to 7 (very positive).
*p < .05, **p < .01, ***p < .001.

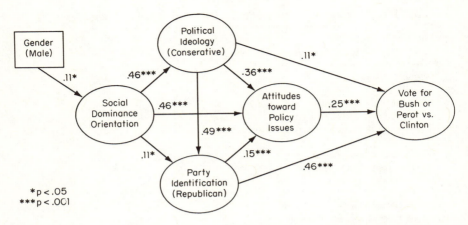

FIGURE 9.1.   Social dominance theory model of voting in the 1992 U.S. presidential election.

and averaged). Republicans, conservatives, and those supporting policies favored by high-SDO people tended to vote for Bush or Perot over Clinton. Moreover, it was not necessary to specify a direct path from gender to voting or to any other variable in order to make the model fit the data $\chi^2(5) = 7.74$, $p = .17$. An alternative model with political ideology as the driving variable in place of SDO failed to fit the data, suggesting that social dominance orientation better explains the gender gap for the kinds of policies measured than conservatism alone.

In a similar study, Pratto, Stallworth, and Conway-Lanz (1995) conducted a poll immediately after Clarence Thomas was confirmed to the Supreme Court. Opinion about this political appointment embodied a number of the ideologies we have found relate positively to social dominance orientation in the United States: meritocracy, conservatism, racism, and sexism (Pratto et al., 1994). Because of Thomas's anti-abortion rights position, his record as Equal Opportunity Commission chief, and Anita Hill's testimony that Clarence Thomas had sexually harassed her, we expected that support for Thomas might show a gender gap.

In October 1991, we telephoned Stanford University undergraduates whose social dominance orientation levels and support for meritocracy we had previously measured and asked them four questions: whether they favored appointing a black to the Supreme Court, whether they favored appointing a conservative to the Supreme Court, whether they believed Anita Hill's testimony that Clarence Thomas had sexually harassed her, and whether they would have voted for Thomas's confirmation if they had been in the Senate. Responses were given on scales from 1 (strongly disagree) to 7 (strongly agree) and the response rate was 100%. Although women ($M = 4.94$) believed Anita Hill's testimony more than men did, $M = 4.17$, $F(1, 162) = 11.3$,

$p < .001$, and were more opposed to Thomas's nomination, $M = 2.69$ for women, $M = 3.62$ for men, $F(1, 162) = 8.84$, $p < .003$, these gender differences could also be accounted for by social dominance orientation.

The social dominance model we fit for the 149 subjects for which we had complete data is shown in Figure 9.2. As usual, men were more social dominance oriented than women. People higher on social dominance orientation tended to believe in meritocracy, oppose appointment of a black to the Supreme Court, favor the appointment of a conservative to the Supreme Court, and disbelieve Anita Hill's testimony. All these ideologies were related to endorsement of Thomas's nomination: support for meritocracy, appointing a conservative, appointing a black, and disbelief of Anita Hill's testimony. Again, no direct path from gender to any variable except SDO was necessary to account for the data; the model shown in Figure 9.2 fit the data, $\chi^2(10) = 9.82$, not significant (n.s.).

The results of these two studies suggest that much of the gender gap in political attitudes (including policy support) and political behavior (including voting) may be driven by individual differences in social dominance orientation that are gender linked. Pratto, Stallworth, and Conway-Lanz (1994) also showed that social dominance models could account for gender differences in

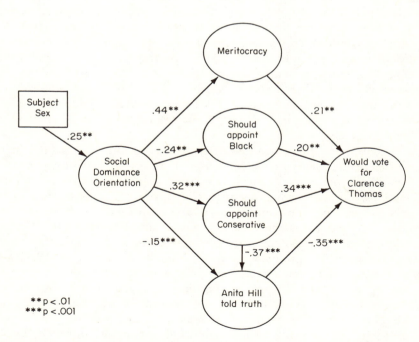

FIGURE 9.2. Social dominance theory model of support for Clarence Thomas's Supreme Court confirmation, October 1991.

support for the 1991 Iraq War, for social welfare programs, and for use of the death penalty.

CAUSES OF THE GENDER GAP IN ELITE POSITIONS

Because support for certain candidates for elite positions such as president and Supreme Court justice is related to SDO, we might also ask whether gender differences on attitudes or values associated with SDO are associated for the gender gap in the attainment of prestigious, elite, authoritative, and militaristic (or diplomatic) social roles. From the perspective of social dominance theory, these roles generally serve to maintain or increase social inequality. Roles that channel valued resources upward (e.g., natural and financial resources, information, property, and health care) or that channel negatively valued resource downward (e.g., toxic waste sites, prison terms), as typically the elite, business, and legal sectors do, we consider to be *hierarchy enhancing*. Similarly, roles and institutions that control the dissemination of ideas that help legitimize hierarchy, such as mainstream media and political leaders, are hierarchy enhancing (e.g., van Dijk, 1993). Roles or institutions that open access to resources (e.g., teachers and librarians) do this less, and those that redistribute resources in a way that is in opposition to the existing status structure (e.g., charity workers, public defenders, and social workers) were consider to be *hierarchy attenuating*. Other roles might be classified as *middlers* — those that neither strongly attenuate nor enhance social hierarchy.

Although definitive research is needed, I strongly suspect that a key feature of male-dominant societies is that men are overrepresented in hierarchy enhancing roles and women are overrepresented in hierarchy attenuating roles. For example, in the United States, currently 75% of lawyers and judges and 92% of police are men, whereas 77% of social service providers (Bureau of Labor Statistics, 1992, pp. 196–199) and a record "high" of 7% of the U.S. Senate are women.

To test this hypothesis in a smaller sample, I categorized, using the definitions of hierarchy role types above, Sample 1 (voters) into hierarchy attenuators, middlers, or hierarchy enhancers based on the respondents' reported occupations. To test whether men were overrepresented among hierarchy enhancers and women were overrepresented among hierarchy attenuators, I performed the χ^2 test of independence on gender and hierarchy role. The test showed that men and women were not represented in the hierarchy roles in proportion to their representation in the sample, with $\chi^2(2) = 19.7$, $p < .001$. Although this sample contained 54% women, attenuators were 67% women, middlers were 60% women, and enhancers were only 27% women.

As a comparison, I conducted the same tests on Samples 2 and 3, collected at colleges in 1990–1992. Student respondents in Samples 2 and 3 (which was the merger of four samples of undergraduates at Stanford University or San Jose State University) indicated their intended careers from a list of 20 that I subsequently categorized as hierarchy enhancing, middler, or hierarchy attenuating. In the college samples, women more intended to pursue hierarchy-attenuating careers and men more intended to pursue hierarchy-enhancing careers, as in Sample 1. In Sample 2, which contained 54% women, intended attenuators were 84% women, intended middlers were 48% women, and intended enhancers were 49% women, with $\chi^2(2) = 30.3, p < .001$. In Sample 3, which contained 57% women, intended attenuators were 74% women, intended middlers were 49% women, and intended enhancers were 59% women, with $\chi^2(2) = 14.78, p < .0001$. These samples show a gender gap in actual or intended role attainment along the hierarchy-enhancing/hierarchy-attenuating dimension.

Social dominance theory predicts that people who are higher on SDO or who hold hierarchy-enhancing beliefs (such as racism) will be found in hierarchy-enhancing roles, whereas people who are low on SDO and who hold hierarchy-attenuating beliefs (such as "we are all God's children") will be found in hierarchy-attenuating roles. For example, Sidanius, Pratto, Martin, and Stallworth (1991) found that college students pursuing majors likely to lead to hierarchy-enhancing careers such as business and law supported hierarchy-enhancing ideologies more than middlers, who supported such ideologies more than students pursuing hierarchy-attenuating careers such as library science and social work. Similarly, Sidanius, Liu, Pratto, and Shaw (1994) found that police officers are much more social dominance oriented than public defenders. Compared to both of these groups, the general public was in the center on social dominance orientation, suggesting that both police and public defenders recruit people with role-appropriate attitudes.

The causes of this pattern, and of the gender gap in hierarchy roles, are several. As noted above, there are often cultural prohibitions on women holding hierarchy-enhancing roles. Under those circumstances, individual preferences probably count for little of the gender gap in role attainment. When people are relatively free to choose their hierarchy role based on their own values and desires, we expect social dominance orientation to predict choice of hierarchy roles. To investigate such self-selection effects, Pratto, Stallworth, Sidanius, and Siers (1995) conducted two experiments in which college students chose between a hierarchy-enhancing or a hierarchy-attenuating job in each of 10 occupations (e.g., police officer, librarian, fundraising, investing, real estate development). We tried to make each job equally appealing and extremely similar in terms of its duties. For example, the hierarchy-enhancing public relations job description read:

> Communications director, Shell Oil. Produce videos, brochures, and other public relations materials that present a positive company image to potential investors and consumers. Maintain contacts with the press. Publicize company actions and intervene to counteract negative publicity. We consider this job vital to the company and its shareholders.

The hierarchy-attenuating public relations job description read:

> Communications director, United Way. Produce videos, brochures, and pamphlets that present our cause to the public and to potential donors. Maintain

contacts with the media. Educate the public about the need for community programs and about ongoing projects. You will be an important part of our program of community service.

Subjects were told to assume that the salary for each position within an occupation would be the same and that they were qualified for all jobs.

In Experiment 1, men chose more hierarchy-enhancing (vs. attenuating) jobs ($M = 4.45$) out of the 10 choices than women did ($M = 2.85$), $F(1, 90) = 9.80, p < .002$ and also had higher SDO scores ($M = 2.71$) than women ($M = 2.22$), $F(1, 155) = 5.48, p < .005$. When subjects' SDO score was covaried out of the number of hierarchy-enhancing jobs chosen, SDO was significantly related to the number of hierarchy-enhancing jobs chosen, $F(1, 93) = 47.7, p < .001$ ($r = .58$), and the gender difference disappeared, $p = .12$. In Experiment 2, we selected subjects extremely high or low on SDO to participate in the experiment, but matched men and women on SDO score. We expected high-SDO people to select hierarchy-enhancing jobs and low-SDO people to select hierarchy-attenuating jobs. For each occupation, low-SDO subjects chose the hierarchy-attenuating jobs over the hierarchy-enhancing jobs, whereas high-SDO subjects showed the opposite pattern. For example, 18 of 24 low-SDO subjects chose the hierarchy-attenuating public relations job described above, whereas 15 of 26 high-SDO subjects chose the hierarchy-enhancing public relations job, $\chi^2(1) = 6.61, p < .01$. Moreover, there was no hint that subject gender influenced job choice. In other words, when SDO levels were equated across sex, there was no gender difference in job preference.

However, personal preference may not be the only factor driving the gender gap in role attainment. In the analyses of the relation between gender and actual or intended occupation role in Samples 1, 2, and 3, the gender gap in role attainment was stronger in the voter sample than in the college samples. To test the relative influence of SDO versus other gender-linked factors' relation to hierarchy role, I regressed the trichotomous role variable on SDO and gender simultaneously. In Sample 1, SDO was positively related to hierarchy-enhancing role, $\beta = .12$, $t(399) = 2.40$, $p < .02$, and so was gender, $\beta = .19$, $t(399) = 3.91$, $p < .0001$. Whether the regression was performed hierarchically with gender or SDO entered first or was performed simultaneously, both gender and SDO had significant relationships to hierarchy role. Unlike in the self-selection experiments, social dominance orientation was unable to account entirely for the gender gap in hierarchy-role attainment in this sample of adults. In Sample 2, two main effects were also found: for SDO, $\beta = .17$, $t(435) = 3.43$, $p < .001$; for gender, $\beta = .14$, $t(435) = 2.78$, $p < .003$. In Sample 3, the regressions of hierarchy role on gender and SDO showed only a main effect for SDO, $\beta = .12$, $t(381) = 2.31$, $p < .02$. There are several possible reasons why SDO was more influential relative to subject's sex in the college samples compared to the voter sample; these include generational shifts in gender role expectations and opportunities for women or the greater ability of college-educated people to choose roles consistent with their own values.

Besides self-selection and gender bias, I suspect that sex stereotypes play a role in perpetuating the gender gap in role attainment. Generally, Americans believe that women are more liberal than men and that women are helpful, compassionate, kindhearted, and devoted to others (Bem, 1974; Ruble, 1983; Spence et al., 1975). Those beliefs may encourage parents, teachers, employers, and others to direct women into hierarchy-attenuating careers or to favor women in hiring decisions for those careers regardless of their individual qualities or preferences. Americans believe men are dominant, forceful, aggressive, ambitious, feel superior and have leadership qualities (Bem, 1974; Ruble, 1983; Spence et al., 1975), so men may be encouraged to apply for elite and authoritative jobs, may be favored in elections for such positions, and the like. In short, sex stereotypes serve as a model of how the world is and become the model of how the world should be (see also Eagly, 1987; Sanday, 1981). The fact that women are overrepresented in the most prototypic hierarchy-attenuating roles (e.g., social worker) and men are overrepresented in the most prototypic hierarchy-enhancing roles (e.g., soldier) may cause people to hold these gender-role associations in mind when considering who to hire for such roles (Eagly & Steffen, 1984).

I therefore predicted that people would try to hire those who have "role-appropriate" social and political attitudes for the positions to be filled. To test these hypotheses, Pratto, Stallworth, Sidanius, and Siers (1995) conducted two hiring experiments in which subjects read the résumés of four recent (fictitious) college graduates and selected the "applicants" for hierarchy-enhancing and hierarchy-attenuating jobs (using descriptions from the previous experiment). We actually created four versions of each applicant by varying their sex and apparent SDO level with information on their résumés (e.g., Rebecca or Michael Davis had either worked as a camp counselor at a preparatory summer camp or for a head start program). In doing so, we controlled the other credentials (e.g., college major and work experience) each applicant had across the applicant's gender and apparent SDO level. Each subject read résumés of a high and low SDO male and a high and low SDO female. Subjects indicated which of these was the best applicant for a set of hierarchy-enhancing and hierarchy-attenuating jobs. As expected, subjects tended to hire high SDO applicants for hierarchy-enhancing jobs and low SDO applicants for hierarchy-attenuating jobs. Also, despite the facts that, in this experiment, applicant sex and apparent SDO were orthogonal, and across conditions, the credentials of the male and female applicants were identical, subjects also tended to hire men for hierarchy-enhancing jobs and women for hierarchy-attenuating jobs. Even in the face of "individuating" value information that seems relevant to the hierarchy role, subjects apparently relied on sex stereotypes to decide what kinds of jobs men and women would do well or should perform.

The self-selection experiments suggests that a gender-linked individual difference, SDO, could drive some of the gender bias in role attainment; the hiring experiments show that sex stereotyping—independently of the preferences or qualifications of applicants—could also drive the bias. My view is that in the real world, both may go on, and moreover, that they feed into one another. Although stereotypes are not always accurate portraits of individuals, stereotypic images of gender and role can influence development of our own self-images and others' impressions and expectations of us (Deaux & Major, 1987). Through their influence on the development of individual personalities, then, stereotypes influence the distribution of people into social roles (e.g., Eccles, 1987; O'Leary, 1974). In particular, if girls are trained to feel good for helping others and boys to feel good for outranking others, the gender-linked personality types are created that are likely to desire hierarchy-attenuating or -enhancing roles. Some preliminary evidence is relevant to this hypothesis. Pratto et al. (1994) found that SDO is negatively related to communality, altruism, and concern for others (emotional empathy). People who assume that their own outcomes are linked to others tend to be more egalitarian and more opposed to group dominance. On the "masculine" side, SDO does not have to do with wanting mere influence; Pratto et al. (1994) found no relationship between SDO and agency or interpersonal dominance. But, the "provider" aspect of the "male" role stereotype may also contribute to the gender gap in role attainment. In college Samples 2 and 3, SDO was positively related to the amount of money subjects intended to make 10 years after graduating from college.

OCCUPATIONAL ROLES AS A VEHICLE FOR THE GENDER GAP IN SOCIAL STATUS

The gender bias in role attainment has implications for the gender gap in prestige and political power because societies (particularly, it seems, male dominance ones) confer different amounts of status on the doers of different tasks (D. E. Brown, 1991).[3] In male-dominant societies, labor is divided between males and females and male tasks are more respected than female tasks, indicating that cultures can use gendered roles to confer more status on men than women (see also Rosaldo, 1974; Sanday, 1974). It is important to note what is arbitrary and what is not about this pattern. The fact that particular roles (e.g., gardening, cooking, house building) belong to men in some societies and to women in others (see D. E. Brown, 1991) gives lie to ideological notions that any particular division of labor is necessary or "natural" or that women contribute no value except babies to the society. For example, the long-held belief that women are incapable of hunting is belied by the examples of the Mbuti, among whom youths, men, and women hunt together with nets (e.g., Turnbull, 1983), and the Agta, whose women hunt with machetes and dogs (Estioko-Griffin & Griffin, 1981; see also Dahlberg, 1981; Slocum, 1975, on female provisioning). Among many African traditional societies, women were the primary food providers (e.g., Boserup, 1986). In male dominance societies, it is quite systematic which sex gets the high-status roles and which roles get high status. The most telling clue that labor divisions by gender can be vehicles for conferring more status on men come from studies that show that, when the gender composition of an occupation changes, the status accompanying that occupation changes so that male or male-dominated occupations still confer the most status. There is evidence that, as women enter male-dominated, high-prestige occupations, the pay and prestige associated with these occupations declines in both industrialized (e.g., Reskin, 1988) and nonindustrialized (e.g., Sanday, 1974) societies. The gender bias in occupational roles is then a very significant proximate cause of the gender gap in social status, income, and political power.

This evidence suggests that it is not the content or consequences of the role, but, rather, the prestige of the people performing the role that connotes privilege. That is, it may well be the case that whatever qualities or behaviors the elite can more easily exhibit become those most valued by members of their society (cf. Dahrendorf, 1968, p. 174). This is not typically how members of a society would understand the relation between valued characteristics and social status or prestige. They, instead, seem usually to accept the notion that those who have the valued quality have somehow earned or deserve prestige or privilege (see Collier, 1988, for an extended discussion).

Thus, further analysis of why status is socially conferred on males is warranted. I wish to add to this discussion by considering the relationship of social dominance orientation to status striving. We define SDO as the desire for one's group to dominate other groups. High-SDO people not only hold legitimizing myths to be true, they also discriminate more against out-group members, especially when they strongly identify with their in-group (Sidanius, Pratto, & Mitchell, 1994) or when their group's status is threatened (Levin & Sidanius, 1993). Because striving for social status and social dominance orientation are linked, we must also reconsider why men are more social dominance oriented than women.

CAUSES OF THE GENDER DIFFERENCE ON SOCIAL DOMINANCE ORIENTATION

As a personality variable concerned with social relationships, it would be quite surprising if social dominance orientation and concomitant attitudes were not responsive to social influence. There is considerable indirect evidence that they are. For example, Sidanius et al. (1991) found that college students' racist attitudes declined over their tenure in school, and the rate of the decline was influenced by the hierarchy role associated with their majors. Law and business students did not decrease in racism as much as the rest of university students. Cross-cultural differences are another form of evidence. The Swedish adolescents studied by Sidanius and Ekehammar (1980) were much more egalitarian than the English and, especially, than the South African adolescents studied by Furnham (1985), as one might expect based on the huge differences in racist and sexist policies in those countries. In a random survey of Los

Angeles, people from Asian and Hispanic backgrounds had higher SDO levels than Euro-Americans and African-Americans (Sidanius, Pratto, & Bobo, 1994), which was also true in the present samples. The hierarchical nature of Hispanic and Asian societies may be reflected in those higher SDO levels; among immigrants, longer stays in the United States were associated with lower SDO levels (Sidanius, Pratto, & Bobo, 1994).

Social dominance theory postulates that people who belong to lower-status groups will have lower levels of social dominance orientation. In addition to the gender differences on SDO, we have evidence of this pattern across two other kinds of group-status designations: ethnic group and sexual orientation. Blacks and hispanics have lower SDO levels than whites, and gays, lesbians, and bisexuals have lower SDO levels than straights (Choudhury & Pratto, 1995). Although we have yet to document the processes that could lead to lower SDO levels in lower-status groups, three come to mind: 1) People may "learn" SDO by generalizing from the legitimizing myths that they learn in their society (e.g., racism, sexism, heterosexism). Because myths that say that one's group is inferior conflict with one's basic need for positive self-regard (cf. Crocker & Major, 1989), low-status group members may reject such myths and become suspicious of similar myths. 2) In a similar way, SDO and belief in legitimizing myths may serve positive identity needs for members of high status groups, so high status group members may "feel better" about social dominance in general. Sidanius, Pratto, and Rabinowitz (1994) and Choudhury and Pratto (1995) have found results compatible with these two predictions in that SDO is positively related to in-group identification for high-status group members, but negatively related for low-status group members. 3) The experience of entitlement and self-knowledge about one's own abilities, ambitions, hard-work, and so forth may lead high status group members to feel that the kind of social standing they have is both normal and deserved.

It may be the case, then, that the status difference between men and women is a cause of the gender difference on SDO. We have reason to believe it is not the only cause because the gender difference on SDO and related variables is thus far invariant across different societies that differ in the relative status of men and women. Sidanius, Ekehammar, and Ross (1979) found no difference in the magnitude of gender differences on social and political attitudes between Swedish and Australian youth. Furnham (1985) found very few gender interactions by nationality in comparing British and South African youths. Sidanius et al. (1991) found no gender interactions by ethnic group on racism measures among 5,600 Texas college students, even controlling for sexism. One gendered construct that correlates negatively with SDO, empathic concern for others (Pratto et al., 1994), was measured by Stimpson, Jensen, and Neff (1992) in U.S., Korean, Thai, and Chinese college students. Stimpson et al. found women to be more concerned about others than men, but found no gender interaction by nationality. In several studies by different researchers, the size of the gender differences on ranking and linking variables was constant across cultures. These cultures vary substantially in their economies and ideologies concerning gender and dominance, but they all have the features of male dominance societies I described above.

In the present samples, I tested whether professional-role socialization mediated gender difference on SDO by testing whether the variance in SDO associated with actual or intended hierarchy role eliminated the gender difference on SDO. In analyses of variance (ANOVAs) on SDO in Samples 1, 2, and 3, hierarchy role and gender each had reliable effects and did not interact. Thus, there were significant gender differences between men and women pursuing the same type of hierarchy role. Similarly, in a random sample of about 1,000 adults, the gender difference on SDO was neither increased nor decreased by educational level, political ideology, abortion rights attitude, and a plethora of other socialization variables—even when all such variables were simultaneously considered (Sidanius, Pratto, & Bobo, 1994). The robustness and constancy of the gender difference on social dominance orientation suggests that this difference is about something even more centrally related to gender in male dominance societies than the cultural relative status difference between men and women, hierarchy role, or political ideology.

REPRODUCTIVE STRATEGIES AND THE GENDER GAP IN STATUS AND SOCIAL DOMINANCE ORIENTATION

At this point, then, the two important aspects of the gender gap in male dominance societies that must be explained are why men are more social dominance oriented than women and why societies confer more status on men, on average, than on women. The inroad to the problem of the gender gap I have not yet used is the family, but it involves all the essential elements: men and women, society, politics, culture, sexual relationships, and economics. The existence of families is of course universal, and, although families vary in form, marriage and children are elements of family life in all societies (e.g., D. E. Brown, 1991). The two chief questions all people might ask themselves then are "Who will my mate (or mates) be?" and "How will my children be cared for?" While some may consider these personal and even "private" choices, the fact is that they influence, and are influenced by, all kinds of social, economic, and political aspects of the surrounding society (cf. Okin, 1989). By considering family relationships, I will outline how evolutionary theory can be brought to bear on the gender gap in social status and social dominance orientation. Rather than taking the view that reproductive aspects of behavior are the distal causes of gender inequality, I discuss them within their cultural context. Postulating this as a dynamic, and not just as a historical, model will allow me to discuss how differences in the degree of gender inequality across societies might occur and what kinds of reproductive patterns characterize nonstratified societies.

Evolutionary theories are fundamentally about the relationship between organisms and their environment. They concern, then, how dynamic systems work and so can serve as a model for understanding social systems. Evolutionary theories are not alternative explanations to "situational" (e.g., cultural, social psychological, historical, structural) theories—in fact, they might be considered the grandparent of situational theories in that they predict that organisms will change their behavior and their features in different environments. In addition, evolutionary theories do not assume that organisms are passive recipients of environmental influence. For social animals, society is a very significant adaptive environment; so, both how creatures are influenced by it and how they create or change it are core concerns of evolutionary theories. This is essentially why evolutionary theories enable one to postulate dynamic models.*

Although it should go without saying, I must also state that evolutionary theories of human behavior do not suppose that humans do not make choices, are "hard wired" or "predestined" to do anything, or that adaptive behaviors are desirable (e.g., Betzig, 1988). But, like psychoanalytic theory, behaviorism, and much of modern psychology, evolutionary approaches can posit that organisms do not always know the (evolutionary) reasons for their behavior. Along with other evolutionary psychologists, it appears to me that some psychological processes or propensities, particularly expectations, preferences, and beliefs, may be the proximate causes of adaptive behaviors. In fact, learning culturally particular attitudes, ideologies, and behavioral repertoires seems necessary for performing behaviors that are adaptive within one's culture.

Another false criticism of evolutionary theories is that they state that anything is adaptive. On the contrary, evolutionary theories do not pretend that everyone does equally well in life. Rather, variance on attributes is necessary to discuss their relationship to the environment or adaptive fitness. To the extent this variance can be attributed to certain features, behaviors, environments, and so forth, the features are said to be "adaptive." Adaptive is not to be equated with moral, right, valuable, coping, optimal, attractive, and the like; evolutionary theories do not prescribe how organisms ought to live (unlike social Spencerian "theories"). I review the processes and tenets of evolutionary theory as they are most relevant to the questions I have raised here. Before continuing, I point out that evolutionary theory did not begin as a genetic theory and in fact is much broader than genetic theory.

Darwin (1871) identified mate choice as an enormously influential act in that, if individual members of a species are differentially selected to be mates, their characteristics would be differentially passed on to the next generation or *sexually selected*. This would change the nature of the future social environment, particularly the kinds of mates available to the next generation. For this reason, sexual selection can give rise to much faster change than natural selection alone (Fisher, 1930). *Homo sapiens sapiens* evolved very quickly to have different brains than other primates, so sexual selection has been used to

---

*Indeed, recent thought on the nature of evolutionary theory might suggest that evolutionary theories must be dynamic, relational models (e.g., Caporael, 1995; Oyama, 1985).

explain many aspects of the ways humans have evolved into the psychological and cultural creatures that we are (e.g., Barkow, 1989; Barkow, Cosmides, & Tooby, 1992; Fox, 1972; Miller, 1993; Parker, 1987).

Trivers's (1972) development of sexual selection in parental investment theory has been employed by many evolutionary social scientists (see Kenrick, Sadalla, Groth, & Trost, 1990; Kenrick, Groth, Trost, & Sadalla, 1993, for social exchange qualifications to the theory). The central thesis is that the sex investing the most in the offspring should be the most selective about mating. This has two major consequences: (1) usually, females will be more choosy than males about mating, for example, about the mate, the timing, and accompanying conditions such as physical, family, or economic conditions; and (2) female mate choice will have more influence on the attributes passed along to the next generation than male mate choice.

There is considerable cross-cultural evidence consistent with the female choosiness thesis in humans (as well as in birds and other mammals). For one, there is more variability in male marriage rates and reproductive success (number of surviving offspring) than in female marriage rates and reproductive success (e.g., Betzig, 1988; Chagnon, 1979; Daly & Wilson, 1978, p. 59; Wilson & Daly, 1992, p. 300). This is presumably because fewer women are rejected as mates than are men. Also, women express greater choosiness in their preferences of potential mate's qualities than men do consistently across many cultures: in the United States (Buss & Barnes, 1986; Coombs & Kenkel, 1966; Kenrick et al., 1990; Pratto, Sidanius, & Stallworth, 1993), Germany (Buss & Angleitner, 1989), France (Murstein, 1976), Canada (Wakil, 1973), Malaysia (Liston & Salts, 1988), and a host of other countries (Buss, 1989b; see reviews by Buss, 1992; Feingold, 1992).

If we assume that investing in one child reduces a man's ability to invest in another (see Trivers, 1972), then parental investment theory suggests that men should also be choosy in their mate selection. In fact, men are not uninterested in the same mate characteristics as women are, they are just slightly less preferential about them (e.g., Buss, 1989b). In humans, female fertility is well concealed, but men who are sexually attracted to infertile women would not have many children, so sexual attraction to women who appear fertile may be adaptive in men (e.g., Buss, 1989b). Physical attractiveness is the one dimension that, cross-culturally, men say is more important in a mate than women do (Buss, 1989b; Buss & Angleitner, 1989; Buss & Barnes, 1986; Coombs & Kenkel, 1966; Kenrick et al., 1990; Liston & Salts, 1988; Murstein, 1976; Pratto et al., 1993; see Buss, 1992; Feingold, 1992, for reviews). It is possible that physical attractiveness serves as a cue for a good mate "investment"; Cunningham (1986) showed that men were more willing to make sacrifices for, invest in, and take risks for, more facially attractive women. Also, one distally observable, distinctly feminine attractiveness feature, low waist-to-hip ratio, is actually adaptively significant in women. Low waist-to-hip ratio is associated with absence of serious diseases, fertile age of life, and fertility in women and is also perceived by men across generations to indicate physical attractiveness, sexiness, and healthiness in women (Singh, 1993). It is not now clear whether any other aspects of feminine attractiveness are actually related to reproductive success, and so there may be other reasons for this "male preference."

Intersexual and Intrasexual Competition

According to evolutionary theory, whenever one sex exerts more mate choice (as generally females do), the other sex is pressured to regain influence by competing with same-sex rivals for selection as mates. This implies that conflict between the sexes can occur due to alternative mating and child-rearing strategies, and that the between-sex conflict can drive within-sex conflicts. For example, Parker (1987) posits that hominid males made the adaptation against female choosiness by controlling access to resources mates would want or need, such as high-protein food and good shelters. Logically, males who secured mates in this way were more likely to father children, and their children were more likely to survive aided by the protein and shelter that their fathers provided. Such a process could easily be played out through material and symbolic culture; men could try to monopolize the economic means to status and societally defined status symbols as a way of attracting or making claims to mates (see also Buss, 1989b, 1994, pp. 215–218; Pratto et al., 1993). That is, men who keep material wealth, status symbols, and so forth for themselves—away from other men and from women in general—could benefit by wooing or claiming women.

Conflict among men would then be expected over social dominance and status, an adaptive reason for male "ranking" behavior. In fact, death by homicide or by legal intervention is far more common among men than among women in the United States, and men in the lowest status ethnic group, blacks (see Sidanius & Pratto, 1993a), have the highest such mortality rate (U.S. Department of Health and Human Services, 1990, pp. 139–140). In nonstratified societies, lower ranked men are often younger men, and several studies show either that there is a population dearth of young men or that they are married at much lower rates than older men (Boserup, 1986, pp. 44–45; Chagnon, 1979; Collier, 1988; Fox, 1972). The particular means by which different societies exclude young men from being able to marry vary widely from denying them jobs to warfare to death from exposure. However, it is clear that societal practices contribute to the marriage and sometimes to mortality inequality among men.

Returning to between-sex conflict, it is clear that male status monopolization entails unequal control of resources (real or symbolic) and so is predicated on unequal power (see also Gailey, 1987; Okin, 1989). Power can be effectively, if expensively, garnered through coercion, so male coercion of females can be expected in male dominance societies. Rape and other violence against women may be signs of such coercion and, in fact, are much more frequent in male dominance societies than in nonstratified societies (Schwendinger & Schwendinger, 1983). But, power can also be effectively held through consensual social mechanisms such as shared ideologies (e.g., Sidanius et al., 1991).

That is, social dominance theory postulates that, when a dominant group is able to convince subordinate group members of its innate superiority (of its "right" to resources it controls) and of the need to follow the dominant group's rules concerning resource acquisition, less coercion will be required to maintain inequality. In male dominance societies, there is a female preference that I suspect makes coercion less "necessary": females show a preference for high-status mates (e.g., Buss, 1992; Feingold, 1992). Within this system of economic, intersexual, and family relationships, male monopolization of status and female selection of high-status mates may be complementary adaptive strategies for the two sexes. In several such societies, higher status men (and women) do have more thriving children (e.g., Betzig, 1993; Chagnon, 1979; Fox, 1972). This does not imply that these strategies, or the social systems they produce, are optimal. Rather, male monopolization of status resources and female preference for high-status mates are adaptive mating strategies to each other. This implies that gender differences in mating strategies may be due to some ancient selected biases or due to responses to the local mating environment or both.

The other mating dimension of particular male concern is paternity certainty. That is, females (unless anesthetized at the time of birth) know that the children they bear are theirs, but males may be less certain about parentage. Parental investment theory postulates that species requiring much care, as humans do, may increase reproductive success to the extent the child receives care. Parental investment theory also suggests that, across species, males should engage in mate-guarding tactics to the extent that they invest in their mate and offspring. Several researchers have suggested various psychological, behavioral, and legal adaptations for males as guards against paternity uncertainty. Strong emotional reactions to sexual jealousy is one mediator. Buss, Larsen, Westen, and Semmelroth (1992) demonstrated that American men can be more easily upset from threats of sexual infidelity than women. Wilson and Daly (1992) postulate that a great deal of homicide and wife battering stems from male sexual jealousy, and that a very large number of human legal systems tolerate physical punishment, including beating and murder, for adultery on the part of women, but not on the part of men. The legal as well as the psychological studies show that socially defined conceptions of "mine" are very important mediators of the devices that men may use to enforce particular child-rearing strategies. Although greater male than female sexual jealousy is widespread, it is very important not to overstate the extent to which it is driven by the "biological fact" of internal fertilization within females. Social arrangements such as *matriliny*, in which children are attributed to the mother's line and men nurture children not only in their wife's home, but in their sisters' homes, should produce less male sexual jealousy. In fact, although male sexual jealousy is not unheard of in nonstratified societies, many of the behaviors presumed to be consequences of it, such as wife battering, murder of wives suspected of infidelity, and abuse of stepchildren, are less common in nonstratified societies (compare Schwendinger & Schwendinger, 1983, with Daly & Wilson, 1988).

Power and the Use of Culture to Enact Mating Strategies

Because humans' parental investments, or child care, are not limited to fertilization and pregnancy, we must consider cultural aspects of reproduction along with biological investment. In particular, we must consider social and political power as a reproductive resource. When people can exert influence over their society, I expect them to try to create cultural environments to be adaptive to them. That is, more powerful people will have more social influence, resulting in social environments that favor their mating strategies. In this light, consider whose mating strategies are facilitated in male dominance societies. In general, men, particularly an elite few, are powerful and have high status. Monopolizing high-status roles for men, and therefore making women desperate for status resources, could be a mating strategy for men, especially for high-status men. Likewise, cultural practices or laws concerning adultery, murder, and divorce often tolerate male sexual jealousy, but not female sexual jealousy; moreover, they show a class bias (see Betzig, 1989; Daly & Wilson, 1988; Dickemann, 1981; see Leacock, 1981; Lepowsky, 1990, on societies that do not have sex-biased adultery customs or laws). Dickemann posits that a number of other sociocultural customs (e.g., periods of engagement, claustration, chastity belts, and veiling) found in male dominance societies are adaptations to increase paternity certainty. Because women who mate with (and, especially, who marry) high-status men differentially benefit from male status monopolization, one could even expect some women to support stratification and the sexist cultural practices that help enable it. Indeed, it is upper-caste women in India (e.g., Dickemann, 1979), elderly upper-class women in China (Ebrey, 1990, p. 217), and elder women in much of Africa (e.g., Dorkenoo & Elworthy, 1992, p. 7; Sanderson, 1981, pp. 19–20) who impose veiling, footbinding, and genital mutilation, respectively, on young girls to make them "marriageable" to high-status men.

SEXUAL POLITICS AND DIVERGENT
REPRODUCTIVE STRATEGIES

The crux of sexual politics is the extent to which different people's reproductive strategies, including mating and child rearing, diverge. Sex differences in parental certainty and pregnancy and lactation are one way that male and female reproductive strategies diverge, but they are only part of the story. Aspects of culture, including divisions of labor, economy, beliefs about ownership and parental responsibility for children, family patterns, economic patterns of exchange, sharing, and ownership, mate selection, codes of sexual behavior, marriage and inheritance customs, and so forth influence the extent to which male and female child-rearing strategies diverge. Rather than being an antidote or add-on to reproductive processes, culture is, then, an integral part of them. For example, if women are expected to raise children, and if raising children effectively bars one from holding powerful roles, acquiring the symbols of status within one's culture (such as money) and so forth, then divergent reproductive strategies lead to inequality between men and women in terms of status and power as well. If, on the other hand, children bring one political power, social prestige, or material wealth, and children are equally attributed to both parents, then child rearing need not lead to sexual inequality.

Because polygyny is so common in human societies, it bears examination in some detail. In terms of reproduction, a given man could hypothetically impregnate many women and so beget more children than any of the women is capable of bearing. Further, in polygynous families, the children of the father and a given mother are not the same set. Hence, the child-rearing strategies and reproductive interests of men and women in polygyny diverge. In particular, the children of one such union are the mother's only "reproductive success," but may not be the father's only "reproductive success," so it is less reproductively costly to him to withdraw support for a given set of those children. If children spend more time with their mother than with their father, it may be less emotionally difficult for the father to withdraw contact and support from the children. When one member of a party is more easily able to withdraw from a social contract, we say that that person has more power. Between men and women, then, polygyny may be characterized by power inequality.

Note, however, that there may be other aspects of social exchange that make the way polygyny is practiced in some societies entail more-equal relationships between men and women than the preceding paragraph suggests. For example, in much of Africa, men control the land, but women and their children do nearly all of the farm labor, which provides for the family. Thus, acquiring more wives can make men richer because, with more laborers, their farm becomes more productive (Boserup, 1986, p. 37). This suggests that, when women are good providers (and not just as mothers), men become motivated to acquire many wives (see Harris, 1993, for a similar argument). Women who provide food and clothing for themselves and for their children are even more of an economic asset, and that practice is not uncommon. A majority of women in such societies prefer polygynous marriage because, since each wife is supposed to provide food and perform domestic chores for her husband, it means each has less housework to do (Boserup, 1986, p. 43). Women may still control the earnings of their own businesses and so enjoy considerable autonomy, including, at times, the ability to earn back their dowry and get out of the marriage (Boserup, 1986, p. 47).

There is considerable variety of opinion as to whether polygyny is associated with equality or inequality among women. In part because polygamy became more prevalent after colonialists abolished domestic slavery in much of Africa, the status of the younger wife or wives is akin to that of an assistant or servant to the first wife (Boserup, 1986, p. 45). In short, lower ranked wives may not enjoy much freedom from doing chores, and the children of lower ranked wives may obtain fewer resources than those of first wives (e.g., Bledsoe, 1993). Moslem law dictates that men may have no more than four wives, and that each wife must be both provided for and treated equally; thus, many African women prefer Moslem polygynous marriage (Boserup, 1986, p. 46).

Whether or not polygyny implies the subjection of women, because humans bear males and females in very nearly equal ratios, polygyny entails unequal reproductive outcomes among men. Male competition over women is thus a central source of political activity. On a gross level, variations in stratification may vary systematically to the extent that societies are polygynous. For example, in contrast to cross-species comparative studies that estimate that early hominid societies had only mild polygyny and dominance (e.g., Alexander, 1989; Barkow, 1989; Daly & Wilson, 1978), some of the first human civilizations were highly polygynous, highly oppressive dominance systems. Betzig's (1986, 1993) study of the first six well-known state civilizations shows that enormously wealthy, despotic men were hugely reproductively successful not only through monopolizing access to women from far and near (tens to thousands of them apiece) and keeping these women submissive to their sexual control, but also through exploiting other men's labor to support their families and to maintain their political predominance. In some contemporary male dominance societies, high-status men are much more often polygynous than low-status men, having either multiple wives (simultaneously or in succession), mistresses or concubines, female slaves who are raped, sexual license with other men's wives, or all of these (e.g., see Chagnon, 1979; Dickemann, 1979, 1981). The enactment of the high-status male mating strategy through societies seems to be able to produce several other characteristics of male dominance societies: inequality within the society (e.g., based on class, ethnicity, family), exploitation of out-groups, unequal sexual freedom or consequent obligations, and economic dependence for women or for their children.

The human opportunity for divergent reproductive strategies is why many aspects of politics, including sexual inequality, stratification within societies, and domination of out-groups, are sexual—not just gendered, but with sexual relationships at their core (see also Betzig, 1986, 1991, 1993; Dickemann, 1979, 1981; Tiger & Fox, 1971). Many of the behavioral strategies that enable polygyny are oppressive. Consider situations in which women choose high-status, but polygynous, mates (see Dickemann, 1979, for an analysis of this female choice). In such societies, many females compete with each other to marry few, very-high-status males. One of the females' chief intrasexual competitive strategies is to submit themselves or their kinswomen to sexual control devices such as footbinding (see Betzig, 1991; Dickemann, 1979, 1981). Thus, the fact that women are more precious as marriage partners in polygynous cultures sometimes produces the ironic effect that women are culturally devalued.

One sexual strategy made attractive by polygyny is to exploit the human and sexual resources of people outside one's group. I suspect that the commonest form of this oppression is based on the male strategy of seeking female mates from outside the local society. Consider the extreme, but common, fact that men raid their neighbors and rape or steal women and girls in modern wars (e.g., Brownmiller, 1975; Chagnon, 1979) and in ancient myths (e.g., Trojan War). Indeed, the rape or kidnapping of out-group women is a dominant symbol of conquest and colonization—recall Romulus's mythical rape of the Sabine women in the founding of Rome and witness the systematic rape in Bosnia (e.g., Rodrigue, 1993) and Rwanda (Ms., 1995) today. Economic exploitation of colonies or within one's society is an adaptive strategy for high-status, polygynous, politically powerful men in at least two ways. First, by definition it means that the fruits of other people's labor can be used to support wives and children of the polygamist (Betzig, 1993). Second, if elite men successfully control the economic system or means of production, other men may end up with too little status to be attractive as mates to women. Consistent with this notion, in the United States, fewer poor men than rich men are married, and poor men have fewer children (e.g., Rockwell, 1976).

Social Dominance Orientation and Mating Strategies

The form of dominant polygyny just described entails the oppression of women and of out-groups, the two hallmarks of human hierarchy that social dominance theory seeks to explain. For men, supporting dominant polygyny may be a mating strategy, so the psychological qualities captured by social dominance orientation may be adaptive for men. That is, men who engage in the behaviors expected of high SDO persons, such as monopolizing status resources, derogating out-group males, assisting political alliances that restrict women's power, and so forth, may have higher reproductive success than men who do not within such social systems.

This suggests that sexual selection pressures may cause the gender difference for social dominance orientation. Exactly how this occurs is not known. One possibility is that early hominids lived in dominant polygynous societies (Alexander, 1989; Barkow, 1989; Daly & Wilson, 1978), so the propensity to oppress women and out-groups could have been sexually selected in early hominid polygyny. That is, the variations in hominid brains and the neural/hormonal system that equipped some hominids with the ability to acquire the emotional and cognitive desire to oppress others may well have been selected in males especially because males with these features fathered and raised more children. Alternatively, men may be taught and learn to be social dominance oriented because it embodies part of what it takes to be viewed as a good father (loyalty, protectiveness, status). Perhaps in either case SDO is only spuriously selected or socialized through its correlation with some other feature. If one assumes that the various male dominance societies from which we have data are essentially equivalent with respect to either proximate or distal selection pressures, then we cannot tell which mechanism causes the sex/gender difference. Pinning down "the cause" of this gender difference appears difficult if not impossible. However, we can test the notion of a reproductive function for SDO within male dominance societies by examining its current relation to mating strategies.

Within male dominance societies, social dominance orientation could be the psychological enabler of oppressive, dominant polygynous behavior. There are several testable hypotheses that follow from this view. They take the form that social dominance orientation will be associated with other psychological polygynous predispositions, but that the degree of association will be different in men and women when the behavioral strategies of males and females in polygyny differ. Recall that the essential element of a polygynous dominance system is a high-status male (or class of males) who oppresses other males and who has sex with many fertile females, whose sexual and economic behaviors are controlled. I predict that SDO should be more positively associated with intention to have many mates in men than in women. Also, sexual jealousy or mate guarding should be more strongly related to SDO in men than in women. If the reason for male sexual jealousy is paternity certainty, then any other tendency to reject children who might not be considered one's own should also be more strongly related to SDO in men than in women. For women in a dominant polygynous system, social dominance orientation is only to their advantage if it helps them gain a very-high-status mate. Therefore, I predict that desire for a high-status mate should more strongly predict SDO among women than among men. Note that predictions concern differences between men and women in the sizes of slopes with SDO, not gender differences in the means or variances on these variables.

I employed four California college samples (Samples 2 through 5 in Table 9.1) to test these hypotheses about SDO and preferences about sexual or family relationships. My samples do not represent the universal test of these predictions one might like, but they do represent a variety of subcultural and socioeconomic backgrounds (see Table 9.1) and consist of young adults who are approaching marrying age. The mate preference results obtained in Sample 2 were remarkably similar to results of both married and unmarried respondents in an independent random survey of Los Angeles area adults (see Pratto et al., 1993) and also to results of international surveys of mate preferences (e.g., Buss, 1989b), so I have reason to believe that these results would replicate in other samples. Respondents in Samples 2 and 3 were San Jose State University or Stanford University students. Sample 4 was a random sample of 723 UCLA undergraduates surveyed by mail in 1989. Sample 5 was 118 San Jose State University students who completed an extensive survey about their ideal mates in fall, 1992.

Sexual Fidelity and Social Dominance Orientation

In an hour-long survey on their desires and expectations of married life, people in Sample 5 answered two complementary questions at different points in the survey about their likely fidelity. One question asked what the probability was that the subject would be sexually faithful in marriage. Subjects were instructed to write their responses in terms of values between 0% and 100%. To test whether SDO was related to sexual infidelity, I regressed SDO on subjects' estimates of their future faithfulness. To test whether this relationship is stronger among men than women, I conducted t tests comparing the size of the slope for women against the size of the slope for men. This tests, independently of differing variances and means on the variables between men and women, the extent to which SDO is related to intended sexual fidelity. As predicted, higher SDO levels were associated with lower estimates of the subjects' own future faithfulness, and the slope was significantly more negative among women than among men (see Table 9.6). In other words, social dominance orientation is less related to intention to be faithful among men than among women.[4]

Respondents in Sample 5 also estimated, again from 0% to 100%, the probability that they would have at least one affair while married. Higher SDO levels on this measure were associated with higher estimates of future affairs, but were significantly more associated among men than among women (see Table 9.6). For a man and a woman at the same SDO level, the man was more likely to say he will be unfaithful. Both results are consistent with my hypothesis that SDO is a psychological enabler of polygyny—having multiple sexual partners for men, but not for women.

Sexual Jealousy and Social Dominance Orientation

My second hypothesis was that measures of sexual jealousy would be more strongly related to SDO among men than among women. I tested this hypothesis by regressing SDO on sexual jealousy measures and comparing slopes

TABLE 9.6. Results Comparing Regressions on Social Dominance Orientation across Males and Females

Regression	Sample	β for Females	β for Males	t	df	p
Own future faithfulness on SDO	5	−4.34	−2.89	−7.26	97	.0005
Own future unfaithfulness on SDO	5	2.25	6.54	−24.28	93	.0005
Sexual jealousy on SDO	2[a]	.89	−1.44	25.5	459	.0005
	3[a]	.07	−1.30	15.0	389	.0005
	5[b]	−4.13	−8.00	22.0	84	.001
Attitude toward in-group adoption on SDO	3	−.30	−.59	1.97	195	.05
SDO on desire for a high-status mate	2	.32	.12	2.30	459	.025
	3	.37	.19	1.96	395	.05
Miscegeny attitude on SDO	2	−.47	−.62	1.73	458	.05
	3	−.33	−.67	3.49	349	.0005
	4	−.21	−.29	1.83	707	.05

Note: p values shown are one tailed. The own faithfulness item was, "What is the probability you will be sexually faithful to your ideal mate while married?" The own unfaithfulness item was, "What is the probability you will have at least one affair while married?" The jealousy and faithfulness items were on 0 to 100 scales; all other scales, including SDO, were on 1-to-7 scales.

[a]Jealousy item was, "What is the probability you would divorce your spouse if he or she had an affair?"

[b]Jealousy item was, "What is the probability your ideal mate would be sexually faithful in marriage?"

between men and women. In Samples 2 and 3, subjects indicated the likelihood (from 0% to 100%) they would divorce their spouse if he or she had an extramarital affair. Lower numbers are taken to indicate greater sexual jealousy because they imply less willingness to allow one's mate to have an alternative sexual relationship. The slopes among men were significantly more negative than among women (see Table 9.6), indicating that the relationship between SDO and this measure of sexual jealousy is stronger for men than for women. In Sample 5, subjects were asked (rated again from 0% to 100%), "What is the probability your ideal mate will be sexually faithful in marriage?" Slopes with this measure and SDO were negative, indicating that higher SDO people are not as confident in their mates' sexual fidelity, perhaps indicating a suspicious nature that could trigger feelings of sexual jealousy. As predicted, the slope was significantly more negative among men than among women (see Table 9.6). So, people who were more social dominance oriented were more sexually jealous, but this was even more true for men than for women.

Paternity Certainty and Social Dominance Orientation

In addition to sexual jealousy, paternity certainty concerns might be exhibited by rejection of children that are not one's "own" (see Daly & Wilson, 1988, on murder and abuse of stepchildren). In Sample 3, subjects rated how comfortable they would feel about adopting children from various ethnic groups. The 1-to-7 scale rating for the subject's own ethnic group was called "attitude toward in-group adoption." I used this measure because this sample was much less comfortable about cross-ethnic adoptions than adoptions within ethnicity. Because people high on SDO are prejudicial in general, I expected that higher SDO people would be less comfortable toward adoption. If discomfort toward adoption taps paternity certainty concerns, there should be a stronger relationship between SDO and attitude toward in-group adoption among men than among women. Both of these expectations were confirmed: The slopes between SDO and adoption attitude were negative, and significantly more among men than women (see Table 9.6). That is, high-SDO men were even less interested than high-SDO women in adopting a child. Paralleling the results on sexual jealousy, these results on adoption indicate that SDO is more related to concerns over whether family members are considered "mine" for men than for women.

Desire for a High-Status Mate and Social Dominance Orientation

Subjects in college Samples 2 and 3 rated how important approximately 30 characteristics were to them in their ideal mate. Factor analyses revealed a primary dimension related to social status, especially among women (see Pratto et al., 1993). I formed a desired mate status measure from the highly loading items: favorable social status, hard working, well educated, ambitious, from a respected family, importance that mate makes desired amount of money and (reverse coded) comfort with marrying a lower status person.

These were rated on scales from completely unimportant to essential (0 to 3 in Sample 2; 1 to 7 in Sample 3). As expected in a society in which men have better access to status than women, women rated the social status dimension higher than men in both samples ($p < .05$), replicating many other studies of mate preferences (e.g., Buss, 1992).

To test whether SDO would be more related to the desire for a high-status mate in women than in men, I regressed SDO on desire for a high-status mate separately for each sex in Samples 2 and 3. All four slopes were reliable at $p < .001$, indicating that SDO and desire for a high status mate are positively related. In both Samples 2 and 3, the slopes were significantly higher among women than among men (see slopes and t tests in Table 9.6). These results show that SDO in women is much more related to desire for a high-status mate than SDO in men is.

These results are all consistent with my hypothesis that SDO helps enable dominant polygyny through the mating strategies of men and women. Among men, the psychological capacity to outrank other men, to exploit outgroups materially and socially, and to control women sexually and materially may propel behavior that is adaptive in male-dominant societies. Among women, SDO may encourage them to select a high-status mate.

This implies that, in polygynous dominance systems, high-status males may benefit the most at the expense of others, but male dominance can be aided by women's behavior that is individually adaptive. Because some women can benefit by marrying high-status men, the theory explains why some women cooperate in their sex's oppression (cf. Dickemann, 1979). In other words, male dominance and out-group oppression may not be attributable solely to one sex or the other, but rather to a dynamically intertwined, complementary, and sometimes cooperative relationship between them. It also indicates that much of "sexual politics" has to do with competition within each sex for mates or resources of the other sex not just to conflict between the sexes (see also Betzig, 1993; Buss, 1994). That is, dominant polygyny not only leads to sexual and political control of females, but also to economic exploitation of low-status males and their reduced ability to become parents or to obtain care for their children. This discussion illuminates exactly why we must consider societal, economic, reproductive, and political factors together in discussing the gender gap, and also why a thorough understanding of politics cannot be established without inclusion of sexuality.

Ideology of Sex and Ethnic Oppression

As another illustration of the relationship between intergroup oppression and both intersexual and intrasexual oppression, consider the cultural beliefs and behavior patterns that are relevant to endogamy. High-status men can be expected to have sexual relations with women outside their own group or class and also to promote sociocultural practices, ideas, and laws that essentially limit women's sexual behavior or limit other male's sexual access to their women, or both. This may be the function of intergroup sexual taboos.

Dickemann (1979) has applied such an analysis to the caste system in India. I believe it also explains sexual, class, and race relations in the United States. Here, statutory rape laws may have been invented to prevent lower status men who had affairs with higher status women from being able to marry them (Thornhill & Thornhill, 1983), "keeping" the high-status women available to high-status men.

An even more long-reaching device is the prohibition on interracial sexual relationships, including, but not limited to, interracial marriage, which was illegal in some states until 1967. Ample evidence indicates that white men used the miscegeny taboo as a pretense to punish black men as they saw fit, especially when blacks' fortunes were rising (Giddings, 1984, chap. 1; Hepworth & West, 1988; Hovland & Sears, 1940). Thus, the miscegeny taboo served as a legitimizing device for maintaining white superiority. The large number of mulattoes during slave times, as well as testimonies of former slaves, indicate that white slave owners raped or sexually coerced their female slaves often (e.g., Fredrickson, 1981; Hooks, 1981; Jones, 1990; White, 1985; Williamson, 1980); thus, the class of politically powerful men who helped establish this prohibition did not actually follow it. In this century, Dollard's (1937) study of "Southerntown" and Griffin's (1960) exploration of the South both documented that some white men had sexual access to black and white women, whereas black men's choices of women of both races were severely limited. White women could not select black lovers without being ostracized or extremely secretive, and a black woman's choices of black lovers were severely restricted if a white man had relations with her. The dual race and sex system afforded greater sexual freedom (and very likely, a larger number of children) to those who had the most political, economic, and legal power: well-off white men (see Davis, 1981, for a similar, but Marxist, analysis of race, class, and sex in the United States).

Social dominance theory predicts that legitimizing ideologies, such as the miscegeny taboo, tend to be supported more by those higher on social dominance orientation. However, because this legitimizing myth more serves high-status men's than women's concerns, I predict that support for the miscegeny taboo will show a stronger relation to SDO among men than among women. I measured support for the miscegeny taboo as the mean of attitudes toward two items, interracial marriage and interracial dating, and regressed it on SDO in Samples 2, 3, and 4. The slopes were significantly more negative among men than among women in all three samples (see Table 9.6). That is, men's SDO levels corresponded more to their opposition to interracial sexual relationships than did women's SDO levels. This analysis parallels the previous analyses in suggesting that SDO is an enabler of oppressive polygyny, but here I have shown this by relating SDO to support for an ideology that has also been an enabler of oppressive polygyny: the miscegeny taboo. Again, I am clearly assuming that a cultural device—spreading a distaste for interracial sexual relationships—could be an adaptive strategy for high-status males. Those disadvantaged by this strategy were not only females, but also low-status males.

The miscegeny taboo and other forms of group prejudice tend to prevent intergroup marriage and thus have a huge impact on the nature of societies. Families not only pass along their genes to their children, they are also the primary vehicle for distributing inherited material wealth and family status, as well as personal characteristics that serve as status cues to others, such as speech style, language(s) spoken, looks, activity preferences, and so forth. When such things are differentially distributed among different groups in a population, then in-group marriage[5] helps to maintain that distribution over generations (e.g., Porterfield, 1982). Prejudice based on ethnicity or class encourages the re-creation of group inequality in every generation of a society. It is exactly through processes such as these that individual preferences and actions influence the social environment not just for the individual and his or her family, but for the rest of society and for other societies as well.

THEORY SUMMARY

Now that I have given examples of most of the pieces, let me briefly summarize social dominance theory's model of human dominance. Social dominance theory seeks to identify the social and psychological processes that contribute to group-based stratification. We have noted that, in addition to "arbitrary group" oppression such as intergroup discrimination based on caste, ethnicity, or class, stratified societies also exhibit inequality for women (Sidanius & Pratto, 1993a). A chief goal of this chapter has been to outline the relationship between intergroup oppression and oppression of women.

Our analysis begins with the view that societies are dynamic systems in which different actors sometimes work toward the same ends and sometimes are at odds. The major dimension along which we consider factors contributing to inequality (versus equality) is in how hierarchy enhancing or hierarchy attenuating they are. For example, we have suggested that certain social roles serve to channel positive resources toward those who already enjoy status, means, and power, and to channel negative resources downward toward those who enjoy little status, material well-being, or power. Here, I have suggested that men predominate in such hierarchy-enhancing roles in part because they hold values that are compatible with those roles and in part because much other social action causes men to be overrepresented in such roles. Pratto, Stallworth, Sidanius, and Siers's (1995) self-selection experiments showed that high- and low-SDO people seek roles compatible with their levels of social dominance orientation. Because more men are high on SDO, self-selection is likely to result in gender differences in attainment of hierarchy-enhancing versus hierarchy-attenuating roles. In Pratto, Stallworth, Sidanius, and Siers's (1995) hiring experiment, subjects hired males more often into hierarchy-enhancing roles than females with the exact same credentials, suggesting that sex stereotyping may contribute to differential hiring rates in hierarchy-enhancing and hierarchy-attenuating roles for men and women. A number of other processes, such as sex-biased job evaluations, may also contribute to different attrition rates from roles for men and women. All of these effects (gender socialization, self-selection, hiring biases, evaluation biases, etc.) may snowball to create the gender gap in role attainment. Ample research suggests that roles are often used to justify differences in pay and status so that roles are an important vehicle for understanding social inequality.

In addition to examining the effects that one's role has on one's status, we postulate that different roles differentially effect relative group standing. By definition, people in hierarchy-enhancing roles help enforce discrimination against lower status members of societies or discrimination in favor of higher status members of societies or both. Thus, individuals in such roles take direct action to distribute social goods unequally and may also operate within institutions that distribute institutionally controlled resources unequally. The aggregate effect of both individual discrimination and institutional discrimination is the perpetuation of group inequality.

One of the most significant social-cognitive processes that contributes to levels of inequality is shared beliefs in ideologies that legitimize inequality. The discussion above about sex stereotypes shows that they may influence the distribution of status and income by perpetuating the gender gap in role attainment. Legitimizing ideologies operate in many other arenas as well. Pratto, Stallworth, and Conway-Lanz (1995) showed that people who believe more in legitimizing ideologies such as nationalism and racism are more supportive of inegalitarian social policies such as going to war. On the other side, those who believe more in hierarchy-attenuating ideologies such as noblesse oblige support egalitarian social policies such as social welfare programs (see also Sidanius & Pratto, 1993b). These studies suggest that ideology is indeed used to legitimize practices regulating social relationships. We are now conducting experiments to test further how people may use ideology to legitimize differential resource allocation.

Social dominance orientation and legitimizing ideologies also play a role in political processes. People who are more social dominance oriented and believe in hierarchy-enhancing ideology and policy also tend to support different political candidates than those who believe in hierarchy-attenuating ideology (Pratto, Stallworth, & Conway-Lanz, 1995; Pratto, Stallworth, & Sidanius, 1995). Politics and other forms of social influence, such as spreading legitimizing beliefs, have indirect effects on the shaping of cultural norms and beliefs pertinent to inequality.

Finally, because we conceive of societies as social systems, we must acknowledge that many of the "outcomes" typical of stratified societies help to perpetuate these processes. For example, when people try to explain why some people are treated better, own more property, are "better" people, and so forth, than others, they may observe the correlation between group membership and its trappings and use relatively simple attribution processes to make up justifications for inequality. For example, the wealthy may appear to have earned their wealth through hard work, the sick may appear to have earned their plagues through disgusting personal habits, and elite groups may appear to have earned their privileged positions by holding opinions that everyone respects. There appear to be few legitimizing ideologies outside of social science theory that reverse the causal directions implied above, such as that members of elite groups were given more opportunity to work and to earn their wealth, that the sick have disgusting personal habits because they are ill, and that people respect elite groups' opinions simply because they are elite. Similarly, when people observe gender gaps in roles, power, attitudes, status, and the like, the "data" they observe may help to create or reinforce their sex stereotypes so that the gender gap is perpetuated through collective memory and beliefs.

The nature of the society can also be described in terms of what roles are available and to whom, what the prevalent ideologies are, how well people's social identity needs are met, and more. Previous research has shown a link between one's social role (Pratto et al., 1994; Sidanius et al., 1991), degree of status threat (Levin & Sidanius, 1993; Sidanius, Pratto, & Mitchell, 1994), degree of positive social identity (Choudhury & Pratto, 1995; Sidanius, Pratto, & Mitchell, 1994; Sidanius, Pratto, & Rabinowitz, 1994) and social dominance orientation. Thus, a number of social factors may contribute to the development of social dominance orientation and related personality types that contribute to group-based inequality. The entire dynamic model is depicted in Figure 9.3.

I noted at the outset that, categorically speaking, men dominate women in almost every society on earth, and that the arenas of this domination are not just intersexual, but also include oppression within the society and against outside groups. This is not coincidental: the oppression of women and the oppression of other social groups are mutually enabling. Based on intersexual competition theory, I suggested that men and women will be in conflict to the extent their mating and child-rearing strategies diverge (see also Buss, 1989a, 1989b). Moreover, intersexual conflict can drive intrasexual conflict. Among women, intrasexual conflict can result in elite women cooperating to reduce other women's sexual, personal, economic, and political freedoms (see Betzig, 1986, 1993; Dickemann, 1979, 1981). Among men, intrasexual conflict can result in economic and prestige ranking, creating stratification (sometimes, but not always, based on class) and outgroup oppression. In short, political strategies are sexual strategies (cf. Fox, 1980; Tiger & Fox, 1971).

This analysis can be fruitfully applied to comparisons across cultures, within societies, and in family dynamics. This theory predicts that cultures that exhibit more inequality in normative sexual relationships will exhibit not only sexual and economic restrictions on women, but also more stratification and more exploitation of out-groups. Within societies, the theory predicts that higher status men will have more mates than lower status men and than women. Within families, it suggests that the more credible the threat of withdrawal of social resources, the more "costly" the lack of paternal responsibility is, or the more female-generated resources are undervalued compared with male-generated resources, the more power the man holds. In other words, there is a dynamic relationship between these levels of analysis. This viewpoint, that individual, family, and societywide processes work as a system,

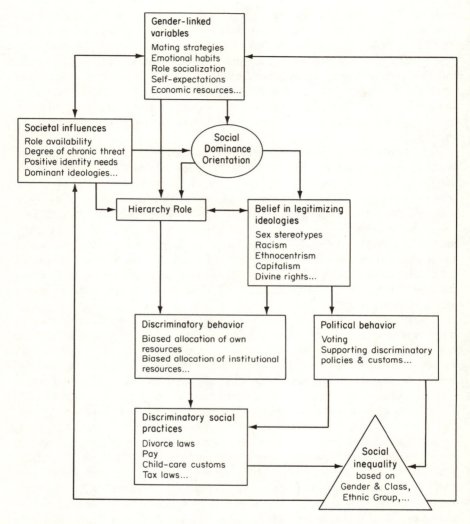

FIGURE 9.3.   General social dominance model of gender and group inequality.

implies that there is no single ultimate cause of male dominance. A social system of male dominance entails status ranking among men, divergent outcomes for men and women, cultural transmission of gender roles and ideologies, institutional discrimination, and a host of other intertwining factors. My viewpoint then suggests that explanations of male dominance that hinge on one variable, such as "men are more aggressive than women," are insufficient. At the same time, it suggests that transforming a society from male dominance to equality or the reverse will require several simultaneous social changes.

If there is one linchpin to understanding sexual politics generally, it is

whether people's child-rearing strategies diverge; when they do, male dominance of women and inequality among men appear to result. This is most
obvious in stratified societies, but inequality for women and inequality among
men also characterize nonstratified societies (cf. Collier, 1988). Rather than
analyzing sexual politics as only concerning the relative status, power, and so
forth between men and women, this analysis suggests that variability within
each sex is quite significant.[6]

Identifying individual advantage in behavior that is disadvantageous for
others, even for same-sex others, is crucial for understanding how humans
create inequality. In addition, it suggests that people with different choices,
different resources, different power bases, and the like may *need* to adapt
differently. As such, individual differences, as in social dominance orientation,
socially valued skills, and so forth, may be quite significant. Presumably,
because people who are lower on social dominance orientation are less sexist,
less interested in personal prestige, more communal, and more interested in
hierarchy attenuation, the nature of their marriages and their child-raising
strategies would differ from those of high SDO people.

The potential for polygyny is one example of a divergent child-raising
strategy: where women are more responsible for their children's care than men
are, but men accrue the economic, political, and reputational benefits of their
children, men will have status and political advantages. However, it seems
more likely that the positive benefits (e.g., regular food, sanitation, and a
home, especially for adults who do not have to produce all those benefits) that
accrue to adults where children are being raised may be the real cause of the
absence of female dominance in human societies. Although even a wealthy
woman could not bear as many children as a wealthy man could father in one
lifetime, human psychology allows people to recognize people as parents and
children who are not their genetic parents or children. As such, it bears mentioning that a form of "female polygyny" might be said to exist in some African
societies in which women take wives. In at least 10 societies, some women
marry women. These female husbands obtain male mates for their wives and
provide material care for the children of these relationships, who are attributed
as the female husband's heirs. In some such marriages, women acquire wives
to continue a father or brother's line, but in others women acquire wives to
the extent they are wealthy, and their wives' children are attributed to their
lineage (see Krige, 1979; O'Brien, 1977). Woman marriage is not then a
romantic or sexual relationship between women, but it is a coparenting relationship. Among these societies, the Ibo have been claimed to be egalitarian
(before colonization; see Van Allen, 1972), the Lovedu have a female leader,
and Lovedu women own and control property and enjoy relatively high status
(e.g., Krige, 1979).

The existence of woman marriage and also of adoption and fosterage
suggest that more attention needs to be paid to the psychological identification
with family members in models of human reproduction, rather than assuming
that genetically related persons "naturally" identify with each other more and
act in each other's interest. A communal, interdependent, empathic orientation

toward children would presumably temper or prevent tendencies to abandon, neglect, or abuse children. It is also important not to assume implicitly or explicitly that birth and nursing are the most deterministic aspects of child care. In many societies, substantial child care happens postweaning, so child-care arrangements are another major area in which male and female strategies may diverge to produce inequality or converge to produce equality.

The child-care arrangements of nonstratified societies for which we have behavioral evidence* support the view that convergent male–female child-care strategies allow for sexual equality and perhaps for general equality within the society as well. Among the Montagnais-Naskapi of Labrador, who typically lived in tent or lodge groups of several "nuclear" families, child care is shared with little regard to whether the child is genetic offspring. Among these people, men and women had equally easy access to divorce, although polygyny was not uncommon, perhaps owing to high mortality rates, especially among men (Leacock, 1981, pp. 49–50). When a Jesuit missionary tried to shame a Naskapi man over his lack of paternity certainty and the "immoral" sexual behavior of his wife, the man replied, "Thou hast no sense. You French people love only your own children; but we all love all the children of our tribe" (Leacock & Goodman, 1976, p. 82; see Leacock, 1981, for other information on the Naskapi).

The Iroquois are famous for their interdependent economic and political arrangements. Men hunted in groups, the composition of which changed frequently, depending on group travel and the location of the game relative to the various hunting bands within the tribe. Women primarily planted and raised food crops, but they elected an elder woman overseer for each season who would supervise the lodge of women working together on each field. The political system had separate councils for men and women, but they were interdependent; for example, the men's council could not meet unless the women voted to give it provisions, which the women controlled (J. K. Brown, 1970). The examples of these societies indicate that, when men and women can be assured that their community will care for all children, they all have an interest in insuring that they contribute to the well-being of the whole community and can enjoy equal economic, sexual, and political freedoms as well.

Evolutionists have applied parental investment theory to understanding the psychologies and mating strategies of human men because human fathers do provide substantial parental care to their children, in fact, more care than any other primates (e.g., Alexander & Noonan, 1979, p. 436). However, applications of this theory need to acknowledge that when one's mate can provide sufficient care for one's child or one's children will be cared for by people other than one's mate or oneself, one need not be as concerned about extracting care from the mate. Thus, in cooperative child-rearing societies, we should expect to see less interest among women in a mate's status, less interest among men in status ranking and paternity certainty, less conflict between

---

*Several ancient societies are thought by some scholars to be egalitarian based on physical evidence and symbol interpretation (see Gisler, 1987; Gimbutas, 1991; Mellaart, 1967).

mates over child-rearing strategies, and perhaps even no gender difference on social dominance orientation. The first three predictions hold true for what Friedl (1975) calls kin-based (nonstratified) societies. Some 20th-century cultures show that interdependence between mates accompanies equality between the sexes. Among the Mbuti pygmies of the Ituri rain-forest in Africa, after the first few years, children are cared for by the whole band (see Turnbull, 1983) and childless couples are given children to adopt. This practice insures that the costs and benefits of children are relatively equal across families. Bush-living !Kung also are sexually egalitarian and have much child care performed by other band members while parents are gathering or hunting (Draper, 1975).

Unlike the Naskapi and !Kung, the Mbuti (Turnbull, 1983) and Tasaday (Nance, 1975) are monogamous and faithful for life. In all four societies, violence against children and women is extremely rare. Perhaps the combined polygyny and polyandry of the Naskapi and !Kung and the absolute monogamy of the Mbuti and Tasaday obviate the male sexual jealousy that is common in male dominance societies and that may contribute to violence against women and children (Daly & Wilson, 1988; Wilson & Daly, 1992). The same is true for rape, which has been hypothesized to be an adaptive mating strategy for men who have so little status that they cannot obtain mates in a "legitimate" way (Thornhill & Thornhill, 1983), that is, via status.

In contrast to the stereotype of rigid socialism, a variety of interdependent family, labor, and economic arrangements are possible within nonstratified systems. In the Naskapi lodge, there were virtually no items that were significantly accumulated, and material goods could not increase a person's status (Leacock, 1981, p. 41). Bush-living !Kung accumulate virtually nothing, but !Kung living in villages have begun to acquire wealth, which is not equally distributed among families, and have begun to become sexist against women (Draper, 1975). The Mbuti and Tasaday own very little and share what they consume. In another egalitarian society, on Vanatinai in the Trobriand Islands, individual men and women possess valued items, but personal wealth is extremely fluid because everyone engages in constant exchange and gift giving (Lepowsky, 1990). Among traditional Hopi, the economic interdependence of men and women is predicated on women's ownership of land and men's responsibility to grow produce on the land (Schlegel, 1990). In two Philippine egalitarian societies, Bacdayan (1977) reports that most labor is done by both sexes, often with nuclear families working together.

Social dominance theory posits that, in male dominance societies, ideologies such as racism and sexism are very instrumental in helping coordinate discriminatory behavior. As shown here, such legitimizing myths are related to policy support (see also Pratto, Stallworth, & Conway-Lanz, 1995; Sidanius & Pratto, 1993b). Conversely, the cultural ideologies of egalitarian people are different than those of male dominance cultures. The Hopi religious/cultural system subsumes male and female into one concept of God (e.g., Schlegel, 1977, 1990), and among both the Hopi (Schlegel, 1990) and the Mbuti (Turnbull, 1983, p. 57), rituals allow both women and men to make fun of the others' sexuality. The Mbuti even have a ritual to teach adolescents the pointlessness of male or female dominance. At the joyous event of a girl's first menstruation, they play tug-of-war, with the men pulling on one side and the women on the other. As soon as one side starts to win, a person from the winning side runs over to help the other side, and so the game goes, with both sides eventually losing (Turnbull, 1983, pp. 45–47). In stark contrast to male dominance societies, none of these nonstratified societies has an internal authority that coerces people to behave in particular ways.

Clearly, a more detailed comparative analysis of cultures is needed to establish that convergent child-rearing systems enable equality (and, as the dynamic model allows, that egalitarian social arrangements of other sorts allow for equality between men and women). Nonetheless, it bears pointing out that even small convergences within male dominance societies may lead to more equality and less conflict between the sexes. For example, Buss and Schmitt (1993) have shown that when men and women think about long-term mates rather than short-term mates, the gender differences in mate preferences are attenuated. Where women are scarce and men have difficulty finding mates, granting women more legal and economic rights can be a means of attracting them, providing advantages for both sexes (e.g., see Matsuda, 1985, on suffrage in the Western frontier states).

Another major problem, however, is to understand why it is so often the case that when nonstratified societies are contacted (or invaded or colonized) by male dominance societies, the relative equality they enjoy disappears (e.g., see Eisler, 1987; Hamamsy, 1957; Leacock & Goodman, 1976; Van Allen, 1972). Several factors have been suggested: the invaders refusing to recognize anyone but men as authorities, economic dependency of the colonized on an economic system that gives the advantage to men, state control over reproduction, competition between invaders and native men over native women, the transformation of cultural beliefs, social and legal devices that disenable persons (particularly women) from controlling the fruits of their own labor, and so forth. A reasonable study of such factors is far beyond the scope of this chapter (but see Hess & Ferree, 1987; Leacock, 1981; Sanday, 1981; Schlegel, 1977; Schwendinger & Schwendinger, 1983; Tiffany, 1979), but is clearly important for understanding equality or inequality in human societies.

There are several general points about models of sexual politics that can be drawn from this theory. First, theories of sexual politics need not omit reproduction, including considerations about child rearing, in order to avoid biological determinism. True evolutionary theories do not require that one "solution" to the problem of reproduction is inevitable. On the contrary, variability across individuals and across species is necessary to postulate selection and thus should be central to any evolutionary theory. In addition, evolution does not preclude behavioral plasticity. However, consideration of our nature, especially considering humans as social animals who require large amounts of socialization to make them viable, does lead one to the conclusion that there are constraints on societies and individuals concerning child care. Thus, a biological view does not need to lead to deterministic predictions, but it suggests that the extreme version of cultural determinism—that absolutely any cultural arrangement is possible—may be wrong. In particular, it is precisely because human children require so much care that we should expect their rearing to have a massive influence on the nature of our societies, including the nature of our work roles, our rules about parenting responsibility, and the like. Conversely, we should expect that a lack of child rearing will also have a massive influence on the nature of our societies. The evolutionary perspective does not, however, presume by whom child care must be accomplished. Avuncular and communal societies provide for children's care by men and women without requiring the status ranking and female inequality typical of stratified societies (e.g., see Friedl, 1975; Leacock, 1981; Lepowsky, 1990; Turnbull, 1983).

Second, because cultures clearly are different adaptive environments, we should also include variability across cultures in evolutionary theories of human behavior, not just as error variance, an afterthought, or an alternative explanation for unexpected results, but as an essential aspect of the models. Given that human beings have to be socialized to make them able to become successful parents, much of enabling children to be reproductively successful involves imparting wisdom, skills, beliefs, polite behaviors, or, in short, culture. These are far from determined by genes or even, apparently, by physical environment. For example, the Mbuti and the Yanamamö are both foraging rain-forest dwellers, but their sexual politics could hardly be more different (see, e.g., Chagnon, 1992; Turnbull, 1983). In addition, the psychological orientations of people toward others, especially whether they strive to dominate them or behave and feel as if the other's outcomes are their own, should not be underestimated in moderating these processes. The variability from person to person in such orientations is quite substantial even within each sex.

Third, deterministic models of sexual politics are inadequate as theories: they are either nonfalsifiable or incompatible with existing data, or both. For this reason, they need not be taken seriously as lessons or proscriptions for sexual politics. For example, the fact that discriminatory behaviors are sometimes individually variable and sometimes normed even within a society should make it apparent that, even if the psychological capacity to oppress has an evolved basis, the philosophic and ethical question of whether individuals choose to oppress is the same as it is in any other social influence theory. If everyone engages in an oppressive behavior, do we hold those individuals accountable? Do we hold individuals accountable for creating discriminatory norms or for perpetuating discriminatory institutions? If only certain people engage in oppressive behavior, does it make sense to infer that they have individual responsibility for their actions? If our societies strongly encourage certain kinds of people to take on roles that are societally defined as oppressive (e.g., drafting men into the military), should we still hold those people accountable for their oppressive behavior?

The same can be said for actions relating to finding a mate and nurturing children. People make choices and take action to become attractive, to force themselves on others, to maintain good mate relationships or to jettison them, to see that their children are nurtured, or to abandon their children. We do not need to assume that because these actions have an adaptive consequence they are determined by the unseen hand of evolutionary selection. To do so uses evolutionary theory to justify the status quo, and we have already seen that adaptive oppression is not equally good for everyone. Further, without more detailed examination of how human culture, society, and both individual and coordinated action influence selection, we underestimate the power we have to affect each other's lives.

The fourth point to be made is that evolutionary models do not need to be reductionistic. There is, quite simply, too much evidence that humans can be reasonably studied using several disciplines and several theoretical constructs. If theories stemming from any of the disciplines are not to be overly stunted, they will all have to become integrative. That is, whereas it may be parsimonious to describe simple behaviors in terms of constructs originating from single disciplines (e.g., culture, economics, biology, or personality). It is hard to see how a reasonably complete understanding of the interesting aspects of human life (e.g., economy, child rearing, symbolic meaning) could be reduced to constructs from a single discipline. Instead, we can invent dynamic theories that use the seemingly most apropos construct to describe each phenomenon, but that specify how the constructs interrelate. In doing so, we may hit upon the most apt description of human life, not by finding an ultimate cause, but by examining how all of these ways of being related. Because so many of the ways we carry the past and present into the future depend not just on our individual natures, but on our relationships (e.g., our shared cultural beliefs, our self- and family concepts, our habits, our stories about who we are), reductionistic theories are useful only for small problems.

I hope the dynamic view I've shown helps obliterate the inappropriate "deterministic" metaphor for life. The lives of people, not automatons, involve blood, food, sickness, labor, joy, conquest, pride, love, hate, humiliation, children, relatives, dirt, conversation, sex, and politics. If we throw out determinism, we can develop an understanding of the dynamic interpersonal, social, sexual, and political processes that shape ourselves and our environments. It seems appropriate that a social-evolutionary perspective would be so useful to a theory of oppression, because oppression, for many people, is a matter of life and death.

Acknowledgments. Portions of this research were presented at the 1992 annual meeting of the American Psychological Society and the 1993 annual meeting of the Western Psychological Association. Please address correspondence to Felicia Pratto, Department of Psychology, Jordan Hall, Stanford University, Stanford, California 94305-2130. I thank Art Aron, David Buss, Laura Carstensen, Jane Collier, Robin Fox, Jeannie Foxtree, John Hetts, Joseph Lopreato, Kelli Keough, Geoffrey Miller, Lisa Stallworth, Cookie Stephan, Jim Sidanius, and Kirsten Stoutemyer for their open-mindedness and criticality in commenting on this research; their careful reading and constructive comments were very helpful to me.

NOTES

1. All of the societies for which we found data are stratified. Sweden, discussed below, was probably the most egalitarian society for which such data are available.

2. Analyses using simultaneous regression of SDO and gender yielded highly similar results in both samples.

3. Friedl (1975) argues that men more often control resources that can be exchanged outside the family and so gain status in that way.

4. In fact, given the constants in the regression equations, the women in this sample intend to be more faithful than the men at every level of SDO for which they could score on the scale.

5. Mating without benefit of marriage (vs. with marriage) does not legally often confer status, titles, family name as much, nor does father–child learning occur at the same rate.

6. Many have claimed that nonstratified societies are actually egalitarian, but most of the ethnographies with which I am familiar suggest that there was status ranking among men in such societies and that women, while not always as dependent, nonproductive, passive, powerless, and so forth as in patriarchical societies, were not accorded as much prestige or power, on the whole, as men. Thus, I suspect that many ethnographers described societies as egalitarian that were not patriarchies, although they describe oppressive behavior by their members (e.g., Chagnon, 1979).

REFERENCES

Alexander, R. D. (1989). Evolution of the human psyche. In P. Mellars & C. Stringer (Eds.), *The human revolution* (pp. 455–511). Edinburgh: Edinburgh University Press.

Alexander, R. D., & Noonan, K. M. (1979). Concealment of ovulation, parental care, and human social evolution. In N. A. Chagnon & W. Irons (Eds.), *Evolutionary biology and human social behavior: An anthropological perspective* (pp. 436–453). North Scituate, MA: Duxbury Press.

Bacdayan, A. S. (1977). Mechanistic cooperation and sexual equality among the Western Bontoc. In A. Schlegel (Ed.), *Sexual stratification* (pp. 270–291). New York: Columbia.

Bakan, D. (1966). *The duality of human existence.* Chicago: Rand McNally.

Barkow, J. H. (1989). *Darwin, sex, and status: Biological approaches to mind and culture.* Toronto: University of Toronto Press.

Barkow, J. H., Cosmides, L., & Tooby, J. (Eds.). (1992). *The adapted mind.* New York: Oxford University Press.

Bem, S. L. (1974). The measurement of psychological androgyny. *Journal of Consulting and Clinical Psychology, 49,* 1129–1146.

Betzig, L. (1986). *Despotism and differential reproduction: A Darwinian view of history.* Hawthorne, NY: Aldine.

Betzig, L. (1988). Mating and parenting in Darwinian perspective. In L. L. Betzig, M. Borgerhoff Mulder, & P. W. Turke (Eds.), *Human reproductive behaviour: A Darwinian perspective* (pp. 3–20). Cambridge, UK: Cambridge University Press.

Betzig, L. (1989). Causes of conjugal dissolution: A cross-cultural study. *Current Anthropology, 30,* 654–676.

Betzig, L. (1991). History. In M. Maxwell (Ed.), *The sociobiological imagination* (pp. 131–140). Albany, NY: State University of New York Press.

Betzig, L. (1993). Sex, succession, and stratification in the first six civilizations: How powerful men reproduced, passed power on their sons, and used power to defend their wealth, women, and children. In L. Ellis (Ed.), *Social stratification and socioeconomic inequality: A comparative biosocial analysis* (pp. 37–74). New York: Praeger.

Bledsoe, C. (1993). The politics of polygyny in Mende education and child fosterage transactions. In B. D. Miller (Ed.), *Sex and gender hierarchies* (pp. 170–192). Cambridge: University of Cambridge.

Block, J. H. (1984). *Sex role identity and ego development.* San Francisco: Jossey-Bass.

Boserup, E. (1986). *Woman's role in economic development.* Brookfield, VT: Gower.

Brown, D. E. (1991). *Human universals.* New York: McGraw-Hill.

Brown, J. K. (1970). Economic organization and the position of women among the Iroquois. *Ethnohistory, 17,* 151–167.

Brownmiller, S. (1975). *Against our will.* New York: Bantam.

Buss, D. M. (1989a). Conflict between the sexes: Strategic interference and the evocation of anger and upset. *Journal of Personality and Social Psychology, 56,* 735–747.

Buss, D. M. (1989b). Sex differences in human mate preferences: Evolutionary hypotheses tested in 37 cultures. *Behavioral and Brain Sciences, 12,* 1–49.

Buss, D. M. (1992). Mate preference mechanisms: Consequences for partner choice and intrasexual competition. In J. H. Barkow, L. Cosmides, & J. Tooby (Eds.), *The adapted mind* (pp. 249–266). New York: Oxford University Press.

Buss, D. M. (1994). *The evolution of desire.* New York: Basic Books.

Buss, D. M., & Angleitner, A. (1989). Mate selection preferences in Germany and the United States. *Personality and Individual Differences, 10,* 1269–1280.

Buss, D. M., & Barnes, M. (1986). Preferences in human mate selection. *Journal of Personality and Social Psychology, 50,* 559–570.

Buss, D. M., Larsen, R. J., Westen, D., & Semmelroth, J. (1992). Sex differences in jealousy: Evolution, physiology, and psychology. *Psychological Science, 3,* 251–255.

Buss, D. M., & Schmitt, D. P. (1993). Sexual strategies theory: An evolutionary perspective on human mating. *Psychological Review, 100,* 204–212.

Bureau of Labor Statistics. (1992). *Employment and Earnings, 39.* Washington, DC: U.S. Government Printing Office.

Caporael, L. R. (1995, February). Sociality: Coordinating bodies, minds, and groups [51 paragraphs]. *Psycoloquy* [on-line serial], Available FTP: Hostname: princeton.edu Directory: /cogsci.ecs.soton.ac.uk/pub/harnad/Psycoloquy/1995. volume.6 File: psych.95.6.01.group-selection.1.caporael.

Chagnon, N. A. (1979). Is reproductive success equal in egalitarian societies? In N. A. Chagnon & W. Irons (Eds.), *Evolutionary biology and human social behavior: An anthropological perspective* (pp. 374–401). North Scituate, MA: Duxbury Press.

Chagnon, N. A. (1992). *Yanomamö: The last days of Eden.* San Diego, CA: Harcourt, Brace, Jovanovich.

Choudhury, P., & Pratto, F. (1995). A group status analysis of ingroup identification and support for group inequality: Ethnicity, sex, and sexual orientation. Unpublished manuscript, Stanford University.

Collier, J. F. (1988). *Marriage and inequality in classless societies.* Stanford, CA: Stanford University Press.

Coombs, R. H., & Kenkel, W. F. (1966). Sex differences in dating aspirations and satisfaction with computer-selected partners. *Journal of Marriage and the Family, 28,* 62–66.

Crocker, J., & Major, B. (1989). Social stigma and self-esteem: The self-protective properties of stigma. *Psychological Review, 96*, 608–630.

Cunningham, M. R. (1986). Measuring physical attractiveness: Quasi-experiments on the sociobiology of female facial beauty. *Journal of Personality and Social Psychology, 50*, 925–935.

Dahlberg, F. (1981). *Woman the gatherer*. New Haven, CT: Yale University Press.

Daly, M., & Wilson, M. (1978). *Sex, evolution, and behavior*. North Scituate, MA: Duxbury Press.

Daly, M., & Wilson, M. (1988). *Homicide*. New York: Aldine de Gruyter.

Dahrendorf, R. (1968). *Essays in the theory of society*. Stanford, CA: Stanford University Press.

Davis, A. Y. (1981). *Women, race, and class*. New York: Vintage.

Darwin, C. (1871). *The descent of man, and selection in relation to sex*. New York: Appleton.

Deaux, K., & Major, B. (1987). Putting gender into context: An interactive model of gender-related behavior. *Psychological Review, 94*, 369–389.

Dickemann, M. (1979). Female infanticide, reproductive strategies, and social stratification: A preliminary model. In N. A. Chagnon & W. Irons (Eds.), *Evolutionary biology and human social behavior: An anthropological perspective* (pp. 321–367). North Scituate, MA: Duxbury Press.

Dickemann, M. (1981). Paternal confidence and dowry competition: A biocultural analysis of Purdah. In R. A. Alexander & D. W. Tinkle (Eds.), *Natural selection and social behavior* (pp. 417–438). New York: Chiron Press.

Dollard, J. (1937). *Caste and class in a southern town*. New York: Doubleday.

Dorkenoo, E., & Elworthy, S. (1992). *Female genital mutilation: Proposals for change*. Report of the Minority Rights Group. Manchester, England: Manchester Free Press.

Draper, P. (1975). !Kung women: Contrasts in sexual egalitarianism in foraging and sedentary contexts. In R. R. Reiter (Ed.), *Toward an anthropology of women* (pp. 77–109). New York: Monthly Review Press.

Eagly, A. H. (1987). *Sex differences in social behavior: A social-role interpretation*. Hillsdale, NJ: Erlbaum.

Eagly, A. H., & Steffen, V. J. (1984). Gender stereotypes stem from the distribution of women and men into social roles. *Journal of Personality and Social Psychology, 46*, 735–754.

Eaton, W. O., & Enns, L. R. (1983). Sex differences in empathy and related capacities. *Psychological Bulletin, 94*, 100–131.

Ebrey, P. (1990). Women, marriage, and the family. In P. S. Roop (Ed.), *Heritage of China: Contemporary perspectives on Chinese civilization* (pp. 197–223). Berkeley, CA: University of California.

Eccles, J. S. (1987). Gender roles and women's achievement-related decisions. *Psychology of Women Quarterly, 11*, 135–172.

Eisler, R. (1987). *The chalice and the blade*. San Francisco: Harper & Row.

Eisler, R., & Loye, D. (1983). The "failure" of liberalism: A reassessment of ideology from a new feminine-masculine perspective. *Political Psychology, 4*, 375–391.

Ekehammar, B., & Sidanius, J. (1982). Sex differences in socio-political attitudes: A replication and extension. *British Journal of Social Psychology, 21*, 249–258.

Estioko-Griffin, A., & Griffin, P. B. (1981). Woman the hunter: The Agta. In F. Dahlberg (Ed.), *Woman the gatherer* (pp. 121–151). New Haven, CT: Yale University Press.

Exposing Abuses. *Ms.* (July/August, 1995), 6, p. 14.

Feagin, J. R., & Feagin, C. B. (1978). *Discrimination American style: Institutional racism and sexism*. Englewood Cliffs, NJ: Prentice Hall.

Feingold, A. (1992). Gender differences in mate selection preferences: A test of the parental investment model. *Psychological Bulletin, 112*, 125–139.

Feshbach, N. D. (1982). Sex differences in empathy and social behavior in children. In N. Eisenberg (Ed.), *The development of prosocial behavior* (pp. 315–338). New York: Academic Press.

Fisher, R. A. (1930). *The genetical theory of natural selection*. Oxford: Clarendon.

Fox, R. (1972). Alliance and constraint: Sexual selection in the evolution of human kinship systems. In B. Campbell (Ed.), *Sexual selection and the descent of man 1871–1971* (pp. 282–331). Chicago: Aldine.

Fox, R. (1980). *The red lamp of incest*. New York: Dutton.

Fredrickson, G. M. (1981). *White supremacy: A comparative study in American and South African history*. New York: Oxford University Press.

Friedl, E. (1975). *Women and men: An anthropologist's view*. New York: Holt, Rinehart, & Winston.

Furnham, A. (1985). Adolescents' sociopolitical attitudes: A study of sex and national differences. *Political Psychology, 6*, 621–636.

Gailey, C. W. (1987). Evolutionary perspectives on gender hierarchy. In B. B. Hess & M. M. Ferree (Eds.), *Analyzing gender* (pp. 32–67). Beverly Hills, CA: Sage.

Giddings, P. (1984). *When and where I enter: The impact of black women on race and sex in America*. New York: Bantam.

Gimbutas, M. A. (1991). *The civilization of the goddess*. San Francisco: HarperCollins.

Goldberg, S. (1973). *The inevitability of patriarchy*. New York: Morrow.

Griffin, J. H. (1960). *Black like me*. New York: Signet.

Hamamsy, L. S. (1957). The role of women in a changing Navaho society. *American Anthropologist, 59*, 101–111.

Harris, M. (1993). The evolution of gender hierarchies: A trial formulation. In D. Miller (Ed.), *Sex and gender hierarchies* (pp. 57–79). Cambridge, UK: Cambridge University Press.

Hepworth, J. P., & West, S. G. (1988). Lynchings and the economy: A time series reanalysis of Hovland and Sears (1940). *Journal of Personality and Social Psychology, 55*, 239–247.

Hess, B. B., & Ferree, M. M. (Eds.). (1987). *Analyzing gender*. Newbury Park, CA: Sage.

Hooks, B. (1981). *Ain't I a woman*. Boston: South End Press.

Hovland, C. R., & Sears, R. R. (1940). Minor studies of aggression VI: A correlation of aggression with economic indices. *Journal of Psychology, 9*, 301–310.

Jones, N. T. (1990). *Born a child of freedom yet a slave: Mechanisms of control and strategies of resistance in antebellum South Carolina*. Hanover, NH: University Press of New England.

Keegan, J. (1993). *A history of warfare*. New York: Knopf.

Kenrick, D. T., Groth, G. E., Trost, M. R., & Sadalla, E. K. (1993). Integrating evolutionary and social exchange perspectives on relationships: Effects of gender, self-appraisal, and involvement level on mate selection criteria. *Journal of Personality and Social Psychology, 64*, 951–969.

Kenrick, D. T., Sadalla, E. K., Groth, G. E., & Trost, M. R. (1990). Evolution, traits, and the stages of human courtship: Qualifying the parental investment model. *Journal of Personality, 58*, 97–116.

Kopinak, K. (1987). Gender differences in political ideology in Canada. *Canadian Review of Sociology and Anthropology, 24*, 23–38.

Krige, E. J. (1979). Woman-marriage, with special reference to the Lovedu — Its significance for the definition of marriage. In S. W. Tiffany (Ed.), *Women and society: An anthropological reader* (pp. 208–237). Montreal: Eden Women's Press.

Leacock, E. B. (1981). *Myths of male dominance*. New York: Monthly Review Press.

Leacock, E., & Goodman, J. (1976). Montagnais marriage and the Jesuits in the seventeenth century: Incidents from the relations of Paul le Jeune. *Western Canadian Journal of Anthropology, 6*, 77–91.

Lepowsky, M. (1990). Gender in an egalitarian society: A case study from the Coral Sea. In P. R. Sanday & R. G. Goodenough (Eds.), *Beyond the second sex: New directions in the anthropology of gender* (pp. 171–223). Philadelphia: University of Philadelphia Press.

Levin, S. L., & Sidanius, J. (1993). *Intergroup biases as a function of social dominance orientation and in-group status*. Unpublished manuscript, University of California at Los Angeles.

Liston, A., & Salts, C. J. (1988). Mate selection values: A comparison of Malaysian and United States students. *Journal of Comparative Family Studies, 19*, 361–370.

Matsuda, M. J. (1985). The West and the legal status of women: Explanations of frontier feminism. *Journal of the West, 24*, 47–56.

Mellaart, J. (1967). *Catal Huyuk: A neolithic town on Anatolia*. New York: McGraw-Hill.

Miller, G. F. (1993). *Evolution of the human brain through runaway sexual selection: The mind as a protean courtship device*. Unpublished doctoral dissertation, Stanford University, Stanford, CA.

Millet, K. (1970). *Sexual politics*. Garden City, NY: Doubleday.

Mitchell, M. (1993). *Attitudes towards the death penalty and use of executions: A social dominance perspective*. Dissertation Abstracts International, 54-06B, 3390, University of California at Los Angeles.

Murdock, G. P. (1949). *Social structure*. New York: Macmillan.

Murstein, B. I. (1976). Qualities of desired spouse: A cross-cultural comparison between French and American college students. *Journal of Comparative Studies, 7*, 455–469.

Nance, J. (1975). *The gentle Tasaday*. New York: Harcourt, Brace, Jovanovich.

Norris, P. (1987). *Politics and sexual equality: The comparative position of women in Western democracies*. Boulder, CO: Rienner.

O'Brien, D. (1977). Female husbands in southern Bantu societies. In A. Schlegel (Ed.), *Sexual stratification: A cross-cultural view* (pp. 109–126). New York: Columbia University Press.

Okin, S. M. (1989). *Justice, gender, and the family*. New York: Basic Books.

O'Leary, V. E. (1974). Some attitudinal barriers to occupational aspirations in women. *Psychological Bulletin, 31*, 809–826.

Oyama, S. (1985). *The ontogeny of information*. Cambridge: Cambridge University Press.

Parker, S. T. (1987). A sexual selection model for hominid evolution. *Human Evolution, 2*, 235–253.

Porterfield, E. (1982). Black-American intermarriage in the United States. *Marriage and Family Review, 5*, 17–34.

Pratto, F., Sidanius, J., & Stallworth, L. M. (1993). Sexual selection and the sexual and ethnic basis of social hierarchy. In L. Ellis (Ed.), *Social stratification and socioeconomic inequality: A comparative biosocial analysis* (pp. 111–136). New York: Praeger.

Pratto, F., Sidanius, J., Stallworth, L. M., & Malle, B. F. (1994). Social Dominance Orientation: A personality variable relevant to social roles and intergroup relations. *Journal of Personality and Social Psychology, 67,* 741–763.

Pratto, F., Stallworth, L. M., Sidanius, J., & Siers, B. (1995). *The gender gap in occupational role attainment. A social dominance approach.* Unpublished manuscript, Stanford University, Stanford, CA.

Pratto, F., Stallworth, L. M., & Conway-Lanz, S. (1995). *Social dominance orientation as a predictor of new political attitudes.* Unpublished manuscript, Stanford University, Stanford, CA.

Pratto, F., Stallworth, L. M., & Sidanius, J. (1995). *The gender gap: Differences in political attitudes and social dominance orientation.* Unpublished manuscript, Stanford University, Stanford, CA.

Reskin, B. F. (1988). Bringing the men back in: Sex differentiation and the devaluation of women's work. *Gender and Society, 2,* 58–81.

Rockwell, R. C. (1976). Historical trends and variations in educational homogamy. *Journal of Marriage and the Family, 38,* 83–95.

Rodrigue, G. (1993, May 14). In Bosnia, shocking reality of policy of rape. *San Francisco Examiner,* pp. A1, A20.

Rosaldo, M. Z. (1974). Woman, culture, and society: A theoretical overview. In M. Z. Rosaldo & L. Lamphere (Eds.), *Women, culture, and society* (pp. 17–42). Stanford, CA: Stanford University Press.

Ruble, T. (1983). Sex stereotypes: Issues of change in the 1970s. *Sex Roles, 9,* 397–402.

Sacks, K. (1979). *Sisters and wives: The past and future of sexual equality.* Westport, CT: Greenwood Press.

Sanday, P. R. (1974). Female status in the public domain. In M. Z. Rosaldo & L. Lamphere (Eds.), *Women, culture, and society* (pp. 189–206). Stanford, CA: Stanford University Press.

Sanday, P. R. (1981). *Female power and male dominance.* Cambridge, UK: Cambridge University Press.

Sanderson, L. P. (1981). *Against the mutilation of women: The struggle to end unnecessary suffering.* London: Ithaca Press.

Schlegel, A. (Ed.). (1977). *Sexual stratification.* New York: Columbia University Press.

Schlegel, A. (1990). Gender meanings: General and specific. In P. R. Sanday & R. G. Goodenough (Eds.), *Beyond the second sex* (pp. 23–41). Philadelphia: University of Pennsylvania Press.

Schwendinger, J. R., & Schwendinger, H. (1983). *Rape and equality.* Beverly Hills, CA: Sage.

Shapiro, R. Y., & Mahajan, H. (1986). Gender differences in policy preferences: A summary of trends from the 1960s to the 1980s. *Public Opinion Quarterly, 50,* 42–61.

Sidanius, J. (1993). The psychology of group conflict and the dynamics of oppression: A social dominance perspective. In S. Iyengar & W. J. McGuire (Eds.), *Explorations in political psychology* (pp. 183–219). Durham, NC: Duke University Press.

Sidanius, J., Cling, B. J., & Pratto, F. (1991). Ranking and linking behavior as a function of sex and gender: An exploration of alternative explanations. *Journal of Social Issues, 47,* 131–149.

Sidanius, J., Devereux, E., & Pratto, F. (1992). A comparison of symbolic racism theory and social dominance theory as explanations for racial policy attitudes. *Journal of Social Psychology, 132*, 377–395.

Sidanius, J., & Ekehammar, B. (1980). Sex-related differences in socio-political ideology. *Scandinavian Journal of Psychology, 21*, 17–26.

Sidanius, J., Ekehammar, B., & Ross, M. (1979). Comparisons of socio-political attitudes between two democratic societies. *International Journal of Psychology, 14*, 225–240.

Sidanius, J., & Liu, J. (1992). Racism, support for the Persian Gulf War, and the police beating of Rodney King: A social dominance perspective. *Journal of Social Psychology, 12*, 685–700.

Sidanius, J., Liu, J. H., Pratto, F., & Shaw, J. S. (1994). Social dominance orientation, hierarchy attenuators and hierarchy-enhancers: Social dominance theory and the criminal justice system. *Journal of Applied Social Psychology, 24*, 338–366.

Sidanius, J., & Pratto, F. (1993a). The inevitability of oppression and the dynamics of social dominance. In P. Sniderman & P. E. Tetlock (Eds.), *Prejudice, politics, and the American dilemma* (pp. 173–211). Stanford, CA: Stanford University Press.

Sidanius, J., & Pratto, F. (1993b). Racism and support of free-market capitalism: A cross-cultural study of the theoretical structure. *Political Psychology, 14*, 383–403.

Sidanius, J., Pratto, F., & Bobo, L. (1994). Social dominance orientation and the political psychology of gender: A case of invariance? *Journal of Personality and Social Psychology, 67*, 998–1011.

Sidanius, J., Pratto, F., & Brief, D. (1995). Group dominance and the political psychology of gender: A cross-cultural comparison. *Political Psychology, 16*, 381–396.

Sidanius, J., Pratto, F., Martin, M., & Stallworth, L. M. (1991). Consensual racism and career track: Some implications of social dominance theory. *Political Psychology, 12*, 691–720.

Sidanius, J., Pratto, F., & Mitchell, M. (1994). Group identity, social dominance orientation and intergroup discriminations: Some implications of social dominance theory. *Journal of Social Psychology, 134*, 151–167.

Sidanius, J., Pratto, F., & Rabinowitz, J. (1994). Gender, ethnic status and ideological asymmetry: A social dominance perspective. *Journal of Cross-Cultural Psychology, 25*, 194–216.

Singh, D. (1993). Adaptive significance of female physical attractiveness: Role of waist-to-hip ratio. *Journal of Personality and Social Psychology, 65*, 293–307.

Slocum, S. (1975). Woman the gatherer: Male bias in anthropology. In R. R. Reiter (Ed.), *Toward an anthropology of women* (pp. 36–50). New York: Monthly Review Press.

Smith, T. W. (1984). The polls: Gender and attitudes towards violence. *Public Opinion Quarterly, 48*, 384–396.

Spence, J. T., Helmreich, R., & Stapp, J. (1975). Ratings of self and peers on sex role attributes and their relation to self-esteem and conceptions of masculinity and femininity. *Journal of Personality and Social Psychology, 9*, 51–77.

Stimpson, D., Jensen, L., & Neff, W. (1992). Cross-cultural gender differences in preference for a caring morality. *Journal of Social Psychology, 132*, 317–322.

Thornhill, R., & Thornhill, N. W. (1983). Human rape: An evolutionary analysis. *Ethology and Sociobiology, 4*, 137–173.

Tiffany, S. W. (Ed.). (1979). *Women and society*. Montreal: Eden Press Women's
    Publications.
Tiger, L. (1970). The possible biological origins of sexual discrimination. *Impact of
    Science on Society, 20*, 29–44.
Tiger, L., & Fox, R. (1971). *The imperial animal*. New York: Henry Holt.
Trivers, R. L. (1972). Parental investment and sexual selection. In B. Campbell (Ed.),
    Sexual selection and the descent of man (pp. 136–179). Chicago: Aldine.
Turnbull, C. M. (1983). *The Mbuti pygmies: Change and adaptation*. San Francisco:
    Holt, Rinehart, & Winston.
U.S. Department of Health and Human Services, National Center for Health Statistics.
    (1990). *United States health and prevention profile, 1989*. Hyattsville, MD:
    Public Health Service.
Van Allen, J. (1972). Sitting on a man: Colonialism and the lost political institutions
    of Igbo women. *Canadian Journal of African Studies, 6*, 165–181.
van Dijk, T. A. (1993). *Elite discourse and racism*. San Diego: Sage.
Vianello, M., & Siemienska, R. (1990). *Gender inequality: A comparative study of
    discrimination and participation*. Newbury Park, CA: Sage.
Wakil, S. P. (1973). Campus mate selection preferences: A cross-national comparison.
    Social Forces, 51, 471–476.
White, D. G. (1985). *Ar'n't I a woman? Female slaves in the plantation south*. New
    York: Norton.
Williams, J. E., & Best, D. L. (1982). *Measuring sex stereotypes*. Beverly Hills, CA:
    Sage.
Williamson, J. (1980). *New people: Miscegenation and mulattoes in the United States*.
    New York: Free Press.
Wilson, M., & Daly, M. (1992). The man who mistook his wife for a chattel. In J. H.
    Barkow, L. Cosmides, & J. Tooby (Eds.), *The adapted mind* (pp. 289–322).
    New York: Oxford University Press.
Wirls, D. (1986). Reinterpreting the gender gap. *Public Opinion Quarterly, 50*, 316–
    330.

10

Male Aggression Against Women:
An Evolutionary Perspective*

BARBARA SMUTS

The worldwide prevalence of male violence toward women has recently become disturbingly evident. Russell's (1984) careful survey of 930 San Franciscan women indicates that one-quarter of American women will experience a completed rape at some time in their lives, and nearly one-half will be victims of attempted or completed rape. Since the age of 14, 27.5% of college women have experienced an attempted or completed rape (Koss, Gidycz, & Wisniewski, 1987). Each year, approximately 1.8 million American wives are beaten by their husbands (Strauss, 1978), and one-eighth of all murders involve husbands killing their wives (Hutchings, 1988).

Although the prevalence of male violence against women varies from place to place, cross-cultural surveys indicate that societies in which men rarely attack or rape women are the exception, not the norm (Broude & Greene, 1978; Levinson, 1989; Sanday, 1981). Cross-culturally, as well as in the United States, male sexual jealousy is the most common trigger for wife beating (Counts, Brown, & Campbell, 1992; Daly & Wilson, 1988).

Why is male aggression against women so common? Why is this aggression so often linked to sex? And why is male aggression against women more frequent and intense in some societies than in others? This chapter examines these issues from an evolutionary perspective, which assumes that, in humans as in many other animals, male aggression against females often reflects male reproductive striving (Burgess & Draper, 1989; Daly & Wilson, 1988). The chapter includes four distinct parts. I begin by considering male aggression against females and female resistance to it in nonhuman primates. This review indicates that male use of aggression toward females, particularly in a sexual context, is common in primates, which suggests that male aggression against women may often represent species-specific manifestations of widespread male reproductive strategies aimed at control of female sexuality. In the second part of the chapter, I use evidence from nonhuman primates, especially apes, as a source of hypotheses concerning how male aggressive coercion may have influenced the evolution of human pair bonds. In speculating about the role of male sexual coercion in human social evolution, I necessarily focus on general patterns that distinguish humans, as a species, from other primates. As Rodseth, Smuts, Harrigan, and Wrangham (1991) argue, the identification of these general, species-specific human social patterns should not be viewed as an end in and of itself, but as a starting point for analysis of cross-cultural diversity. Thus, in the third section of the chapter, I use both evolutionary theory and comparative analysis involving other primates to generate a series of hypotheses to help explain variation across cultures in male aggression toward women. The fourth and final section discusses the implications of an evolutionary approach to male aggression against women and considers possible directions for future research.

Although an evolutionary analysis assumes that male aggression against women reflects selection pressures operating during our species' evolutionary history (Burgess & Draper, 1989; Daly & Wilson, 1988), it in no way implies that male domination of women is genetically determined or that frequent male aggression toward women is an immutable feature of human nature. In some societies, male aggressive coercion of women is very rare, and, even in societies with frequent male aggression toward women, some men do not show these behaviors (e.g., Counts, 1991). Thus, the challenge is to identify the situational factors that predispose members of a particular society toward or away from the use of sexual aggression. I argue that an evolutionary framework can be very useful in this regard.

MALE AGGRESSION AND FEMALE RESISTANCE IN PRIMATES

Male reproductive success is limited by the ability to fertilize females; for this reason, in most animals males provide no parental care, but focus instead on gaining additional opportunities to mate (Trivers, 1972). Males typically benefit by mating with any female who is potentially fertile, whereas females do not benefit by mating with every male who comes their way. Females benefit from being choosy about their mates because some males provide better genes than others or because some males are better able or more willing to provide the female with resources, parental care, protection, or other benefits that aid female reproduction (Trivers, 1972).

Male eagerness to mate, combined with female reluctance to reproduce with any male who comes along, creates an obvious sexual conflict of interest that is virtually universal (Hammerstein & Parker, 1987). Sometimes males improve their chances of mating by offering benefits to females, such as food, protection, or assistance in rearing young (Smuts & Gubernick, 1992; Trivers, 1972). But, sometimes males attempt to overcome female resistance by employing force or the threat of force. *Male sexual coercion* can be defined formally as "male use of force, or its threat, to increase the chances that a female will mate with the aggressor or to decrease the chances that she will mate with a rival, at some cost to the female" (Smuts & Smuts, 1993). Sexual coercion and female resistance to it are important phenomena to examine in other animals because the outcomes of these struggles can illuminate the balance of power between the sexes and how it varies under different circumstances. Here, I focus on sexual coercion in nonhuman primates. I first present some examples of male sexual coercion and the costs it imposes on females, and I then consider how females resist male attempts to control them forcefully.

Male Sexual Coercion

In many monkeys and apes, during the period when the female is in estrus (i.e., when she is fertile and sexually receptive), she receives significantly more aggression from males, and often receives more wounds, than at times when she is not in estrus (see Smuts & Smuts, 1993, for references). Rhesus monkeys provide a clear example. These Asian macaques live in large, multimale, multifemale troops, and adult males are about 20% larger than adult females. In a recent study of female mate choice in a provisioned, free-ranging colony of rhesus monkeys in Puerto Rico, Manson (1994) found that females in estrus consistently approached peripheral and low-ranking males in order to mate with them. When a female associated with a low-ranking male, however, she was vulnerable to aggression by high-ranking males; these males disrupted the pair by chasing or attacking the female on average between three and six times per day. Manson found a direct relationship between the amount of time an estrous female spent with low-ranking males and the rate at which she received aggression from other males. Despite this risk, females persisted in their attempts to mate with the males of their choice.

Rhesus males attempt to control females mainly when the females are in estrus, and they show less aggression toward females at other times. In some other primates, such as hamadryas baboons, males try to maintain control over females all the time (Kummer, 1968). Hamadryas baboons form small groups containing a single breeding male, several adult females, and their immature offspring. Several of these one-male units associate in larger units called *bands*, which also include a number of "bachelor" males without females of their own, who are eager to mate. Day in and day out, the breeding males persistently herd their females away from these bachelor males. Whenever a female strays too far from her male, he will threaten her by staring and raising his brows. If she does not respond instantly by moving toward him, he will attack her with a neck bite (Kummer, 1968). The neck bite is usually symbolic—the male does not actually sink his teeth into her skin—but the threat of injury is clear.

Male sexual coercion also appears to be a prominent feature of the societies of wild chimpanzees. Chimpanzees live in large communities with 8–20 adult males and many females and young (Goodall, 1986; Nishida & Hiraiwa-Hasegawa, 1987). Male chimpanzees remain in their natal communities and are therefore related to one another; females typically transfer between communities at sexual maturity. When a female chimpanzee undergoes sexual cycles (which happens for only a few months once every 5 years or so), the males in her group compete for opportunities to mate with her, especially as she nears ovulation, when her sexual swelling reaches its maximum size (Hasegawa & Hiraiwa-Hasegawa, 1983; Tutin, 1979). When many males are present, the most dominant, or alpha male, usually prevents any other males from mating with her. Low-ranking males therefore try to lure estrous females into the forest, away from other chimps, where they can mate in peace. These consorts may last for several weeks and, at Gombe, are responsible for roughly one-third of all conceptions. If the female is willing to go, as she sometimes is, then the pair simply sneaks away. But, if the female is unwilling, the male will employ what Goodall (1986, p. 453) terms "a fair amount of brutality" to try to force her to accompany him. He will repeatedly perform aggressive displays around her to induce her to follow him and, if she still does not follow, will attack her. It is impossible to tell how many consorts involve reluctant females forced to accompany males because, in cases in which the female apparently willingly follows the male, she may do so because of aggression received from him in the past. Indeed, Goodall reports a high frequency of "unprovoked" attacks on females in the early phases of sexual swelling, which she interprets as a male tactic to intimidate the female so she will be less likely to resist future efforts to mate with her. Goodall concludes that, unless a male chimpanzee is very old or ill, he can usually force an unwilling female to consort with him through these efforts.

Although male chimpanzees use aggression to force reluctant females to accompany them, the use of force during the sexual act is rare in this species and in most other nonhuman primates. Orangutans are a striking exception. Among wild orangutans, most copulations by subadult males (e.g., Galdikas, 1985; Mitani, 1985) and nearly half of all copulations by adult males (Mitani, 1985) occur after the female's fierce resistance has been overcome through aggression. Orangutan females' solitary habits, unique among anthropoid primates, may help to explain their vulnerability to forced copulations (see below).

Male primates use of force to increase sexual access to females can also involve infanticide (Hrdy, 1979). In a wide variety of nonhuman primates, males kill infants sired by other males (Hausfater & Hrdy, 1984; Struhsaker & Leland, 1987). Because a return to sexual cycling is inhibited by lactation, death of the infant typically brings the mother into estrus sooner than would occur otherwise, and, in many instances, the infanticidal male subsequently mates with the mother. Infanticide may be considered a form of sexual coercion because it involves the use of force to manipulate the female's sexual state and mating behavior to the male's advantage, while imposing a cost on the female (Smuts & Smuts, 1993).

Costs to Females of Male Sexual Coercion

The reproductive costs to females of male aggression in general and sexual coercion in particular appear to be considerable. As indicated above, females are frequently wounded, sometimes severely, during male aggression in the mating context, but quantitative data on rates and severity of wounding are scarce (Smuts & Smuts, 1993). Occasionally females die as a result of male aggression (olive baboons: personal observation, 1978; rhesus macaques: Lindburg, 1983; chimpanzees: Goodall, 1986).

The costs of infanticide are easier to measure. Among gray langurs, when a usurper replaced the resident male, 40% of the infants present and 34% of infants born shortly afterward were killed ($n = 115$ infants in 12 troops; Sommer, 1994). Since male takeovers occur on average every 26.5 months (Sommer & Rajpurohit, 1989), infanticide is clearly an important source of infant mortality. In red howlers, 44% of all infant mortality is due to infanticide (Crockett & Rudran, 1987). Watts (1989) gives a similar figure (37%) for mountain gorillas.

Male aggression also inflicts numerous, more subtle costs on females related to reduced foraging efficiency, the energetic efforts of maintaining vigilance against male violence, and constraints imposed on female ability to form social relationships, including restrictions on female mate choice (Smuts & Smuts, 1993). When we look closely, we find that, in many primates, hardly an aspect of female existence is not constrained in some way by the presence of aggressive males.

Female Strategies to Resist Male Aggression

Female primates employ a variety of means to resist male aggression, including sexual coercion (reviewed in Smuts & Smuts, 1993); these tactics include physiological responses that alter the timing of reproduction in ways that thwart infanticide by males (Hrdy, 1977, 1979). Most interesting for our purposes, however, are strategies of resistance based on social relationships. In rhesus monkeys, females form strong, lifelong bonds with their female kin, and females cooperate to protect their female relatives against male aggression (Bernstein & Ehardt, 1985; Kaplan, 1977). This pattern of forming long-term bonds with female kin is common in Old World monkeys, and in all of these "female-bonded" species (Wrangham, 1980), females band together against males (Smuts, 1987).

Male aggression is constrained in female-bonded species not just because of the threat of female coalitions, but also because females in these groups influence the outcome of male–male competition for dominance. In rhesus macaques and vervet monkeys, for example, a male's quest to achieve and maintain high dominance status is strongly influenced by the support of high-ranking females (Chapais, 1983; Raleigh & McGuire, 1989). The males' reliance on female support makes them reluctant to challenge dominant females (Chapais, 1983; Keddy, 1986).

Female primates also reduce their vulnerability to male aggression by forming long-term, friendly relationships with particular males. For instance, in savanna baboons, each female forms long-term relationships or "friendships" (Smuts, 1985) with one or two particular adult males (Altmann, 1980; Ransom, 1981; Seyfarth, 1978; Smuts, 1985; Strum, 1987). Males protect their female friends and those females' infants against aggression by other troop members, including other males, and a female's bond with one or two particular males reduces the amount of harassment she receives from other males. The female, in turn, often shows marked preferences for mating with her friends (Smuts, 1985).

These examples indicate that, far from being helpless victims of male control, female primates typically have several means of resisting males and asserting their own interests. The advantage males gain (in most species) through their larger size is countered by the fact that females cooperate against males, whereas males seldom cooperate against females (see below for important exceptions). It is also balanced by the female tendency to form long-term bonds with particular males who help to protect them and by "king-making" power, which constrains male use of force against them. Note that all of these ways in which females resist or prevent male coercion involve supportive social relationships—sometimes with other females, sometimes with males, and sometimes with both.

We return to the issue of female resistance to male coercion below in a discussion of cross-cultural diversity. I wish first, however, to examine how male sexual coercion in our closest primate relatives, the apes, influences their social systems. This discussion will set the stage for a consideration of the role of male sexual coercion in human social evolution.

Male Sexual Coercion in Apes: Effects on the Social System

As discussed above, male orangutans and chimpanzees show considerable aggression toward potential mates. In addition, male chimpanzees attack strange females from neighboring communities. Young, sexually cycling, nulliparous female chimpanzees typically transfer, either temporarily or permanently, to neighboring communities; while there, they mate with community males (Goodall, 1986; Nishida, 1979; Nishida & Hiraiwa-Hasegawa, 1985; Pusey, 1979). Males welcome these females and sometimes even protect them from hostility by resident females. In dramatic contrast, when chimpanzee males encounter mature, anestrous females (i.e., lactating mothers) from another community, they typically respond with intense, sometimes lethal aggression (Bygott, 1972; Goodall, 1986; Goodall et al., 1979; Nishida & Hiraiwa-Hasegawa, 1985). These attacks often inflict severe injuries and sometimes result in the death of the mother or her infant. Goodall (1986) speculates that if the death of a female's mother makes the daughter more likely to leave her natal group, then lethal attacks on mothers may facilitate recruitment of their adolescent daughters to the attacker's group. If she is correct, then these attacks can be viewed as sexual coercion (although in this instance the target of violence is not the males' potential mate, but her mother).

Whatever the reason for the brutal attacks on strange females, they clearly occur regularly and thus constitute an important selection pressure influencing the behavior of female chimpanzees. Female chimpanzees forage, often on their own with dependent young, in dispersed, but overlapping, home ranges. Males range more widely and cooperate in the defense of a community range that encompasses the ranges of several females. As adults, and often after transferring from their natal communities, female chimpanzees become clearly identified with a particular community (i.e., with a particular group of males) (Goodall, 1986; Nishida & Hiraiwa-Hasegawa, 1987). Although female dispersion is probably a product of feeding competition (Wrangham, 1975, 1979), the fact that females "belong" to a particular male community, rather than range and associate freely regardless of community boundaries, is probably a response to violence by males from neighboring communities. This conclusion is supported by observations indicating that infants of lactating females with ambiguous community identity are especially vulnerable to infanticide by males (Kawanaka, 1981; Nishida, 1990; Nishida & Kawanaka, 1985; Nishida, Takasaki, & Takahata, 1990).

Less information is available on male aggression against females in gorillas, bonobos, and gibbons compared with orangutans and chimpanzees. The available data suggest, however, that in at least some of these apes, as in chimpanzees, male aggression has influenced not only female behavior, but also the form of the social system itself.

The case is clearest for mountain gorillas, which live in family groups with, typically, one breeding "silverback" male and several unrelated females and their young (Stewart & Harcourt, 1987). In these apes, almost all infants that lose the protection of a silverback male (in most cases, because he had recently died) are soon killed by other males (Watts, 1989). In contrast, infants living in a group with a silverback male are rarely killed (Watts, 1989). These observations provide strong support for the hypothesis that infanticide is the selective force responsible for group living in gorillas (Watts, 1983, 1989; Wrangham, 1979, 1982, 1987). Because females rely for protection primarily on the silverback male rather than on other females (Watts, 1989), the gorilla social system is based not on bonds between related females, but on bonds between (usually unrelated) females and the adult males(s) in the group (Stewart & Harcourt, 1987).

Male sexual coercion, in the form of infanticide, may also explain the monogamous social system of gibbons and siamangs. Van Schaik and Dunbar (1990) evaluate several alternative hypotheses to explain monogamy in large primates in which males do not help to care for infants (including gibbons and siamangs). After testing the predictions of each hypothesis against the available data, they conclude that protection from male infanticide is the best explanation for the evolution of monogamy in gibbons and siamangs. Because direct evidence for gibbon infanticide is thus far lacking, this proposal needs further testing.

The social system of bonobos, or pygmy chimpanzees, is similar in many ways to that of chimpanzees, and, as in chimpanzees, males are slightly larger than females (Nishida & Hiraiwa-Hasegawa, 1987). It is therefore surprising to find that male aggression against females is apparently quite rare in this species. We do not know why. One possibility is that the stronger female–female bonds found among bonobos compared with chimpanzees thwart male aggression (Smuts & Smuts, 1993). Too little is known about bonobos to give much weight to this hypothesis, however.

In summary, male violence toward females or their young has strongly influenced female choice of associates in chimpanzees and gorillas and possibly in gibbons and bonobos as well. In the fourth great ape, the orangutan, females cannot afford to associate with other adults owing to the costs of feeding competition (Rodman, 1984; Wrangham, 1979), and they apparently pay a severe price for their solitary habits—frequent forced copulations, which either do not occur, or occur much less often, in the other apes. These conclusions suggest that it is critical to consider how male aggression against females and young may have influenced social evolution in ancestral hominids.

MALE SEXUAL COERCION AND THE EVOLUTION OF HUMAN PAIR BONDS

Pair bonds (long-term, more-or-less-exclusive mating relationships) that are embedded within a multimale, multifemale group distinguish humans from all other primates (Alexander & Noonan, 1979; Rodseth, Wrangham, Harrigan, & Smuts, 1991), and pair bonds have long been considered a critical development in human social evolution (Washburn & Lancaster, 1968). Most reconstructions of human evolution have assumed that pair bonds evolved to facilitate the exchange of resources between the sexes (e.g., Lovejoy, 1981; McGrew, 1981; Tanner, 1981; Washburn & Lancaster, 1968; Zihlman, 1981), often with a particular emphasis on the need for increased male parental investment in the form of meat (Foley, 1989; Galdikas & Teleki, 1981; Lancaster & Lancaster, 1983; Lovejoy, 1981). These scenarios assume that females benefited from pair bonds because they gained meat from males. Given the importance of male sexual coercion among nonhuman primates, and especially among our closest living relatives (chimpanzees, gorillas, and orangutans), however, we should carefully consider the alternative hypothesis that pair bonds benefited females initially because of the protection mates provided against other males (including protection from infanticide; Alexander & Noonan, 1979; Smuts, 1985; van Schaik & Dunbar, 1990). Consider the following hypothetical scenario.

Based on our knowledge of the significance of male–male alliances in modern humans, we know that, at some point during hominid evolution, male cooperation became increasingly important. This trend may have occurred in response to increased intergroup competition (Alexander & Noonan, 1979) or because of the need to cooperate during hunting and in intragroup competition for power, resources, and mates. Nonhuman primate studies demonstrate that cooperation among allied males is facilitated when the most dominant males tolerate some mating activity by their lower ranking allies. This toleration is a clear pattern among male coalition partners in chimpanzees (de Waal, 1982; Goodall, 1986; Nishida, 1983), hamadryas baboons (Abegglen, 1984; Kummer, 1968; Kummer, Gotz, & Angst, 1974; Sigg, Stolba, Abegglen, & Dasser, 1982), and savanna baboons (Smuts, 1985). I suggest that, among hominids, the kind of tolerance we see among male allies in nonhuman primates became formalized as each male began to develop a long-term mating association with a particular female or females (a trend foreshadowed in savanna baboons). This tolerance does not imply an absence of male mating competition within the group since some males would undoubtedly continue to have larger numbers of mates than others (as is true among humans today). Even low-ranking males might obtain significant mating privileges, however, if their support was sufficiently important to high-ranking males during intragroup or intergroup competition.

Truly exclusive mating relationships would not evolve unless they also benefited females, and it is in this context that male sexual coercion becomes relevant. I assume that, as among many nonhuman primates that live in multimale, multifemale groups, hominid females were vulnerable to sexual coercion, including infanticide by males. Among chimpanzees, males of all ranks attack females, but protection of females against other males involves mainly the alpha male since lower ranking males hesitate to direct aggression up the hierarchy (de Waal, 1982; Goodall, 1986). This pattern was likely to change once males began to claim particular females as mates and to respect the mating relationships of their allies. Respect for an ally's mating relationship would include inhibition against attacking his mate and his mate's offspring, particularly when the ally was present. Similarly, as males attempted to develop long-term relationships with particular females, they would be likely to protect those females and the females' offspring against aggression by other males.

Once males began to respect the mating privileges of their allies and to offer protection to their long-term female associates, a female who pursued a promiscuous strategy would become increasingly vulnerable to sexual coercion and infanticide, for two reasons.[1] First, she would not have one particular male associate who was prepared to defend her against other males. Second, the "respect" that served to inhibit male aggression against their allies' mates (and allies' mates' children) would not apply to her. Thus, she and her offspring would be attacked more often and protected less often. The implication is that, once males benefited from more-or-less-exclusive mating bonds with particular females, females would find noncompliance with male demands for these relationships to be very costly, just as female chimpanzees find resistance to male consort overtures costly. The benefits to females of maintaining a promiscuous mating pattern would have to be quite large to compensate for these costs. In other words, as male efforts to establish pair bonds increased, females were forced to reduce promiscuous mating in exchange for male protection from harassment by other males. At the same time, females probably became more vulnerable to aggression from their mates because other males would be less likely to interfere owing to the costs of disrupting male–male alliances. Viewed in this light, human pair bonds, and therefore human marriage, can be considered a means by which cooperating males agree about mating rights, respect (at least in principle) one another's "possession" of particular females, protect their mates and their mates' children from aggression by other men, and gain rights to coerce their own females with reduced interference by other men.

This scenario is, of course, speculative, as are all attempts to reconstruct human social evolution. It can never be proven correct; its value lies in its advantages as a heuristic device. One advantage is its focus on conflicts between spouses, an important aspect of marriage that is typically ignored when these relationships are approached from the perspective of more traditional, "economic" models of human pair bonding. A second advantage is the way in which the "male coercion scenario" can integrate several important aspects of human sociality within a single theoretical framework. Consider, for example, the fact that, in a wide variety of societies, women are particularly vulnerable to male violence, including abduction, rape, and infanticide, when they lack the protection of a mate (e.g., Bailey & Aunger, 1989; Chagnon, 1983; Hill & Kaplan, 1988; Murphy & Murphy, 1985). The special vulnerability of "unattached" women is dramatically illustrated by Biocca's account of a Brazilian woman kidnapped by the Yanomamos (Biocca, 1968, cited in Mathieu, 1989). When men from another village tried to rape the kidnapped woman, no Yanomamo male would protect her because she was not yet married to one of them. Similarly, the Mundurucus recite a myth in which a woman said to "have no owner" is gang raped (Murphy & Murphy, 1985, p. 133). In the same vein, among the Azandes, rape of an unmarried woman is not treated seriously, but, if she is married, the husband has the right to kill the rapist (Sanday, 1981). Hill and Kaplan report that survivorship among Ache children whose fathers have died or deserted the mother is significantly lower than that of other children, primarily owing to homicide by other men. Consistent with this evidence, many societies emphasize the importance of protection of women by male kin and husbands from aggression by other men (e.g., Irons, 1983; Lewis, 1990). Among Awlad'Ali Bedouins, for example, women are commonly referred to as *wliyya*, which means "under the protection" (Abu-Lughod, 1986, pp. 80–81). Also consistent with the male coercion scenario is the fact that most human societies sanction male aggression against their wives in response to suspected or actual adultery and the fact that this type of aggression appears to be very common (e.g., Counts et al., 1992; Daly & Wilson, 1988; Levinson, 1989).

A third advantage of the coercion hypothesis is that, in contrast to hypotheses that focus on the division of labor between men and women, it invokes selection pressures common to other animals and thereby facilitates comparisons between human and nonhuman social relations. For example, like orangutan chimpanzee females, women traveling alone are extremely vulnerable to assault by males. Like savanna baboon females, women develop special relationships with particular males who offer them protection against other males. Like hamadryas or gorilla females, in exchange for this protection women are generally expected to mate more-or-less exclusively with their protector. And, like rhesus monkey females, women are often subject to severe aggression when caught courting, or copulating, with other males. Thus, humans combine many of the different aspects of sexual coercion and female counterstrategies found in other primates.

These similarities offer the possibility of employing the comparative method to investigate aspects of human female–male relationships, including variation in the frequency and intensity of male aggression against females. Below, I use comparative evidence from nonhuman primates to generate several hypotheses concerning factors responsible for variation in male aggression against women, particularly variation in women's vulnerability to wife beating, which is better documented than other forms of male aggression against women (Counts, 1990b; Counts et al., 1992). Since the majority of wife beatings reflect the husband's attempts to discourage wifely infidelity (Counts et al., 1992; Daly & Wilson, 1988), I often deal with instances of male sexual coercion as defined above. It is important to emphasize that I use ethnographic examples to illustrate, not to test, the hypotheses developed below. Formal evaluation of these hypotheses remains a task for the future.

MALE AGGRESSION TOWARD WOMEN: SOURCES OF VARIATION

Hypothesis 1: Male Aggression Toward Women Is More Common When Female Alliances Are Weak

As indicated above, in many Old World monkeys, females remain in their natal groups their whole lives and ally with related females to chase and attack aggressive males. In contrast, among apes, in which females disperse from their natal kin, females rarely form coalitions with other females to inhibit male aggression. Human females tend to follow the ape pattern, both in terms of dispersal from kin (see below) and in terms of the weak tendency to form female coalitions against men (Begler, 1978; Rodseth, Smuts et al., 1991; Rodseth, Wrangham et al., 1991). Yet, in spite of this general pattern, much variation exists across cultures in the degree of female cooperation against males. At one extreme are some patrilocal societies, in which women's ties with natal kin are virtually severed after marriage and young married women live as strangers in a household ruled by the authority of their husband's male kin (Lamphere, 1974). In these societies, in which the wife is viewed as a competitor by her female affines, the husband's female kin not only fail to support the wife against male coercive control, they often actively encourage it (e.g., Gallin, 1992; Lateef, 1990; Wolf, 1974). Similarly, in polygynous societies that do not practice sororal polygyny, conflicts of interest between cowives often preclude the development of strong cooperative relationships among them (Lamphere, 1974).

At the other extreme are societies in which bonds among maternal female kin remain strong throughout life, such as the Navajo (Lamphere, 1974). Kerns (1992) provides a striking example of the significance of these female bonds in the reduction of male aggressive coercion of women. In the black Carib community in Belize that she studied, married women typically reside near their mothers, and, if a husband beats his wife, neighbors immediately alert her mother. The mother's arrival on the scene, combined with the shaming gaze of other female witnesses, is usually sufficient to stop the beating. It is interesting that, in this community, even unrelated women will help one another because, they say, "We're all women and it could happen to any of us." Women clearly recognize the importance of alliances with female kin, and they point out that women who live away from their mothers are more vulnerable to abuse. Some other societies in which related women cooperate to inhibit male aggression include the Wape (Mitchell, 1990), Nagovisi (Nash, 1990), Mundurucu (Murphy & Murphy, 1985), and !Kung (Draper, 1992).

Even in the absence of strong bonds between related women, situations that foster female cooperation may lead to coalitions against males. In a cross-cultural statistical analysis of factors associated with wife beating, Levinson (1989) reports that the existence of female work groups was significantly associated with reduced frequency of wife beating because, according to Levinson, these groups afford women both social support and economic independence from their husbands. This finding calls to mind Wolf's (1975) evidence indicating that cooperation among Taiwanese women who formed informal women's circles could inhibit mistreatment of wives even in this extremely patriarchal society.

Hypothesis 2: Wife Beating Is More Common When Females Lack Support From Natal Kin

Among nonhuman primates, females in female-bonded monkey groups receive aid against male aggression not only from female kin, but also from brothers and sons (prior to the males' dispersal to other groups) and older males (who may be their fathers) with whom they have long-term, affiliative relationships (e.g., Kaplan, 1977; Smuts, 1985). In contrast, among apes and other nonhuman primates in which females leave their natal groups, few or no kin are available to intervene on their behalf when they are attacked by males (Smuts & Smuts, 1993).

Among humans, also, availability of support from kin may be an important factor influencing female vulnerability to male aggression, particularly wife beating. As an initial hypothesis, we might predict that, as in nonhuman primates, residence patterns will determine availability of kin support, and that wife beating will therefore be more common in patrilocal societies than in matrilocal ones. Levinson's (1989) cross-cultural analysis, however, shows that patrilocal versus matrilocal residence does not have a significant effect on the frequency of wife beating. There are at least three possible reasons for the failure to find a significant relationship. First, residence patterns do not provide a sufficiently fine-grained indication of the proximity of kin; women in patrilocal societies may be only a few hours travel from kin; or they may be separated by several days travel (Brown, 1992; Counts, 1990b; Murdock, 1949). Second, among humans, individuals can maintain ties with kin even when they do not live near one another, so proximity to kin does not predict patterns of cooperative relationships to the extent that it does in nonhuman primates (Rodseth, Smuts et al., 1991; Rodseth, Wrangham et al., 1991). Third, extensive cross-cultural variation exists in the willingness of nearby kin to intervene to protect a woman from wife beating. For example, in Oceania, among indigenous Fijians (Aucoin, 1990) and Palauans (Nero, 1990), a woman's kin readily offer her sanctuary from an abusive husband, but among Indo-Fijians (Lateef, 1990) and in Kaliai, Papua New Guinea (Counts, 1990a), the woman's family is reluctant to take her in, supposedly because of the additional economic burden she inflicts.[2] Thus, the hypothesis should be modified to predict reduced wife beating when a woman's kin are both willing and able to protect her from her husband's attacks. Campbell (1992), for example, describes two patriarchal Muslim cultures, the Mayottes and an Iranian group. Among the Mayottes, a woman's kin intervene to protect her and wife beating is rare, whereas is Iran her kin do not intervene and wife beating is common. Thus, to explain variation in the frequency of wife beating, we need to examine not only whether a woman's kin are close enough to help her, but why nearby kin help more in some societies than in others. Since aid by male kin to protect a daughter or sister against her husband involves conflict between men, the nature of male–male relationships is one potential source of variation in the willingness of male kin to intervene.

Hypothesis 3: Male Aggression Toward Women Is More Common When Male Alliances Are Particularly Important and Well Developed

In humans, the relative weakness of female coalitions is paralleled by unusually strong male coalitions (Rodseth, Wrangham et al., 1991). Male reliance on alliances with other males in competition for status, resources, and females is a universal feature of human societies (Flinn & Low, 1986; Foley, 1989; Rodseth, Smuts et al., 1991; Rodseth, Wrangham et al., 1991). There can be no doubt that men benefit reproductively from bonds with other men, including alliances used in both intra- and intergroup competition. On the other hand, men also benefit from bonds with women, including bonds with female kin and with wives. I consider each in turn.

Female kin may contribute to a man's reproductive success directly, through cooperative relationships (e.g., Ortner, 1981), and indirectly, through increments to his inclusive fitness. For men, maintaining bonds with male allies on one hand and protecting related women on the other may often represent conflicting goals. If a man's daughter or sister is being beaten by one of his friends, should he defend her or ignore the beating and maintain good relations with his friend? The ethnographic record indicates that societies may vary systematically in this regard.

Consider, for example, the findings of Begler (1978), who analyzed the outcomes of male–female disputes (specifically, who came to whose aid) in a variety of societies. Among Australian aborigines, although people claimed that a woman's kin would come to her aid if she were beaten, this assistance was never provided in any of the descriptions of disputes Begler found in the literature. In other cultures, such as the !Kung San and Mbuti, men appear to be more willing to side with their female kin or wives in disputes, and this willingness to intervene is associated with less-frequent wife beating in these societies (Begler, 1978; Draper, 1992). Other societies fall somewhere in between. The Efe of the Ituri Forest provide an example: According to Bailey (1989), when men and women fight, usually bystanders do not go to the aid of either party; they simply remove spears and knives from the vicinity and let the couple fight it out.

Why are men in some societies, such as those mentioned above, reluctant to intervene to protect female kin? Meggitt claims that, in the Australian aborigine group he studied, men fail to support female kin because "most men are more concerned to maintain male solidarity than to redress the wrongs done to women" (Meggitt, 1962, p. 92, cited in Begler, 1978). This claim is further supported by two additional findings from Begler's analysis of Australian aborigine disputes. First, men consistently sided with the losing party in a fight between two men in order to prevent injury to the weaker party, which indicates an emphasis on preserving balanced relations among men. Second, Begler describes numerous cases in which a man who was confronted by a dispute over a women between two men, both of who were his allies, attacked the woman rather than taking sides. This situation sometimes resulted in injury or death of the woman, leading one ethnographer to conclude that "male opinion regarded it as better to attack a woman, and perhaps cause her death, than allow men to fight over her. In general, men were reluctant to support female interest against male interest" (Hiatt, 1965, p. 140, cited in Begler, 1978).

These examples suggest that when male alliances are particularly important, men may be less likely to support female kin who are victims of wife beating. Gregor's (1990) analysis of gang rape among the Mehinakus, a South American tribe, suggests a similar trade-off. He claims that the custom of punishing by gang rape those women who have viewed the men's sacred flutes "expresses men's loyalties to one another, and their willingness to betray the ties of affection, kinship, and economic dependence that link them to the women" (Gregor, 1990, p. 493). When men do support female kin against aggression by other men, the price may be high, as illustrated by Chagnon's example of how one man's rescue of his sister from an abusive husband provoked severe fighting among Yanomamo men from the same village (Chagnon, 1983, p. 174).

Just as men face trade-offs involving bonds with female kin versus bonds with other men, they may face similar trade-offs involving bonds with wives versus bonds with other men. Across cultures, much variation exists in the degree of cooperation and emotional intimacy found between husbands and wives (Irons, 1979, 1983; Whiting & Whiting, 1975). Whiting and Whiting describe two types of societies, ones in which the marital relationship is "intimate" and ones in which it is "aloof." The Aka of Africa are a good example of a society characterized by marital intimacy: Women and men are usually monogamous, men are involved in child care, and mates work, eat, and sleep together (Hewlett, 1991). In contrast, the marital relationship among the Rwala Bedouins is aloof: Polygyny is common, men have little interaction with their children, and mates work, eat, and sleep apart (Musil, 1928, cited in Katz & Konner, 1981). In their statistical analysis of features associated with these two types of marital relationships, the Whitings found that aloof relationships were positively associated with a tendency for men to spend most of their time with other men, apart from women, with the formation of fraternal interest groups (i.e., strong bonds among cohorts of related men; Otterbein, 1970) and with the glorification of male attributes associated with effective warriors (Whiting & Whiting, 1975, p. 194). These findings suggest two conclusions:

1. Men face a trade-off between the development of bonds with wives and the development of bonds with other men; in other words, the elaboration of strong marital bonds interferes with the development of effective male alliances and vice-versa (cf. Irons, 1979, 1983). This tension between male–female and male–male bonds is evident in such cultures as the Awlad'Ali Bedouins, for which open display of affection toward a wife results in ridicule by a man's allies (Abu-Lughod, 1986).

2. The trade-off between male–female and male–male bonds will depend, at least in part, on the importance of male alliances in intergroup warfare. When these alliances are critical, men apparently sacrifice the benefits of developing affiliative bonds with their wives in order to maximize the benefits of male cooperation. In contrast, we may speculate that, under other conditions, including perhaps lower rates of intergroup conflict and particular types of subsistence strategies, men benefit relatively more from development of affiliative bonds with women.

Since affiliation cannot be compelled, but must be earned through providing benefits and inhibiting costs, I hypothesize that men will be less likely to beat their wives in societies in which marital bonds are emphasized and will be more likely to beat their wives in societies in which these bonds are sacrificed in favor of male alliances. Whiting and Whiting (1975) found no relationship between the frequency of wife beating and whether husbands and wives sleep together or apart (their measure of marital intimacy). However, sleeping patterns provide at best an indirect measure of marital intimacy, and more direct measures are required to test this hypothesis. In addition, it is probably important to scale marital intimacy as a continuous, rather than a dichotomous, variable. Examples of societies characterized by high husband–wife intimacy and very low rates of wife beating include the Aka (Hewlett, 1991), the !Kung San (Draper, 1992), and the Wape of New Guinea (Mitchell, 1990).[3]

It is also important to consider the effect of male alliances on other forms of male aggression toward women, such as rape. Otterbein (1979) reports a statistically significant, positive cross-cultural association between the frequency of rape and the existence of fraternal interest groups. In many instances, however, the rapes apparently involved women from enemy groups. Thus, the correlation between fraternal interest groups and rape may simply reflect the fact that both of these variables are associated with warfare. Within groups, the relationship between strong male alliances and rape may be quite complex. On one hand, "gangs" of young men are notoriously dangerous to women, both in traditional societies (e.g., New Guinea highlands; Gelber, 1986) and in industrial societies (e.g., fraternity gang rape; Sanday, 1990). On the other hand, male alliances may also be a particularly effective means of protecting women from aggression, including rape, by men from other groups or by bachelors from within the group (Irons, 1983). Among the Efe of the Ituri Forest, for example, Bailey and Aunger (1989) report that male allies from the same patriclan escort women between camps and villages with bows and arrows in hand in order to defend them from harassment or capture by males from other clans.

Reliance on this type of protection entails costs as well as benefits for women. First, men may use their alliances with other men to prevent actions that may benefit the women, but at a cost to the men. The Efe society again provides a good example: Bailey (1988, p. 62) reports that when an Efe woman leaves her group to live in a village with a Bantu man (which represents an increase in status and resources for the woman), her clansmen cooperate to "rescue" her from the village and return her to her own people. Second, because protection of women by groups of allied men is often conditional on the woman's conformance to cultural ideals of proper female behavior, it is used to control women as well as to protect them. Examples include such societies as the Mundurucu and Mehinaku of South America, in which women who choose to travel along relinquish all rights to retaliation if they are sexually assaulted (Gregor, 1990; Murphy & Murphy, 1985). Similarly, in the United States today, rape is less likely to be punished by the male-dominated legal system if the victim dresses in ways considered provocative or if she has a history of sexual activity (Estrich, 1987). Finally, as argued above, marriage itself can be considered a means by which cooperating males agree about mating rights. In virtually all the world's cultures, mating rights entail not only the exclusion of other men from sexual access to a man's wife—a means of protecting women from rape by other men—but also the husband's right to have sex with his wife regardless of her consent—a means of legitimizing rape by the husband (Finkelhor & Yllo, 1985). Thus, male alliances provide women with important benefits, but at the same time inflict significant costs.

How and why the ratio of these costs and benefits varies across societies is an important question for future research.

Hypothesis 4: Female Vulnerability to Wife Beating Will Generally Increase as Male Relationships Become Less Egalitarian

Across cultures, men (and other kin) appear particularly reluctant to intervene on behalf of a female relative when the cause of a husband–wife dispute is the woman's infidelity (or suspected infidelity; Abu-Lughod, 1986; Aucoin, 1990; Counts, 1992; Lateef, 1990; Lewis, 1990; Miller, 1992). In many societies, men (at least in their public actions) condemn adulterous behavior by all women, including their female kin. Yet, in other societies, although men may be considerably distressed by their own wives' adultery, male aggression in response to female adultery is not considered legitimate, and men protect their female kin from wife beating (e.g., !Kung San; Draper, 1992). To understand this cross-cultural variation, we need to examine the complex dilemma that men face in responding to adulterous activity by women.

From an evolutionary perspective, the ideal situation for each man is to prevent adultery by his own wife or wives while he pursues adulterous relations with other men's wives. With the exception of extreme despots (Betzig, 1986), however, a man can neither successfully enact nor publicly espouse this strategy because it directly conflicts with the strategies of other men, including his allies. Men must therefore compromise their ideal strategies. One common compromise seems to involve overt support for sanctions against female adultery combined with varying degrees of covert circumvention of those sanctions. One important manifestation of overt support for sanctions against female adultery is a man's willingness to allow his own female kin to be beaten by another man for sexual transgressions, including adultery.

Cooperating with other men to enforce sanctions against female adultery also involves trade-offs. On the one hand, through cooperation, a man can often reduce his own vulnerability to cuckoldry. On the other hand, when a man cooperates with other men in this way, he also typically reduces his opportunities to gain additional offspring through adulterous matings. The ratio between these costs and benefits should vary, in turn, depending on two related factors:

1. *The degree of political inequality among men.* Collier and Rosaldo (1981) contrast two basic types of male relationships in traditional societies. In some societies, few opportunities exist for some men to accumulate political power and resources at the expense of other men, and egalitarian relationships prevail among men (e.g., Draper, 1992). Under these conditions, no man can consistently manipulate and control the behavior of other men. In contrast, in other societies, some men can accumulate political power and resources at the expense of other men and can use these sources of power to impose their will

on others. In these societies, men exhibit nonegalitarian relationships (Collier & Rosaldo, 1981).

The degree of equality among men should influence the trade-offs men face in their attempts to control female adultery. When relationships among men are nonegalitarian, powerful men can use their alliances with one another to manipulate the system to their own advantage. Specifically, they can enforce sanctions against others' adulterous behavior and guard their own mates while they simultaneously gain access to the mates of lower status men (e.g., Betzig, 1986). Men in power can thus increase the benefits of controlling female sexuality while they decrease the costs of reduced mating opportunities. In contrast, when male relationships are highly egalitarian, the costs and benefits of male cooperation to control female sexuality fall on all men roughly equally, so men should be less motivated to create and enforce sanctions against female adultery.

2. *The degree of variation in the ability of different men to invest in their offspring.* Differences in male ability to invest in offspring will tend to vary directly with differences in male power. At one extreme, we can imagine a society in which all men have similar abilities to invest in offspring. Under these conditions, the loss of an offspring through cuckoldry would be balanced by the gain of an offspring through adultery, and men would be less motivated to cooperate with one another to prevent female adultery.[4] At the other extreme, imagine a society in which some men can invest much more in offspring than others. Under these conditions, men with the greatest ability to invest (i.e., high-status men) should be particularly concerned with protecting themselves from cuckoldry and will therefore cooperate to support sanctions against adultery by their own women (cf. Dickemann, 1981).

Several predictions follow from these theoretical considerations. In societies in which relationships between men are fairly egalitarian and in which individual differences in male ability to provide parental investment are slight, men will gain less from cooperating to promote sanctions against female adultery, will tend to rely more on individual tactics to prevent cuckoldry, and will tend to support their female kin in disputes with their husbands. As a result, women will have more sexual freedom and be less vulnerable to wife beating. The !Kung San provide a good example (Draper, 1992; Shostak, 1981).

In contrast, in societies characterized by individual differences both in male power and in male ability to invest in young, powerful men will promote sanctions against female adultery among their women and will not support female relatives in conflicts with their husbands over female adultery (except, perhaps, in those unusual cases in which female relatives marry lower status men). Thus, the sexuality of high-status women will be rigidly controlled (Dickemann, 1981), and they will be vulnerable to wife beating (e.g., Lateef, 1990).[5] At the same time, women of low status will be victims of sexual coercion and exploitation by high-status men (e.g., Betzig, 1986, 1995). In these societies, even low-status men may support sanctions against female adultery because of the benefits associated with mimicry of elite cultural ideals.

In societies at the extreme of this end of the continuum, often character-ized as "honor and shame societies," high-status men not only refuse to protect their female kin from wife beating in response to adultery, but actually beat, or even kill, their own female kin for this transgression (Campbell, 1964; Lateef, 1990; Peristiany, 1966). This act benefits the women's kin in two ways. First, it demonstrates the family's commitment to the code of female chastity and fidelity, which protects their ability to obtain husbands for their women in the future. Second, it prevents the need for punishment of the wayward woman by her husband's family, which would result in interfamily feuding and the disruption of valuable marital alliances.

I therefore hypothesize that egalitarian relationships among men (as de-fined above) are likely to be associated with relatively tolerant attitudes toward female sexuality, including a tendency for male kin to protect women from being beaten by their husbands for sexual offenses, whereas hierarchical rela-tionships among men are likely to be associated with rigid control of female sexuality, including a tendency for men to refuse to support female kin who have committed sexual infractions. In short, as male relationships become increasingly egalitarian, women gain both increased sexual freedom and re-duced vulnerability to spousal aggression (Draper, 1992).

Hypothesis 5: Women Will Be More Vulnerable to Male Aggression as Male Control of Resources Increases

In nonhuman primates, females rely on their own efforts to obtain food and do not depend on males for any material resources (other than, in a few species, very occasional food sharing). In human societies, in contrast, women typically depend on men for at least some critical resources. Both evolutionary theorists and cultural anthropologists often emphasize the cooperative nature of the division of labor in humans: Women gather and men hunt; men plow the fields and women harvest the food. What these accounts ignore is the widespread existence of sexual asymmetries in the control of resources, includ-ing food, land, money, tools, and weapons, that allow men to use resources as a means of controlling women (e.g., Burgess & Draper, 1989; Sacks, 1975; Tabet, 1982). Once women become dependent on men for resources, their vulnerability to male coercive control increases for two reasons. First, as dis-cussed above, the more resources men invest in their mates and their mates' children, the more important it is for men to ensure paternity certainty; this situation in turn increases their motivation to control female sexuality (Dicke-mann, 1981), which may include the use of coercive methods (e.g., Lateef, 1990). Second, as women's dependence on men for resources increases, the alternatives to remaining with a coercive mate decline, reducing the woman's power to negotiate the terms of the relationship (e.g., Iron, 1983; Lateef, 1990; Counts, 1992).[6]

Lateef (1990) provides a particularly vivid example of the interaction between male aggression toward women and female economic dependence on men. The Indo-Fijian society that she studied shares many characteristics of the northern Indian Hindu society from which it stems, including patrilocal residence, patrilineal inheritance, and patriarchal rule by senior males. The vast majority of her female informants had experienced or had been threatened with male violence, either by male kin or by husbands, and "violence pervades the lives of young women" (Lateef, 1990, p. 48). Because of restrictions related to purdah (seclusion of women from public observation), women are generally unable to work outside the home and are entirely dependent on their husbands for economic support. The woman's parents often depend on sons for support, and brothers are hard-pressed to provide additional economic support for sisters who might flee their husbands because of abuse. Thus, if a woman does leave her husband, she often ends up on welfare; in fact, a much larger proportion of Indo-Fijian women are on welfare compared to ethnic Fijian women, who can gain support from their families in the event of marital disputes. According to Lateef (1990, p. 60), many women faced with the task of trying to raise children without male economic support choose to remain in violent marriages. Her account reminds me of an Indian woman I knew in East Africa. This young woman had been severely beaten by her husband. Finally, her family took her back, but, in order to earn her keep, she had to work 12 hours a day in the family-owned store. When not working, she was restricted to the family compound. Because the failure of her marriage was shameful to her and her family, she could never marry again. She had nothing to look forward to but endless years of drudgery living in an extremely circumscribed world. With tears in her eyes, she described her existence as "a living death." When a similar fate confronts wives who leave their husbands, it is not surprising that many of them remain with their husbands in spite of the beatings they may suffer.

Cross-cultural analyses generally support the hypothesis that male control of resources makes women more vulnerable to male aggression. Schlegel and Barry (1986), for example, report a statistically significant cross-cultural association between reduced female contribution to subsistence and increased frequency of rape. Women's contribution to subsistence is unlikely to be the best measure of male control of resources, however, since women may work very hard but still not control the fruits of their labors (Friedl, 1975). Levinson (1989) reports a more germane result: Across cultures, a statistically significant positive association exists between the degree of male control over the products of family labor and the frequency of wife beating.

This relationship between male control of resources and the frequency of wife beating does not necessarily hold, however, in industrial societies or societies undergoing modernization. In the United States, for example, the relationship between the frequency of wife beating and the wife's economic dependence on her husband is curvilinear; beatings are most frequent when women are very dependent, less common when female economic dependence is intermediate, and again frequent when female economic dependence is minimal (Levinson, 1989). Similarly, in traditional societies undergoing rapid economic change, including expansion of women into the labor market, increased female economic autonomy is sometimes associated with increased wife beating (Counts, 1992; Miller, 1992; Nero, 1990). The evidence suggests that, when economic dependence on men decreases, women are more likely to defy male attempts to control them, and some men may respond by resorting to violence. This finding cautions us against the naive hope that changes in a single variable will reduce women's vulnerability to male aggression. Rather, we must consider how numerous variables, including the ones suggested here, interact to increase or decrease the frequency of male aggression against women.

DISCUSSION

The evidence reviewed above suggests that, far from being an immutable feature of human nature, male aggression toward women varies dramatically depending on circumstances. In particular, I have hypothesized that male use of aggression against women will reflect varying costs and benefits of different male reproductive strategies and female counterstrategies, such as mustering support from relatives or leaving a violent relationship. Below, I briefly discuss some of the implications of a strategic view of male aggression against women and indicate possible directions for future research.

Gender Ideology

Cultural anthropologists have provided ample documentation of the ways in which gender ideology — cultural beliefs about the nature of men and women and proper sex-typed behavior — both reflects and helps to sustain particular types of male–female relationships (e.g., Abu-Lughod, 1986; Gregor, 1990; Llewelyn-Davis, 1981). Gender ideology supports male aggression against women in myriad ways. For example, as indicated above, many, perhaps most, of the world's cultures subscribe to the belief that a husband (but not a wife) has the right, indeed often even the duty, to beat a spouse who commits or is suspected of committing adultery (see Counts et al., 1992; Daly & Wilson, 1988). Another example involves the belief that a woman who ventures out on her own is looking for sexual adventure and is therefore fair game for sexual assault by any man (e.g., Lewis, 1990; Murphy & Murphy, 1985). These and similar strongly held beliefs reflect cultural legitimization of a man's right, under certain conditions, to beat or rape a woman with impunity, and they undoubtedly influence individual behavior. If, for example, a woman believes that she deserves to be beaten or raped because of her actions, or if she at least thinks that everyone else believes it, she will almost certainly be less likely to perform those actions; similarly, a man who shares these beliefs will be more likely to act coercively.

From an evolutionary perspective, these cultural beliefs are hypothesized to be products of individual strategic behavior. In other words, they can be viewed as reflections of the reproductive interests of the most powerful individuals in a given society. For example, in a classic article, Ortner (1978) analyzes variation in cultural ideologies related to women and sexuality. She concludes that in prestate societies, women are generally considered dangerous to men, but, in state-level societies, they are said to be in danger from men, which justifies male protection and guardianship. "Before they were polluting, and this had to be defended against, but now they are said to be pure, and to need defending" (Ortner, 1978, p. 26). Ortner is puzzled as to why this shift in ideology should occur. An evolutionary perspective, including the discussion above of how variation in male–male relationships influences male reproductive strategies, suggests a possible answer.

In many prestate societies, in which relationships between men tend to be more egalitarian than in state societies, men often face opportunities to have sex with one another's wives (see above). Women as sexual beings are therefore sources of danger to men in two respects. First, if the woman is his wife, the man is vulnerable to cuckoldry. Second, if the woman is someone else's wife, the temptation to adultery threatens a man's own well-being because of potential retaliation and also threatens male solidarity by creating a source of conflict between men. Thus, it is not surprising that, in these societies, women are often portrayed as dangerous and polluting, and it is their sexuality that makes them so.[7] By portraying women in this way, men blame women for male sexual exploits and direct attention away from the real source of danger—the underlying sexual competition between men that continuously threatens male solidarity (Collier & Rosaldo, 1981).

In state-level societies, on the other hand, female sexuality is much more rigidly controlled because high-status men (those who presumably contribute the most to the creation and maintenance of cultural ideology) effectively protect their women from sexual access by other men (see above and Dickemann, 1981). Thus, we find an ideology that focuses on women as pure, in danger of being spoiled, and in need of male protection. To go one step beyond Ortner, I suggest that in these societies the notion of women as dangerous and polluting is not eliminated altogether; rather, it is now shifted to the low-status women who are vulnerable to sexual exploitation by high-status men—thus the ideology of the virgin and the whore. From a male point of view, the virgin is one's own wife, or daughter, or sister, whereas the whore is the lower status woman whose sexual availability enables high-status men to enjoy the benefits of promiscuity without incurring the costs. By depicting these women as whores, high-status men can attribute their sexual exploits to the women's voracious sexuality, drawing attention away from the coercive tactics they employ to gain access to these women.

In some cases, such as the example just given, "strategic" interpretations of cultural ideology may appear fairly straightforward. In other cases, however, advocates of an evolutionary approach must confront the paradoxical fact that less-powerful people whose interests do not appear to be advanced by particular cultural beliefs nevertheless often seem to share them. For example, not only men, but women, too, sometimes express the belief that adulterous wives deserve to be beaten (e.g., Aucoin, 1990; Counts, 1992; Lateef, 1990). Among the Awlad'Ali Bedouins of Egypt, "women claim . . . that 'real men'

. . . beat their wives when the wives do stupid things," and women want husbands who are dominant men (Abu-Lughod, 1986, p. 89).

One possible interpretation of these paradoxical beliefs is provided by Lateef (1990), who argues that Indo-Fijian women benefit by conforming to a male-dominated social system because they have no alternatives to their economic dependence of men. Similarly, among the Awlad'Ali Bedouins, women must rely on husbands for protection. Given this reality, it is no wonder that women prefer as husbands men who demonstrate their protective abilities by maintaining control over their dependents. In other words, women's adoption of cultural values that appear to go against their own interests may in fact be necessary for survival (Mathieu, 1990) or for successful reproduction (Dickemann, 1981). In addition, when the exigencies of daily life foster female competition for scare resources, including favors dispensed by men, women may advocate cultural beliefs that allow men to coerce other women (Gallin, 1992; Lateef, 1990). The existence of reproductive conflicts of interest between women and how these conflicts may prevent female cooperation and thereby help to maintain male domination are important topics that require further analysis by evolutionary biologists and feminists alike (Hrdy, 1981).

The Role of Male Aggression in Maintaining Dominance over Women

In a recent cross-cultural review of women's status, Mukhopadhyay and Higgins (1988) urge cultural anthropologists to examine the role of male aggression in the maintenance of sociocultural systems of male dominance over women. This task will not be easy because of the difficulty in distinguishing cause from effect: Are men able to coerce women because they dominate women in so many other ways, or does male aggression play a central role in establishing dominance over women to begin with? To complicate the analysis further, the answer to this question probably varies from society to society.

These difficulties are apparent in many ethnographic accounts. Lateef (1990), for example, reports that Indo-Fijian women informants claimed that fear of male violence was the reason they complied with constraints on their behavior. However, she also argues that the family ideology, which places women in a subordinate role, is the main mechanism for enforcing male dominance, and that male violence plays only a supplementary role (Lateef, 1990). Burbank (1992) argues from her Australian aborigine evidence that frequent male aggression does not prevent women from doing what they want and that it does not inevitably promote asymmetries in power between the sexes.

Gregor, in contrast, claims that, in small-scale, technologically simple societies, the "fact that men can overwhelm women in violent encounters is recognized . . . and looms large in gender politics" (Gregor, 1990, p. 480). He provides a vivid example from his own fieldwork among the Mehinakus of South America. Among the Mehinakus, as among some other indigenous societies in South America (Murphy & Murphy, 1985) and New Guinea (Gelber, 1986), men conduct sacred rituals in the men's house, which is segregated from women, and women who violate this space are (in theory, at least) punished by gang rape. According to Gregor, the men rationalize the rape as follows: "The tradition is good, it makes the women afraid of us. . . . They are afraid of the men's penises! So they just stay in the houses" (keeping the women in the houses is a metaphor for keeping them under control and in their place; Gregor, 1990, p. 487).[8]

Gregor's conversations with village women indicate that they experience the threat of male violence as pervasive, and they frequently have nightmares in which they are the victims of male aggression. This finding is particularly striking in light of the fact that wife beating is extremely rare in this society, and no gang rapes had apparently occurred for many years. Presumably, the threat of gang rape alone was sufficient to make women frightened of men. As a result, according to Gregor, women are more likely to obey men in other domains. Gregor concludes his analysis of gang rape by saying,

> It at once expresses the subordinate status of women and the solidarity of men. . . . It is the sanction by which men as a group keep women as a group from participating in the religious and political systems as equals. . . . It is an overwhelming and supremely effective symbol of gender inequality. (Gregor, 1990, pp. 492–493)

Clearly, additional empirical evidence is required to determine the extent to which use of male force, or its threat, contributes to male dominance over women in various domains. An evolutionary perspective would tend to support Gregor's contention that male aggression against women functions as an important sanction controlling female behavior because of the potentially enormous costs to women of physical injury at the hands of men. Note that the males' superior fighting ability is not the ultimate (evolutionary) cause of male dominance over women. As I have argued elsewhere (Smuts, 1995), male reproductive striving is the ultimate cause of male dominance over women; men's superior fighting ability is simply one means to this end.

Female Sexuality

Researchers working from an evolutionary perspective have characterized female sexuality as both lower in intensity and less oriented toward sexual variety than male sexuality (e.g., Symons, 1979). Symons argues that these sex differences reflect genetically based differences in female and male psychologies as a result of sexual selection. For example, men are said to be more highly motivated to seek multiple sexual partners because in this way they can father numerous offspring, whereas women are said to be less interested in sexual variety per se because their reproductive success depends less on multiple partners than it does on adequate investment by a single, investing male.

Hrdy (1979, 1981) has challenged some of these characterizations of female sexuality by pointing out that nonhuman primate females are often both highly sexually motivated and highly promiscuous. It is possible that, relative to many nonhuman primate females, human females are less promiscuous and appear to be less sexually motivated in part because of the effects of male aggression on female sexuality.

Anthropological evidence indicates that, in a wide variety of societies around the world, the expression of female sexuality evokes negative sanctions, often including physical punishment by husbands or male relatives (Daly & Wilson, 1988). Examples include the frequent beating of adulterous wives (see above); the abandonment or killing of girls found not to be virgins at marriage (Lewis, 1990); and beatings for immodest behavior, such as transgressing purdah, revealing too much of the face or ankle, or speaking to or even looking at unrelated men (e.g., Abu-Lughod, 1986; Counts, 1992; Lateef, 1990; Lewis, 1990). In a variety of cultures, women have had their genitals cut out or sewn together to discourage sexual activity; their movements curtailed by mutilation of the feet, the threat of rape, and confinement to guarded harems; their noses bitten off in culturally sanctioned responses to adultery; and their bodies beaten and mutilated during gang rapes considered a normal part of adolescent male sexuality (Daly, 1978; Dickemann, 1981; Gelber, 1986; Lewis, 1990; Murphy & Murphy, 1985). Assertive female sexuality leads to abandonment of wives among the Yanomamos and to gang rape among the Mundurucus (Chagnon, 1983; Murphy & Murphy, 1985). In some cultures, force is considered an integral part of normal marital sex; the man's struggle to overcome a frightened and resistant woman heightens his sexual satisfaction (e.g., Levine, 1959; Miller, 1992). Because of these and other similar practices, women associate sex with danger.[9]

These and other countless examples of cultural constraints on female sexuality support Rubin's claim that male-dominated systems foster a kind of female sexuality that responds to male needs and desires rather than one that has needs and desires of its own (Rubin, 1975, p. 182). In other words, both the objective, observable expression of female sexuality and women's subjective experience of their own sexuality are so influenced by repression and fear of violent coercion that, in most societies, it is impossible to identify the "intrinsic" nature of female sexuality based on female behavior. It seems premature, for example, to attribute the relative lack of female interest in sexual variety to women's biological nature alone in the face of overwhelming evidence that women are consistently beaten for promiscuity and adultery.

An advocate of the traditional sociobiological view of female sexuality might respond that, precisely because sex has been dangerous for women, evolution has favored a reduced female sex drive. Four arguments can be marshaled against this view. First, if female sexuality is muted compared to that of men, then why must men all over the world go to extreme lengths to control and contain it? Second, since the extent to which female sexuality is repressed and subject to violent constraints varies tremendously across societies, it would make no sense for women to evolve an inherently muted sexuality. Third, women can gain important reproductive benefits from mating with multiple partners (Hill & Kaplan, 1988), a point often ignored in evolutionary analyses (Hrdy, 1986). Fourth, evidence from nonhuman primates and from women in societies with relatively few coercive constraints on female sexual behavior, such as the !Kung San or modern Scandinavia, indicate the existence of an active, assertive female sexuality that is excited by, among other things, sexual variety (Hrdy, 1981; 1986; Shostak, 1981). I do not call attention to these considerations in order to argue that, in the absence of constraints, female sexuality would be just like male sexuality. Rather, my goal is to emphasize the need to investigate how the experience and expression of female sexuality varies, at both psychological and behavioral levels, depending on the extent and nature of the constraining influence of male strategies. Until these investigations provide new evidence, the nature of female sexuality must remain an open question.[10]

Behavioral Flexibility and Evolutionary Analysis

Feminist anthropologists have rightly criticized simplistic biological arguments that explain social relations between men and women, including male dominance over women, as direct and inevitable consequences of genetically determined differences in the physical and psychological natures of the sexes (e.g., Collier & Rosaldo, 1981; Quinn, 1977). As Bleier (1984) has eloquently argued, these explanations remove gender asymmetries in power from the political arena, reducing them to inevitable, if regrettable, manifestations of immutable natural laws that can then be used to rationalize and justify sexual oppression. I have tried to show here that a biological, evolutionary perspective on relations between the sexes does not necessarily depend on deterministic assumptions, nor does it inevitably draw conclusions that support the status quo. On the contrary, my purpose has been to show that a responsible evolutionary analysis is both political and conditional, and therefore potentially radical, in its implications. Specifically, I have argued that men use aggression to try to control women, and particularly to try to control female sexuality, not because men are inherently aggressive and women inherently submissive, but because men find aggression to be a useful political tool in their struggle to dominate and control women and thereby enhance their reproductive opportunities. I have also argued that male use of aggression as a tool is not inevitable, but conditional; that is, under some circumstances, coercive control of women pays off, whereas under other circumstances it does not.

What makes the above analysis different from other perspectives that emphasize the conditional nature of male aggression toward women is its emphasis on individual reproductive success as the ultimate goal of both male sexual coercion and female resistance to it. This assumption provides a useful theoretical framework for analyzing the costs and benefits of different courses of action. To the extent that this evolutionary framework proves useful in helping to identify the conditions that favor male aggression toward women, it can also contribute to the formulation of strategies to alter those conditions.

Conclusion: Future Research Directions

The analyses described above suggest several fruitful directions for future research. First and most fundamentally, to evaluate hypotheses to explain cross-cultural variation in the frequency of male aggression toward women we need quantitative information on actual rates and intensities of wife beating, rape, and other aggressive acts. Collection of this information will require behavioral observations and careful, systematic interviews with reliable informants.

Second, as Begler (1978) advocated some time ago, if we want to understand why men sometimes feel free to use aggression against women and sometimes do not, we must pay attention not only to gender ideology (i.e., what people say people should do), but also to what people actually do, especially in domains in which behavioral outcomes are particularly telling. Begler's accounts of who actually supports whom in disputes between men and women are salient examples of the value of behavioral observations. Anthropologists have argued at great length about the extent to which men dominate women in all human cultures and about whether male domination in particular arenas implies male domination in others (e.g., Mukhopadyay & Higgins, 1988; Ortner, 1991; Quinn, 1977; Whyte, 1978). There is only one way to answer these questions: We need behavioral observations that tell us who wins when conflicts of interest arise between the sexes and why they win.

Third, in order to identify the factors that favor or disfavor male aggression against women, we need information on the costs and benefits—that is, the consequences—of these acts (or the absence of these acts). This information will often be very difficult to obtain; how can we tell, for example, whether a given instance of wife beating decreased the chances that the woman would continue to see her lover? At the very least, it would be useful to gain more information from informants concerning their own perceptions of the consequences of different acts. Only a small minority of the ethnographies that I reviewed include specific accounts of how the people involved were affected by male aggression.

Fourth, I have argued that the form and frequency of male aggression toward women is related to the nature of men's relationships with one another. Many critical questions related to this hypothesis remain unexplored. For example, does the impact of male cooperation on relations between the sexes vary depending on the purposes of that cooperation (i.e., intergroup competition, intragroup competition, more efficient food procurement)? Does it matter whether or not male alliances involve mainly kin? Are there circumstances under which men simultaneously develop cooperative bonds with other men and intimate, noncoercive relationships with women? I have also argued that the nature of female relationships influences female vulnerability to male aggression. Thus, we need to explore carefully the complex and subtle ways in which different types of relationships influence one another.

Fifth, much more information is needed concerning female resistance to acts of male aggression and female counterstrategies that inhibit or prevent aggression. I am painfully aware that, although this chapter focuses on behaviors that affect women, it deals mostly with actions by men, not by women. This reflects in part the difficulty of gleaning information about female strategies from a literature that remains somewhat male biased. I hope that by emphasizing the prominence of male aggression against women cross culturally, the chapter will help to focus attention on the strategies that women employ to protect themselves from men.

Sixth, although this chapter has focused on cross-cultural variation in male aggression against women, it is equally important to investigate variation among individuals within a given society. All of the hypotheses presented here could be modified to help to account for intracultural variation in male aggression against women. For example, within a society, some women threatened by their husbands will receive more support from their kin than others, and these differences could help to explain individual differences in women's vulnerability to wife beating.

Finally, to understand variation in men's and women's tendencies to be perpetrators and victims of intersexual aggression both across and within societies, it will be critical to consider not only variations in current circumstances, but also individual differences in previous experience that may lead people to respond to similar circumstances in different ways. An evolutionary perspective on developmental processes may prove very useful in this regard (e.g., Chisholm, 1988; Draper & Harpending, 1988; Smuts, 1992).

Acknowledgments. This paper was inspired by the pioneering work of Mildred Dickemann, Sarah Hrdy, and Richard Wrangham, who recognized the costs that male reproductive strategies impose on females. I thank Judith Brown, David Gubernick, Sarah Hrdy, and Patty Gowaty for valuable comments, and Mildred Dickemann, Lars Rodseth, and Robert Smuts for extensive feedback on an early draft. I also thank several contributors to *Sanctions and Sanctuary* (Counts et al., 1992) for sharing their chapters with me in advance of publication. This work was supported in part by National Science Foundation grant BNS-8857969.

NOTES

1. *Promiscuous* is a technical term used by biologists to describe mating behavior involving multiple partners; no connotation of wanton or indiscriminate sex is implied.

2. A fourth possible reason is that Levinson's patrilocal sample includes societies with claustration, an alternative to wife beating that is preferred by those who can afford it as a more effective and less damaging means of ensuring wifely fidelity (Mildred Dickemann, personal communication, 1991).

3. To complicate the argument further, it seems likely that when a man's most important alliances are those he establishes with affinal kin through exchange of women (e.g., Levi-Strauss, 1949/1969), aggression toward wives will be inhibited, at least to some extent, by the desire to maintain these alliances. For example, Aucoin (1990) describes how, among Fijians, a husband who has beaten his wife disrupts

relations between exogamous clans. To reestablish good relations, he must perform a ritual act of atonement to the wife and her kin. I suspect that one important factor determining whether strong links among affines inhibit or promote male violence toward wives is the nature of the act that evokes the husband's aggression; if the provocation involves failure to conform to cultural ideals of proper female behavior, especially sexual transgressions, the woman may be blamed for disrupting good relations between affines, and her kin may support the husband's right to beat her (see text). In contrast, if the husband beats the woman for, in the eyes of her kin, "no good reason," then he may be blamed for disrupting affinal relations, and the woman may be supported by her kin (e.g., Abu-Lughod, 1986).

4. For the sake of simplicity, this argument assumes that men do not easily discriminate offspring resulting from adulterous unions and thus cannot withdraw parental investment from those offspring. If men can withdraw investment from offspring of these unions, the benefits to men of adultery decrease (because the resulting offspring will suffer from reduced male parental investment), but the costs of being cuckolded also decrease (because men will not suffer the costs of investing in other men's offspring). Without knowing the precise relationship between these benefits and costs, it is impossible to specify how ability to detect cuckoldry will influence male proclivity to support general sanctions against female adultery.

5. This argument converges in important ways with that developed by Dickemann to explain purdah, claustration, and other forms of control of female sexuality in stratified societies (Dickemann, 1981). It broadens Dickemann's argument, which focuses on the importance to high-status men of protecting their parental investment, in its emphasis on the trade-offs entailed in male cooperation to control female adultery in different types of societies, and the effect of these trade-offs on the male tendency to ally with or against their female kin during spousal disputes over female adultery.

6. This evidence suggests the possibility that male economic provisioning of women and children evolved not only because it increased the fitness of their own offspring (the traditional explanation, which views male provisioning as a form of parental investment), but also because it increased their control over female sexuality (a different explanation that views male provisioning as a form of mating effort).

7. Ortner (1981) points out that many tribal societies stress male "purity," that is, sexual abstinence, before major undertakings like hunting or raids on other groups. Perhaps this custom has arisen to decrease the risks of sexually motivated conflicts between men prior to events that depend on male cooperation.

8. Among another South American tribe, the Mundurucu, men also state explicitly that they use the penis as a weapon during gang rape (Murphy & Murphy, 1985).

9. It is not necessary for a woman to experience male aggression herself in order to become afraid: Growing up in a society in which she sees other women subjected to similar acts, or in which she is simply warned repeatedly of the dangers associated with female sexuality, is sufficient to arouse deep-rooted fear (Brownmiller, 1975; Gregor, 1990; Mathieu, 1989; McKee, 1992).

10. Symons (1979) disagrees. He cites evidence concerning lesbian sexuality to argue that, in the absence of male influence, female sexuality would be expressed primarily in the context of long-term, monogamous relationships, and that women would show little interest in sexual variety. He suggests that sexual behavior among homosexual men and women provides important insights into the essential nature of male and female sexuality because, with partners of the same sex, sexual behavior is free from the compromises imposed by the need to respond to the very different and usually conflicting needs of the opposite sex.

Symons's claim that lesbian sexuality reflects female sexuality free from the constraining influence of male interests rests on the implicit assumption that all women need to do to avoid this influence is cease interacting sexually with men. This assumption seems wrong for two reasons. First, lesbians, like all women in male-dominated societies, grow up in a sociocultural context that imposes powerful constraints on the development and expression of their sexuality. These developmental experiences influence female psychology in deeply rooted ways that cannot be erased simply by choosing to avoid sex with men. Second, lesbians remain vulnerable to male sexual coercion. Thus, Symons's analysis, like that of many other evolutionarily minded researchers, is flawed by his failure to acknowledge the systematic domination of women by men and how this domination influences female sexuality.

REFERENCES

Abegglen, J. J. (1984). *On socialization in hamadryas baboons.* Cranberry, NJ: Associated University Press.

Abu-Lughod, L. (1986). *Veiled sentiments: Honor and poetry in a Bedouin society.* Berkeley, CA: University of California Press.

Alexander, R. D., & Noonan, K. M. (1979). Concealment of ovulation, parental care, and human social evolution. In N. Chagnon & W. Irons (Eds.), *Evolutionary biology and human social behavior* (pp. 436–453). North Scituate, MA: Duxbury Press.

Altmann, J. (1980). *Baboon mothers and infants.* Cambridge, MA: Harvard University Press.

Aucoin, P. M. (1990). Domestic violence and social relations of conflict in Fiji. *Pacific Studies, 13,* 23–43.

Bailey, R. C. (1988). The significance of hypergyny for understanding subsistence behaviour among contemporary hunters and gatherers. In B. V. Kennedy & G. M. LeMoine (Eds.), *Diet and subsistence: Current archaeological perspectives* (pp. 57–65). Calgary: University of Calgary Press.

Bailey, R. C. (1989). *Time allocation of Efe Pygmy men and women of the Ituri Forest, Zaire. Cross-cultural studies in time allocation* (Vol. 3). New Haven, CT: Human Relations Area Files.

Bailey, R. C., & Aunger, R. (1989). Significance of the social relationships of Efe Pygmy men in the Ituri Forest, Zaire. *American Journal of Physical Anthropology, 78,* 495–507.

Begler, E. B. (1978). Sex, status, and authority in egalitarian society. *American Anthropologist, 80,* 571–588.

Bernstein, I. S., & Ehardt, C. L. (1985). Agonistic aiding: Kinship, rank, age, and sex influences. *American Journal of Primatology, 8,* 37–52.

Betzig, L. (1986). *Despotism and differential reproduction: A Darwinian view of history.* Hawthorne, NY: Aldine de Gruyter.

Betzig, L. (1995). Medieval monogamy. *Journal of Family History, 20,* 181–216.

Biocca, E. (1968). *Yanoama: Recit d'une femme Bresilienne enlevee par les Indiens.* (Gabrielle Cabrini, Trans.). Paris: Plon.

Bleier, R. (1984). *Science and gender: A critique of biology and its theories on women.* New York: Pergamon Press.

Broude, G. J., & Greene, S. J. (1978). Cross-cultural codes on 20 sexual attitudes and practices. *Ethnology, 15,* 409–430.

Brown, J. K. (1992). Introduction: Definitions, assumptions, themes and issues. In D. Counts, J. K. Brown, & J. C. Campbell (Eds.), *Sanction and sanctuary: Cultural perspectives on the beating of wives* (pp. 1–18). Boulder, CO: Westview Press.

Brownmiller, S. (1975). *Against our will: Men, women, and rape.* New York: Simon and Schuster.

Burban, V. K. (1991). Fight! Fight! Men, women, and interpersonal aggression in an Australian Aboriginal community. In D. Counts, J. K. Brown, & J. C. Campbell (Eds.) (1992). *Sanction and sanctuary: Cultural perspectives on the beating of wives.* Boulder, CO: Westview Press.

Burgess, R. L., & Draper, P. (1989). The explanation of family violence: The role of biological, behavioral, and cultural selection. In L. Ohlin & M. Tonry (Eds.), *Family violence, crime and justice: A review of research* (Vol. 11, pp. 59–116). Chicago: University of Chicago Press.

Bygott, J. D. (1972). Cannibalism among wild chimpanzees. *Nature, 238,* 410–411.

Campbell, J. (1964). *Honour, family, and patronage: A study of institutions and moral values in a Greek mountain community.* Oxford: Clarendon Press.

Campbell, J. C. (1992). Cultural contexts versus Western social sciences. In D. Counts, J. K. Brown, & J. C. Campbell (Eds.), *Sanction and sanctuary: Cultural perspectives on the beating of wives* (pp. 229–249). Boulder, CO: Westview Press.

Chagnon, N. A. (1983). *Yanomamo: The fierce people* (3rd ed.). New York: Holt, Rinehart and Winston.

Chapais, B. (1983). Adaptive aspects of social relationships among adult rhesus monkeys. In R. A. Hinde (Ed.), *Primate social relationships: An integrated approach* (pp. 171–175). Oxford: Blackwell.

Chisholm, J. (1988). Toward a developmental evolutionary ecology of humans. In K. MacDonald (Ed.), *Sociobiological perspectives on human development.* New York: Springer-Verlag.

Collier, J. F., & Rosaldo, M. Z. (1981). Politics and gender in simple societies. In S. B. Ortner & H. Whitehead (Eds.), *Sexual meanings: The cultural construction of gender and sexuality* (pp. 275–329). Cambridge, UK: Cambridge University Press.

Counts, D. A. (1990a). Beaten wife, suicidal woman: Domestic violence in Kaliai, West New Britain. *Pacific Studies, 13,* 151–169.

Counts, D. A. (1990b). Domestic violence in Oceania: Conclusions. *Pacific Studies, 13,* 25–254.

Counts, D. A. (1992). "All men do it." Wife beating in Kaliai, Papua New Guinea. In D. Counts, J. K. Brown, & J. C. Campbell (Eds.), *Sanction and sanctuary: Cultural perspectives on the beating of wives* (pp. 63–76). Boulder, CO: Westview Press.

Counts, D., Brown, J. K., & Campbell, J. C. (Eds.). (1991). *Sanction and sanctuary: Cultural perspectives on the beating of wives.* Boulder, CO: Westview Press.

Crockett, C. M., & Rudran, R. (1987). Red howler monkey birth data II: Interannual, habitat and sex comparisons. *American Journal of Primatology, 13,* 369–384.

Daly, M. (1978). *Gynecology: The metaethics of radical feminism.* Boston: Beacon Press.

Daly, M., & Wilson, M. (1988). *Homicide.* Hawthorne, NY: Aldine de Gruyter.

de Waal, F. B. M. (1982). *Chimpanzee politics: Power and sex among apes.* New York: Harper and Row.

Dickemann, M. (1981). Paternal confidence and dowry competition: A biocultural analysis of purdah. In R. D. Alexander & D. W. Tinkle (Eds.), *Natural selection and social behavior: Recent research and new theory* (pp. 439–475). New York: Chiron Press.

Draper, P. (1992). Room to maneuver: !Kung women cope with men. In D. Counts, J. K. Brown, & J. C. Campbell (Eds.), *Sanction and sanctuary: Cultural perspectives on the beating of wives* (pp. 43–61). Boulder, CO: Westview Press.

Draper, P., & Harpending, H. (1988). A sociobiological perspective on the development of human reproductive strategies. In K. MacDonald (Ed.), *Sociobiological perspectives on human development* (pp. 340–372). New York: Springer-Verlag.

Estrich, S. (1987). *Real rape.* Cambridge, MA: Harvard University Press.

Finkelhor, D., & Yllo, K. (1985). *License to rape: Sexual abuse of wives.* New York: Free Press.

Flinn, M., & Low, B. (1986). Resource distribution, social competition, and mating patterns in human societies. In D. Rubenstein & R. W. Wrangham (Eds.), *Ecological aspects of social evolution* (pp. 217–243). Princeton, NJ: Princeton University Press.

Foley, R. A. (1989). The evolution of hominid social behavior. In V. Standen & R. A. Foley (Eds.), *Comparative socioecology* (pp. 473–494). Oxford: Blackwell.

Friedl, E. (1975). *Women and men: An anthropologist's view.* New York: Holt, Rinehart and Winston.

Galdikas, B. M. F. (1985). Subadult male orangutan sociality and reproductive behavior at Tanjung Puting. *American Journal of Primatology, 8,* 87–99.

Galdikas, B. M. F., & Teleki, G. (1981). Variations in subsistance activities of male and female pongids: New perspectives on the origins of human labor divisions. *Current Anthropology, 22,* 241–256.

Gallin, R. S. (1992). Wife abuse in the context of development and change: A Chinese (Taiwanese) case. In D. Counts, J. K. Brown, & J. C. Campbell (Eds.), *Sanction and sanctuary: Cultural perspectives on the beating of wives* (pp. 219–227). Boulder, CO: Westview Press.

Gelber, M. G. (1986). *Gender and society in the New Guinea highlands: An anthropological perspective on antagonism toward women.* Boulder, CO: Westview Press.

Goodall, J. (1986). *The chimpanzees of Gombe: Patterns of behavior.* Cambridge, MA: Harvard University Press.

Goodall, J., Bandora, A., Bergmann, E., Busse, C., Matama, H., Mpongo, E., Pierce, A., & Riss, D. (1979). Inter-community interactions in the chimpanzee population of the Gombe National Park. In D. A. Hamburg & E. R. McCown (Eds.), *The great apes* (pp. 13–53). Menlo Park, CA: Benjamin/Cummings.

Gregor, T. (1990). Male dominance and sexual coercion. In J. W. Stegler, R. A. Shweder, & G. Herdt (Eds.), *Cultural psychology* (pp. 477–495). Cambridge, UK: Cambridge University Press.

Hammerstein, P., & Parker, G. A. (1987). Sexual selection: Games between the sexes. In J. W. Bradbury & M. B. Anderson (Eds.), *Sexual selection: Testing the alternatives* (pp. 119–142). New York: John Wiley and Sons.

Hasegawa, T., & Hiraiwa-Hasegawa, M. (1983). Opportunistic and restrictive matings among wild chimpanzees in the Mahale Mountains, Tanzania. *Journal of Ethology, 1*, 75–85.

Hausfater, G., & Hrdy, S. B. (Eds.). (1984). *Infanticide: Comparative and evolutionary perspectives*. Hawthorne, NY: Aldine de Gruyter.

Hewlett, B. (1991). *Intimate fathers: The nature and context of Aka Pygmy paternal infant care*. Ann Arbor, MI: University of Michigan Press.

Hiatt, L. R. (1965). *Kinship and conflict: A study of an aboriginal community in northern Arnhem land*. Canberra: Australian National University.

Hill, K., & Kaplan, H. (1988). Trade-offs in male and female reproductive strategies among the Ache: Parts 1 and 2. In L. Betzig, P. Turke, & M. Borgerhoff Mulder (Eds.), *Human reproductive behavior* (pp. 277–305). Cambridge, UK: Cambridge University Press.

Hrdy, S. B. (1977). *The langurs of Abu: Female and male strategies of reproduction*. Cambridge, MA: Harvard University Press.

Hrdy, S. B. (1979). Infanticide among animals: A review, classification, and examination of the implications for the reproductive strategies of females. *Ethology and Sociobiology, 1*, 13–40.

Hrdy, S. B. (1981). *The woman that never evolved*. Cambridge, MA: Harvard University Press.

Hrdy, S. B. (1986). Empathy, polyandry, and the myth of the coy female. In R. Bleier (Ed.), *Feminist approaches to science* (pp. 119–146). New York: Pergamon Press.

Hutchings, N. (1988). *The violent family: Victimization of women, children, and elders*. New York: Human Sciences Press.

Irons, W. (1979). Investment and primary social dyads. In N. A. Chagnon & W. Irons (Eds.), *Evolutionary biology and human social behavior: An anthropological perspective* (pp. 181–213). North Scituate, MA: Duxbury Press.

Irons, W. (1983). Human female reproductive strategies. In S. Wasser (Ed.), *Social behavior of female vertebrates* (pp. 169–213). New York: Academic Press.

Kaplan, J. R. (1977). Patterns of fight interference in free-ranging rhesus monkeys. *American Journal of Physical Anthropology, 47*, 279–288.

Katz, M., & Konner, M. (1981). The role of the father: An anthropological perspective. In M. Lamb (Ed.), *The role of the father in child development* (pp. 155–186). New York: John Wiley and Sons.

Kawanaka, K. (1981). Infanticide and cannibalism in chimpanzees with special reference to the newly observed case in the Mahale Mountains. *African Studies Monographs, 1*, 69–99.

Keddy, A. C. (1986). Female mate choice in vervet monkeys (*Cercopithecus aethiops sabaeus*). *American Journal of Primatology, 10*, 125–134.

Kerns, V. (1992). Preventing violence against women: A Central American case. In D. Counts, J. K. Brown, & J. C. Campbell (Eds.), *Sanction and sanctuary: Cultural perspectives on the beating of wives* (pp. 125–138). Boulder, CO: Westview Press.

Koss, M. P., Gidycz, C. A., & Wisniewski, N. (1987). The scope of rape: Incidence and prevalence of sexual aggression and victimization in a national sample of higher education students. *Journal of Consulting and Clinical Psychology, 55*, 162–170.

Kummer, H. (1968). *Social organization of hamadryas baboons*. Chicago: University of Chicago Press.

Kummer, H., Gotz, W., & Angst, W. (1974). Triadic differentiation: An inhibitory process protecting pair bonds in baboons. *Behaviour, 49,* 62–87.

Lamphere, L. (1974). Strategies, cooperation, and conflict among women in domestic groups. In M. Z. Rosaldo & L. Lamphere (Eds.), *Women, culture, and society* (pp. 97–112). Stanford, CA: Stanford University Press.

Lancaster, J. B., & Lancaster, C. S. (1983). Parental investment: The hominid adaptation. In D. J. Ortner (Ed.), *How humans adapt: A biocultural odyssey* (pp. 33–56). Washington, DC: Smithsonian Institution.

Lateef, S. (1990). Rule by the *Danda*: Domestic violence among Indo-Fijians. *Pacific Studies, 13,* 43–62.

Levi-Strauss, C. (1969). *The elementary structures of kinship.* Boston: Beacon Press. (Original work published 1949)

Levine, R. (1959). Gusii sex offenses: A study in social control. *American Anthropologist, 61,* 956–990.

Levinson, D. (1989). *Family violence in cross-cultural perspective.* Newbury Park, CA: Sage.

Lewis, D. E. (1990). Tungara conjugal jealousy and sexual mutilation. *Pacific Studies, 13,* 115–126.

Lindburg, D. G. (1983). Mating behavior and estrus in the Indian rhesus monkey. In P. K. Seth (Ed.), *Perspectives on primate biology* (pp. 45–61). New Delhi: Today and Tomorrow.

Llewelyn-Davis, M. (1981). Women, warriors, and patriarchs. In S. B. Ortner & H. Whitehead (Eds.), *Sexual meanings: The cultural construction of gender and sexuality* (pp. 330–358). Cambridge, UK: Cambridge University Press.

Lovejoy, C. O. (1981). The origin of man. *Science, 211,* 341–350.

Manson, J. (1994). Male aggression: A cost of female mate choice in Cayo Santiago rhesus macaques. *Animal Behaviour, 48,* 473–475.

Mathieu, N. (1989). When yielding is not consenting: Material and psychic determinants of women's dominated consciousness and some of their interpretations in ethnology, Part I. *Feminist Issues, 9,* 3–49.

Mathieu, N. (1990). When yielding is not consenting: Material and psychic determinants of women's dominated consciousness and some of their interpretations in ethnology, Part II. *Feminist Issues, 10,* 51–90.

McGrew, W. G. (1981). The female chimpanzee as a human evolutionary prototype. In F. Dahlberg (Ed.), *Woman the gatherer* (pp. 35–73). New Haven, CT: Yale University Press.

McKee, L. (1992). Men's rights/women's wrongs: Domestic violence in Ecuador. In D. Counts, J. K. Brown, & J. C. Campbell (Eds.), *Sanction and sanctuary: Cultural perspectives on the beating of wives* (pp. 139–156). Boulder, CO: Westview Press.

Meggitt, M. J. (1962). *Desert people: A study of the Walbiri Aborigines of Central Australia.* Sydney: Angus and Robertson.

Miller, B. D. (1992). Wife-beating in India: Variations on a theme. In D. Counts, J. K. Brown, & J. C. Campbell (Eds.), *Sanction and sanctuary: Cultural perspectives on the beating of wives* (pp. 173–184). Boulder, CO: Westview Press.

Mitani, J. C. (1985). Mating behavior of male orangutans in the Kutai Reserve. *Animal Behaviour, 33,* 392–402.

Mitchell, W. E. (1990). Why Wape men don't beat their wives: Constraints toward domestic tranquility in a New Guinea society. *Pacific Studies, 13,* 141–150.

Mukhopadhyay, C. C., & Higgins, P. J. (1988). Anthropological studies of women's status revisited: 1977–1987. *Annual Review of Anthropology, 17,* 461–495.

Murdock, G. P. (1949). *Social structure.* New York: Macmillan.

Murphy, Y., & Murphy, R. F. (1985). *Women of the forest* (2nd ed.). New York: Columbia University Press.

Musil, A. (1928). *The manners and customs of the Rwala Bedouins.* New York: Charles Crane.

Nash, J. (1990). Factors relating to infrequent domestic violence among the Nagovisi. *Pacific Studies, 13,* 127–140.

Nero, K. L. (1990). The hidden pain: Drunkenness and domestic violence in Palau. *Pacific Studies, 13,* 63–92.

Nishida, T. (1979). The social structure of chimpanzees of the Mahale Mountains. In D. A. Hamburg & E. R. McCown (Eds.), *The great apes* (pp. 73–122). Menlo Park, CA: Benjamin/Cummings.

Nishida, T. (1983). Alpha status and agonistic alliance in wild chimpanzees (*Pan troglodytes schweinfurthii*). *Primates, 24,* 318–336.

Nishida, T. (1990). A quarter century of research in the Mahale Mountains: An overview. In T. Nishida (Ed.), *The chimpanzees of the Mahale Mountains: Sexual and life history strategies* (pp. 3–35). Tokyo: University of Tokyo Press.

Nishida, T., & Hiraiwa-Hasegawa, M. (1985). Responses to a stranger mother-son pair in the wild chimpanzee: A case report. *Primates, 26,* 1–13.

Nishida, T., & Hiraiwa-Hasegawa, M. (1987). Chimpanzees and bonobos: Relationships among males. In B. B. Smuts, D. L. Cheney, R. M. Seyfarth, R. W. Wrangham, & T. T. Struhsaker (Eds.), *Primate societies* (pp. 165–177). Chicago: University of Chicago Press.

Nishida, T., & Kawanaka, K. (1985). Within-group cannibalism by adult male chimpanzees. *Primates, 26,* 274–284.

Nishida, T., Takasaki, H., & Takahata, Y. (1990). Demography and reproductive profiles. In T. Nishida (Ed.), *The chimpanzees of the Mahale Mountains: Sexual and life history strategies* (pp. 63–97). Tokyo: University of Tokyo Press.

Ortner, S. B. (1978). The virgin and the state. *Feminist Studies, 4,* 19–37.

Ortner, S. B. (1981). Gender and sexuality in the hierarchical societies: The case of Polynesia and some comparative implications. In S. B. Ortner & H. Whitehead (Eds.), *Sexual meanings: The cultural construction of gender and sexuality* (pp. 359–409). Cambridge, UK: Cambridge University Press.

Ortner, S. B. (1991, Winter). Gender hegemonies. *Cultural Critique, 14,* 35–80.

Otterbein, K. (1970). *The evolution of war.* New Haven, CT: Human Relations Area Files.

Otterbein, K. (1979). A cross-cultural study of rape. *Aggressive Behavior, 5,* 425–435.

Peristiany, J. G. (Ed.). (1966). *Honour and shame: The values of Mediterranean society.* Chicago: University of Chicago Press.

Pusey, A. E. (1979). Intercommunity transfer of chimpanzees in Gombe National Park. In D. A. Hamburg & E. R. McCown (Eds.), *The great apes* (pp. 465–480). Menlo Park, CA: Benjamin/Cummings.

Quinn, N. (1977). Anthropological studies on women's status. *Annual Review of Anthropology, 6,* 181–225.

Raleigh, M. J., & McGuire, M. T. (1989). Female influences on male dominance acquisition in captive vervet monkeys, *Cercopithecus aethiops sabaeus. Animal Behavior, 38,* 59–67.

Ransom, T. W. (1981). *Beach troop of the Gombe*. Lewisburg, PA: Bucknell University Press.

Rodman, P. S. (1984). Foraging and social systems of orangutans and chimpanzees. In P. S. Rodman & J. G. H. Cant (Eds.), *Adaptations for foraging in nonhuman primates: Contributions to an organismal biology of prosimians, monkeys, and apes* (pp. 134–160). New York: Columbia University Press.

Rodseth, L., Smuts, B. B., Harrigan, A. M., & Wrangham, R. W. (1991). The human community as a primate society: Reply to comments. *Current Anthropology, 32*, 429–433.

Rodseth, L., Wrangham, R. W., Harrigan, A. M., & Smuts, B. B. (1991). The human community as a primate society. *Current Anthropology, 32*, 221–254.

Rubin, G. (1975). The traffic in women: Notes on the "political economy" of sex. In R. R. Reiter (Ed.), *Toward an anthropology of women* (pp. 157–210). New York: Monthly Review Press.

Russell, D. E. H. (1984). *Sexual exploitation: Rape, child sexual abuse, and workplace harassment*. Newbury Park, CA: Sage.

Sacks, K. (1975). Engels revisited: Women, the organization of production, and private property. In R. R. Reiter (Ed.), *Toward an anthropology of women* (pp. 211–234). New York: Monthly Review Press.

Sanday, P. R. (1981). The socio-cultural context of rape: A cross-cultural study. *Journal of Social Issues, 37*, 5–27.

Sanday, P. R. (1990). *Fraternity gang rape*. New York: New York University Press.

Schlegel, A., & Barry, H. (1986). The cultural consequences of female contributions to subsistence. *American Anthropologist, 88*, 142–150.

Seyfarth, R. M. (1978). Social relationships among adult male and female baboons, II. Behavior throughout the female reproductive cycle. *Behaviour, 64*, 227–247.

Shostak, M. (1981). *Nisa: The life and words of a !Kung woman*. Cambridge, MA: Harvard University Press.

Sigg, H., Stolba, A., Abegglen, J. J., & Dasser, V. (1982). Life history of hamadryas baboons: Physical development, infant mortality, reproductive parameters and family relationships. *Primates, 23*, 473–487.

Smuts, B. B. (1985). *Sex and friendship in baboons*. Hawthorne, NY: Aldine de Gruyter.

Smuts, B. B. (1987). Gender, aggression, and influence. In B. B. Smuts, D. L. Cheney, R. M. Seyfarth, R. W. Wrangham, & T. T. Struhsaker (Eds.), *Primate societies* (pp. 400–412). Chicago: University of Chicago Press.

Smuts, B. B. (1995). The evolutionary origins of patriarchy. *Human Nature, 6*, 1–32.

Smuts, B. B. (1992). Psychological adaptations, development and individual differences. *Behavioral and Brain Sciences, 15*, 401–402. (Commentary on R. Thornhill and N. W. Thornhill, "The Evolutionary Psychology of Men's Coercive Sexuality.")

Smuts, B. B., & Gubernick, D. J. (1990). Male–infant relationships in nonhuman primates: Paternal investment or mating effort? In B. Hewlett (Ed.), *The father's role: Cultural and evolutionary perspectives* (pp. 1–29). Hawthorne, NY: Aldine de Gruyter.

Smuts, B. B., & Smuts, R. W. (1993). Male aggression and sexual coercion of females in nonhuman primates and other mammals: Evidence and theoretical implications. In P. J. B. Slater, J. S. Rosenblatt, M. Milinski, & C. T. Snowden (Eds.), *Advances in the study of behavior* (Vol. 22, pp. 1–63). New York: Academic Press.

Sommer, V. (1994). Infanticide among the langurs of Jodphur: Testing the sexual selection hypothesis with a long-term record. In S. Parmigiani & F. vom Saal (Eds.), *Infanticide and parental care* (pp. 155–198). Chur, Switzerland: Harwood Academic Publishers.

Sommer, V., & Rajpurohit, L. S. (1989). Male reproductive success in harem troops of Hanuman langurs (*Presbytis entellus*) near Jodphur (Rajasthan/India). *Behavioral Ecology and Sociobiology, 16*, 245–248.

Stewart, K. J., & Harcourt, A. H. (1987). Gorillas: Variation in female relationships. In B. B. Smuts, D. L. Cheney, R. M. Seyfarth, R. W. Wrangham, & T. T. Struhsaker (Eds.), *Primate societies* (pp. 155–164). Chicago: University of Chicago Press.

Strauss, M. A. (1978). Wife-beating: How common and why? *Victimology, 2*, 443–458.

Struhsaker, T. T., & Leland, L. (1987). Colobines: Infanticide by adult males. In B. B. Smuts, D. L. Cheney, R. M. Seyfarth, R. W. Wrangham, & T. T. Struhsaker (Eds.), *Primate societies* (pp. 83–97). Chicago: University of Chicago Press.

Strum, S. C. (1987). *Almost human.* New York: Random House.

Symons, D. (1979). *The evolution of human sexuality.* New York: Oxford University Press.

Tabet, P. (1982). Hands, tools, weapons. *Feminist Issues, 2*, 3–62.

Tanner, N. (1981). *On becoming human.* Cambridge, UK: Cambridge University Press.

Trivers, R. L. (1972). Parental investment and sexual selection. In B. Campbell (Ed.), *Sexual selection and the descent of man, 1871–1971* (pp. 136–179). Chicago: Aldine.

Tutin, C. E. G. (1979). Mating patterns and reproductive strategies in a community of wild chimpanzees (*Pan troglodytes schweinfurthii*). *Behavioral Ecology and Sociobiology, 6*, 39–48.

van Schaik, C. P., & Dunbar, R. I. M. (1990). The evolution of monogamy in large primates: A new hypothesis and some crucial tests. *Behaviour, 115*, 30–62.

Washburn, S. L., & Lancaster, C. S. (1968). The evolution of hunting. In R. B. Lee & I. DeVore, *Man the hunter* (pp. 293–303). Chicago: Aldine.

Watts, D. P. (1983). *Foraging strategies and socioecology of mountain gorillas (Pan gorilla beringei).* Unpublished doctoral dissertation, University of Chicago.

Watts, D. P. (1989). Infanticide in mountain gorillas: New cases and a reconsideration of the evidence. *Ethology, 81*, 1–18.

Whiting, J. W., & Whiting, B. B. (1975). Aloofness and intimacy between husbands and wives: A cross-cultural study. *Ethos, 3*, 183–207.

Whyte, M. K. (1978). *The status of women in preindustrial societies.* Princeton, NJ: Princeton University Press.

Wolf, M. (1975). *Women in Chinese society.* Stanford: Stanford University Press.

Wrangham, R. W. (1975). *The behavioural ecology of chimpanzees in Gombe National Park, Tanzania.* Unpublished doctoral dissertation, Cambridge University.

Wrangham, R. W. (1979). On the evolution of ape social systems. *Social Science Information, 18*, 334–368.

Wrangham, R. W. (1980). An ecological model of female-bonded groups. *Behaviour, 75*, 262–300.

Wrangham, R. W. (1982). Kinship, mutualism, and social evolution. In King's College Sociobiology Group (Eds.), *Current problems in sociobiology* (pp. 269–290). Cambridge, UK: Cambridge University Press.

Wrangham, R. W. (1987). Evolution of social structure. In B. B. Smuts, D. L. Cheney, R. M. Seyfarth, R. W. Wrangham, & T. T. Struhsaker (Eds.), *Primate societies* (pp. 282–296). Chicago: University of Chicago Press.
Zihlman, A. H. (1981). Women as shapers of the human adaptation. In F. Dahlberg (Ed.), *Woman the gatherer* (pp. 75–120). New Haven, CT: Yale University Press.

11

The Confluence Model
of Sexual Aggression:
Feminist and Evolutionary Perspectives

NEIL M. MALAMUTH

The research that I describe in this chapter was initially inspired by the feminist movement and was designed to test some of the ideas put forth by its writers. Later, however, both in response to findings emerging from the research and in light of my growing interest in evolutionary psychology, my colleagues and I began also to conceptualize some of the work in the framework of evolutionary psychology. In this chapter, I attempt to summarize key points of the feminist and evolutionary analyses concerning causes of sexual coercion and relate them to the research we conducted.

About a decade ago, feminist colleagues who were quite familiar with our research suggested I critique a number of evolutionary-based articles that had been recently published on the topic of rape. In their view, these articles promoted a "biologically deterministic" and dangerous perspective that needed to be challenged. Although I had some interest in the relevance of evolutionary concepts to issues of sex and aggression (e.g., Malamuth, Feshbach, & Jaffe, 1977), it was with the goal of critiquing this approach that I proceeded to read carefully recent evolutionary analyses of rape and general discussions of evolutionary psychology. To my surprise, I found these to be quite illuminating and certainly not "biologically deterministic." Later, when I spent close to three years on the faculty of the University of Michigan, Ann Arbor, I had the opportunity to further my understanding of this area, particularly in the context of my association with David Buss, one of the leading theoreticians and researchers in the developing field of evolutionary psychology. With time, I became convinced that the evolutionary approach provided avenues for significant developments in our research program.

THE FEMINIST VIEW OF COERCIVE SEX

Throughout history, sexual coercion severely hampered the choices and opportunities available to women, both in sexual and other life spheres (Brownmiller, 1975). It is not surprising, therefore, that the modern feminist movement has focused on this topic as one of the main issues. Although there have been some writers who have emphasized somewhat different perspectives (e.g., MacKinnon, 1987), most feminists have defined rape and other forms of sexual coercion as motivated not by sexuality, but by a desire to assert power over women. Violence is a tactic used to assert that power. The implication is that sexual coercion is an expression of a more generalized strategy to dominate and control women. The origins of sexual coercion are viewed within a framework that emphasizes group conflict. Accordingly, males have constructed a patriarchal (male-dominated) social system and engage in behaviors designed, consciously or unconsciously, to maintain their control (Brownmiller, 1975; Clark & Lewis, 1977; Sanday, 1981). It is also suggested that men's physical size and strength, as well as sexual anatomy, led to the realization that women could be controlled and traumatized by using sex as a tool of domination (Brownmiller, 1975). The feminist view is aptly illustrated in the following quotation:

> Most people understand that lynchings and pogroms are motivated by political objectives: preserving white and gentile supremacy. Similarly, the aim of violence against women—conscious or not—is to preserve male supremacy. Early feminist analysts of rape exposed the myths that it is a crime of frustrated attraction, victim provocation, or uncontrollable biological urges, perpetrated only by an aberrant fringe. Rather, rape is a direct expression of sexual politics, an assertion of masculinist norms, and a form of terrorism that preserves the status quo. (Caputi & Russell, 1990, p. 34)

Feminists contend that, in order to maintain a hierarchical system, women and men are inculcated with certain attitudes, roles, emotions, perceptions, and desires. Females are conditioned to favor dependency, powerlessness, and submission; males are conditioned to favor aggressivity and dominance. Characteristics such as tenderness and empathy are encouraged for females and discouraged for males (e.g., Weis & Borges, 1973). The need for males to conform to "masculine" self-concepts of mastery over women, as well as the fear of one's own "feminine" side, result in males' devaluation of women, hostility toward them, and sexual arousal from dominating them. Since feminists attribute the origins of rape and other forms of violence to socialization within patriarchical cultures, they view individual differences among men as reflections of varied learning experiences, varied degrees of internalization of patriarchical values, and the extent to which violence is required and available to create and maintain dominance. This view is articulated in the following:

> All men learn to dominate women, but only some men batter them. Violence is only one of the many ways in which men express their socially structured right to control and chastise. For some men, a sense of owning women is combined with a belief in the right to use force. For others, however, violence is a morally unacceptable way to maintain their dominant status. In still other cases men may not need to use violence to dominate. Verbal abuse, withholding affection, or withdrawing resources may suffice. (Schechter, 1982, p. 219)

Women are viewed as having been selected for male domination because their reproductive capacity has been an important "commodity" that males wanted to control for a variety of reasons. For example, in a society in which property rights were based on familial lines, it was important to know who your offspring were. Controlling female sexuality ensures paternal certainty[1] (e.g., Clark & Lewis, 1977). In addition, women's weaker physical strength made them vulnerable to control by men (Brownmiller, 1975).

According to feminists, a radical restructuring of society is necessary in order to end rape and other forms of violence against women. It is essential that men's self-esteem not be based on domination of women or of other men. What is required to reach this goal is a political and economic system that deemphasizes competition and encourages cooperation and sharing of resources (e.g., Schechter, 1982).

Although the feminist views summarized above provided a rich source of ideas for our research, I believe that these views have not provided sufficient explanation of the origins of factors contributing to male dominance, which is perceived to cause violence against women. Why have men constructed patriarchal cultures that teach the types of roles described above, and why have women not constructed cultures that provide a breeding ground for female dominance? For a variety of empirical and theoretical reasons, I do not believe that explanations that rely only on the role of physical strength (Brownmiller, 1975) or on the mothering role of females (e.g., Chodorow, 1978; Dinnerstein, 1976) are sufficient. It is also necessary to incorporate differences that may have evolved in the "minds" of men and women. Such mental differences create the potential for men's motivation, under some environmental conditions, to dominate women and the lack of women's motivation to dominate men similarly.[2] As indicated below, understanding the origins of males' motives for dominance within the evolutionary framework should not be confused with the common fallacy that such a theory suggests that such dominance is inevitable or "natural."[3]

AN EVOLUTIONARY PERSPECTIVE

There are several excellent introductions to the developing field of evolutionary psychology (e.g., Buss & Schmitt, 1993; Wright, 1994). I present here a brief overview of the field, focusing on issues most relevant to this chapter.

General Overview

Darwin's evolutionary theory posits that living organisms are formed by *natural selection*, a continuous process of differential reproductive success by which certain "design" differences are transmitted to subsequent generations. Evolutionary psychology applies current knowledge of evolutionary processes to understanding the human mind[4] and behavior. Within the past two to three decades, considerable strides have been made within this field that enable better understanding of humans and their social interactions (Buss, 1995; Crawford, 1989).

The basic underlying "force" that designed the human mind is natural selection, that is, reproductive success or "fitness." According to evolutionary psychology, to understand the human mind today it is essential analyze the psychological mechanisms (i.e., information-processing algorithms or decision rules) that evolved in ancestral environments.[5] These mechanisms continue to guide our reactions (i.e., emotions, thoughts, behaviors) in contemporary environments. According to the version of evolutionary psychology emphasized here, the mind is composed primarily of many "domain[6]-specific" mechanisms rather than general mechanisms relevant to many domains (Buss, 1995; Cosmides & Tooby, 1987). Although under ancestral environments these mechanisms contributed to reproductive success and were therefore transmitted to subsequent generations, in current environments they may or may not contribute to any type of "success." While the mind was designed by natural selection processes operating in ancestral environments to promote fitness, people are not presumed to strive consciously to achieve the goal of fitness. In other words, people do not consciously "choose" their actions in order to promote fitness, but the types of mind mechanisms that evolved in ancestral environments and that can be "activated" in current environments were naturally selected because in those earlier environments they had fitness-favoring consequences.

Adaptations are responses that were naturally selected (i.e., increased reproductive success) in the evolutionary history of our species. Human responses may be adaptations, by-products of adaptations, or *noise* (e.g., mutations, genetic drift, etc.). Much effort is directed within this approach, by formulating testable hypotheses, to understanding which of these three possibilities particular behaviors represent (Buss, 1995). Because a behavior may have been adaptive in evolutionary environments, and therefore contributed to the current structure of the mind, does not mean that such a behavior is desirable, moral, or inevitable.[7]

Some people fail to understand properly the implications of this approach. They falsely believe that it suggests that humans are *hard wired* or do not make choices.[8] On the contrary, evolutionary approaches focus on the interaction between organisms and their environments and how organisms change their behavior in different environments. In humans, behavior is viewed as highly flexible in that the mind is very much attuned to situational information and can take a variety of forms precisely because we have complex, situation-contingent psychological mechanisms. In our species, social interactions are a very crucial part of the environment. Cultures that humans create reflect characteristics of the human mind and also shape the behaviors elicited in social environments.

It is important to note that the question is not whether evolutionary principles apply to human behavior and the psychology underlying it, but which evolutionary model is more accurate (Symons, 1992). The only alternatives offered to the theory that humans evolved by the same principles as other species is the belief that God created us or that we were put here by some extraterrestrial beings (Buss, 1990). No other viable scientific theory currently exists regarding the origins of life and of the human mind.

Within the evolutionary framework, however, there are various alternatives. One difference in evolutionary-based models is between those conceptualizing the human mind as a general information processor and those emphasizing specific mechanisms relevant to particular domains. Similarly, there may be various competing "minitheories" to explain any particular phenomenon, all derived from the evolutionary metatheory. These are then tested empirically to evaluate which best fit the data. Theories emphasizing the role of learning or culture are not alternatives to theories encompassing the role of evolutionary processes since what can be learned and how learning takes place are determined by the characteristics of the evolved mind of a species. Rather, learning theories focus on one aspect of a more comprehensive model of human nature and its interaction with the environment. Such a comprehensive theory needs to incorporate understanding of the design of the mind, as formed by evolutionary processes and as it interacts with the physical and social environment, including the cultures created by those minds (Buss, 1990, 1995).[9]

Individual Differences

With respect to individual differences, evolutionary psychology often focuses on the developmental learning environments experienced by each person (the ontogenetic histories of humans are not uniform), although there is also recognition of inherited differences that may affect interactions with the environment. It is important to note that evolutionary selective pressures[10] have been essentially the same for all humans in most domains in which problem-solving adaptations (e.g., how to regulate heat, how to detect cheaters, etc.) occurred. Therefore, psychological mechanisms are generally universal for all humans (i.e., species typical) (Tooby & Cosmides, 1990). However, their behavioral manifestations are not invariant or *fixed*. Such mechanisms process environmental information (e.g., the likely consequences of various behaviors). Their expression (in behavior) is expected to vary, both developmentally and contemporarily, with the nature of the environment. To understand the role of experience, however, it is essential to understand the learning mechanisms pertaining to differing domains (e.g., the role of experience may have different effects in areas such as deception detecting, mate selection, anger control, etc.). These mechanisms evolved in human minds within ancestral environments. Tooby and Cosmides (1992) have written extensively about the inadequacy of typical learning or socialization explanations that fail to consider the role of such mechanisms, showing how these often create the illusion of explanation.

Individuals' long-term "occupancy" of differing roles or situations can also be important (Buss, 1991). For example, a man who is married to a woman who gets a great deal of attention from other men may frequently show jealousy as compared to a man whose wife seldom receives much attention. Both, however, may have the same underlying jealousy mechanisms. Or, a man who is frequently rejected by women may appear to be habitually "feeling rejected" as compared to one who is relatively seldom rejected. Individual differences in feeling rejected here are not necessarily due to inherited or developmental differences (although these can directly or indirectly be contributors as well), but to being frequently in recurring environmental conditions that activate the relevant mechanisms. However, the threshold for activation of the mechanisms may become adjusted or recalibrated. In the example above, the man may become relatively prone to perceiving rejection or being suspicious of women's intentions so that he indeed feels rejected in circumstances that would not elicit that reaction in other men (Malamuth & Brown, 1994).

Gender Differences

In terms of gender similarities and differences, males and females are expected to have the same psychological mechanisms in those domains in which natural selection processes favored the same "solutions" to adaptive problems regardless of the solver's gender. Correspondingly, mechanisms are expected to differ in domains for which differing solutions or strategies have been more successful in evolutionary history for the different sexes (Buss, 1994). One of these areas is sexuality, for which the natural selection processes differed somewhat for males and females, resulting in sexual dimorphism in relevant psychological mechanisms (Buss & Schmitt, 1993).

Social Dominance Orientation

While the discussion below focuses on mechanisms directly relevant to sexual aggression or coercion, it should be noted that the evolutionary approach provides a useful theoretical model regarding the origin of dominance by one group over another, which according to feminist theory, is the basis for male sexual aggression against females. Rather than viewing reproductive capacity as just another resource that men try to control, evolutionary theories have emphasized reproductive strategies as underlying the evolution of mechanisms supporting social hierarchy generally (e.g., see chapters by Pratto and by Buss in this volume, as well as Pratto, Sidanius, & Stallworth, 1993). Both individual dominance mechanisms (directly relevant to within-group hierarchy) and *coalitional* mechanisms (directly relevant to the formation of alliances with others) need to be considered in a model designed to account for one group's dominance over another.

MECHANISMS DIRECTLY RELEVANT TO SEXUAL COERCION

Below, I attempt to outline an evolutionary-based model of sexual coercion. Although I draw various ideas from the writings of other researchers, the model presented contains some new elements not described elsewhere.

Three types of mechanisms may be directly relevant to male use of aggression or coercion against females in the sexual domain. The first type is the mechanisms underlying sexuality. This type is largely independent of the other two classes of mechanisms, which are hypothesized to be interrelated: one guides coercion while the other underlies dominance of the opposite gender.[11]

Mechanisms Underlying Sexuality

The psychological mechanisms governing male sexuality are not the same as those guiding female sexuality; this is due to the different reproductive consequences for the two genders in ancestral environments of sexual behavior. These created differences in the type of "mating strategies" most adaptive for each gender (Symons, 1979).

Differences in mating strategies can be traced to the minimum "parental investment" required to produce an offspring (Trivers, 1972). In our species, the parental investment required to produce offspring is much greater for females (i.e., nine months for females vs. minutes for males). Given that females can only produce a maximum of 20 offspring in a lifetime, having sex with a relatively large number of males is unlikely to have adaptive advantages. It is generally far better to invest more in each offspring by carefully selecting a mate with good genes who will participate in the raising of the offspring. For males, having intercourse with a larger number of fertile females was likely to be correlated with reproductive success since in ancestral environments contraceptive devices were not available, and the upper limit for siring offspring has been much higher than for females. Even totally "uninvested" sex may therefore have had favorable reproductive consequences.

In light of these differences, men and women differ considerably in their orientation to *impersonal sexuality*, that is, sex not associated with affection and bonding that typically characterize long-term relationships (Symons, 1979). Although males are capable of "personal sex" involving bonding emotions such as love, the psychological mechanisms underlying their sexual behavior also foster impersonal sex to a greater degree than females. Similarly, although females are capable of impersonal sexuality, their psychological mechanisms are relatively more consonant with personal sex. In ancestral environments, reproductive success for males was correlated with having sex with a large number of fertile females,[12] whereas for females reproductive success was more a function of sex with the carefully selected "right" men, such as those who possessed various economical, political, or psychological resources (Buss, 1994).

If male sexuality were unconstrained by real-life exigencies such as competition and threats from other men, rejection by females, and limited resources, the mechanisms governing this domain would result in sex with many fertile women. Such desires are indeed revealed in the sexual fantasies of men (B. Ellis & Symons, 1990). To reiterate, the male mind is "primed" by evolution, to a greater degree than the female mind, to engage in impersonal sex that does not involve emotional bonds.

Sexuality Mechanisms and Sexual Coercion

It may be said that the sexuality mechanisms in the minds of men set the stage for the occurrence of coercive sexuality. Because of their greater capacity for impersonal sex, men can be fully sexually functional in the face of an unwilling sexual partner who has no emotional desire for or bonds with the male (e.g., Malamuth & Check, 1983). The progeny of such sex would be likely to contribute to the man's reproductive success even if the man is also having intercourse with willing partners.

The male potential for coercive sex is not simply a function of body differences such as physical strength or anatomical ability to "penetrate," as emphasized by some feminists (e.g., Brownmiller, 1975). It is just as feasible for a woman to coerce a man to engage in oral sex by threatening him with a gun as for a man to similarly coerce a woman. There is also a crucial difference of minds. Even in situations in which the potential for females to coerce males is as high as for males to coerce females, it is expected that gender differences will occur even if males and females were raised in the identical environments. This is particularly true when environmental conditions are conducive to coercive sex. Wartime is a good example (Brownmiller, 1975). For instance, in the recent conflict in Bosnia, many men raped women, but it is doubtful that many women coerced men. These men were, in most cases, probably unlikely to commit such atrocities under peacetime conditions. Similarly, in Japan, a country where the known rate of rape is very low under peacetime conditions, during World War II very large numbers of men had coercive sex with Korean women.

Overall, the evolutionary approach suggests that the highly controversial assertion made by some feminists that "all men are real or potential rapists" (Clark & Lewis, 1977, p. 140) has some validity, but only if their developmental and current environments do not strongly discourage such acts. In the identical environmental conditions that prompt many men to commit coercive sex, it is expected that the minds of women would not prompt them to coercion.

Individual differences among men in their proneness to impersonal sexuality may help predict their likelihood of engaging in coercion, particularly in the context of an environment that discourages such acts. In such an environment, the role of other mechanisms that interact with the sexuality mechanisms may be particularly important.

Mechanisms Underlying Hostility/Dominance

Conflict often occurs in the context of human interactions. From the perspective of evolutionary psychology, conflict between individuals is related to the degree to which their reproductive interests are at odds (e.g., Alexander, 1979; Hamilton, 1964). Coercion is one of the tactics that may be used to deal with conflict. Coercion typically involves using force to attain one's interests at the expense of others. The human system appears to contain an interrelated "network" of responses (Berkowitz, 1993), including emotions (e.g., anger, hostility, jealousy, etc.), attitudes (e.g., acceptance of the use of violence), and motor tendencies (e.g., impulsivity) that may be "mobilized" to activate behavioral tactics that serve coercive goals.

Buss (1989) studied one important aspect of such a hypothesized network of responses. His work focused on the sources of male and female anger and upset as part of analyzing conflict between the sexes. He provided support for the hypothesis that both genders will be angered by aspects of the other gender's evolutionary-based reproductive strategy that conflict with their own gender's reproductive strategy. In the case of males, these include females' selective withholding of sex from them. Negative emotions such as anger are hypothesized to serve as signals that cause people to act in ways that reduce the interference with their own reproductive-based strategies. When such negative emotions occur recurrently, at critical stages in one's development, or both, they may lead to a relatively fixed hostile personality. Such a personality, calibrated to respond relatively violently to even mild provocations, can be adaptive within the context of certain threatening environments, although it can obviously be counterproductive when individuals are no longer in such environments.

Within the evolutionary framework, one important source of potential conflict between male and female interests stems from male uncertainty of parenthood. Since only females give birth to children, a male may be uncertain that a child being born was conceived by him, whereas the woman can be certain that the child to which she is giving birth was conceived by her. Consequently, natural selection operated on those male characteristics that served to increase the likelihood that the men are investing in their own offspring. If a man had intercourse with more than one woman prior to each woman becoming pregnant, it did not affect the maternity certainty of each woman. However, if a woman had intercourse with more than one man prior to her becoming pregnant, it reduced the paternal certainty of each of the men. This resulted in the evolution within the male mind of a psychology with greater proprietary feelings. Men are predicted to be more likely to dominate, monopolize, and control the sexuality of women. The extent to which men try to accomplish this and the methods they use differ, depending on social conditions, but the underlying psychological mechanisms are universal in male minds (Daly & Wilson, 1987; Symons, 1979; Wilson & Daly, 1992).

Dominance/Hostility Mechanisms and Sexual Coercion

Although males would be motivated to dominate the sexual behavior of women directly, they may also be motivated to control other facets of women's lives, such as with whom women interact, because this increases their ability to control the woman's sexual behavior.

There may be a set of emotions (e.g., anger, etc.), attitudes (acceptance of the use of violence), and other responses that forms an interrelated network of characteristics (Berkowitz, 1993) that is mobilized to assert dominance when a man perceives[13] blocked access to or domination of a desired female. These may be become relatively fixed or characterological if such perceived experiences occur at critical periods in one's development, are sufficiently recurrent, or both. Such responses may have had reproductive consequences for some men in ancestral environments by limiting female choice, just as rage that "energized" violence in response to a perceived threat by a competitor may have also had improved fitness in these environments.

Integrating Different Mechanisms

Evolutionary psychologists have sought to determine whether mechanisms affecting sexual coercion are the result of the direct consequences of rape on fitness (i.e., an adaptation) or incidental *by-products* (i.e., side effects) of other mechanisms that relate to general sexual or coercive strategies designed to promote benefits and reduce costs. The question has been addressed by focusing both on perpetrators (R. Thornhill & N. W. Thornhill, 1992) and victims (N. W. Thornhill & R. Thornhill, 1990). I believe that it is also essential to consider whether the integration or interaction of different mechanisms may have their own fitness consequences. It may well be that natural selection processes operate at the level of specific mechanisms, but they may also operate at the level of the interaction or integration of different mechanisms, conferring on each a further fitness benefit. Consider, as an analogy, the modularity of the brain in such an area as vision. It has been well established that there is a high level of specialization of modules for perception (e.g., form, color, movement, etc.) and comprehension, processes that occur simultaneously (Zeki, 1992). Each of these mechanisms is controlled by different areas in the brain. The functioning of each mechanism may be impaired independently of the mechanisms with which it integrates (Restak, 1994). Fitness advantages are likely to occur at the level of the integrated act that combines activities of the separate units involved in vision, as well as at the level of individual mechanisms.

With respect to rape, researchers continue to debate whether such coercion was likely to have had direct fitness consequences in ancestral environments. Some evolutionary psychologists posit reasons why such consequences may not have occurred (e.g., Symons, 1979). However, I believe that it is useful to consider more complex models that include "algorithms" that allow for flexibility and take into account men's alternative strategies in the face of different environmental experiences or input. For example, in discussing why rape may not have fitness consequences, Symons indicates that a female's "best" choice is often a male who succeeds in competition with other males; he most likely will be her suitor. Symons is suggesting a linear correlation between opportunities to mate with females and being successful in fitness terms without resorting to the use of force against females. But, such a model does not incorporate "nonlinear" relationships in which, for males who were relatively unsuccessful in attracting females (perhaps at critical stages relatively early in life), the algorithms affecting sexual arousal and other processes may be altered more in favor of coercive sex because, for these unsuccessful males, such a strategy may indeed have had better fitness consequences in ancestral environments.[14] Similarly, men may benefit from using mixed mating strategies. These could include having mutually consenting sex with some women, such as members of one's own tribe, and having coercive sex with other women, such those abducted from neighboring groups. Such abduction seems to have been quite common in our species' evolutionary history (Chagnon, 1994).

COMPARING AND INTEGRATING THE FEMINIST AND EVOLUTIONARY APPROACHES

Table 11.1 presents a brief summary of some key points of the feminist and evolutionary approaches as they pertain to the topic of sexual coercion. While feminists have emphasized the role of men's desire to dominate women as the basic underlying factor causing rape and other forms of violence against women (a form of group domination), evolutionary psychology provides a model of the design of mind differences between the genders that helps explain the origin of such an orientation to dominance.

According to evolutionists, as noted above, the basic underlying "force" that designed the human mind is natural selection, that is, reproductive success within ancestral environments. Many feminists have argued that rape is essentially one of many forms of male assertion of power over women and have emphasized that it is not a "sexual" act. In contrast, evolutionary theorists have emphasized that mechanisms governing sexuality in the male mind play an important role in motivating rape. It is important to recognize that this view differs from the traditional psychiatric view of rape as a product of aberrant or "pent up" sexuality. Rather, the evolutionary approach emphasizes that the male mind generally possesses characteristics that enable coercive sex to occur in various circumstances. This view is similar to that of many feminists who have argued that rapists and "normal" men differ in degree of coercion, but not in kind (e.g., Clark & Lewis, 1977). Whereas feminists

TABLE 11.1.   Feminist and Evolutionary Theories as They Pertain
to Sexual Coercion

Issue	Feminist Theory	Evolutionary Theory
Basic "force" behind rape:	Men's desire to dominate women due to group conflict	Directly contributing to fitness or by-product of other mechanisms
Purpose of rape:	Ultimate form of domination	In ancestral environments, attain sexual access to desired females
Why women as targets?	Reproductive and other commodities useful to men for property transmission and other functions; also, women vulnerable targets	Sexual desire is proximate mechanism. In ancestral environments, rape may have contributed to reproductive success
Why men rape?	Socialization (i.e., learning)	Natural selection (ultimate cause) interacting with "learning" environments (proximate cause)
Mechanisms causing and supporting rape:		Impersonal sexual orientation
	Attitudes, sex roles, emotions, perceptions, and arousal processes that facilitate and justify male domination	

have explained the origin of such male motivation and behavior in cultural socialization terms, evolutionists contend that even with the identical socialization experiences men and women would differ considerably in this domain. Although the occurrence of coercive sex is certainly not viewed as inevitable, the existence of underlying mechanisms that contribute to such acts differs in the minds of males and females.

Consequently, the role of learning can only be properly understood in the framework of the mind that translates environmental input into behavior, both throughout the lifespan and in the immediate situation. Women are targeted by men for domination not only because they bear the "commodity" of new life and are physically weaker, but because sexual desire is one of the proximate mechanisms motivating rape. In ancestral environments, such coercive sex may have increased men's reproductive success under some circumstances[15] since having intercourse was highly correlated with pregnancy prior to the advent of contraceptive devices. Both the feminist and evolutionary approaches view coercive sex not as "crazy behavior," but as fulfilling certain functions for the aggressors. Feminists have considered one set of interrelated sociopolitical and psychological mechanisms (i.e., asserting dominance, feeling superior, etc.), while evolutionists have emphasized how the fitness consequences in ancestral environments formed such proximate feelings and other reactions. In general, then, the feminist approach largely views rape as a by-product of men's desire to dominate women, while the evolutionary approach sees mechanisms underlying male sexuality as being fundamental to rape specifically and to men's motivation for control or domination generally.

THE CONFLUENCE MODEL OF SEXUAL AGGRESSION

To reiterate, the feminist approach described above has emphasized the role of dominance/hostility mechanisms. The evolutionary approach has been interpreted here as stressing both sexuality mechanisms (i.e., impersonal sexual orientation) and incorporating dominance/hostility mechanisms that may be mobilized in response to "blocked" goals. The research described below empirically tests the role of both sets of mechanisms as contributors to sexual aggression. Although the development of this line of work was initially inspired by the writings of feminists, it was later developed on the basis of the empirical findings, as well as other theoretical influences. While not initially designed to test an evolutionary-based model directly, the findings bear out well predictions that may be derived from such an approach.

Malamuth, Sockloskie, Koss, and Tanaka (1991) proposed a model of the characteristics of aggressors that suggests that coercive sex may be conceptualized as resulting from the convergence of (1) relatively high levels of "impersonal" sex and (2) hostile, dominating characteristics (also see Malamuth, Heavey, & Linz, 1993). According to this model, the ontogeny of coerciveness can often be traced to early home experiences and parent–child interactions. Family interactions lay the foundation, or may serve as "triggers" at critical formative periods (Draper & Harpending, 1982), for enduring cognitive (Dodge, Bates, & Pettit, 1990), emotional/attachment (Kohut, 1977), and behavioral (Patterson, DeBaryshe, & Ramsey, 1989) responses. Home environments that include violence between parents and child abuse, especially sexual abuse (Fagan & Wexler, 1938), may lead to developmental processes that later affect aggression against women. For example, individuals experiencing this type of home environment may develop negative views of male–female relationships, which may foster a relatively impersonal orientation to sexuality, a hostile "schema" about social relationships, or both, particularly with the opposite gender.

Abusive home environments may also interfere with the mastery of critical developmental skills such as managing frustration, delaying gratification, negotiating disagreements, and forming a prosocial identity (Newcomb & Bentler, 1988). Such processes may contribute to the well-documented pattern by which abusive home environments also increase the likelihood that the individual may associate with delinquent peers and participate in antisocial behaviors during adolescence (Patterson et al., 1989).

These early childhood and adolescent characteristics may develop into adult characteristics that can lead to sexual aggression. Malamuth et al. (1991) have described these characteristics as forming two "paths" or constellations of factors: the impersonal sex path and the hostile masculinity path.

The impersonal sex path   Association with a subculture of delinquent peers may contribute to and be a "marker" for a noncommittal, game-playing orientation in sexual relations (Elliott & Morse, 1989; Newcomb & Bentler,

1988). We have labeled this orientation the promiscuous/impersonal sex path. Boys who develop a high emphasis on sexuality and sexual conquest as a source of peer status and self-esteem may use a variety of means to induce females into sexual acts. Of course, some boys and men have this orientation to sexuality without having had a visible delinquent background (Kanin, 1984). Moreover, some males have a promiscuous sexual orientation without using coercive tactics.

This impersonal sex construct is similar to the concept used by evolutionary psychologists in the context of studying *sociosexuality*, which refers to individual differences in the willingness to engage in sexual relations without closeness or commitment (Gangested & Simpson, 1990; Simpson & Gangested, 1991). *Unrestricted* sexuality individuals report having sex earlier in relationships, more than one concurrent sexual relationship, many one-time partners in the past, and sex with partners on only one occasion, and they foresee many partners in the future. *Restricted* individuals, on the other hand, tend to insist on the development of closeness and commitment before engaging in sex, and they possess the opposite set of behavioral characteristics. Simpson and Gangested supported the above profiles with research that gathered independent reports provided by people's sexual partners.

A noncommittal orientation to sexuality may contribute not only to sexual aggression, but to other types of conflict in relationships later in life with women. Men with such an orientation appear relatively unlikely to be "faithful" in monogamous relationships. In monogamous relationships, this may be a source of distress that can lead to arguments and physical aggression.

The hostile masculinity path   The second path hypothesized to be relevant to sexual aggression involves a personality profile we have labeled *hostile masculinity*. It combines two interrelated components: (1) an insecure, defensive, hypersensitive, and hostile/distrustful orientation, particularly toward women; and (2) gratification from controlling or dominating women. This profile is hypothesized to lead men to use sex as a means of asserting dominance over and venting hostilities toward women. The hostility may also allow these men to overcome inhibitions, such as sympathy for the victim, that might ordinarily mitigate their use of coercive tactics (Malamuth, 1986).

An important component and early precursor of the hostile masculinity path is feelings and perceptions of rejection, hurt, and anger. The highly hostile masculine male may be afraid of rejection and anxious about relationships with women, as revealed in some of the scales assessing this path. In particular, many of the items on the Hostility Toward Women scale measure insecure and defensive reactions such as "I have been rejected by too many women in my life" and "I am sure that I get a raw deal from the women in my life." Further, Lisak and Roth (1988) compared sexually aggressive and nonaggressive college students and focused on the factors underlying their anger and power motivations. They concluded that sexually aggressive men were more likely to perceive themselves as having been hurt by women, including perceptions of being deceived, betrayed, and manipulated. They also found that variables assessing such hurt correlated highly with items assessing anger toward women and a desire to dominate them. It is not clear at this stage whether such hurt feelings represent some degree of objective reality, with the more aggressive men having experienced more rejection, or whether they are "hypersensitive" to the same type of experiences shared with the nonaggressive men, or both. No matter the case, these feelings and perceptions may be conceptualized in terms of the evolutionary psychological notion that sexual aggression is more likely among men who feel like "losers" in attempts to attract and control sexually desirable women (e.g., Symons, 1979).

The control and power possessed by a woman by virtue of her sexual appeal may be particularly threatening to such a man. The use of coercion against women may reduce anxieties about being rejected (Malamuth et al., 1977) by enabling the male to take charge and assume dominance. Coercive sex reduces her control over him by eliminating her ability to exercise choice. The feelings of hostility toward women included in this construct may be associated with a desire to denigrate women and therefore make them less powerful or potentially controlling. Sexual aggression may also confirm to the man that he is living up to the expectations of "male superiority" by being the one who "calls the shots" in this very personally vulnerable arena.

We believe that a variety of characteristics that have been shown to be predictors of sexual aggression (e.g., Malamuth, 1986) are aspects of the hostile masculinity path. These include sexual arousal in response to aggression, sexual dominance motives, hostility toward women, and attitudes facilitating aggression against women (Burt, 1980). We believe that these are components of a controlling, adversarial male orientation toward females that is likely to be expressed in diverse ways.

The interaction of the two paths   Malamuth et al. (1991) hypothesized that the degree to which a person possesses characteristics of the hostile path will determine whether an impersonal sexual orientation leads to sexual aggression. In other words, the hostility path may moderate the relationship between impersonal sex and sexual aggression. If true, this should appear statistically as an interaction effect.

Testing Model with a National Sample

Using latent-variable structural equation modeling,[16] Malamuth et al. (1991) tested a model, shown in Figure 11.1, based on the theoretical framework described above. Data from a large, nationally representative sample of male students in any form of post–high school education was used.

This model describes how early home experiences of parental violence, child abuse, or both begin a process that, through two different trajectories, may lead to coercive behavior toward women. As discussed above, the first step in this progression is involvement in delinquent activity. This delinquent activity is the hypothesized starting point for both trajectories. In the hostile path, delinquency leads to the development of attitudes that support violent

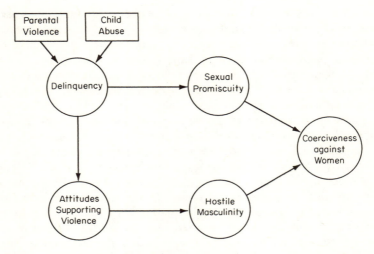

FIGURE 11.1.   Model of the characteristics of men who are coercive against women as proposed by Malamuth et al. (1991).

behavior. These attitudes are associated with controlling, self-absorbed, "one-upmanship" personality characteristics. These may partially emanate from a perception of having been rejected by desired women, resulting in the development of hostile feelings toward them. Hostile masculinity is predictive of both sexual and nonsexual coercion against women, as well as stress in relationships with them.

The second trajectory described by this model involves the association of delinquency with high levels of impersonal sexuality. Such sexuality, when combined with high levels of hostile masculinity, was expected to predict increased use of coercion against women. Based on our theorizing that sexual aggression partly reflects general conflict in relations with women, a common latent factor underlying sexual and nonsexual coercion of women was also hypothesized.

Although the development of this model was guided by the theory outlined above, the initial model was refined using half of the available sample and then cross validated using the second half of the sample. This model fit the data well in both sample halves with one exception: A consistent relationship between delinquency and attitudes supporting violence was not found. This path was significant in only one of the sample halves. This suggests that the hostile masculinity and sexual promiscuity paths may be relatively independent sets of characteristics. The abusive home environment and the delinquency experiences we studied consistently contributed only to the promiscuity path. Attitudes supporting violence against women and the other characteristics of the hostile masculinity path may stem from experiences other than those studied in this research.

As noted in the discussion of the interaction of the two paths, Malamuth et al. (1991) hypothesized that the presence of hostile masculinity would moderate the extent to which sexual promiscuity leads to sexual aggression. Statistically, we examined this prediction using hierarchical multiple regression with component scores on hostile masculinity and sexual promiscuity. As expected, it revealed a significant interaction between sexual promiscuity and hostile masculinity when predicting sexual aggression.[17] No interaction was found when predicting nonsexual aggression.

To explore this interaction further, subjects were divided into three groups based on their level of hostile masculinity and sexual promiscuity. A 3 × 3 analysis of variance was performed with sexual aggression scores as the dependent variable. This analysis yielded significant effects for hostile masculinity, sexual promiscuity, and their interaction. Trend analyses within each level of sexual promiscuity revealed no effects within the lowest level, a linear trend of increasing sexual aggression within the middle level, and a quadratic trend of increasing sexual aggression within the highest level. The group that was high on both sexual promiscuity and hostile masculinity reported higher levels of sexual aggression than all other groups.

Replicating and Extending the Confluence Model

Recently, we have been involved in research aimed at refining and extending the confluence model (Malamuth, Linz, Heavey, Barnes, & Acker, 1995). In this research, we used this model in a 10-year longitudinal study to predict difficulties in men's relations with women. We began this research with the hypothesis that the same two-path causal structure would be useful for the longitudinal prediction of sexual aggression, as well as for the prediction of general dysfunction in relations with women. As discussed above, it is our belief that the factors leading to sexually aggressive behavior (e.g., tendencies to dominate, monopolize, control, and manipulate women) are indicative of a pattern of relating to women in social relationships generally. We therefore expected that the factors specified in the confluence model of sexual aggression would also be predictive of a fairly wide range of relationship problems with women. In particular, we expected that the paths comprising the confluence model would predict general distress in romantic relationships, as well as heightened levels of physical and verbal aggression.

This study followed up approximately 150 men who had participated in several of the studies conducted approximately 10 years earlier. We therefore had two assessment phases, divided by about 10 years. Four primary outcome measures were assessed in the later assessment. First, men were asked to report on their level of sexual aggression during the 10 years subsequent to their initial participation by using a modified version of the scale by Koss and Oros (1982). Nonsexual aggression was assessed with regard to the subject's current or most recent romantic partner using the physical and verbal aggression subscales of the Conflict Tactics Scale (Straus, 1979) and the verbal aggression subscale of the Spouse Specific Assertiveness Inventory (O'Leary & Curley,

1987). Finally, general distress in the subject's current or most recent relationship was assessed using several measures of relationship quality and stability.

We had three primary goals in this study. First, we wished to replicate conceptually the model of sexual aggression developed by Malamuth et al. (1991) using a new sample of men. Second, we wanted to evaluate the utility of this model for predicting sexual aggression, relationship distress, and nonsexual aggression within a longitudinal framework. Third, we sought to refine further several aspects of the confluence model, including the specific nature of the sexuality characteristics associated with sexual coercion and the possible role of an interrelated network of characteristics relevant to hostile masculinity.

In this study, we employed a path analytic approach to test models rather than using structural equations modeling. To parallel the constructs used in earlier research (Malamuth et al., 1991), we formed a composite using the manifest indicators of the latent variables.

We began by successfully replicating the model developed by Malamuth et al. (1991) using cross-sectional data. Next, we tested an extended model, adding the longitudinal data. We hypothesized that the same general causal structure would be useful for longitudinal prediction of conflict in relationships with women. Further, we expected that we could predict better who would later in life be in conflict with women by knowing who had been sexually aggressive earlier, as well as who continued to show characteristics associated with hostile masculinity and impersonal sexuality. The measure of conflict with women used in this model was composed of measures of sexual aggression, nonsexual aggression, and relationship distress. The predictions were borne out, and this model generally fit the data well. This provides further support for the usefulness of the two-path causal structure in understanding conflict with women.

Having established the usefulness of the model for longitudinal prediction of conflict with women, we attempted to refine several aspects of the model using the measures collected at the second assessment. For example, we sought to explore further the role of sex drive in sexual aggression and to examine the role of general hostility in aggression.

Various theorists have argued that more sexually aggressive men have a higher sex drive (e.g., L. Ellis, 1989). In our model, we suggested that it is a particular orientation to sexuality or a particular "mating strategy" that characterizes sexual aggressors rather than primarily heightened sex drive. We therefore hypothesized that indicators of impersonal sex would be associated with increased sexual aggression, but that other sex drive indicators would not. Analyses from our longitudinal study generally supported this contention, although there were some ambiguities in the data. The findings showed that sexual aggression earlier in life was predictive of impersonal sexual relations in such forms as sexual arousal when looking at attractive unknown women and having more extra-relationship affairs later in life. By contrast, early sexual aggression did not predict responses reflective of sex drive generally, such as the degree of pleasure derived from sex, the frequency of sex with a woman, or the number of orgasms per week.

Finally, we used the data from the longitudinal study to test successfully a hierarchical model that suggests some of the factors contributing to sexual aggression (e.g., proneness to general hostility) underlie various types of conflict and aggression in intimate relations, whereas other factors (e.g., hostility to women, sexual dominance) are more specific to sexual aggression itself. As part of this model, we also demonstrated the importance of such variables as perceived threats to one's masculinity (i.e., sex-role stress) as hypothesized antecedents of hostile masculinity.

Recent Replications and Extensions

Two recent studies have provided additional evidence highlighting the utility of the confluence model of sexual aggression. Christopher, Owens, and Stecker (1993) successfully replicated the two-path model, but also added some additional variables. Particularly noteworthy was the addition, as part of the path we have labeled hostile masculinity, of a variable specifically measuring perceived negative experiences in relationships with women. The addition consisted of elements similar to the "rejection-hurt-anger" pattern described above. This variable was found to have a significant impact on sexually aggressive behavior.

In another recent study, Dean and Malamuth (1995) have shown that the hostile masculinity path is an excellent predictor not only of the profile of sexual aggressors, but also of those men who imagine aggressing sexually but have not actually engaged in such behavior. Imagined aggression was assessed in two ways: by men's self-reported likelihood of aggressing sexually if assured of avoiding negative consequences to themselves (Malamuth, 1989a, 1989b) and by a scale of sexually aggressive fantasies (Greendlinger & Byrne, 1987). As suggested by a number of investigators (e.g., Buss, 1990; B. Ellis & Symons, 1990), fantasies may actually provide more insight into the psychological mechanisms underpinning feelings, thoughts, and actions than do behaviors. This is because behaviors are often constrained by real-life exigencies (e.g., potential punishment, damage to reputation, etc.), whereas fantasies are private and far less likely to be inhibited by fear of the consequences.

Conclusion

The findings of the research described above provide considerable confirmation of hypotheses derived from both feminist and evolutionary writers. A series of studies focusing on the correlates of sexual aggression yielded findings consistent with feminists' contentions regarding the role of factors such as sex-role stress, attitudes promoting violence against women, hostility toward women, and dominance motives. Further, both cross-sectional and longitudinal studies showed that these form part of an interrelated constellation of variables, labeled hostile masculinity, that consistently predicted individual differences in men's sexually aggressive behavior. Although the role of a more general construct labeled general hostility (which encompassed variables such as emotional susceptibility to negative affect and impulsivity) was also shown to contribute to sexual aggression, its influence was found to be mediated by the more specific mechanisms included within hostile masculinity.

These data are also consistent with the evolutionary approach, particularly the findings suggesting that the hostile masculinity constellation is related to a self-perception of having been rejected by many desired women. The evolutionary approach provides a model for the reasons that such a constellation may become mobilized in some men under certain circumstances. In ancestral environments, activation of such mechanisms may have contributed to reproductive success, although it is unlikely to have the same consequences in contemporary environments. To reiterate, this does not suggest that such behaviors are desirable or justified. Just as recognizing that being able to kill under some circumstances probably contributed to reproductive success in our species, so, too, sexual coercion under some circumstances may have increased fitness.

Additional support for the evolutionary approach is provided by the findings that the profile of sexual aggressors is best described by the confluence of hostile masculinity and impersonal sexuality constellations. It supports well the idea that the orientation to sexuality it describes sets the stage for coercive sex. Some feminists had strongly discounted the role of sexuality in motivating rape, a belief that is not supported by our findings or those of other researchers (e.g., Palmer, 1988). However, feminists could reconceptualize the meaning of the impersonal sexuality constellation, suggesting that it reflects a relatively dehumanized orientation to women that disinhibits aggressivity.

I believe that to understand the causes of sexual coercion adequately, it is necessary to develop a comprehensive, "vertically integrated" model that includes multiple-level complementary explanations of ultimate and proximate causes (Barkow, 1989). In developing such a model of the characteristics of sexual aggressors, it is important to consider the following: (1) specieswide mechanisms resulting from natural selection that mediate between environmental stimuli and the person's behavior; (2) genderwide differences in certain psychological mechanisms; (3) cultural and subcultural differences in ideology, social climate, and so on; and (4) individual variability within males (e.g., genetic, hormonal, experiential, etc.). In a research area focusing on such a critical problem as sexual coercion, it will be particularly important to demonstrate that such an integrated model not only serves heuristic purposes, but that it performs well in such areas as predicting the likelihood that a person will aggress, generating new hypotheses that otherwise would not have been made, and guiding more-effective prevention and treatment programs. Although we believe that our research program has taken some steps in this direction and that it has benefited considerably from the writings of both feminists and evolutionary psychologists, there is still a long road ahead.

Acknowledgments The author would like to thank Sara Melzer, Shuli Ersler, Jeffrey Valle, Timna Horowitz, Zipora Malamuth, and David Buss for very helpful comments on earlier drafts of this chapter. The research summarized here was supported by a grant from the National Institute of Mental Health.

NOTES

1. As discussed below, emphasis on men's concern over paternal certainty is also critical to evolutionary theorizing. Whereas feminists see the concern as a product of a particular economic-political system of property ownership, evolutionists posit that it is a universal feature of the male "mind." Such a feature evolved because men who had such a concern were "naturally selected," as opposed to those who did not possess such a concern.

2. There are, however, relatively unusual environmental conditions for which some of the "traditional" male and female roles may be reversed in some ways (e.g., see Cook, 1991). This highlights how ecologically or situationally flexible certain mechanisms are, as well as the interaction between nature and nurture.

3. This is the "naturalistic fallacy." Although cancer or ulcers may be the natural result of certain interactions between our physiological system and environmental influences, this does not mean we should consider them inevitable or fail to utilize accumulating medical knowledge to prevent them. Accordingly, since various types of power relationships are clearly within the range of human potential, they may all be considered equally natural. However, they are not equally desirable within a given value system, and knowledge about the conditions that facilitate different types of relations may be used to facilitate the emergence of those considered more desirable.

4. The brain describes the physiological entity, whereas the mind is denominated as the psychological entity.

5. Current environments in "modern" technological societies are radically different in many respects from the type of environments that were a relatively stable feature during most of human evolutionary development. Although evolutionary processes continue, of course, in current environments, the processes of natural selection typically take many generations to change features of the human mind significantly. Therefore, evolutionary psychology contends that it is particularly important to present in a historical context the development of the mind within ancestral environments, sometimes referred to as environments of evolutionary adaptiveness (EEA).

6. A *domain* refers to an area in which a "problem" occurs that requires some adaptive solution. Examples of domains include areas with problems of how to regulate body heat, how to differentiate allies from enemies, how to detect cheaters, how to fight parasites, how to obtain mates, how to obtain food, and so on.

7. Consider the example of our taste receptors, which evolved in ancestral environments as a means of selecting between substances that provided nutritious value (e.g., as often indicated by the sweetness in ripe fruit) versus those that were harmful to us (e.g., as often indicated by the bitterness in poisons). In today's environments, capitalization of these taste buds has been used to develop substances such as processed sugar, which also activates our sweetness mechanisms, but may actually be harmful rather than beneficial to our health.

8. This is a confusion that often appears in the writings of some feminists. There

is the misunderstanding that, if a behavior has an "innate" basis, then it is immutable. For example, Burbank (1994) writes that feminists "have identified aggression against women as a major social problem . . . but insofar as it is 'seen as a socially produced and often socially legitimized cultural phenomenon,' not necessarily as an indicator of innate or immutable male aggressiveness" (p. 3).

The confusion here is twofold. First, it is important to recognize that all potential human behaviors have an innate basis (e.g., the capacity to fly by flapping one's hands is not within our species' range of potential behavior no matter how much cultural training we have, but the capacity to learn to build an airplane is within our range of innate potentiality). Second, there is an inappropriate dichotomizing of causes as innate versus learned. This is not true even in what we typically think of as physiological processes. For example, whenever our immune system encounters a new virus, it is forever changed. It has thus "learned" from its experience (Gazzaniga, 1992). The commonality is that all human behaviors are a function of the interaction of genetically transmitted potential for a limited set of acts and environmental input. However, in different domains, there are differing degrees of flexibility vis-à-vis the role of environmental influences (e.g., Buss, 1990). If one uses the analogy to a computer program, some are quite simple, with a particular input eliciting a specific output. Some may be highly complex, with many "if–then" alternatives. Such complex programs may include rules regarding how to select among alternative outputs as a function of the consequences of previous outcomes. Such rules therefore enable "learning" from experience. The experience may also result in modifications in the basic rules originally found in the program. Similarly, all human learning requires genetically based programs of rules that specify how to process experiential information.

9. Again using the analogy of a computer program, it is only possible to understand how the input to the program affects the output by understanding the underlying rules of the program that govern how input may be processed.

10. The term *selective pressures* refers to natural selection favoring particular characteristics. For example, if females choose relatively intelligent males as mates, thereby resulting in a correlation between males' intelligence levels and their reproductive success, then there are selective pressures for more intelligent males.

11. Independent of the line of research described, L. Ellis (1989) has also proposed that rape is motivated by "the sex drive and the drive to posses and control (especially in regard to sex partners)" (p. 104). There are several important differences between the model we have developed and that of Ellis. A discussion of the similarities and differences is beyond the scope of this chapter.

12. These generalizations are, of course, oversimplifying some complexities. For example, females may prefer to mate with males who show signs of willingness to commit to monogamous relationships. Therefore, a man who develops a "reputation" for being highly promiscuous may not be chosen as a mate by some females, thereby creating a selection pressure for males who are not taking advantage of every mating opportunity.

13. The emphasis here is on a person's perceptions or feelings rather than on the objective situation. Thus, a man who feels relatively "entitled" to be desired by various women may feel more rejected in the same situation than a man who does not have a feeling of entitlement. Similarly, a relatively high orientation to impersonal sexuality may create more opportunities for rejection experiences if the man seeks many short-term relationships.

14. Research by Yates, Barbaree, and Marshall (1984) supports the view that, in

contemporary environments, when men are angered by being "put down" by a woman, they become more sexually aroused to coercive sex.

15. Coercive sex is likely to have potential negative consequences for the perpetrator, including direct harm from the woman or her kin, damage to their reputation, and the like. However, evolutionists suggest that there may have been recurring circumstances in our evolutionary history during which the "net benefit" on men's fitness may have been selected for a mating strategy that includes the potential of coercive sexuality.

16. Such modeling may be described as combining techniques similar to factor analysis and path analysis. The former technique enables extraction of the common variance among several ways of measuring the same construct, whereas the latter technique examines the links among the constructs.

17. The fact that sexually aggressive men are characterized by both high levels of impersonal sexuality and hostile masculinity indicates that a simple "sex deprivation" model is not accurate. It may be that an impersonal sexual orientation, which is typically associated with desires for a relatively large number of sexual partners, creates a high likelihood of rejection experiences, even for men who are quite successful in attracting female partners. Such experiences may contribute to the development of the emotional pattern associated with hostile masculinity, although a relatively heightened sensitivity to rejection may lead to a subjective perception of frequent rejections irrespective of the objective reality.

REFERENCES

Alexander, R. D. (1979). *Darwinism and human affairs*. Seattle, WA: University of Washington Press.

Barkow, J. H. (1989). *Darwin, sex, and status: Biological approaches to mind and culture*. Toronto: University of Toronto Press.

Berkowitz, L. (1993). Towards a general theory of anger and emotional aggression: Implications of the cognitive-neoassociationistic perspective for the analysis of anger and other emotions. In R. S. Wyer & T. K. Srull (Eds.), *Perspectives on anger and emotion. Advances in social cognition* (Vol. 6, pp. 1–46). Hillsdale, NJ: Erlbaum.

Brownmiller, S. (1975). *Against our will: Men, women and rape*. New York: Simon and Schuster.

Burbank, V. K. (1994). *Fighting women: Anger and aggression in aboriginal Australia*. Berkeley, CA: University of California Press.

Burt, M. R. (1980). Cultural myths and supports for rape. *Journal of Personality and Social Psychology, 21*, 217–230.

Buss, D. M. (1989). Conflict between the sexes: Strategic interference and the evocation of anger and upset. *Journal of Personality and Social Psychology, 56*, 735–747.

Buss, D. M. (1990). Evolutionary social psychology: Prospects and pitfalls. *Motivation and Emotion, 14*, 265–286.

Buss, D. M. (1991). Evolutionary personality psychology. *Annual Review of Psychology, 42*, 459–491.

Buss, D. M. (1994). *The evolution of desire: Strategies of human mating*. New York: Basic Books.

Buss, D. M. (1995). Evolutionary psychology: A new paradigm for psychological science. *Psychological Inquiry, 6,* 1–30.

Buss, D. M. (1996). Sexual conflict: Evolutionary insights into feminism and the "battle of the sexes." In D. M. Buss & N. M. Malamuth (Eds.), *Sex, power, conflict: Evolutionary and feminist perspectives.* New York: Oxford University Press.

Buss, D. M., & Schmitt, D. P. (1993). Sexual strategies theory: An evolutionary perspective on human mating. *Psychological Review, 100,* 204–232.

Caputi, J., & Russell, D. E. H. (1990, Sept.–Oct.). "Femicide": Speaking the unspeakable. *Ms. Magazine,* 34–37.

Chagnon, N. A. (August, 1994). How important was "marriage by capture" as a mating strategy in the EEA? *Human Behavior and Evolution Society Newsletter, 3*(3), 1–2.

Check, J. V. P. (1985). *The Hostility Towards Women Scale.* Unpublished doctoral dissertation, University of Manitoba, Winnipeg, Manitoba, Canada.

Check, J. V. P., & Malamuth, N. M. (1983). Sex role stereotyping and reactions to depictions of stranger v. acquaintance rape. *Journal of Personality and Social Psychology, 45,* 344–356.

Chodorow, N. (1978). *The reproduction of mothering: Psychoanalysis and the sociology of gender.* Berkeley, CA: University of California Press.

Christopher, F. S., Owens, L. A., & Stecker, H. L. (1993). Exploring the dark side of courtship: A test of a model of premarital sexual aggressiveness. *Journal of Marriage and the Family, 55,* 469–479.

Clark, L., & Lewis, D. (1977). *Rape: The price of coercive sexuality.* Toronto: The Women's Press.

Cook, H. B. K. (1991). *Small town, big hell: An ethnographic study of aggression in a Margariteno community.* Unpublished doctoral dissertation, University of California, Los Angeles.

Cosmides, L., & Tooby, J. (1987). From evolution to behavior: Evolutionary psychology as the missing link. In J. Dupre (Ed.), *The latest on the best: Essays on evolution and optimality* (pp. 277–306). Cambridge, MA: Massachusetts Institute of Technology Press.

Crawford, C. B. (1989). The theory of evolution: Of what value to psychology? *Journal of Comparative Psychology, 103,* 4–22.

Daly, M., & Wilson, M. (1987). *Homicide.* New York: Aldine.

Dean, K., & Malamuth, N. M. (1995, in preparation). *Characteristics of men who aggress sexually and of men who imagine sexually aggressing: Risk and moderating variables.*

Dinnerstein, D. (1976). *The mermaid and the minotaur: Sexual arrangements and human malaise.* New York: Harper and Row.

Dodge, K. A., Bates, J. E., & Pettit, G. S. (1990). Mechanisms in the cycle of violence. *Science, 250,* 1678–1683.

Draper, P., & Harpending, H. (1982). Father absence and reproductive strategy: An evolutionary perspective. *Journal of Anthropological Research, 38,* 255–273.

Elliott, D. S., & Morse, B. J. (1989). Delinquency and drug use as risk factors in teenage sexual activity. *Youth and Society, 21,* 32–60.

Ellis, B., & Symons, D. (1990) Sex differences in sexual fantasy. *Journal of Sex Research, 27,* 527–555.

Ellis, L. (1989). *Theories of rape.* New York: Hemisphere.

Fagan, J., & Wexler, S. (1988). Explanations of sexual assault among violent delinquents. *Journal of Adolescent Research*, *3*, 363–385.

Gangested, S. W., & Simpson, J. A. (1990). Toward an evolutionary history of female sociosexual variation. *Journal of Personality*, *58*, 69–96.

Gazzaniga, M. S. (1992). *Nature's mind: The biological roots of thinking, emotions, sexuality.* New York: Basic Books.

Gilmore, D. D. (1990). *Manhood in the making: Cultural concepts of masculinity.* New Haven, CT: Yale University Press.

Greendlinger, V., & Byrne, D. (1987). Coercive sexual fantasies of college men as predictors of self-reported likelihood of rape and overt sexual aggression. *Journal of Sex Research*, *23*, 1–11.

Hall, G. C. N., & Hirschmann, R. (1991). Toward a theory of sexual aggression: A quadripartite model. *Journal of Consulting and Clinical Psychology*, *59*, 662–669.

Hamilton, W. D. (1964). The genetical evolution of social behavior, I and II. *Journal of Theoretical Biology, 7*, 1–52.

Kanin, E. J. (1984). Date rape: Unofficial criminals and victims. *Victimology: An International Journal*, *2*, 95–108.

Kohut, H. (1977). *The restoration of the self.* New York: International University Press.

Koss, M. P., Gidycz, C. A., & Wisniewski, N. R. (1987). The scope of rape: Incidence and prevalence of sexual aggression and victimization in a national sample of students in higher education. *Journal of Consulting and Clinical Psychology*, *55*, 162–170.

Koss, M. P., & Oros, C. J. (1982). Sexual experiences survey: Reliability and validity. *Journal of Consulting and Clinical Psychology*, *50*, 455–457.

Lisak, D., & Roth, S. (1988). Motives and psychodynamics of self-reported, nonincarcerated rapists. *Journal of Personality and Social Psychology*, *55*, 795–802.

MacKinnon, C. A. (1987). *Feminism unmodified: Discourses on life and law.* Cambridge, MA: Harvard University Press.

Malamuth, N. M. (1986). Predictors of naturalistic sexual aggression. *Journal of Personality and Social Psychology*, *50*, 953–962.

Malamuth, N. M. (1989a). The attraction to sexual aggression scale: Part 1. *Journal of Sex Research*, *26*, 26–49.

Malamuth, N. M. (1989b). The attraction to sexual aggression scale: Part 2. *Journal of Sex Research*, *26*, 324–354.

Malamuth, N. M., & Brown, L. M. (1994). Sexually aggressive men's perceptions of women's communications: Testing three explanations. *Journal of Personality and Social Psychology*, *67*, 699–712.

Malamuth, N., & Check, J. (1983). Sexual arousal to rape depictions: Individual differences. *Journal of Abnormal Psychology*, *92*, 55–67.

Malamuth, N., Feshbach, S., & Jaffe, Y. (1977). Sexual arousal and aggression: Recent experiments and theoretical issues. *Journal of Social Issues*, *22*, 110–133.

Malamuth, N. M., Heavey, C., & Linz, D. (1993). Predicting men's antisocial behavior against women: The "interaction model" of sexual aggression. In G. N. Hall, R. Hirschmann, J. R. Graham, & M. S. Zaragoza (Eds.), *Sexual aggression: Issues in etiology and assessment and treatment* (pp. 63–97). New York: Hemisphere.

Malamuth, N. M., Linz, D., Heavey, C. L., Barnes, G., & Acker, M. (1995). Using the confluence model of sexual aggression to predict men's conflict with women: A 10-year follow-up study. *Journal of Personality and Social Psychology, 69,* 353–369.

Malamuth, N. M., Sockloskie, R., Koss, M. P., & Tanaka, J. (1991). The characteristics of aggressors against women: Testing a model using a national sample of college students. *Journal of Consulting and Clinical Psychology, 52,* 670–681.

Newcomb, M. D., & Bentler, P. M. (1988). *Consequences of adolescent drug use: Impact on the lives of young adults.* Beverly Hills, CA: Sage.

O'Leary, K. D., & Curley, A. D. (1987). *Spouse specific assertion and aggression.* Unpublished manuscript, State University of New York, Stoney Brook.

Palmer, C. (1988). Twelve reasons why rape is not sexually motivated: A skeptical examination. *Journal of Sex Research, 25,* 512–530.

Patterson, G. R., DeBaryshe, B. D., & Ramsey, E. (1989). A developmental perspective on antisocial behavior. *American Psychologist, 44,* 329–335.

Pratto, F. (1996). Sexual politics: The gender gap in the bedroom, the cupboard, and the cabinet. In D. M. Buss & N. M. Malamuth (Eds.), *Sex, power, conflict: Evolutionary and feminist perspectives.* New York: Oxford University Press.

Pratto, F., Sidanius, J., & Stallworth, L. M. (1993). Sexual selection and the sexual and ethnic basis of social hierarchy. In L. Ellis (Ed.), *Social stratification and socioeconomic inequality: A comparative biosocial analysis* (pp. 111–136). New York: Praeger.

Restak, R. M. (1994). *The modular brain.* New York: Macmillan.

Sanday, P. R. (1981). The sociocultural context of rape: A cross-cultural study. *Journal of Social Issues, 37,* 5–27.

Schechter, S. (1982). *Women and male violence.* Boston, MA: South End Press.

Simpson, J. A., & Gangested, S. W. (1991). Individual differences in sociosexuality: Evidence for convergent and discriminant validity. *Journal of Personality and Social Psychology, 60,* 870–883.

Straus, M. (1979). Measuring intrafamily conflict and violence: The Conflict Tactics (CT) Scales. *Journal of Marriage and the Family, 41,* 75–85.

Symons, D. (1979). *The evolution of human sexuality.* Oxford: Oxford University Press.

Symons, D. (1992). On the use and misuse of Darwinism in the study of human behavior. In J. Barkow, L. Cosmides, & J. Tooby (Eds.), *The adapted mind* (pp. 137–162). New York: Oxford University Press.

Thornhill, N. W., & Thornhill, R. (1990). An evolutionary analysis of psychological pain following rape: 1. The effects of victim's age and marital status. *Ethology and Sociobiology, 11,* 155–176.

Thornhill, R., & Thornhill, N. W. (1983). Human rape: An evolutionary analysis. *Ethology and Sociobiology, 4,* 1–74.

Thornhill, R., & Thornhill, N. W. (1992). The evolutionary psychology of men's coercive sexuality. *Behavioral and Brain Sciences, 15,* 363–421.

Tooby, J., & Cosmides, L. (1990). On the universality of human nature and the uniqueness of the individual. The role of genetics and adaptation. *Journal of Personality, 58,* 17–68.

Tooby, J., and Cosmides, L. (1992). The psychological foundations of culture. In J. Barkow, L. Cosmides, & J. Tooby (Eds.), *The adapted mind* (pp. 1–45). New York: Oxford University Press.

Trivers, R. L. (1972). Parental investment and sexual selection. In B. Campbell (Ed.), *Sexual selection and the descent of man* (pp. 1871–1971). Chicago: Aldine.

Weis, K., & Borges, S. S. (1973). Victimology and rape: The case of the legitimate victim. *Issues in Criminology, 8,* 71–115.

Wilson, M., & Daly, M. (1992). The man who mistook his wife for a chattel. In J. H. Barkow, L. Cosmides, & J. Tooby (Eds.), *The adapted mind.* New York: Oxford University Press.

Wright, R. (1994). *The moral animal: Why we are the way we are: The new science of evolutionary psychology.* New York: Pantheon.

Yates, E., Barbaree, H. E., & Marshall, W. L. (1984). Anger and deviant sexual arousal. *Behavior Therapy, 15,* 287–294.

Zeki, S. (1992, September). The visual image in mind and brain. *Scientific American, 267,* 68–76.

12

Sexual Conflict: Evolutionary Insights into Feminism and the "Battle of the Sexes"

DAVID M. BUSS

In every age the battle of the sexes is largely a battle over sex.
Donald Symons (1979)

Sex, power, conflict, coercion, control, manipulation—these are all strong words that evoke powerful emotions. Why is sex so often linked with these other words? This chapter starts with two fundamental assertions. First, much conflict between the sexes is about *sex* (Symons, 1979). Second, conflicts about *power* often center on sexuality and control over sexual access. In this chapter, I argue that evolutionary psychology affords critical insights into the nature and operation of conflicts between the sexes generally, and particular aspects of feminist positions more specifically.

POTENTIAL POINTS OF CONVERGENCE BETWEEN FEMINIST AND EVOLUTIONARY PERSPECTIVES

Although the evolutionary literature and feminist literature historically have been isolated from each other, recent work by feminist evolutionists show that the two perspectives might not be as incompatible as some have believed (see Gowaty, 1992; Hrdy, 1981; Lancaster, 1991; Smuts, 1992, 1995). It is perhaps astonishing that feminists and evolutionary psychologists focus on many of the same topics. Perhaps none are as central to both feminists and evolutionary psychologists as *sex, power,* and *conflict.* It is even more astonishing that the two perspectives, despite their relative insularity from one another, seem to converge on many key points.

Before describing these points of convergence, it is critical to note that neither feminism nor evolutionary psychology represent monolithic or singular perspectives. Both represent a diversity of positions. Just as there is a diversity of competing evolutionary hypotheses, all stemming from the same basic theoretical framework, there is a diversity of feminist perspectives. Thus, my description of the points of convergence would most likely be endorsed only by some feminists and some evolutionary psychologists.

A further qualification is that evolutionary psychology and feminism differ qualitatively in ways that render the two incomparable. Evolutionary psychology is a science geared toward understanding and accounting for what exists. In contrast, feminism typically contains both a position of what exists (e.g., the notion of "patriarchy" as a central causal force that results in the oppression of women) and a social/political agenda (e.g., increasing women's economic equality). In comparing evolutionary psychology with feminism, therefore, there are at least two points of departure. One is comparing the evolutionary and feminist positions on the causal forces accounting for what exists. A second involves highlighting some ways in which evolutionary psychology might shed light on various aspects of feminist political agendas.

In describing feminist perspectives, I rely heavily on authors such as Faludi (1991), Gowaty (1992), hooks (1984), Jagger (1994), MacKinnon (1987), Ortner (1974), Smuts (1995), and Wolf (1991). In describing evolutionary perspectives, I rely heavily on Daly and Wilson (1988), Tooby and Cosmides (1992), Symons (1979), and my own work (Buss, 1989a, 1994, 1995). The following represent key points of potential convergence between the two perspectives.

Men tend to control resources and power worldwide. Scientists have tried for years to discover a culture in which men did not dominate women in the domains of overt political power and material resources. Although many people have heard rumors about cultures in which women dominate men, none have ever been documented in the literature. Indeed, feminist anthropologists who have spearheaded the search conclude that such cultures do not exist (Ortner, 1974). Of course, societies clearly differ in their degree of social and economic inequality between the sexes.

The generalization that men tend to wield power and control resources, however, should not obscure the fact, that in nearly every culture, women contribute substantially to the economic resources. In hunter-gatherer societies, for example, women sometimes contribute 60%–80% of the calories through gathering (Tooby & DeVore, 1987). Furthermore, women often exert considerable power through various means, including exerting preferential mate choice, divorcing men under certain conditions, controlling or regulating men's access to women's sexuality, and influencing their sons, lovers, fathers, sisters, and grandchildren (Buss, 1994). In addition, women exert power in subtle ways that may be missed by male researchers. Sarah Hrdy (1981), for example, noted benefits of female sexuality and Barbara Smuts (1995) described the importance of female coalitions—both of which are important phenomena previously missed by male researchers. Thus, although there is general agreement that most or all cultures are "patriarchal" in the sense of men's domination in the domains of resources and overt power, this generalization should not obscure the many ways in which women accrue resources and exert control.

The generalization is further compromised by individual differences within each sex. Many men lack power and resources, and some women wield tremendous power and possess substantial resources. Just as there are impoverished homeless men who fail to attract women over whom they might be dominant, there are women such as Margaret Thatcher and Madonna who wield considerable power and influence. Thus, generalizations about male dominance over women must be qualified by these within-sex differences.

With these qualifications, the greater male control of resources seems to be a generalization agreed on by both feminist and evolutionary scholars. Within the United States, for example, women tend to earn less income than men (Faludi, 1991). Men occupy more positions of overt leadership within the political arena, including the Senate, the House of Representatives, and the presidency and its cabinet. The same trend holds true within major corporations in nearly every sphere of business activity. Thus, although the individual exceptions must qualify this generalization, men do seem to dominate in the realm of resource control.

Men often control women through resources. If men possess the resources that women want or need, then men can use those resources to control women. In the mating domain, men use their resources to attract women (Buss, 1994). Within relationships, women lacking economic resources often feel at the mercy of their husbands or boyfriends for fear of the loss of those resources (Wilson & Daly, 1992). As in other domains, the *golden rule* probably applies: He who has the gold makes the rule.

Men's control of women often centers on their sexuality and reproduction. In a cross-cultural perspective, the ways in which men attempt to control women's sexuality is nothing short of bewildering (Dickemann, 1981; Wilson & Daly, 1992). Veiling a woman's face is an attempt to conceal a woman's sexual signals from other men. Placing women in harems gives a king or emperor potentially exclusive sexual and reproductive access to those women. Forms of genital mutilation, such as clitoridectomy and infibulation, seem designed to dissuade women from seeking sexual pleasure or pursuing sexual relationships with men other than their husbands, although these methods of controlling women's sexuality are often used by the woman's own kin and may even be undergone "voluntarily" by a women to enhance her desirability to men. Within our own culture, men, and especially jealous men, control women's sexuality by restricting contact with other men, monopolizing all of a woman's time, threatening harm to the woman or a rival man for cues to infidelity, and insisting that the woman wear possessive ornamentation (Buss, 1988). Despite the variability of the tactics men employ, it is clear that men's attempts to control women often center on their sexuality, and both feminists and evolutionary psychologists agree on this point (e.g., MacKinnon, 1987; Smuts, 1995).

Men's sexual aggression circumvents women's choice. Sexual aggression by men, ranging from verbal sexual harassment to touching a woman's body without her permission to forced sexual intercourse, effectively interferes with a woman's control of her sexuality. Sexual aggression is a cost that is inflicted primarily by men on women (Malamuth, Sockloskie, Koss, & Tanaka, 1991; Studd & Gattiker, 1991). There are exceptions, of course, such as in prisons where men are the aggressors and other men are the victims. Nonetheless, sexual aggression, sexual harassment, and sexual coercion are costs that are typically inflicted by men on women, with the effect of reducing a woman's control over her own sexuality (Smuts, 1992). In addition, they sometimes cause shame, guilt, humiliation, and lowered self-esteem, all of which may reduce a woman's subjective sense of efficacy (Thornhill, chap. 4).

Some men think of women as property to be owned and used. The tendency of men to view women as property is so pervasive that Wilson and Daly (1992) entitled one of their chapters on the topic, "The Man Who Mistook His Wife for a Chattel." Proprietariness involves rights to sell, exchange, or dispose of one's property and to demand recompense if there is theft or damage of the property (Wilson & Daly, 1992). There is considerable evidence that some men view women in this way. Indeed, many laws involving a spouse's sexual infidelity are written in language that implies that another man is unlawfully poaching (Daly & Wilson, 1988). Among some cultures, women are literally purchased like cattle by men who then demand a refund if they are not satisfied (see Buss, 1994, for a summary). Kings, despots, and emperors throughout human history routinely stocked harems with hundreds or thousands of women, who were kept under guard by eunuchs (Betzig, 1992). In sum, there is considerable evidence to suggest that some men view women as personal property—a point agreed on by both feminists and evolutionary psychologists.

This is not to deny that women sometimes view men in exploitative ways, as objects to be controlled and manipulated in various ways for their own purposes. Indeed, there is considerable evidence that women sometimes view men as "success objects," perceive the sexual encroachment by a rival woman on her mate to be a violation of her proper entitlements, act to fend off rivals from encroachment, and so on (Buss, 1994). Nonetheless, there seems to be a fundamental asymmetry. At no point in recorded history have women purchased men as husbands, raided neighboring villages to capture men as mates, or placed men into harems for their exclusive sexual access. One cannot, of course, rule out the possibility that if women had more power and control they might act in ways analogous to men. But there is no evidence that they have ever done so, nor do women in positions of power act in the sexually proprietary way that men do.

Women, as well as men, often participate in perpetuating oppression. Women may participate in men's control of them in various ways. Women may adopt and espouse an ideology that reinforces men's control (Smuts, 1992, 1995), socialize their sons and daughters in ways that perpetuate men's control (Low, 1989), and preferentially select men as mates who will exert such control (Buss, 1989a, 1994). Although some feminists view women as entirely helpless victims of a ruthlessly male-dominated society (e.g., Mac-Kinnon, 1987), many recognize that women also participate in the perpetuation of male control (Smuts, 1995; Wolf, 1993).

In summary, there are a number of fundamental observations about which feminists and evolutionary psychologists more or less seem to agree. These include the worldwide tendency of men to control resources, men's use of these resources to control and manipulate women, men's focus on women's sexuality as a locus of control, some men's use of sexual aggression as a means of circumventing women's choices, men's view of women in proprietary terms, and the role that women sometimes play in perpetuating oppression. In the remainder of this chapter, I argue that evolutionary psychology has much to contribute to feminist psychology by providing a deeper understanding of why these phenomena occur. In order to understand why these phenomena occur, the analysis must start with the origins of sex differences for it is in these differences that the sources of conflict reside.

HUMAN EVOLUTIONARY HISTORY: THE LOCUS OF SEX DIFFERENCES

Evolutionary psychology predicts that males and females will be the same or similar in those domains in which the sexes have faced the same or similar adaptive problems. Both sexes have sweat glands because both sexes have faced the adaptive problem of thermal regulation. Both sexes have similar taste preferences for fat, sugar, salt, and particular amino acids because both sexes have faced similar food consumption problems. Both sexes develop callouses when they experience repeated rubbing on their skin because both sexes have faced the adaptive problem of damage due to environmental friction. Both sexes appear to have cognitive and emotional mechanisms designed to detect cheaters and foster reciprocal relationships (Cosmides, 1989).

In other domains, men and women have faced substantially different adaptive problems over human evolutionary history. In the physical realm, for example, women have faced the problem of childbirth; men have not. Women, therefore, have evolved particular adaptations that are lacking in men, such as a cervix that dilates to 10 centimeters just prior to giving birth, mechanisms for producing labor contractions, and the release of oxytocin in the bloodstream during the delivery.

Men and women have also faced different information-processing problems in some adaptive domains. Because fertilization occurs within the woman, for example, men have faced the adaptive problem of uncertainty of paternity in putative offspring. Men who failed to solve this problem risked investing resources in children who were not their own. We are all descendants of a long line of ancestral men whose adaptations (i.e., psychological mechanisms) led them to behave in ways that increased their likelihood of paternity and decreased the odds of investing in children who were putatively theirs, but whose genetic fathers were other men. This does not imply, of course, that men were or are consciously aware of the adaptive problem of compromised paternity.

Women faced the problem of securing a reliable or replenishable supply of resources to nourish them through pregnancy and lactation, especially when food resources were scarce (e.g., during droughts or harsh winters). We are all descendants of a long and unbroken line of women who successfully solved this adaptive challenge, for example, by preferring mates who showed the ability to accrue resources and the willingness to channel them to particular women (Buss, 1994). Those women who failed to solve this problem failed to survive, imperiled the survival chances of their children, and hence failed to become our ancestors.

Evolutionary psychologists predict that the sexes will differ in precisely those domains in which women and men have faced different sorts of adaptive problems (Buss, 1994). To an evolutionary psychologist, the likelihood that the sexes are psychologically identical in domains in which they have recurrently confronted different adaptive problems over the long expanse of human evolutionary history is essentially zero (Symons, 1992). The key question, therefore, is not, Are men and women psychologically different? Rather, the key questions about sex differences, from an evolutionary psychological perspective, are (1) In what domains have women and men faced different adaptive problems? (2) What are the sex-differentiated psychological mechanisms of women and men that have evolved in response to these sex-differentiated adaptive problems? (3) Which social, cultural, and contextual inputs moderate the magnitude of expressed sex differences.

SEXUAL SELECTION

Although many nonbiologists equate evolution with "natural selection" or "survival selection," Darwin sculpted what he believed to be a second theory of evolution—the theory of sexual selection. *Sexual selection* is the causal process of the evolution of characteristics due to reproductive advantage, which accrues through mate competition. Sexual selection occurs in two forms. First, members of one sex can successfully out-compete members of their own sex by a process of *intrasexual competition*. Whatever characteristics lead to success in these same-sex competitions—greater size, strength, cunning, or social skills—they can evolve or increase in frequency by virtue of the reproductive advantage that accrues to the winners through increased access to more numerous or more desirable mates.

Second, members of one sex can evolve preferences for desirable qualities in potential mates by a process of *intersexual selection*. If members of one sex exhibit some consensus about which qualities are desirable in the other sex, then members of the other sex who possess the desirable qualities will gain a competitive mating advantage. Hence, the desirable qualities—whether morphological features such as antlers, plumage, or muscle mass, or psychological features such as kindness, the desire to make investments as a parent, a lower threshold for risk taking, or the ability to acquire resources—can evolve by virtue of the reproductive advantage attained by those who are preferentially chosen for possessing the desirable qualities. Among humans, both causal processes—preferential mate choice and same-sex competition for access to mates—are prevalent among both sexes and probably have been throughout human evolutionary history (Buss, 1994).

PSYCHOLOGICAL SEX DIFFERENCES

While a detailed analysis of hypotheses about psychological sex differences that follow from sexual asymmetries in mate selection and intrasexual competition is well beyond the scope of this article (see Buss, 1994), a few of the most obvious differences in adaptive problems are discussed next.

The problem of paternity uncertainty. Because fertilization occurs internally within women, men are always less that 100% "certain" (again, no conscious awareness implied) that their putative children are genetically their own. Some cultures have phrases to describe this, such as "mama's baby, papa's maybe." Women are always 100% certain that the children they bear are genetically their own.

The problem of identifying reproductively valuable women. Since women's ovulation is concealed and there is no evidence that men can detect when women ovulate, ancestral men had the difficult adaptive challenge of assessing the relative fertility of women. Although ancestral women would also have faced the problem of identifying fertile men, the problem is considerably less severe (1) because most men remain fertile throughout their life span, whereas fertility is steeply age graded among women and (2) because women invest more heavily in offspring, they in effect become the limiting resource for reproduction and hence men seeking sexual access more intensely competed for them. Thus, there is rarely a shortage of men willing to contribute the sperm necessary for fertilization, whereas from men's perspective there is a pervasive shortage of fertile women.

The problem of identifying men able to invest. Because of the tremendous burdens of a nine-month pregnancy, childbirth, and subsequent lactation, women who selected men who were able to invest resources in them and their offspring would have been at a considerable advantage in survival and reproductive currencies compared to women who were indifferent to the investment capabilities of the man with whom they chose to mate. Women who were not aware of the potential benefits they could gain by identifying and selecting men with resources would have suffered by being less able to acquire food, protection, and shelter during vulnerable periods of pregnancy.

The problem of identifying men willing to invest. Having resources is not enough. Copulating with a man who had resources but who displayed a hasty postcopulatory departure would have been detrimental to the woman, particularly if she became pregnant and faced raising a child without the aid and protection of an investing father. A man with excellent resource-accruing capacities might channel resources to another woman or pursue short-term sexual opportunities with a variety of women. A woman who had the ability to detect a man's willingness to invest in her and her children would have an adaptive advantage relative to women who were oblivious to a man's proclivity to invest.

The problem of gaining sexual access to women. Because of the large asymmetry between men and women in their *minimum obligatory parental investment*—a nine-month gestation and parturition for women versus an act of sexual intercourse for men—the direct reproductive benefits of gaining sexual access to a variety of mates would have been much higher for men than for women throughout our evolutionary history (Symons, 1979; Trivers, 1972). Therefore, in social contexts in which some short-term mating or polygynous mating were possible, men who succeeded in gaining sexual access to a variety of women, other things being equal, would have experienced greater reproductive success than men who failed to gain such access (see also Greiling, 1993, for adaptive benefits to women of short-term mating).

These are just a few of the adaptive problems that women and men have confronted differently or confronted to differing degrees. Other examples of sex-linked adaptive problems include those of coalitional warfare, coalitional defense, hunting, gathering, combating sex-linked forms of reputational damage, embodying sex-linked prestige criteria, and attracting mates by fulfilling the differing desires of the other sex—domains that have consequences for mating, but are sufficiently wide ranging to span a great deal of social psychology (Buss, 1994). It is in these domains that evolutionary psychologists anticipate the most pronounced sex differences—differences in *solutions* to sex-linked adaptive problems in the form of evolved psychological mechanisms.

PSYCHOLOGICAL SEX DIFFERENCES IN DOMAINS PREDICTED BY THEORIES ANCHORED IN SEXUAL SELECTION

When Maccoby and Jacklin (1974) published their classic book more than 20 years ago on the psychology of sex differences, knowledge was spotty and methods for summarizing the literature were largely subjective and interpretive (Eagly, 1995). Since that time, a veritable explosion of empirical findings has occurred, along with quantitative meta-analytic procedures for evaluating them (e.g., Eagly, 1995; Feingold, 1990; Hall, 1978; Hyde, 1996; Oliver & Hyde, 1993; Rosenthal, 1991). Although new domains of sex differences continue to surface, such as the recently documented female advantage in spatial location memory (Silverman & Eals, 1992), the domains in which we find large, medium, small, and no sex differences are starting to emerge more clearly.

A few selected findings illustrate the heuristic power of sexual selection theory. In examining these findings, we use the widely adopted *d* statistic as the index of magnitude of effect. Cohen (1977) proposes a rule of thumb for evaluating effect sizes: .20 as "small," .50 as "medium," and .80 as "large." As Hyde (in Chapter 5) points out, sex differences in the intellectual and cognitive ability domains tend to be small. Women's verbal skills tend to be slightly higher than men's ($d = .11$). Sex differences in math also tend to be small ($d = .15$), with men showing only a slight advantage. Most tests of general cognitive ability, in short, reveal small sex differences.

Two primary exceptions to the general trend of small sex differences in the cognitive abilities' domain occur with spatial rotation (men perform better) and spatial location memory (women perform better). Spatial rotation ability is essential for successful hunting, in which the trajectory and velocity of a spear must match correctly the trajectory of an animal as each moves with different speeds through space and time. The d for spatial rotation ability is .73. Other sorts of skills involved in hunting also show large magnitudes of sex differences, such as throwing velocity ($d = 2.18$), throwing distance ($d = 1.98$), and throwing accuracy ($d = .96$; Ashmore, 1990). Skilled hunters, as good providers, are known to be sexually attractive to women in current and traditional tribal societies (Hill & Hurtado, 1989; Symons, 1979).

Women, in contrast, consistently perform better at spatial location memory tasks ($d = .72$, averaged across Study 1 and Study 2, from Silverman & Eals, 1992). This female advantage is consistent with the hypothesis that ancestral women specialized in foraging and gathering—activities that would be greatly aided by accurate recall of the locations of fruit-bearing trees, blooming bushes, and edible plants. The recent finding of a female advantage in this domain of spatial ability—going in the opposite direction of the sex difference in spatial rotation ability—provides powerful evidence of the domain specificity of sex differences.

Large sex differences also appear reliably for precisely those aspects of sexuality and mating predicted by evolutionary theories of sexual strategies (Buss & Schmitt, 1993). Oliver and Hyde (1993), for example, document a large sex difference in attitudes toward casual sex ($d = .81$). Similar sex differences have been found with other measures of men's desire for casual sex partners, a psychological solution to the problem of seeking sexual access to a variety of partners (Buss & Schmitt, 1993; Symons, 1979). For example, men state that they would ideally like to have more than 18 sex partners in their lifetimes, whereas women state that they would desire only 4 or 5 ($d = .87$; Buss & Schmitt, 1993). In another study that has been replicated twice, 75% of men but 0% of women approached by an attractive stranger of the opposite sex consented to a request for sex (Clark & Hatfield, 1989).

Women tend to be more exacting than men, as predicted, in their standards for a short-term mate ($d = .79$; Buss & Schmitt, 1993). Women tend to place greater value on good financial prospects in a mate—a finding confirmed in a study of 10,047 individuals residing in 37 cultures located on 6 continents and 5 islands around the world (Buss, 1989b). Women more than men especially disdain qualities in a potential mate that signal inability to accrue resources, such as lack of ambition ($d = 1.38$) and lack of education

(d = 1.06; Buss & Schmitt, 1993). Women desire physical protection abilities more than men, both in short-term mating (d = .94) and in long-term mating (d = .66; Buss & Schmitt, 1993).

Men and women also differ in the weighting given to cues that trigger sexual jealousy. Men and women were presented with the following dilemma: "What would upset or distress you more: (1) imagining your partner forming a deep emotional attachment to someone else or (2) imagining your partner enjoying passionate sexual intercourse with that other person." Men expressed greater distress about the second scenario, for which sexual infidelity, rather than emotional infidelity, is highlighted; women showed the opposite pattern. The difference between the sexes in which scenario was more distressing was 43%, with a d of .98 (Buss, Larsen, Westen, & Semmelroth, 1992). These sex differences have been replicated by different investigators (Wiederman & Allgeier, 1993), using physiological as well as written recording devices (Buss et al., 1992), and have been replicated in other cultures (Buunk et al., in press).

These sex differences were predicted a priori by psychological theories based on sexual selection. They represent only a sampling from a larger body of supporting evidence. The sexes also differ substantially in a wide variety of other ways that are predicted by sexual selection theory, such as engaging in physical risk taking (Wilson & Daly, 1985), perpetrating homicides (Daly & Wilson, 1988), inferring sexual intent in others (Abby, 1982), perceiving the upset that people experience on being the victims of sexual aggression (Buss, 1989a), and committing violent crimes of all sorts (Daly & Wilson, 1988). As noted by the anthropologist Donald Brown: "It will be irresponsible to continue shunting these [issues] aside, fraud to deny that they exist" (Brown, 1991, p. 156). Evolutionary psychology sheds light on why these differences exist.

IMPLICATIONS OF EVOLVED SEX DIFFERENCES FOR THE BROADER DISCOURSE

Strong sex differences occur reliably in domains closely linked with sex and mating, as predicted by psychological theories based on sexual selection (Buss, 1994). Within these domains, the psychological sex differences are patterned in a manner that maps precisely onto the adaptive problems men and women have been predicted to have faced over human evolutionary history. Indeed, in most cases, the evolutionary hypotheses about sex differences were generated a decade or more before the empirical tests of them were conducted and the sex differences discovered. These models thus have heuristic and predictive power and have consequences for the broader discourse on sex differences.

Neither sex can be considered "inferior" or "superior." Neither women nor men can be considered superior or inferior to the other, any more than a bird's wings can be considered superior or inferior to a fish's fins or a kangaroo's legs. Each sex possesses mechanisms designed to deal with its own adaptive challenges — some similar and some different — and so notions of superiority or inferiority with regard to evolved sex differences are logically incoherent from the vantage point of evolutionary psychology. The metatheory of evolutionary psychology is descriptive, not prescriptive—it carries no normative or prescriptive values.

Sex differences are not intractable or unchangeable. Contrary to common misconceptions about evolutionary psychology, documenting that sex differences originated through a causal process of sexual selection does not imply that the differences are unchangeable or intractable. On the contrary, understanding their origins provides a powerful heuristic to identify the contexts in which the sex differences are most likely to be manifested (e.g., in the context of mate competition) and hence a guide to effective loci for intervention if change is judged to be desirable.

Evolutionary psychology does not justify the status quo; instead, it points to contexts for effective intervention. Although some worry that inquiries into the existence and evolutionary origins of sex differences will lead to justification for the status quo, it is hard to believe that attempts to change the status quo can be very effective if we remain ignorant of the sex differences that actually exist, the causal forces that gave rise to them, and the contexts in which they are expressed. Knowledge is power, and attempts to intervene in the absence of knowledge may be like a surgeon operating with a blindfold—there may be more harm than healing (Tooby & Cosmides, 1992).

The perspective of evolutionary psychology jettisons the outmoded dualistic thinking inherent in much current discourse by getting rid of the false dichotomy between "biological" and "social." It offers a truly interactionist position that specifies the particular features of social context that are especially critical for processing by our evolved psychological mechanisms. No other theory of sex differences has been capable of generating the large number of precise, detailed, patterned sex differences outlined by theories emerging from evolutionary psychology (e.g., Bailey, Gaulin, Agyei, & Gladue, 1994; Buss & Schmitt, 1993; Daly & Wilson, 1988; Ellis & Symons, 1990; Gangestad & Simpson, 1990; Greer & Buss, 1994; Kenrick & Keefe, 1992; Symons, 1979). Thus, those interested in change ignore evolutionary psychology only at their peril. Evolutionary psychology possesses the heuristic power to guide investigators to the particular domains in which the most pronounced sex differences, as well as similarities, will be found. Those grappling with the existence and implications of psychological sex differences cannot afford to ignore the evolutionary origins of these sex differences. One of the most important implications of evolved psychological sex differences pertains to men's control over resources, a critical aspect of what is sometimes called *patriarchy*.

EVOLUTIONARY ORIGINS OF
MALE RESOURCE CONTROL OR PATRIARCHY

Feminist scholars often trace the roots of women's oppression to *patriarchy*, a term referring to men's dominance over women in the family specifically and in society more generally (Lerner, 1986, pp. 238–239; Smuts, 1995). I dislike the term "patriarchy" because it qualifies as a *panchreston*, something that means different things to different people and purports to explain everything, but really explains nothing. More concretely, the patriarchy is typically defined so broadly and vaguely that it subsumes many different sorts of phenomena, each with their own causal dynamics. In a recent paper, Barbara Smuts (1995) focused primarily on the topic of sexual aggression as the central component of patriarchy and only incidentally on men's control over resources and the causal origins of male resource control. The current chapter, in contrast, focuses more heavily on male control of resources, the causal origins of male resource control, and the consequences of this control for sexuality. Although it is obvious that sexual aggression and control of resources have interesting and complex links, it is equally clear that the causal origins and dynamics of each are different. Thus, subsuming male resource control and male sexual aggression (and a variety of other phenomena) under the umbrella term of patriarchy may have the unintended consequence of clouding rather than clarifying the causal analysis. Moreover, conflating long-term control over sexuality (by spouse or kin) with short-term control through rape or sexual aggression is problematic since these are likely to be products of different selective forces.

A reasonable scientific question pertains to the origins of the phenomena subsumed under the term patriarchy. Although historically some feminists have offered speculations about the origins of male control and domination (e.g., by tracing it to the fact that men are larger and stronger than women), no consensus has been reached. Most feminists simply take patriarchy as a given, as a starting point from which analysis proceeds, and do not consider its origins (Smuts, 1995; Stewart, personal communication, 1991).

Elsewhere, I have argued that men's control over resources can be traced, in large part, to the coevolution of women's mate preferences and men's competitive strategies (Buss, 1989b, 1994). Findings from the largest study ever conducted on what men and women desire in a mate (10,047 subjects from 37 cultures around the world) provide unequivocal evidence that women universally place a greater premium than do men on the resource base and resource acquisition potential of a prospective mate (Buss, 1989b). These preferences, operating repeatedly over thousands of generations, have led women to favor as mates men who possess status and resources and to disfavor as mates men who lack these assets. Men in human evolutionary history who failed to acquire resources were more likely to have failed to attract women as mates.

Women's preferences thus established an important set of ground rules for men in their competition with one another. Based on sexual selection theory, the desires of one sex establish the critical dimensions along which members of the opposite sex compete. Since ancestral men tended to place a premium on women's physical appearance, for example, this established attractiveness as a major dimension along which women compete with one another. The $53 billion cosmetic industry within the United States, which is overwhelmingly a female-consumer industry, is a testament to the magnitude of this form of intrasexual competition among women.

Analogously, women's desires for men with resources established the acquisition of resources as a major dimension of men's competition with each other. Modern men have inherited from their ancestors psychological mechanisms that not only give priority to resources and status, but also lead men to take risks to attain resources and status. Men who failed to give the goals of status and resources a high personal priority and failed to take calculated risks to best other men also failed to attract mates. This sort of competition carries a large price tag in male–male violence and homicide, as well as in earlier death on average. The earlier death of men across cultures, in other words, is due directly to a long history of male–male intrasexual competition in which men rather than women selected riskier strategies. We are all the descendants of men who succeeded in out-competing other men. As their descendants, modern men carry with them the psychological mechanisms that led to their success.

Women's preferences and men's strategies of intrasexual competition co-evolved, just as men's preferences and women's strategies of intrasexual competition coevolved. Men may have started controlling resources to attract and control women, and women's preferences in a mate may have followed. Alternatively, women's preferences for a successful, ambitious, and resourceful mate selected men's competitive strategies of risk taking, status striving, derogation of competitors along dimensions of status, the formation of coalitions to gain resources, and an array of individual efforts aimed at besting other men on the dimensions that women desire. Most likely, the men's competitive strategies and women's mate preferences coevolved together. The intertwining or interplay of these coevolved mechanisms in men and women created the conditions for men to dominate in the domain of resources.

The hypothesis that women have played a causal role in men's control of resources, through the influence of their mate preferences on men's competitive strategies, strikes some as "blaming the victim." Not only do women suffer from men's control over resources, now it seems like they are getting blamed for it as well. The inference of blame, however, does not follow from the identification of women's participation in one aspect of the causal chain. From the vantage point of evolutionary psychology, neither sex deserves blame. Instead, we are all the end products of a long causal process that involved the coevolution of women's preferences and men's intrasexual competition tactics. As products of this process, men and women are equally blame worthy or blame free. Issues of blame are irrelevant in the evolutionary psychological analysis of the origins of men's control of resources.

The evolutionary origins of men's monopolization of resources are not simply an incidental historical footnote of passing curiosity. Rather, it has a profound bearing on the present because it reveals some of the primary causes of men's continuing control of resources. Women today continue to want as mates men who have resources, and they continue to reject as mates men who lack resources. These preferences are expressed repeatedly by women in dozens of studies conducted on tens of thousands of individuals in scores of countries worldwide (Buss, 1989b, 1994). They are expressed countless times in everyday life. In any given year, the men women marry earn more than men of the same age women do not marry (see Buss, 1994). Women who earn more than their husbands divorce at double the rate of women whose husbands earn more than they do (see Buss, 1994). Furthermore, men continue to form alliances and compete with other men to acquire the status and resources that make them desirable to women. The forces that originally caused the resource inequity between the sexes—namely, women's preferences and men's competitive strategies—contribute to maintaining resource inequality today.

This analysis of resource inequality does not deny the existence of other contributing causes such as the sexist practice of giving women and men unequal pay for the same work. Nor does this analysis imply that men's greater control of resources is inevitable or justifiable (see also Smuts, 1995). But, if change is deemed desirable, as it clearly is by many, the perspectives of evolutionary psychology help by identifying the specific causal factors responsible for originating and maintaining gender inequality in resources. Failure to identify these critical causal loci and ignoring them because they are upsetting strip away a powerful source of knowledge that would otherwise make change more possible.

WHY WOMEN'S SEXUALITY LIES AT THE CORE OF CONFLICT

Feminists' and evolutionists' conclusions converge in their implication that men's efforts to control female sexuality lie at the core of their efforts to control women. Our evolved sexual strategies account for why this occurs and why control of women's sexuality is a central preoccupation of men (Smuts, 1992). Over the course of human evolutionary history, men who failed to control women's sexuality—for example, by failing to attract a mate, failing to prevent cuckoldry, or failing to keep a mate—experienced lower reproductive success than men who succeeded in controlling women's sexuality (Buss, 1994). We come from a long and unbroken line of ancestral fathers who succeeded in obtaining mates, preventing their infidelity, and providing enough benefits (or inflicting enough deterrent costs) to keep them from leaving. We also come from a long line of ancestral mothers who successfully secured investing mates, acted to prevent the siphoning of a mate's resources to other women, and granted sexual access to men who provided beneficial resources.

CONFLICTS AND CONFLUENCES OF INTEREST: ARE ALL MEN REALLY UNITED WITH OTHER MEN TO CONTROL WOMEN?

Feminist theory sometimes portrays men as being united with all other men in their common purpose of oppressing all women (Dworkin, 1987; Faludi, 1991). But, the evolution of human mating suggests that this cannot be true because men and women compete mainly against members of their own sex. Men strive to control resources at the expense and to the exclusion of other men. Men deprive other men of their resources, exclude other men from positions of status and power, and derogate other men in order to make them less desirable to women. That roughly 70% of all homicides involve men victimizing other men reveals the sorts of costs men incur as a result of competing with other men (Daly & Wilson, 1988). That men on average die six years earlier than women is further testimony to the penalties men pay for this struggle with their own sex.

Women do not escape the damage inflicted by members of their own sex. Women compete with each other for access to high-status men, have sex with other women's husbands, and lure men away from their wives. Women slander and denigrate their rivals, especially those who pursue short-term sexual strategies (Buss & Dedden, 1990). Women and men are both victims of the sexual strategies of their own sex and so can hardly be said to be united with all members of their own sex for some common goal.

The primary exception to this is when men form coalitions that function as subgroups within the broader culture (see, e.g., Chagnon, 1983; Smuts, 1995). These coalitions are sometimes used to control women's sexuality, as illustrated by the phenomenon of brutal gang rape (Smuts, 1992). Furthermore, men's coalitions may sometimes be used to exclude women from power—for example, when exclusive men's clubs or lodges in which business is transacted explicitly prevent women from joining. These same coalitions, however, are also directed against other men and their coalitions. In business, politics, and warfare, men form coalitions for their own benefit at the expense of other coalitions of men. Among the Yanomamo of Venezuela, as a concrete example, men form coalitions to raid neighboring villages (Chagnon, 1983). These conditions thus inflict costs on both men and women—on women in the form of a forcible capture and on men in the sense that their wives, daughters, and sisters are forcibly taken from them, and, in addition, some of these men are killed.

It must also be recognized that both men and women benefit from the strategies of the opposite sex. Men provide resources to certain women (e.g., their wives, sisters, daughters, and mistresses). A woman's father, brothers, and sons all benefit from her selection of a mate with status and resources. Contrary to the view that men and women are united with all members of their own sex for the purpose of oppressing the other sex, each individual is united in interests with some members of each sex and is in conflict with some members of each sex. Simple-minded views of a conspiracy by one sex or the other have no foundation in reality.

CONSEQUENCES FOR THE GENDER WARS

This analysis has important consequences for the scientific agenda of understanding conflict between the sexes and for the feminist political agenda of gaining greater equality for women in the home and workplace. In this section,

I examine a few of these consequences by offering insights into phenomena that seem to be at the core of much conflict.

Same-sex competition is intimately linked with conflict between the sexes. It should be clear from this analysis that conflict between the sexes cannot be divorced from same-sex competition. Consider, for example, the fact that women tend to compete with one another in the realm of physical appearance. This no doubt harms women in many ways. As the feminist Naomi Wolf (1991) observes, the constant bombardment with images of flawless models may create unrealistic expectations and may damage women's self-esteem (see also Kenrick, Guttieres, & Goldberg, 1989, on contrast effects). This phenomenon, according to an evolutionary psychological analysis, can ultimately be traced to men's mate preferences. Over human evolutionary history, men have imposed their desire for attractiveness on women because physical attractiveness provides a set of proximate cues to health and youth, and hence to fertility. Men with these preferences outreproduced other men who lacked such preferences, or who had alternative preferences, such as for women who were prepubescent or postmenopausal. Since men today are the descendants of men who carried this mate preference, they continue to impose this pressure on women.

The same analysis, however, suggests that women are competing primarily against other women. A woman enhances her own beauty at the expense of other women because she improves her own odds of attracting a desirable man at a cost to her competitors. One woman's gain is another's loss in the mating domain. Thus, this phenomenon, although it undoubtedly damages some women, cannot be solely laid at the doorstep of men; enhancement of physical attractiveness is a tactic performed by a woman for her own competitive advantage.

Some feminists, such as Wolf (1991), decry the obsession with female beauty and strive to change people's values so that they place greater emphasis on personal qualities such as intelligence, complexity, sense of humor, and empathy. Because values are able to be manipulated to some degree, these changes may work to some degree. When they do work, however, they will simply change the dimensions along which women compete with each other. If all men were suddenly convinced to value physical strength supremely in a mate and to be indifferent to other dimensions of physical attractiveness, then women would, over time, compete with one another to build their muscles, wear clothing that showed off bulging biceps, and show off their strength by opening jars and arm wrestling with other women. Women would derogate other women not so much by impugning their appearance or sexuality, but by denigrating their strength and physical prowess. Women who were lacking muscle mass would suffer discrimination by men on the mating market.

Although changing the dimensions that are valued does not alter the fundamental dynamics of same-sex competition or the anguish felt by those shunned for lacking the desired characteristics, it does change the content of intrasexual competition, which may be deemed desirable by some (especially, for example, by those lacking desired qualities using the current criteria for mate selection). The value that men place on physical attractiveness seems especially galling to some women. Part of the reason for this is that attractiveness is so undemocratically distributed. Part of the reason is that there is not much that one can do to change it (although the high rates of makeup usage and cosmetic surgery suggest that women do seek to change what they can, at least sometimes). Intelligence, empathy, kindness, and sense of humor, in contrast, seem subjectively more alterable, more under one's control, more subject to self-improvement. Furthermore, these other qualities may not be as immediately apparent or assessable, and hence those lacking them might not be immediately excluded from further consideration. Nonetheless, the dynamics of sexual selection operate with equal force despite these subjective impressions. Conflict between the sexes cannot be divorced from same-sex competition unless one does not participate in heterosexual mating.

Women, as well as men, exploit the desires of the other sex. Prostitution provides a good example of the exploitation of the desires of others, and in fact the feminist community is split on this issue. From one perspective, prostitution exists because of a powerful male desire for sexual variety, combined with the inability of some men to attract women as mates. From a related but different perspective, some women are able to pursue a strategy of exploiting men's sexual desires to extract money and other resources in exchange for sex. In countries or states where prostitution is legal or semilegal, some women choose to pursue this profession (Burley & Symanski, 1981). A woman who chooses prostitution may do so because of restricted alternative strategies of resource acquisition, such as an inability to secure other forms of lucrative employment or a failure to attract a sufficiently investing mate. Alternatively, some women choose prostitution because if provides a quick and lucrative source of income and hence may be seen as a desirable option relative to a nine-to-five job or a demanding husband. The fact that some women choose prostitution, of course, does not negate the fact that some women are forced or coerced into prostitution.

Prostitution is sometimes viewed as a symbol of male oppression, but it can be viewed alternatively as expanding women's range of options to pursue a wider variety of strategies of resource acquisition. Some are adamantly against prostitution and argue that it is a "patriarchal institution" (MacKinnon, 1987). Alternatively, women who oppose prostitution can be viewed as engaging in a battle with other women about what strategies of resource acquisition are judged acceptable. Typically, women who oppose prostitution are in better positions to pursue alternative means of resource acquisition, either through their careers or through marrying a man with resources.

Prostitutes, like women who pursue short-term sexual strategies, pose a threat primarily to other women. Their presence, for example, may deter some men from pursuing marriage in presumptively monogamous societies, which often entails a long-term commitment of resources to one woman. As Symons (1979) observes:

> To the extent that heterosexual men purchase the services of prostitutes and pornographic masturbation aids, the market for the sexual services of non-

prostitute women is diminished and their bargaining power vis-à-vis men is weakened. . . . In fact, feminist prostitutes and many nonprostitute, heterosexual feminists are in direct competition, and it should be no surprise that they are often to be found at one another's throats. (pp. 259–260)

Even if they do not deter marriage, prostitutes may siphon off resources that might otherwise go to a man's wife and her children. Thus, prostitution benefits some women at the expense of other women. The elimination of prostitution, therefore, functions to strip some women of one strategy of resource acquisition—the strategy of exploiting men's desire for sexual variety.

Similar arguments can be made about related phenomena, such as pornography and sexually explicit performers such as Madonna. Madonna is able to exploit men's sexual desires and make millions of dollars by doing so. Those who argue for laws restricting these phenomena (e.g., MacKinnon, 1987) effectively deprive some women of what would otherwise be a profitable resource acquisition strategy, and arguably one that may be preferred by some women instead of subjecting themselves to a controlling husband (Burley & Symanski, 1981). In fact, some women say that they turn to prostitution to avoid the drudgery of marriage. Maylay women in Singapore, for example, sometimes become prostitutes to avoid the hard work expected of wives, which includes gathering firewood and laundering clothes (Burley & Symanski, 1981). Among the Amhara and Bemba, prostitutes earn enough through casual sex to hire men to do the work that is normally expected of wives (Burley & Symanski, 1981). The immediate acquisition of resources, in short, is a considerable benefit to women who engage in temporary sexual liaisons (Buss & Schmitt, 1993; Smith, 1984).

But increases in women's resource equality should reduce their need to use their sexuality as a means to secure resources. As Donald Symons (1979) notes, "Women's increasing political and economic equality will reduce their sexual vulnerability as well as their need to use sex for economic and political gain or security" (p. 274). Thus, achieving economic equality remains a goal that may unite feminists who endorse women's freedom to use their bodies and feminists who oppose other women's use of their bodies for pornography or prostitution.

When women gain access to resources. A key part of the feminist agenda is for women to gain equal access to financial resources. Were women to gain equal access to resources, they would not have to depend on men for those resources. Consequently, equal resource acquisition would free women to pursue a broader range of life options. Thus, from a woman's perspective, access to more resources can only have positive outcomes.

What happens when women have resources of their own? Some feminists have argued that when women gain access to resources themselves, then their mate preferences will shift (Alice Eagly, personal communication, 1994). Not only will women not value resources in a mate as much, they argue, but their own resources will free them to value the more "frivolous" characteristics that men value, such as physical appearance. The data do not support these predicted shifts. Several separate studies have come to a singular conclusion on the effects of women's resources on their desire for men with resources—it does not change them (see Buss, 1994, for summaries). Women with more resources do not place any greater value on physical attractiveness than women with fewer resources. Nor do resource-laden women ignore the resources of a potential mate. In fact, in two studies, women with more resources placed more value on a potential mate's resources than did women with fewer personal resources (Buss, 1989b; Townsend, 1989; Wiederman & Allgeier, 1992). Furthermore, studies of cultures that show greater relative economic equality between the sexes show sex differences in desire for mates with resources of the same magnitude as cultures that show great economic disparities between the sexes (Buss, 1989b).

Despite the lack of evidence that women do not shift their desires in a mate to devalue resources when they themselves possess resources, it is clearly too early to tell what would happen when more women gained full economic equality. As Martin Daly points out (personal communication, 1994), evolutionary psychological accounts generally expect context sensitivity with regard to resource conditions. Thus, were a shift in women's desires to occur as their own economic conditions changed, this would not be incompatible with evolutionary models, but it would require a more complex depiction of our evolved desires.

CONCLUSION

Feminist and evolutionary theories centrally focus on issues of sex, power, and conflict. These perspectives converge in several key points: Men tend to control resources worldwide; men's control of women often centers on control of women's sexuality and reproduction; men sometimes display a proprietary psychology toward women, viewing them as property to be controlled, owned, and used; and women as well as men sometimes participate in perpetuating women's oppression.

Evolutionary psychology provides insights into why these phenomena occur. Since differential reproduction is the engine that drives evolutionary change, activities surrounding reproduction have been the frequent targets of selection. Moreover, since differential reproduction implies a relative metric, competition and conflict have been the norm over evolutionary time, not the exception. Because men's and women's strategies sometimes interfere with one another, conflict between the sexes ensues. Because men's and women's strategies commonly interfere with members of their own sex, conflict among women and conflict among men ensues.

Although it would be naive to believe that all human conflict can be eliminated, an evolutionary psychological analysis provides several paths toward producing greater harmony between the sexes. To use a physiological metaphor, we have evolved callous-producing mechanisms, but we can design our environments to be relatively free of friction, thus preventing the development of callouses. Analogously, men and women have evolved mating mechanisms that, when activated, produce psychological strife, but in principle, with enough knowledge, we could design environments that are more free of conflict.

While evolutionary psychology does not offer a panacea to these problems, it does offer several avenues to pursue these goals. One is simply greater understanding. In my own research, I have found the disturbing result that men seriously underestimate how upsetting sexual aggression is to women victims (Buss, 1989a). Conversely, women overestimate how upsetting sexual aggression is to male victims. Becoming better educated about the nature of these psychological sex differences may be one small step toward reducing conflict between the sexes.

A second avenue for change is that evolutionary psychology provides a heuristic to identify the contexts most likely to trigger conflict between the sexes. In my own research, for example, I have examined the cues that cause men to infer greater sexual interest on the part of a woman than may be the case. We have been able to identify three cues that cause this interpretive error—a woman smiling at a man, being friendly to a man, and going to a bar alone. On the other hand, we have also identified signals that do *not* appear to cause misunderstanding, such as dancing closely and prolonged eye contact. This work thus reveals the contexts in which intervention would be most likely to succeed at reducing conflict between the men and women. For example, men could be apprised of the finding that, as a group, they tend to overinterpret the sexual intentions of a woman who smiles at them and thus may want to be more cautious before acting on the basis of a mere smile. After all, the woman might simply be trying to be friendly (Abby, 1982).

A third avenue for change lies with understanding that the fundamental desires of women and men differ in some domains, perhaps most notably in the sexual domain. Indeed, fulfilling each other's evolved desires may be one of the most powerful keys to harmony between a man and a woman (Buss, 1994). Those who fulfill each other's desires have more harmonious relationships that are marked by kindness, affection, and commitment (Buss, 1991). Our evolved desires, in short, provide the essential ingredients for solving the elusive mystery of harmony between the sexes.

We are the first species with the capacity to control our own destiny. The prospect of designing our destiny remains excellent to the degree that we comprehend our evolutionary past. Only by examining the complex repertoire of human sexual strategies can we know where we came from. Only by understanding why these human strategies have evolved can we control where we are going.

Acknowledgments. The author thanks the members of the Prestige Group for extremely helpful comments on earlier versions of this chapter: Todd DeKay, Bruce Ellis, Judith Flynn, Arlette Greer, Heidi Greiling, Karen Parker, Sarah Moldenhouer, Todd Shackelford, and David Schmitt. The author is also deeply indebted to Neil Malamuth, Barb Smuts, and Donald Symons for providing incisive reactions to this chapter specifically and for dialogues, now spanning years, on these issues.

REFERENCES

Abby, A. (1982). Sex differences in attributions for friendly behavior: Do males misperceive females' friendliness? *Journal of Personality and Social Psychology, 32,* 830–838.

Ashmore, R. D. (1990). Sex, gender, and the individual. In L. A. Pervin (Ed.), *Handbook of personality: Theory and research.* New York: Guilford Press.

Bailey, J. M., Gaulin, S., Agyei, Y., & Gladue, B. A. (1994). Effects of gender and sexual orientation on evolutionarily relevant aspects of human mating psychology. *Journal of Personality and Social Psychology, 66,* 1074–1080.

Betzig, L. (1992). Roman polygyny. *Ethology and Sociobiology, 13,* 309–349.

Brown, D. (1991). *Human universals.* Philadelphia: Temple University Press.

Burley, N., & Symanski, R. (1981). Women without: An evolutionary and cross-cultural perspective on prostitution. In R. Symanski, *The immoral landscape: Female prostitution in Western societies* (pp. 239–274). Toronto: Butterworth.

Buss, D. M. (1988). From vigilance to violence: Mate guarding tactics. *Ethology and Sociobiology, 9,* 291–317.

Buss, D. M. (1989a). Conflict between the sexes: Strategic interference and the evocation of anger and upset. *Journal of Personality and Social Psychology, 56,* 735–747.

Buss, D. M. (1989b). Sex differences in human mate preferences: Evolutionary hypotheses tested in 37 cultures. *Behavioral and Brain Sciences, 12,* 1–49.

Buss, D. M. (1991). Conflict in married couples: Personality predictors of anger and upset. *Journal of Personality, 59,* 663–688.

Buss, D. M. (1994). *The evolution of desire: Strategies of human mating.* New York: Basic Books.

Buss, D. M. (1995). Evolutionary psychology: A new paradigm for psychological science. *Psychological Inquiry, 6,* 1–30.

Buss, D. M., & Dedden, L. (1990). Derogation of competitors. *Journal of Social and Personal Relationships, 7,* 395–422.

Buss, D. M., Larsen, R., Westen, D., & Semmelroth, J. (1992). Sex differences in jealousy: Evolution, physiology, and psychology. *Psychological Science, 3,* 251–255.

Buss, D. M., & Schmitt, D. P. (1993). Sexual strategies theory: An evolutionary perspective on human mating. *Psychological Review, 100,* 204–232.

Buunk, B., Angleitner, A., Oubaid, V., & Buss, D. M. (in press). Sexual and cultural differences in jealousy: Tests from the Netherlands, Germany, and the United States. *Psychological Science.*

Chagnon, N. (1983). *Yanomamo: The fierce people.* New York: Holt, Rinehart, and Winston.

Clark, R. D., & Hatfield, E. (1989). Gender differences in receptivity to sexual offers. *Journal of Psychology and Human Sexuality, 2,* 39–55.

Cohen, J. (1977). *Statistical power analysis for the behavioral sciences.* San Diego, CA: Academic Press.

Daly, M., & Wilson, M. (1988). *Homicide.* New York: Aldine de Gruyter.

Dworkin, A. (1987). *Intercourse.* New York: Free Press.

Eagly, A. H. (1995). The science and politics of comparing women and men. *American Psychologist, 50,* 145–158.

Ellis, B. J., & Symons, D. (1990). Sex differences in sexual fantasy: An evolutionary psychological approach. *Journal of Sex Research, 27,* 527–556.

Faludi, S. (1991). *Backlash: The undeclared war against American women*. New York: Crown.

Feingold, A. (1990). Gender differences in effects of physical attractiveness on romantic attraction: A comparison across five research paradigms. *Journal of Personality and Social Psychology, 59*, 981–993.

Gangestad, S. W., & Simpson, J. A. (1990). Toward an evolutionary history of female sociosexual variation. *Journal of Personality, 58*, 69–96.

Gowaty, P. A. (1992). Evolutionary biology and feminism. *Human Nature, 3*, 217–249.

Greer, A., & Buss, D. M. (1994). Tactics for promoting sexual encounters. *Journal of Sex Research, 31*, 185–201.

Greiling, H. (1993, June). *Women's short-term sexual strategies*. Paper presented at the Conference on Evolution and the Social Sciences, London School of Economics, London, England.

Hall, J. A. (1978). Gender effects in decoding nonverbal cues. *Psychological Bulletin, 85*, 845–852.

Hill, K., & Hurtado, M. (1989). Hunter-gathers of the new world. *American Scientist, 77*, 437–443.

hooks, b. (1984). *Feminist theory: From margin to center*. Boston: South End Press.

Hrdy, S. (1981). *The woman that never evolved*. Cambridge, MA: Harvard University Press.

Hyde, J. S. (1996). Where are the gender differences? Where are the gender similarities? In D. M. Buss & N. M. Malamuth (Eds.), *Sex, power, conflict: Evolutionary and feminist perspectives*. New York: Oxford University Press.

Jagger, A. (1994). *Living with contradictions: Controversies in feminist social ethics*. Boulder, CO: Westview Press.

Kenrick, D. T., Gutierres, S. E., & Goldberg, L. (1989). Influence of erotica on ratings of strangers and mates. *Journal of Experimental Social Psychology, 25*, 159–167.

Kenrick, D. T., & Keefe, R. C. (1992). Age preferences in mates reflect sex differences in reproductive strategies. *Behavioral and Brain Sciences, 15*, 75–133.

Lancaster, J. (1991). A feminist and evolutionary biologist looks at women. *Yearbook of Physical Anthropology, 34*, 1–11.

Lerner, G. (1986). *The creation of patriarchy*. Oxford: Oxford University Press.

Low, B. (1989). Cross-cultural patterns in the training of children: An evolutionary perspective. *Journal of Comparative Psychology, 103*, 313–319.

Maccoby, E. E., & Jacklin, C. N. (1974). *The psychology of sex differences*. Stanford, CA: Stanford University Press.

MacKinnon, C. (1987). *Feminism unmodified*. Cambridge, MA: Harvard University Press.

Malamuth, N. M., Sockloskie, R., Koss, M., & Tanaka, J. (1991). The characteristics of aggressors against women: Testing a model using a national sample of college women. *Journal of Consulting and Clinical Psychology, 59*, 670–681.

Oliver, M. B., & Hyde, J. S. (1993). Gender differences in sexuality: A meta-analysis. *Psychological Bulletin, 114*, 29–51.

Ortner, S. B. (1974). Is female to male as nature is to nurture? In M. Z. Rosaldo & L. Lamphere (Eds.), *Women, culture, and society* (pp. 67–88). Stanford, CA: Stanford University Press.

Rosenthal, R. (1991). *Meta-analytic procedures for social research* (Rev. ed.). Newbury Park, CA: Sage.

Silverman, I., & Eals, M. (1992). Sex differences in spatial abilities: Evolutionary theory and data. In J. Barkow, L. Cosmides, & J. Tooby (Eds.), *The adapted mind: Evolutionary psychology and the generation of culture* (pp. 533–549). New York: Oxford University Press.

Smith, R. (1984). Human sperm competition. In R. L. Smith (Ed.), *Sperm competition and the evolution of mating systems* (pp. 601–659). New York: Academic Press.

Smuts, B. B. (1992). Male aggression against women. *Human Nature, 3,* 1–44.

Smuts, B. B. (1995). The evolutionary origins of patriarchy. *Human Nature, 6,* 1–32.

Studd, M., & Gattiker, U. E. (1991). The evolutionary psychology of sexual harassment in organizations. *Ethology and Sociobiology, 12,* 249–290.

Symons, D. (1979). *The evolution of human sexuality.* New York: Oxford University Press.

Symons, D. (1992). On the use and misuse of Darwinism in the study of human behavior. In J. Barkow, L. Cosmides, & J. Tooby (Eds.), *The adapted mind: Evolutionary psychology and the generation of culture* (pp. 137–159). New York: Oxford University Press.

Thornhill, N. (1996). Psychological adaptation to sexual coercion in victims and offenders. In D. M. Buss & N. M. Malamuth (Eds.), *Sex, power, conflict: Evolutionary and feminist perspectives* (pp. 90–104). New York: Oxford University Press.

Tooby, J., & Cosmides, L. (1992). Psychological foundations of culture. In J. Barkow, L. Cosmides, & J. Tooby (Eds.), *The adapted mind: Evolutionary psychology and the generation of culture* (pp. 19–136). New York: Oxford University Press.

Tooby, J., & DeVore, I. (1987). The reconstruction of hominid behavioral evolution through strategic modeling. In W. G. Kinzey (Ed.), *The evolution of human behavior: Primate models* (pp. 183–237). Albany, NY: State University of New York Press.

Townsend, J. M. (1989). Mate selection criteria: A pilot study. *Ethology and Sociobiology, 10,* 241–253.

Trivers, R. (1972). Parental investment and sexual selection. In B. Campbell (Ed.), *Sexual selection and the descent of man* (pp. 136–179). New York: Aldine de Gruyter.

Wiederman, M. W., & Allgeier, E. R. (1992). Gender differences in mate selection criteria: Sociobiological or socioeconomic explanation? *Ethology and Sociobiology, 13,* 115–124.

Wiederman, M. W., & Allgeier, E. R. (1993). Gender differences in sexual jealousy: Adaptationist or social learning explanation? *Ethology and Sociobiology, 14,* 115–140.

Wilson, M., & Daly, M. (1985). Competitiveness, risk taking, and violence: The young male syndrome. *Ethology and Sociobiology, 6,* 59–73.

Wilson, M., & Daly, M. (1992). The man who mistook his wife for a chattel. In J. Barkow, L. Cosmides, & J. Tooby (Eds.), *The adapted mind: Evolutionary psychology and the generation of culture* (pp. 289–322). New York: Oxford University Press.

Wolf, N. (1991). *The beauty myth.* New York: Morrow.

Wolf, N. (1993). *Fire with fire.* New York: Ballantine.

Name Index

Subject Index

Acquaintance rape, 94, 95, 115, 116
  alcohol factor in, 138–39, 141, 143–56
  labeling as "rape," 122
  objective boundaries and, 98
Adaptationist approach, 90–101, 200, 219, 272–73, 302–3
  domain-specific, 272–73, 300–301
  See also Natural selection
Adultery
  cross-cultural responses to women's, 247–48
  gender differences, 13–14, 203
  and pollution beliefs, 252
  sex-biased customs, 16, 147, 203, 204, 240, 241, 251, 252–53, 255
  social dominance, orientation and, 208–9
  See also Paternity certainty
Against Our Will (Brownmiller), 131, 162
Aggression
  alcohol consumption and male, 138, 139, 143, 145, 149
  female resistance strategies, 235–38, 257–58
  gender-differences analysis, 113–14, 128
  hostile vs. instrumental, 128–29

and human pair bonds evolution, 238–41
hypotheses on conditions for, 241–51
male fantasies of, 287
and male hostility toward women, 282–83
and male-male vs. male-female bonds, 245
and male physical size, 12–13, 270
and male resource control, 249–50
male socialization for, 270–71
mechanisms underlying, 277–79
sexual coercion as, 233–41
variables in, 251–58
women victims, 231–60, 270–71
See also Power; Rape; Violence
Alcohol consumption, 138–56
  cross-cultural beliefs about, 153
  and gender role norms, 143–44, 153–54
  and misperceptions of sexual intent, 148–51
  and sexual arousal, 99, 100
  and sexual assault, 138–45, 152–54
Anorgasmia, 115
Attractiveness
  as mating criterion, 43–47, 96, 201–2, 307, 311–12
  as sexual harassment factor, 65–66